Donald Trump and American Populism

New Perspectives on the American Presidency
Series Editors: Michael Patrick Cullinane and Sylvia Ellis, University of Roehampton

Published titles
Constructing Presidential Legacy: How We Remember the American President
Edited by Michael Patrick Cullinane and Sylvia Ellis

Presidential Privilege and the Freedom of Information Act
Kevin M. Baron

Forthcoming titles
Obama v. Trump: The Politics of Rollback
Clodagh Harrington and Alex Waddan

Series website: https://edinburghuniversitypress.com/new-perspectives-on-the-american-presidency.html

DONALD TRUMP AND
AMERICAN POPULISM

Richard S. Conley

EDINBURGH
University Press

Edinburgh University Press is one of the leading university presses in the UK. We publish academic books and journals in our selected subject areas across the humanities and social sciences, combining cutting-edge scholarship with high editorial and production values to produce academic works of lasting importance. For more information visit our website: edinburghuniversitypress.com

Edinburgh University Press Ltd
The Tun – Holyrood Road, 12(2f) Jackson's Entry, Edinburgh EH8 8PJ

First published in hardback by Edinburgh University Press 2020

Typeset in 11/13 Sabon by
IDSUK (DataConnection) Ltd

A CIP record for this book is available from the British Library

ISBN 978 1 4744 5006 5 (hardback)
ISBN 978 1 4744 5007 2 (paperback)
ISBN 978 1 4744 5008 9 (webready PDF)
ISBN 978 1 4744 5009 6 (epub)

Contents

List of figures and tables   vi

1. Populist disrupter-in-chief   1

2. The populist precedent   58

3. The roots of Trump's populism   158

4. 2016: The year of the populists   203

5. The populist-elect and the permanent campaign   246

6. The populist as policymaker   281

7. The populist in peril   302

8. Epilogue: Quo vadis?   341

Bibliography   351

Index   422

Figures and tables

Figure 2.1 Conceptualizing and Comparing Populist Candidates, Presidents, and Movements   78

Figure 2.2 Recurrent Structures in Presidential Authority in Skowronek's Political Time Framework   148

Figure 2.3 Trump's Potential Placement in "Political Time"   151

Figure 7.1 The Perils of Trump's Presidency   307

Table 5.1 Post-Election Rallies, December 2016   250

Table 5.2 Post-Inauguration Rallies, 2017   268

Table 6.1 Executive Orders by Policy Area, 2017–18   286

Table 6.2 Executive Memoranda by Policy Area, 2017–18   293

1

Populist disrupter-in-chief

The corrupt establishment knows that we are a great threat to their power. They know if we win their power is gone, and it's returned to you the people . . . But it all depends on whether we let the corrupt media decide our future, or we let the American people decide our future.

—Donald Trump, October 13, 2016

I. Introduction

On November 8, 2016 Republican standard-bearer Donald J. Trump shook the American political landscape to its foundations, from the peninsula of the Sunshine State north to Coal Country and west across the fruited plain. In light of Democrats' relative advantage in delegate-rich states in the northeast and California, his Electoral College victory was tantamount to drawing an inside straight at a poker table somewhere at a remote, Native-owned casino in "flyover territory." Indeed, bettors in Las Vegas and abroad staked the odds *against* a Trump victory at five to one on Election Day.[1] Written off by pundits, disdained by the media, derided by Democrats, and scorned by so-called "establishment" primary rivals in the Grand Old Party (GOP) for whom he invented flippant and insulting sobriquets, the idiosyncratic and irascible business mogul seemingly surprised everyone—save perhaps himself—by narrowly prevailing in key swing states including Florida, Michigan, North Carolina, Ohio, Pennsylvania, and Wisconsin to carry the Electoral College 304–227 over rival Hillary Clinton.

---

[1] Lucinda Shen, "Here's how much you could have won betting on Trump's presidency." *Fortune*, November 9, 2016. http://fortune.com/2016/11/09/donald-trump-president-gamble/

Trump dismissed critics who immediately called into question the legitimacy of his victory. His detractors underscored that he lost the popular vote by nearly 2.9 million ballots, the largest margin in U.S. history.[2] Holding steadfast in the Machiavellian messaging that characterized his campaign, the president-elect ignited a Twitterstorm within days of his victory by drawing upon a central component of his populist political instincts, conspiracy theory, to provide an alternative narrative to Clinton's future book *What Happened*. Rejecting the thesis of Russian interference in the election, dismissing the impact of the late October reopening of the Federal Bureau of Investigation (FBI) inquiry into the former Secretary of State's handling of emails, and shrugging off allegations of collusion between members of his campaign and the Kremlin in Moscow, Trump contended instead, without any empirical evidence, that "[i]n addition to winning the Electoral College in a landslide, I *won the popular vote* if you deduct the millions of people who voted illegally."[3]

Several months later in January 2017, during his first White House interview, the president doubled down on his belief in rampant voter fraud by illegal immigrants, particularly in Democratic states such as New York and California that overwhelmingly backed Clinton and were essentially responsible

[2] Of the four other presidents who won the Electoral College but lost the popular vote, John Quincy Adams prevailed in the Electoral College in 1824 with 38,000 fewer popular votes than Andrew Jackson, who won a plurality; in 1876 Samuel Tilden culled 254,000 more popular votes than Rutherford B. Hayes, who won the Electoral College when the delegations for Florida, Louisiana, South Carolina and Oregon cast ballots for him in exchange for an end to federal troops in the South, thus ending Reconstruction in the Compromise of 1877; in 1888 Benjamin Harrison lost the popular vote to Grover Cleveland by nearly 91,000 votes; and in 2000 George W. Bush lost the popular vote to Al Gore by nearly 544,000 votes.

[3] @realDonaldTrump, "In addition to winning the Electoral College in a landslide, I won the popular vote if you deduct the millions of people who voted illegally." *Twitter*, November 27, 2016, 12:30 p.m. https://twitter.com/realdonaldtrump/status/802972944532209664. Emphasis added.

for the popular/electoral vote disjuncture.[4] Trump's unsubstantiated and widely refuted allegations were apparently tied to an *Infowars* story claiming that three million illegal aliens had cast votes unlawfully in 2016.[5] Whether Trump believed the uncorroborated report was perhaps less significant than the immediate furor his comments created. The media became instantaneously distracted and suspended discussion of front-page newspaper stories questioning the president's business income in light of prohibitions under the Emoluments Clause in Article I, Section 9 of the Constitution.[6] Trump clearly did not consider the costs of vilifying illegal immigrants without facts. But the president's red herring had successfully, if temporarily, sidetracked the media from the expanding Russia collusion narrative of his critics, derailed public attention from pressing legal questions, and rallied his supporters by indicting his old political opponent "Crooked Hillary" anew—even if the election had been over for nearly three months.

Trump's specious chronicle of the 2016 popular vote for the presidency represents paramount elements of a populist political

---

[4] Philip Bump, "Why did Trump lose the popular vote? Because he didn't care about it. And because they cheated." *Washington Post*, January 26, 2017. https://www.washingtonpost.com/news/politics/wp/2017/01/26/why-did-trump-lose-the-popular-vote-because-he-didnt-care-about-it-and-because-they-cheated/?noredirect=on&utm_term=.6353f3f54e11

[5] Katie Forster, "Donald Trump's false claim about illegal votes based on unverified tweet posted on conspiracy website." *The Independent* (UK), November 28, 2016. https://www.independent.co.uk/news/world/americas/donald-trump-millions-illegal-aliens-voted-greg-phillips-three-million-tweet-infowars-alex-jones-a7443006.html

[6] Andrew Restuccia, "Trump's baseless assertions of voter fraud called 'stunning'." *Politico*, November 27, 2016. https://www.politico.com/story/2016/11/trump-illegal-voting-clinton-231860. Maryland and the District of Columbia filed a lawsuit regarding Trump's international hotel in Washington, DC. See Ann E. Marimow and Jonathan O'Connell, "Trump can profit from foreign government business at his hotel, if he doesn't do favors in return, Justice Dept. says." *Washington Post*, June 11, 2018. https://www.washingtonpost.com/local/public-safety/obscure-no-more-the-emoluments-clause-is-back-again-in-a-federal-court/2018/06/09/cf052832-6a72-11e8-9e38-24e693b38637_story.html?utm_term=.8d31666b1862

style that he plays like a finely tuned instrument. The recurrent themes include the unending recrimination of elites and political foes, unseemly personal invectives, the misrepresentation of facts tied to anti-intellectual discourse, calculated semiotics focused on the abjection of the "foreign" or "other" as he defines it, and conspiracy narratives and the invention of bogeymen to rationalize challenges, setbacks, and defeats. Improvisational and unpredictable, Trump's unapologetically truculent and imperious approach to governance, often via instantaneous phone messaging and unilateralism, generates optics of chaos while fostering ample uncertainty and angst, especially for those who find themselves in the president's oratorical crosshairs.

Extended repartees on Twitter are often electronic salvos fired by the thin- (if nicely tan-) skinned chief executive in the early morning hours after presumably stewing about perceived personal slights. As the president explained years before, "When someone attacks me, I always attack back . . . except 100x more. This has nothing to do with a tirade but rather, a way of life!"[7] Indeed as Trump biographers Charlie Laderman and Brendan Simms suggest, Trump's worldview is such that life is "combat," and an interminable struggle without a clear victory—for him personally or for the nation—is intolerable.[8] Social media posts, press conferences, and post-election rallies bordering on the Founders' worst fears of demagoguery are replete with verbal assaults *du jour* on the media, including allegations of unfair coverage and "fake news" reporting by individual journalists and entire networks, notwithstanding Fox News until August 2019.[9] No one—from cabinet secretaries, judges, and members of Congress on either

---

[7] @realDonaldTrump, "When someone attacks me, I always attack back . . . except 100x more. This has nothing to do with a tirade but rather, a way of life!" *Twitter*, November 11, 2012, 5:56 a.m. https://twitter.com/realdonaldtrump/status/267626951097868289?lang=en

[8] Charlie Laderman and Brendan Simms, *Donald Trump: The Making of a World View* (New York: I. B. Tauris, 2017), pp. 4–5.

[9] Caitlin O'Kane, "'Fox isn't working for us anymore': President Trump promises to find a new outlet." *CBS News*, August 29, 2019. https://www.cbsnews.com/news/fox-news-donald-trump-tweet-fox-isnt-working-for-us-anymore-2019-08-28/

side of the aisle to despots like Kim Jong-Un and longstanding allies in Europe or Canada—escapes the president's rhetorical wrath if he senses an affront to his character or self-proclaimed mission to "Make America Great Again." Elites of any stripe are the low-hanging fruit for Trump's strategic rants.

At first glance, some of the president's social media tactics appear as ad hoc as they are inexplicable. Examples include his impromptu involvement in controversies such as the national anthem in the National Football League (NFL) that are peripheral to his policy agenda to the bizarre reposting of a tweet by a British extremist party leader featuring a Muslim migrant assailing a Dutch boy that prompted outrage in the United Kingdom.[10] Closer analysis, however, reveals another dimension to Trump's populist style: a focus on challenging not only political elites but also cultural elites. Attacks on cultural elites are aimed at galvanizing his base as much as promises to restore economic prosperity to those who have suffered decades of abuse by inept leaders.

Three years into Trump's presidency, one observation is straightforward: A central component to his populist campaigning and leadership style is the *spectacle*, in which "particular details stand for broader and deeper meanings,"[11] gestures overshadow results, and performance outweighs and often obfuscates facts. "The artifice of his authenticity and infantilization of discourse," writes Robert Singh, "were integral to his appeal. The very characteristics attracting obloquy—insults, assaults on 'politically correct' taboos, genitalia references, violent language—testified to his outspoken credentials as credibly effecting 'change' to an ossified politics-as-usual."[12] Often as disorienting, discordant, and confounding in

---

[10] Elizabeth Landers and James Masters, "Trump retweets anti-Muslim videos." *CNN*, November 30, 2017. https://edition.cnn.com/2017/11/29/politics/donald-trump-retweet-jayda-fransen/index.html

[11] Bruce Miroff, "The Presidency and the Public: Leadership as Spectacle." In Michael Nelson (ed.), *The Presidency and the Political System*, 4th edition (Washington, DC: Congressional Quarterly Inc., 1995), pp. 274, 278.

[12] Robert Singh, "'I, the People': A Deflationary Interpretation of Populism, Trump, and the United States Constitution." *Economy and Society* 46, no. 1 (2017): 26.

logic and syntax as a script from Eugène Ionesco's theater of the absurd, Trump's histrionics are deliberately calculated to lend legitimacy to his populist panache. "Populist trust," Maxine Molyneux and Thomas Osborne contend,

> can be generated by idiocy in that such a personal style is both an individualizing yet also hard-to-fake device for signaling trust on the lines of "if I am this absurd (or, if Trump, this out of line), I must be genuine".[13]

If the president's assaults on decency and his politically incorrect discourse leave the Washington patriciate breathlessly discomfited, the malodorous plebeians condemned for shopping at Walmart by uppity, if now-disgraced, FBI agents like Peter Strzok wryly clamor that Trump is doing exactly the job they elected him to undertake: upsetting the apple cart of the entrenched elite, lambasting a putatively dishonest media, and taking aim at a supposedly self-interested permanent political class that manipulates institutional rules to the detriment of the forgotten voter. As a result, little if anything in the president's quiver of rhetorically sharp arrows, including personal demonization of political foes and the delegitimization of democratic processes and political institutions, formal or informal, is off-limits. As *Wall Street Journal* correspondent Gerald Seib asserts,

> Disruptor-in-chief is a title Mr. Trump likely would accept, with pride. Disrupting the status quo is what he does. He set out to disrupt the Republican Party, then the presidential-election process, and, ultimately, Washington. He has done it all.[14]

---

[13] Maxine Molyneux and Thomas Osborne, "Populism: A Deflationary View." *Economy and Society* 46, no. 1 (2017): 6.

[14] Gerald F. Seib, "On the world stage, Trump remains disruptor-in-chief." *Wall Street Journal*, June 7, 2017. https://www.wsj.com/articles/on-the-world-stage-trump-remains-disruptor-in-chief-1496677230

II. *The populist phenomenon in perspective: comparative and historical challenges to the political establishment*

Populism, Cas Mudde and Cristóbal Rovira Kaltwasser assert, "is a label seldom claimed by people or organizations themselves. Instead, it is ascribed to others, most often with a negative connotation."[15] Critics of populism frequently characterize the phenomenon as the politics of grievance focused less on problem-solving and more on assigning blame to elites or scapegoating some disadvantaged group for the ordinary citizen's woes.

If populism is a disruptive force in the political arena as the Trump presidency suggests, it is because the approach focuses on the politics of conflict and privileges polarization rather than consensus-building. The political style dichotomizes society into two opposing groups, elites and ordinary citizens, and pits them against one another. Populists claim to represent the "people" outside the prevailing governing structure, which they view as corrupted. They clamor for direct democracy, favor majoritarianism, deprecate mediated institutions, and are prone to de-emphasize if not directly challenge minority rights in both the Madisonian sense and in terms of race and ethnicity. They are inclined to reduce complex problems to some least common denominator and lure supporters with simplified solutions. With an anti-intellectual tendency to abnegate facts, science, and reason, populists often descend into the realm of conspiracy theory to explain complex social, economic, and political challenges. Nostalgia for the past, or a preoccupation with the return to some golden moment in time, may also inform populist rhetoric. Nativism is also a frequent hallmark of the populist narrative and can pivot variably on religiosity and/or racial and ethnic differentiation. Populist nationalism concentrates on the articulation of national identity and the construction of claims to represent some component of "the people" as an underdog within

---

[15] Cas Mudde and Cristóbal Rovira Kaltwasser, *Populism: A Very Short Introduction* (New York: Oxford University Press, 2017), p. 2.

the nation.[16] Populists may employ ultra-nationalist rhetoric as a means of scapegoating and excluding certain groups (e.g., ethnic, racial) from the nation-state and decisionmaking power within it. Finally, populist nationalists may accentuate national sovereignty and the inviolability of the nation-state within the international order.[17]

Such common, though not mutually exclusive, features of populism are discernible contemporaneously within a comparative frame. Trump's victory in the United States in 2016 represented one of many swells in the storm surge of grassroots discontent that catapulted successful populist candidates to victory elsewhere around the globe. In the last decade the populist wave, and its unevenly destabilizing effects on governing institutions, economic markets, and state–society relations, has washed ashore in both established democracies and developing nations. The tsunami effectively left established political orders in the flotsam and jetsam of an undulating tide of disillusioned and disgruntled voters. Populists' particularism, Joseph S. Nye, Jr., posits, "makes it an unlikely candidate for a broad ideological movement that enthusiasts proclaim." Yet the contemporary vanguards of populism share one fundamental element of cohesion first and foremost: the "common denominator is *resentment* of powerful elites."[18]

Let us consider briefly the comparative context. Across the Atlantic Emmanuel Macron, despite his technocratic roots in the French *appareil politique*, transformed a fledgling candidacy into a mass, independent populist movement, unprecedented since

---

[16] Benjamin de Cleen and Yannis Stavrakakis. "Distinctions and Articulations: A Discourse Theoretical Framework for the Study of Populism and Nationalism." *Javnost—The Public: Journal of the European Institute for Communication and Culture* 24, no. 4 (2017): 301–19.

[17] Benjamin de Cleen, "Populism and Nationalism." In Cristóbal Rovira Kaltwasser, Paul Taggart, Paulina Ochoa Espejo, and Pierre Ostiguy (eds.), *The Oxford Handbook of Populism* (New York: Oxford University Press, 2017), pp. 342–62.

[18] Joseph S. Nye, Jr., "Populism is likely to continue in the United States." "Symposium: Why Is Populism on the Rise and What Do the Populists Want?" *The International Economy* (Winter 2019): 12. Emphasis added.

Charles de Gaulle's victory in 1960, to conquer the Élysée in 2017. Macron claimed to "speak directly for 'the people,' eschewing the role of democratic intermediaries" and painting other parties as detached, self-interested, and corrupt. "Macron was able to succeed because such views were common in France, as they are in many countries experiencing a populist revolt."[19] From the very moment he assumed the presidency of the Fifth Republic, however, Macron seemingly abjured his populist campaign by pursuing "austerity measures that directly affected everyday French citizens,"[20] including social security taxes and cuts to housing subsidies. The result was a dramatic loss in public support just three months into his term. The backlash culminated in widespread social unrest and spontaneous riots in the fall of 2017 by the radical *gilets jaunes* or yellow vest movement. The proximate cause for the civil disorder was a hike in fuel taxes that galvanized opposition to Macron's policies as out of touch with the voters he courted just months before.[21]

A year earlier in 2016, across the Channel from *douce France* to the white cliffs of Dover, a different populist saga had already began to unfold in the United Kingdom (UK). The island nation voted narrowly in a referendum, 52–48 percent, to leave the European Union (EU) in the so-called Brexit vote. The balloting cast a long shadow on the future prospects for British unity, as England and Wales voted to sever ties with the Continental economic and political project while Scotland and Northern Ireland voted to remain. Regardless, the outcome was undeniably a redoubtable slap at the British elite. "Voters thought politicians, business leaders, and intellectuals had lost their right to control the system.

---

[19] Harvey Feigenbaum, "Macron the populist." *Social Europe*, February 5, 2019. https://www.socialeurope.eu/macron-the-populist

[20] Maxence Lambrecq, "Pourquoi Emmanuel Macron s'effondre dans les sondages." *Europe1*, August 27, 2019. https://www.europe1.fr/politique/pourquoi-emmanuel-macron-seffondre-dans-les-sondages-3419846. Translated by author.

[21] See Yann Algan *et al.*, "Qui sont les Gilets jaunes et leurs soutiens?" *Observatoire du Bien-être* 3, February 14, 2019. http://www.sciencespo.fr/cevipof/sites/sciencespo.fr.cevipof/files/-Qui-sont-les-Gilets-jaunes-et-leurs-soutiens-1.pdf

Voters thought the elite had contempt for their values—for their nationalism and interests."[22] Economic stagnation in the Euro-zone, combined with the rise of nationalist sentiment connected to the EU's response to refugee crises precipitated by human catastrophes such as the Syrian Civil War, contributed to the outcome.

Indignation at political elites in the UK only deepened following the referendum as Prime Minister Theresa May sought unsuccessfully to negotiate an exodus with intransigent European leaders and a recalcitrant opposition in Westminster. She was ultimately forced to resign in July 2019 amidst domestic and international stalemate. Mounting exasperation with the political class was evident in the stunning gains for Nigel Farage's Brexit Party two months earlier in the 2019 European Parliament elections. Farage, a firebrand nationalist, cobbled together the party just six weeks before the vote and gained 32 percent of the ballots in Britain with the promise to confront the Conservative and Labour parties domestically if a "no deal" exit from the EU were not implemented.[23] Regardless, with May's resignation the task of negotiating Brexit fell, however briefly, to Boris Johnson, a flamboyant conservative leader known for his gaffes and no-holds-barred offensive commentary. His nationalist rhetoric at times resembles elements of Trump's populist style as much as his uncanny hairstyle. Echoing Trump's call to "Make America Great Again," in his first speech to Parliament in July 2019 Johnson vowed that Brexit would make Britain the greatest place on earth.[24] Johnson's pledge to withdraw the UK from the EU by October 31, 2019, if necessary without securing a settlement with Continental leaders, led to the crumbling of his majority and

---

[22] John Mauldin, "3 reasons Brits voted for Brexit." *Forbes*, July 6, 2016. https://www.forbes.com/sites/johnmauldin/2016/07/05/3-reasons-brits-voted-for-brexit/#1a286d501f9d

[23] Tom Kibasi, "Nigel Farage's victory gives him the whip hand over British politics." *The Guardian*, May 27, 2019. https://www.theguardian.com/commentisfree/2019/may/27/nigel-farage-brexit-party-elections

[24] Guy Faulconbridge and Kylie MacLellan, "'I'll make Britain great again, PM Johnson says, echoing Trump." *Reuters*, July 25, 2019. https://www.reuters.com/article/us-britain-eu-ill-make-britain-great-again-pm-johnson-says-echoing-trump-idUSKCN1UK0OG

a call for new elections just six weeks after assuming the prime ministership—the third such national election since the Brexit referendum, which ultimately gave the Tories the majority needed for Johnson to make good on his promise. The UK formally exited the European Union on January 31, 2020.

From Eastern and Central Europe to South America the populist wave proved more alarming for its challenge to democratic norms and the scapegoating of minorities for economic and social challenges. While in the Ukraine in 2019 voters elected a comedian, Volodymyr Zelenskiy, "as an anti-establishment gesture, or simply as a joke,"[25] the populist onslaught in Poland and Hungary was scarcely a laughing matter. Illiberal "reforms" undertaken at the behest of the Polish Law and Order Party and Hungarian Prime Minister Victor Orbán's Fidesz Party raised the specter of authoritarianism in two countries struggling to consolidate democracy since the fall of the Berlin Wall thirty years ago. As Anna Grzymala-Busse notes, "after populists gained power, they proceeded to politicize and neuter the constitutional courts, limit media access and freedoms, rewrite electoral laws, and divide society into 'better' and 'worse' sort of citizens."[26] Similarly, in Latin America, Jair Bolsonaro's victory in Brazil in 2018 provoked angst about a new anti-democratic spirit gripping one of the most ethnically diverse countries in the Western Hemisphere. Dubbed the "Trump of the Tropics," Bolsonaro drew upon the theme of corruption, seized on the disintegration of the Left, and fed off political scandals that resulted in the impeachment of President Dilma Rousseff in 2016 to garner support.[27] He openly attacked political elites and threatened

[25] Katya Soldak, "Ukrainian humor: A comedian is elected president." *Forbes*, April 21, 2019. https://www.forbes.com/sites/katyasoldak/2019/04/21/ukrainian-humor-a-comedian-is-elected-president/#4129dffcd140

[26] Joshua Tucker, "Will global populism continue to erode democracies?" *Washington Post*, September 13, 2017. https://www.washingtonpost.com/news/monkey-cage/wp/2017/09/13/will-global-populism-continue-to-erode-democracies/

[27] Daniel Gallas, "Dilma Rousseff impeachment: How did it go wrong for her?" *BBC News*, May 12, 2016. https://www.bbc.com/news/world-latin-america-36028247

the arrest of adversaries, called minorities lazy and criminal, took aim at homosexuals by contending that Brazil should not become a "gay tourism paradise," and argued he would not recognize any electoral outcome other than his own victory.[28]

A. Trump, populism, and American political eras

Whatever Trump's rhetorical or other bonds to contemporary populist homologues abroad, the president's populist mold is an amalgam of similar themes his American predecessors have emphasized since the 1800s. The stylistic inheritance includes movements and/or individuals seeking to capitalize on anti-elitism and socio-economic angst dating to the Second Party Era. Most individual populist candidates have failed in their bids for the presidency and most movements have proven ephemeral. Still, as Nye asserts:

> Populism is not new and it is as American as pumpkin pie. Some populist reactions are healthy for democracy (think of Andrew Jackson in the nineteenth century or the Progressive era at the beginning of the last century), while other nativist populists such the anti-immigrant Know-Nothing Party in the nineteenth century or Senator Joe McCarthy and Governor George Wallace in the twentieth century have emphasized xenophobia and insularity. The recent wave of American populism includes both strands.[29]

Indeed, anti-elitism and nativism are two key elements of the populist style as it has been expressed intermittently over the Republic's 230-year political history, complemented by majoritarian tendencies, a focus on the common man and claims to

---

[28] See Danielle Brant, "Bolsonaro Uses Same Fascist Tactics as Trump, Says Yale Professor." *Folha de S. Paulo* (English version), October 4, 2018. https://www1.folha.uol.com.br/internacional/en/world/2018/10/bolsonaro-uses-same-fascist-tactics-as-trump-says-yale-professor.shtml; Tom Phillips and Anna Jean Kaiser, "Brazil must not become a 'gay tourism paradise', says Bolsonaro." *The Guardian*, April 25, 2019. https://www.theguardian.com/world/2019/apr/26/bolsonaro-accused-of-inciting-hatred-with-gay-paradise-comment

[29] Nye, "Why Is Populism on the Rise, and What Do the Populists Want?," p. 13.

grassroots support, and anti-intellectual discourse. It is vital to emphasize that American populism is not wedded solely to the left or to the right of the political spectrum. "While populist ire is typically aimed at wealthy elites," argues Joseph Lowndes, "populists tend to prefer the language of popular sovereignty to class, blurring distinctions in a broad definition of *the people*."[30] The tie that binds populists across time—and figures and movements with motivations as different as Andrew Jackson, William Jennings Bryan and the People's Party of the 1890s, to Ross Perot and Donald Trump—is the articulation of the concept of the ordinary, hardworking "people" facing an entrenched elite at odds with their interests. There is also a predisposition by populists to revert to the rhetoric of nativism and identify a scapegoat to blame for the woes of the downtrodden. As Lowndes further elaborates,

> American populism dwells ambivalently in the discursive lineage of the classical/grotesque binary as it has always been couched in beliefs in Enlightenment ideals of progress, and in celebration of more bourgeois understandings of the production of wealth than the redistribution thereof ... Populist identity thus distinguishes itself against those seen as exploitative elites above and parasitic dependents below, which are depicted as imprudent, excessive, wasteful, and indolent.[31]

The key to understanding the variant of American populism is the way in which its protagonists frame the nature of the conflict and seek to polarize the electorate. For example, in the progressive era populists like Bryan and the People's Party defined the "people" as farmers and small merchant producers whose diminishing fortunes had been overlooked by a government whose "functions have been basely surrendered by our

---

[30] Joseph Lowndes, "Populism in the United States." In Cristóbal Rovira Kaltwasser, Paul Taggart, Paulina Ochoa Espejo, and Pierre Ostiguy (eds.), *The Oxford Handbook of Populism* (New York: Oxford University Press, 2017), p. 232.
[31] Ibid., p. 237.

public servants to corporate monopolies."[32] In recent decades, for Ross Perot (and Donald Trump) elites sold out farmers and steelworkers with bad trade deals like the North American Free Trade Agreement (NAFTA). The alleged benefactors comprised Mexicans working in *maquiladoras* south of the border and illegal immigrants who traversed that border to take jobs away from Americans stateside.

In the post-World War II era, populism on the political right has manifested frequently as a reaction to social change. As Berlet and Lyons assert, this strain of populism "posits a noble hard-working middle group constantly in conflict with lazy, malevolent, or sinful parasites at the top and bottom of the social order."[33] In attacking a privileged elite populists take aim at marginalized segments of population who do not qualify as members of the "people," more commonly identified with white workers and small businessmen. To elaborate,

> the populist world view sees a division not between rich and poor but between producers and parasites. And that's why Trump's supporters hold in equal contempt Wall Street financiers who got a bailout and undocumented immigrants who broke the law.[34]

It is also why two decades earlier Ross Perot lambasted elites in Washington for selling ordinary Americans short with deficit spending and free trade deals while intimating that blacks on welfare were freeloading off hardworking taxpayers.

One may reach back into time to consider the only populist prior to Trump to accede to the nation's highest political office to compare these dynamics historically. Andrew Jackson— a towering icon of nineteenth-century politics to whom Trump

---

[32] "People's Party Platform, 1896." http://www.digitalhistory.uh.edu/disp_textbook.cfm?smtID=3&psid=4067

[33] Chip Berlet and Matthew N. Lyons, *Right-Wing Populism in America: Too Close for Comfort* (New York: Guilford Press, 2000), p. 348.

[34] Mara Liasson, quoting Michael Lind of the New America Foundation, "Nativism and economic anxiety fuel Trump's populist appeal." *NPR*, September 4, 2015. https://www.npr.org/sections/itsallpolitics/2015/09/04/437443401/populist-movement-reflected-in-campaigns-of-sanders-and-trump

clumsily attempts to compare himself—took up the mantle of the common man following the "corrupt bargain" perpetrated by a cabal of crooked elites, including House Speaker Henry Clay, in the smoke-filled parlors of Congress to rob him of the presidency in 1824.

> Politically Andrew Jackson's Democratic Party coalition was made up of farmers, emergent industrial wage workers, and slave owners—all depicted as the "producing classes" of society. "Producers" understood themselves in contrast, on the one hand, to the idle rich such as bankers and land speculators, and on the other, to people of color, stereotyped as parasitic and/or predatory figures at the other end of the economic spectrum.[35]

Upon winning the White House in 1828, Jackson's subsequent war on the Bank of the United States, an institution he characterized as a representation of favoritism toward foreign and domestic economic elites against the common man, solidified his electoral base. The longer-term effect of Jackson's politics of conflict was the rise of a new political party, the Whigs, founded essentially on personal contempt for the Tennessean as the nation edged ever closer to civil strife over slavery.

Apart from his diatribes against corrupt elites in Washington, Trump's hardline stance against illegal immigration also brings to mind a time and political movement over a century-and-a-half ago notable for anti-immigration, nativist fervor linked to socioeconomic fears. If Trump's critics suggest that his pledge to build a wall at the southern border with Mexico and his intemperate and uncharitable comments about illegal immigrants are reflective of a deeper narrative of racism and xenophobia he foments via coded language, the Know-Nothing Party (formally the American Party) of the 1850s did not mince words in its virulent disdain for foreigners—especially Irish Catholics—attempting to build a life in America. Drawing support from disaffected Whigs, the American Party nominated Millard Fillmore as its unsuccessful

---

[35] Joe Lowndes, "Populist Persuasions." *The Baffler*, October 31, 2018. https://thebaffler.com/latest/populist-persuasions-lowndes

nominee for the presidency in 1856. Its platform included the mandate that "Americans must rule America" and proposed a "change in the laws of naturalization, making a continued residence of twenty-one years . . . and excluding all paupers or persons convicted of crime from landing upon our shores."[36] While avoiding the slavery issue, the Know-Nothings attracted support from anti-Catholic, anti-immigration elements of the electorate in opposition to unresponsive politicians.[37] At the core of the Know-Nothings' foreboding was a Papist conspiracy bent on changing the social fabric of the nation by inundating the United States with immigrants loyal to the Catholic Church and not to the Constitution. White Anglo-Saxon Protestants would be overrun eventually, altering the character of the nation forever.

Such an admixture of anti-elitism and nativism is evident in Trump's populist style, though Irish and German immigrants are not his target. And it is not always the president himself who hatches conspiracy theories about those who oppose his policies on the southern border. But he lays the groundwork for speculation and provides ample fodder for imagination. Trump casts efforts to halt illegal crossings with reference to the enforcement of existing law while simultaneously highlighting the damage that undocumented workers, particularly illegals with criminal records, cause to the economy, the body politic, and grieving "angel families" who have been victimized by the loss of loved ones. The president belittles his immediate predecessors for failing to address border security. Some conservative media figures have taken Trump's comments and run with them into a different realm to resurrect nativist sentiments reminiscent of Know-Nothingism. With the apparent blessing of the president's advisors, commentators on Fox News, including Laura Ingraham, peddle the conspiratorial "great replacement theory" whereby Democratic politicians

---

[36] American Party Platform, 1856, Articles III and IX. *HistoryHub*, http://historyhub.abc-clio.com/Support/Display/2144524?sid=2146163&cid=31&view=&tab=3

[37] Bruce Levine, "Conservatism, Nativism, and Slavery: Thomas R. Whitney and the Origins of the Know-Nothing Party." *Journal of American History* (September 2001): 456.

"want to replace you, the American voters, with newly amnestied citizens and an ever increasing number of chain migrants" as a means of creating a permanent majority. For his part, Fox News host Tucker Carlson opined that "Latin American countries are changing election outcomes here by forcing demographic change on this country."[38] To the degree that Trump employs anti-illegal immigration measures (largely through unilateral action) as a form of economic nationalism linked to an "America First" platform, it is a policy stance—as former chief strategist to the president, Steve Bannon, remarked—"that works for the vulgarians, that works for the hobbits, that works for know-nothings, that works for the peasants with the pitchforks" against elites who putatively regard working-class Americans who support Trump as intellectually inferior.[39]

Nativism and nationalist revival in the populist narrative, whether on the left or the right of the political spectrum, is commonly linked to the idealization of the nation's past in the bid to recover a real or imagined greatness in the halcyon days of a lost era. The restoration of American pre-eminence hinges on wresting power from political elites, attacking the administrative state, and empowering the forgotten voter. Trump's focus on returning manufacturing jobs from overseas, resuscitating the coal, steel and energy industries, and nixing international trade deals unfair to the United States purposefully hearkens back to images of the grandeur of American industrial might in the nineteenth century. Who better to resurrect the successful exploits of those captains of industry with thousands of employees under their tutelage like J. P. Morgan, Andrew Carnegie, Henry Ford, and Andrew Mellon than the iconic New York real estate mogul

---

[38] Courtney Hagle, "How Fox News pushed the white supremacist 'great replacement' theory." *MediaMatters*, August 5, 2019. https://www.mediamatters.org/tucker-carlson/how-fox-news-pushed-white-supremacist-great-replacement-theory

[39] Frances Stead Sellers and Aaron Blake, "Stephen Bannon's apparent references to anti-immigrant Know-Nothing Party don't seem so coincidental anymore." *Washington Post*, February 2, 2017. https://www.washington-post.com/news/the-fix/wp/2017/02/02/stephen-bannons-apparent-references-to-anti-immigrant-know-nothing-party-dont-seem-so-coincidental-anymore/

who rails against the economic ravages of globalization on the middle class? On the cultural side, Trump frequently emphasizes patriotism, reverence for the flag, and the nation's Christian heritage as a form of American exceptionalism that elites have attempted to unstitch from the seams of the nation's intricate weave. That narrative, including the president's staunch support for Israel, has bolstered his support among Evangelicals, despite their trepidations about his personal conduct.[40]

At first glance a comparison of Trump to William Jennings Bryan's populism in the decade before and immediately after the turn of the twentieth century might seem curious. After all, Bryan's progressive agenda was squarely opposed to those emblematic "robber barons" (and the bankers who supported them) who he thought bore responsibility for the plight of the downtrodden. Unlike Trump, few questioned Bryan's commitment to Christian doctrines that he employed as a benchmark of moral authority. Yet the deeper theme of restoration of a glorious past connects Trump to Bryan, however oddly. For the latter, a return to an agrarian society—not industrialization—was the cornerstone of American wealth, progress, and social cohesion. Seizing upon the fervent debate over monetary policy in the 1896 election, Bryan trumpeted the cause of indebted farmers and small merchants against wealthy, moneyed elites with his opposition to the gold standard. "Bryan's populist rhetoric," argues Troy Murphy,

> consistently defends a democratic ideal, expressed in part through the nobility of "plain people" and the moral fabric of agrarian communities, against the attacks of a rapidly changing world and the "force" of a supposed elite, whether those elites are the bankers of 1896 or the scientists of 1925.[41]

[40] Melissa Quinn, "Tony Perkins: Trump gets a 'mulligan' over Stormy Daniels from Evangelicals." *Washington Examiner*, January 23, 2018. https://www.washingtonexaminer.com/tony-perkins-trump-gets-a-mulligan-over-stormy-daniels-from-evangelicals

[41] Troy M. Murphy, "William Jennings Bryan: Boy Orator, Broken Man, and the 'Evolution' of America's Public Philosophy." *Great Plains Quarterly* 40, no. 2 (2002): 85. Murphy's reference to 1925 regards the Scopes Monkey Trial involving the teaching of evolution in public schools to which Bryan was opposed on religious grounds.

Ultimately economic displacement and social anxiety drove support for the populist narrative of Bryan (unsuccessfully in 1896) as they did for Trump (successfully in 2016). Like Philippe Bridau in Balzac's *The Black Sheep*, one central and unflagging impulse in the populist style is to recover a vanished inheritance and restore the national family, or at least its forgotten siblings, to prominence and wealth.

Trump's bond to other twentieth-century populists underscores how *style* supplants substance in comparisons across time. Despite very different policy stances, Trump and the "Kingfish"—Huey Pierce Long of Louisiana—share qualities of "a politician of special character: a charismatic mass leader, one whose power exceeded the ordinary bounds of democratic politics, one who threatened to alter the very structure of American politics."[42] Long's "Share Our Wealth" plan was the product of both his unbridled political ambition and quest for the presidency in 1936 stemming from the belief that Franklin Roosevelt's New Deal had failed to address sufficiently the predicament of the common man during the Depression. Long's redistributive program echoed exhortations now heard among Democrats jockeying for the White House in 2020, like Bernie Sanders or Elizabeth Warren: levying taxes on the highest wage earners, implementing a more progressive tax scheme, providing governmental health care benefits and free education, and guaranteeing paid vacation, among others.[43] As a major power broker, the Kingfish's threat to Roosevelt's re-election may well have prompted the president's efforts to cement a "second" New Deal in the summer of 1935.[44]

Regardless, the strands of Long's populist narrative intertwine with Trump's insofar as they sew together the threads of economic

---

[42] Alan Brinkley, "Huey Long, the Share Our Wealth Movement, and the Limits of Depression Dissidence." *Louisiana History: The Journal of the Louisiana Historical Association* 22, no. 2 (Spring 1981): 118.

[43] See Henry M. Christman (ed.), Kingfish to America, Share Our Wealth: Selected Senatorial Papers of Huey P. Long (New York: Schocken Books, 1985).

[44] See Edwin Amenta, Kathleen Dunleavy, and Mary Bernstein, "Stolen Thunder? Huey Long's 'Share Our Wealth,' Political Mediation, and the Second New Deal." *American Sociological Review* 59, no. 5 (1994): 678–702.

anxiety and anti-intellectualism. As Alan Brinkley notes, dissidents of the 1930s like Huey Long (and Father Charles Coughlin) were suspicious of an increasingly dominant corporate culture able to control their own lives and the lives of others. As outsiders themselves, they began "speaking for outsiders."[45] They were particularly adept at

> appealing to one of the fundamental anxieties of any modern, industrial society: the fear of lost autonomy, of powerlessness; the terrifying sense—and the more terrifying in a time of economic distress—of losing control, of discovering that one's fate is in the hands of forces one cannot affect or even know. Virtually all members of modern society suffer such anxieties in some form, to some degree; Long and Coughlin, however, were appealing to those afflicted with such fears with special intensity.[46]

To Long's critics he was a "shameless demagogue" who "appealed to the wild unthinking radical fringe."[47] The anti-intellectual component of his rhetoric dismissed socio-economic complexity and replaced specificity with promises that emphasized what his supporters would obtain in a transactional politics. "The Kingfish," writes Ernest Bormann, "was vague about how the plan would work or how it would be translated into action. His explanation was always simple and plausible." At the same time, "he could employ evidence, logic, ridicule, humor and pathos with skill and in ingenious proportion."[48] Such a description of the slain senator from the Pelican State could be equally applied to Trump's "Make America Great Again" rallies before and after the 2016 election.

Trump's style connects emotively to contemporary populists like Barry Goldwater, George Wallace, and H. Ross Perot in both the realm of anti-intellectualism and matters of race.

---

[45] Alan Brinkley, "Comparative Biography as Political History: Huey Long and Father Coughlin." *The History Teacher* 18, no. 1 (1984): 12.

[46] Ibid., p. 13.

[47] Alden Hatch, *Franklin D. Roosevelt* (New York: Henry Holt, 1947), p. 221.

[48] Ernest Bormann, "Huey Long: Analysis of a Demagogue." *Today's Speech* 2, no. 3 (1954): 18–19.

Populists often float conspiracy theories onto which their supporters latch and subsequently embellish. Trump, of course, spoke of 2016 as a "rigged" election and thereafter "deep state" conspiracies to oust him from office. In 1964 Goldwater railed against the evils of big government and communism. Some in support of his presidential campaign, including members of the John Birch Society, ultimately interpreted such rhetoric in artful ways to advance the remarkable folly that President Dwight Eisenhower had been a shill for the Soviets. Goldwater spent significant time and resources combating a theme that gained traction like a runaway train and enabled the media to paint him further as part of the lunatic fringe. In 1968 Alabama Governor George Wallace viewed the civil rights movement as a chief component of a broader communist conspiracy that included the liberal establishment (judges, Congress, and the academy) and the national news media. Finally, Perot's extensive history of engaging in conspiracy theory comprised not only plots by shadowy figures to assassinate him but also sabotage of his family by incumbent President George H. W. Bush in 1992. "Conspiracy theories were always part of his [Perot's] appeal,"[49] writes John F. Harris. Yet,

> Belief in conspiracies conveys at best poor understanding and at worst mental instability. Trump has displayed the same weakness, endorsing the "vaccines cause autism" myth, the "Obama born in Kenya" canard, the "Clintons killed Vince Foster" rumor, the "Rafael Cruz involved in the JFK assassination" nonsense and many more crackpot theories.[50]

Populists' expression of nativist tendencies also frequently occasions charges of racism and xenophobia from veiled language or outright hostility toward minorities. Notwithstanding Wallace, an

---

[49] John F. Harris, "Ross Perot—The father of Trump." *Politico*, July 9, 2019. https://www.politico.com/story/2019/07/09/ross-perot-the-father-of-trump-1404720

[50] Mona Charen, "Ross Perot's lessons for today." *RealClearPolitics*, September 2, 2016. https://www.realclearpolitics.com/articles/2016/09/02/ross_perots_lessons_for_today_131686.html

avowed segregationist, the truth is in the eye of the beholder. Following in the footsteps of Goldwater and Perot, Trump paints what psychologists describe as an "ambiguous image." The rhetoric he employs may be conceptualized in a way similar to Rubin's vase, where at one glance there appears to be a single flower container while at another glimpse one might perceive two faces as the vase fades into the background.[51] The duck/rabbit illusion is another example of the illusion of reversible images in which one's focus on the left- or right-hand side of the image determines which animal is perceived.[52] The point is that both perceptions cannot be processed visually at the same time. The intersection of the populist style and racial rhetoric is sometimes as perplexing as these cognitive puzzles, since the interpretation of what the image *really* is must be left to the observer who attempts to make sense of it.

One the one hand it is difficult to typecast Goldwater as a racist and a sympathizer of white nationalists. He was a member of the National Association for the Advancement of Colored Persons (NAACP) and the Urban League. Unlike Trump, Goldwater was a conviction politician of a libertarian stripe. He opposed civil rights legislation on principled, Tenth Amendment grounds that federal intervention was unnecessary and the matter should be left to the states. On the floor of the Senate, Goldwater stated before his vote against the 1964 Civil Rights Act that

> I am unalterably opposed to discrimination or segregation on the basis of race, color, or creed or on any other basis; not only my words, but more importantly my actions through years have repeatedly demonstrated the sincerity of my feeling in this regard.[53]

On the other hand, his stance on civil rights earned him the unwelcome endorsement of the Ku Klux Klan. Richard Rovere

---

[51] "Optical Illusion, Rubin's Vase, 1915." https://www.sciencesource.com/archive/Optical-Illusion--Rubin-s-Vase--1915-SS2529214.html

[52] See "Duck-Rabbit." https://www.illusionsindex.org/i/duck-rabbit

[53] *New York Times*, "Text of Goldwater speech on civil rights." June 16, 1964. https://www.nytimes.com/1964/06/19/archives/text-of-goldwater-speech-on-rights.html

maintains that while Goldwater made no racist appeals during the 1964 presidential election, in the south the movement "appears to be a racist movement and almost nothing else" and Goldwater spoke of race "in an underground, or Aesopian, language—a kind of code that few in his audiences had any trouble deciphering."[54] Such is a frequent charge against Trump.

In a similar vein, Perot's various comments on the campaign trail in 1992 suggested the undertones of racism to some and overt racism to others, though there was no evidence he had ever expressed animus toward blacks or other minorities in his long career as an entrepreneur. Nevertheless his use of the phrase "you people" to African American voters resulted in "one of the most reviled racial epithets for Black people during his address to the NAACP's annual convention in 1992."[55] Moreover, at a debate with vice-presidential candidate Al Gore Perot railed against NAFTA by showing pictures of Mexicans living in cardboard boxes, a stereotype at which many took umbrage.[56] Finally, in a televised interview with David Frost, Perot used racial stereotypes to blame blacks for exploiting welfare programs paid for by hard-working Americans. Perot imitated the alleged thinking of African American men on the subject in a particularly offensive way:

> I'm just kind of a dumb dude who never finished fourth grade. I'm wandering around the streets with my baseball hat on backward and $150 tennis shoes I knocked another kid out to get. I'm looking for real trouble to prove that I am a man. Well, how do I define what a man is? I define what a man is from the rap music I hear . . . A man

[54] Richard H. Rovere, "The Campaign: Goldwater." *The New Yorker*, October 3, 1964. https://www.newyorker.com/magazine/1964/10/03/the-campaign-goldwater

[55] Bruce C. T. Wright, "Ross Perot dies 27 years after his infamous NAACP 'You People' speech." *NewsOne*, July 9, 2019. https://newsone.com/3881919/ross-perot-dies-you-people-naacp-speech/

[56] Patrick J. McDonnell and Juanita Darling, "Perot's debate statements strike raw nerve in Mexico. Reaction: Blunt exchange impresses many, but Texan comes under fire for what is seen as stereotypical descriptions of poverty." *Los Angeles Times*, November 11, 1993. https://www.latimes.com/archives/la-xpm-1993-11-11-mn-55573-story.html

is defined in that culture as a breeder who gets the woman pregnant and then she gets welfare.[57]

Despite the Texas billionaire's crude characterization of African American men, Steve Chapman contends that "Perot didn't make the blatant appeals to white racism that Trump does."[58] Critics of Trump suggest that the president's rhetoric speaks for itself, as the commander-in-chief paints images of Mexican illegal immigrants as "bad hombres," rapists, and drug dealers and lauds the "good people on both sides" of the 2018 Charlottesville, Virginia clashes between Antifa (anti-fascist) and white supremacist groups over the removal of Confederate statues. Democratic hopefuls in the 2020 election now routinely and reflexively call the president racist and a white supremacist.[59] Even before his election, detractors point to Trump's backing by the leader of the Ku Klux Klan (who, incidentally, endorsed George H. W. Bush, though Bush rejected his endorsement). According to David von Drehle, "[h]e'd do enough dog whistling to attract [David] Duke's endorsement— though he would pretend not to know who Duke was."[60] The president's supporters, of course, reject such arguments as

[57] Quoted in Kenneth J. Neubuck and Noel Cazenave, *Welfare Racism: Playing the Race Card against America's Poor* (New York: Routledge, 2001), pp. 156–7.

[58] Steve Chapman, "Ross Perot paved the way for Donald Trump." *Chicago Tribune*, July 9, 2019. https://www.chicagotribune.com/columns/steve-chapman/ct-column-ross-perot-trump-chapman-20190709-4ihr3754xrghfohle5jmg7z-vsi-story.html

[59] Faris Bseiso, "Yang says 'no choice' but to call Trump a white supremacist." *CNN*, August 9, 2019. https://www.cnn.com/2019/08/09/politics/yang-trump-white-supremacist/index.html; Brett Samuels, "2020 Democrats feel more emboldened to label Trump a racist." *The Hill*, August 17, 2019. https://thehill.com/homenews/campaign/457730-2020-democrats-feel-more-emboldened-to-label-trump-a-racist

[60] David Von Drehle, "Ross Perot walked so Trump could run." *Washington Post*, July 9, 2019. https://www.washingtonpost.com/opinions/before-donald-trump-there-was-ross-perot/2019/07/09/284bf7e0-a27b-11e9-bd56-eac6bb02d01d_story.html

overblown hyperbole from the Left. Trump, from their perspective, takes aim at political opponents like the "Squad"[61] via tweets or soundbites for the radical policy views of these members of Congress, including their embrace of platforms like the "Green New Deal," not for their race.[62] Their race or ethnicity is purportedly subordinate to their own outrageous commentary on matters like Israel—even as the president tells them to "go back to where they are from" and all but one member of the group was born in the United States.[63] Alas, Trump's continual acclaim of economic gains for minorities, carefully crafted speeches celebrating minorities on special occasions,[64] and defense by those inside and outside the Beltway who flatly refute charges of racism against him fall on deaf ears among his detractors.[65] Survey data underscore that nine of ten Democrats believe he is a white supremacist. At the same time, an equal proportion of Republicans dismiss such allegations

[61] The "Squad" includes freshmen Democratic members of the 116th Congress Alexandria Ocasio-Cortez (NY-14), Ilhan Omar (MN-5), Rashida Tlaib (MI-13), and Ayanna Pressley (MA-7).

[62] See Andrew C. McCarthy, "Trump and the 'racist tweets'." *National Review*, July 16, 2019. https://www.nationalreview.com/2019/07/donald-trump-and-the-racist-tweets/

[63] Bianca Quilantan and David Cohen, "Trump tells Dem congresswomen: Go back where you came from." *Politico*, July 14, 2019. https://www.politico.com/story/2019/07/14/trump-congress-go-back-where-they-came-from-1415692

[64] See DeNeen L. Brown and Cleve R. Wootson, Jr., "Trump ignores backlash, visits Mississippi Civil Rights Museum and praises civil rights leaders." *Washington Post*, December 9, 2017. https://www.washingtonpost.com/news/post-politics/wp/2017/12/09/amid-backlash-trump-set-to-attend-private-gathering-as-civil-rights-museum-opens-in-mississippi/

[65] See Michael Von Schoik, "Trump 'is not a racist' at all: Ben Carson." *Fox Business News*, July 21, 2019. https://www.foxbusiness.com/economy/trump-is-not-racist-at-all-ben-carson; Philip M. Bailey, "Sen. Mitch McConnell: President Donald Trump 'is not a racist'." *Louisville Courier-Journal*, July 16, 2019. https://www.courier-journal.com/story/news/politics/2019/07/16/mitch-mcconnell-president-donald-trump-is-not-racist/1746316001/; Holman W. Jenkins, "Prove the tweets were racist." *Wall Street Journal*, July 23, 2019. https://www.wsj.com/articles/prove-the-tweets-were-racist-11563923093

as fabrications and hysteria linked to "Trump Derangement Syndrome."[66]

To return to the ambiguous image metaphor, there are few who have problems discerning whether Trump is the rabbit or the duck, a vile racist or a champion of equal opportunity. To which "people" does he plead in his populist narrative? One segment of voters sees only the foreground image and shrugs off intemperate rhetoric as incidental to race; another segment focuses only on the background and concludes he is a white supremacist as evil as Hitler and contends that detention facilities for illegals on the southern border are equivalent to Nazi extermination camps like Auschwitz. The semantics of presidential rhetoric obviously solidify these perceptions through polarizing individual and collective interpretation.[67] Observations are filtered through the lens of partisanship, ideology, and normative conceptions of presidential leadership in a 50/50 nation unable to make the Gestalt switch.

III. Trump's populist presidency: savior, Satan, or Samson?

There is certainly no dearth of opinion on the president's inimitable job performance at the midpoint of his term. But in order to comprehend the polarizing effects and broader implications of Trump's leadership approach, it is critical to assess how his populist campaigning and governing styles converge with longstanding perspectives of the modern presidency, per se. Across the spectrum of voters, journalists, scholars, and pundits, evaluations of Trump, like those of any individual president, naturally intersect not only with partisan inclinations but also with

---

[66] Ian Haney López, "Why do Trump's supporters deny the racism that seems so evident to Democrats?" *Los Angeles Times*, August 13, 2019. https://www.latimes.com/opinion/story/2019-08-13/trump-voters-racism-politics-white-supremacy; David Smith, "'Trump derangement syndrome': The week America went mad." *The Guardian*, July 22, 2019. https://www.theguardian.com/us-news/2018/jul/21/trump-derangement-syndrome-putin-summit-republicans

[67] On the role that semantic information may play in perception of ambiguous images, see Janet Davis, H. R. Schiffman, and Suzanne Greist-Bousquet, "Semantic Context and Figure-Ground Organization." *Psychological Research* 52, no. 4 (1990): 306–9.

normative assessments of what the exercise of executive power *should be* within the American political structure. As scholar Michael Nelson suggests, three countervailing, allegorical models of presidential power have emerged across time since Franklin Roosevelt fundamentally altered expectations of the chief executive and ushered in the modern era of the presidency: Savior, Satan, and Samson.[68] Trump's populist leadership style, which defies ostensible ideological dogma and is founded in majoritarian eccentricity and limitless anti-elite narratives, rooted in a preoccupation with self-flattery, and grounded in a neo-nativism peppered with conspiracy theory, arguably reinforces each of these perspectives in a particularly exaggerated way.

A. Savior versus sage: Trump the populist and Madison the pluralist

Trump supporters are most likely to view the president's unorthodox comportment and policy goals through the lens of the Savior model. This perspective emphasizes the primacy of the presidential office in furtherance of the public good and general welfare. Its foundational roots reach back to the seminal debates about the Republic's formation at the Constitutional Convention, and are notably located in Alexander Hamilton's essay in Federalist #70. Hamilton posited that

> Energy in the Executive is a leading character in the definition of good government. It is essential to the protection of the community against foreign attacks; it is not less essential to the steady administration of the laws; to the protection of property against those irregular and high-handed combinations which sometimes interrupt the ordinary course of justice; to the security of liberty against the enterprises and assaults of ambition, of faction, and of anarchy.[69]

---

[68] Michael Nelson, "Evaluating the Presidency." In Michael Nelson (ed.), *The Presidency and the Political System*, 4th edition (Washington, DC: Congressional Quarterly, Inc., 1995), pp. 3–28.

[69] Federalist #70, "The Executive Department Further Considered." From the *New York Packet*, Tuesday, March 18, 1788. http://avalon.law.yale.edu/18th_century/fed70.asp

From the Savior standpoint the president acts as the primary custodian of the national interest. In foreign policy the president is endowed with key prerogatives due to his constitutional status as commander-in-chief and chief diplomat. Among those, as Hamilton asserted in a plea for a unitary executive in Federalist #70, are "secrecy and despatch." In the contemporary era, the president is expected to act as "chief legislator" in the domestic realm and set the legislative agenda to promote the general welfare and support the overlooked, powerless citizens with little influence over policy outcomes. "Members of Congress," explains Michael Nelson, "cater to wealthy and influential interests within their constituencies." Sitting atop the political order at the other end of Pennsylvania Avenue from Capitol Hill, the president is able to "mobilize the unorganized and inarticulate and speak for national majorities against special interest groups."[70]

The Savior model takes a benign view of presidential power and favors action over the status quo, innovation over inertia. In the modern era, the concept very much is tied to the legacy of Franklin D. Roosevelt and his remarkable record of legislative leadership in his first "100 days" in office at a time of unprecedented socio-economic upheaval during the Great Depression.[71] In "Song of the South," the country music group Alabama captured the notion of FDR as redeemer-in-chief in the memorialization of the yellow-dog Democratic states of the old Confederacy that benefited mightily from the programs of the *New Deal*: "the cotton was short and the weeds were tall, but Mr. Roosevelt is gonna' save us all." All subsequent chief executives stand "in the shadow" of FDR in the search for greatness and in the quest to make an indelible imprint on the office in honor of the voters who elected them, despite vastly different governing contexts and leadership philosophies.[72]

[70] Nelson, "Evaluating the Presidency," p. 5.
[71] Richard E. Neustadt, "The Contemporary Presidency: The Presidential 'Hundred Days'—An Overview." *Presidential Studies Quarterly* 31, no. 1 (2001): 121–5.
[72] William E. Leuchtenburg, *In the Shadow of FDR: From Harry Truman to George W. Bush* (Ithaca, NY: Cornell University Press, 2001).

How does the Savior model correspond to Trump's populist presidency? Among his core constituents, the Oval Office is viewed as the last, best hope of liberating the masses from an unshakable, corrupt elite in the swamp of Washington, standing up to dishonest media that are biased against Republicans and conservatives, reversing economic dislocation and socio-cultural change, and inhibiting foreign powers from taking advantage of the United States. There is a certain narrative of victimization that infuses the president's simplified rhetoric, rather ironically since conservatives often portray progressives and liberals as obsessed with unfair treatment and discrimination, particularly among minority groups. Nevertheless Trump supporters display a particular indignation against the "establishment," an ill-defined, catch-all notion of elites within government who putatively employ convoluted rules and procedures to advance self-serving policies anathema to the nation's well-being. If the president's overbearing rhetoric threatens the legitimacy of other branches of government, discredits informal institutions like the media charged with holding public officials accountable, or undermines international organizations and bilateral trade relationships, his fitful speechmaking, malicious tweets, and Delphic policy stances emphasize decades of the "little guy's" abuse by the permanent political class in Washington and nefarious foreign leaders bent on unfair international commerce practices. To achieve his ends, Trump employs a common feature of populist leadership that "mobilizes the antagonism of 'the people' against the established order, drawing for this purpose on rhetorical traditions of popular protest."[73]

Most critically, Trump's bold proclamation at the Republican National Convention in Cleveland, Ohio in 2016 that "[n]obody knows the system better than me, which is why I alone can fix it" is a prima facie rejection of the tenets of *indirect* democracy and the Founders' confidence in the virtues of legislative government. Trump and his base of voters rebuff the fundamental notion of

---

[73] Margaret Canovan, "Two Strategies for the Study of Populism." *Political Studies* 30, no. 4 (1982): 549.

mediated power.[74] Such a perspective conflicts incontrovertibly with the Founders' emphasis on the balance of power between the branches and the virtues of channeling temporary, popular passions through elective institutions with intricate checks and balances. As James Madison noted eloquently in Federalist #51, "Ambition must be made to counteract ambition."[75]

Distrustful of Congress and the courts, Trump and his supporters casually reject such foundational, republican theories and champion an institutional partisanship that elevates the presidency above other branches of government. Forswearing the idea of "separated institutions sharing powers,"[76] Trump and his proponents hold firmly that the chief executive can and should act, unilaterally through *direct action* if necessary and in the perceived national interest—and most disturbingly, even if the rules must be twisted or violated. During the 2016 Republican primaries, 90 percent of Trump supporters agreed that "public officials don't care much what people like me think"; 83 percent concurred that "the old way of doing things no longer works and we need radical change"; and most critically, 84 percent contended that "what we need is a leader who is willing to say or do anything to solve America's problems."[77] It comes as no surprise that once Trump took up residence at the White House in 2017, a survey by the American Values Project found that 66 percent of Republican backers of Trump agreed that "because things have gotten so far off track in this country, we need a leader who is willing to break some rules if that's what it takes to set things right."[78]

---

[74] Molyneux and Osborne, "Populism: A Deflationary View," p. 3. Emphasis added.

[75] Federalist #51. http://avalon.law.yale.edu/18th_century/fed51.asp.

[76] Richard E. Neustadt, *Presidential Power and the Modern Presidents* (New York: Free Press, 1964), p. 42.

[77] Quinnipiac University Poll, April 5, 2016. https://poll.qu.edu/national/release-detail?ReleaseID=2340

[78] David Smith, "Survey: Two in three Trump supporters want a president who breaks the rules." *The Guardian*, December 5, 2017. https://www.theguardian.com/us-news/2017/dec/05/republican-trump-supporters-survey-american-values-rule-breaker

B. Satan, psychology, and presidential pathology

By contrast, those who embrace the Satan view of the presidency share deep trepidations about, and profound suspicions of, executive power generally. From this perspective, Trump's singular behavior and populist rhetoric amplify fears, rational or otherwise, of impending tyranny. Such concerns of despotism in the executive are as old as the impassioned debates in Philadelphia in 1787 that were heavily influenced by the colonial experience under King George III. Cato (George Clinton of New York) wrote in Anti-Federalist #67 about the probable excess of executive ambition and opined "that he [the president] may be great and glorious by oppressing his fellow citizens, and raising himself to permanent grandeur on the ruins of his country."[79] Subscribers to the Satan model would gladly take their chances of foundering on Scylla's rocky shoals of institutional immobilism than be subsumed in Charybdis's whirlpool of despotism, war, and civic strife that accompanies presidential pre-eminence. "Our three 'greatest' Presidents," Nelson Polsby asserts, "were reputedly Washington, Lincoln, and Franklin Roosevelt. The service of all three is intimately associated with three incidents in American history when the entire polity was engaged in total war."[80]

Fears of an out-of-control executive are scarcely unfounded in the post-World War II era. The calamitous and failed presidencies of Lyndon Johnson and Richard Nixon drove some scholars, including Arthur Schlesinger, who had once lauded the Savior model, to become increasingly concerned about the ascendency of an "imperial presidency."[81] Central to this apprehension were the excesses of the Johnson and Nixon presidencies in light of their contempt for constitutional limits

---

[79] Anti-Federalist #67. http://www.thisnation.com/library/antifederalist/67.html

[80] Nelson W. Polsby, "Against presidential greatness." *Commentary*, January 1, 1977. https://www.commentarymagazine.com/articles/against-presidential-greatness/

[81] Arthur M. Schlesinger, Jr., *The Imperial Presidency* (Boston: Houghton Mifflin, 1973).

on executive power, both in the domestic and foreign policy realms. As Nelson explains:

> In foreign affairs the power of these presidents sustained a large-scale war in Vietnam long after public opinion had turned against it. The power of the president as "chief legislator," in Rossiter's phrase, prompted such hasty passage of Great Society social welfare programs that their flaws, which might have been discovered between the president and Congress, were not found until later . . . Finally, in 1972 and 1973, a host of abuses of presidential power, which have been grouped under the umbrella term *Watergate*, occurred, forcing Nixon's resignation in August 1974.[82]

In the years following Nixon's departure from the political scene in August 1974, a resurgent Congress passed a host of laws and engaged in significant internal restructuring in the quest to restore balance between the branches and curb presidential excess.[83] Yet, as Andrew Rudalevige highlights, the legal institutions of "Congress's 'resurgence regime' proved to be built on sand—and, like sand, eroded away, leaving a new landscape."[84] Apprehension about presidential arrogation of congressional authority, from the trampling of the war power to unilateral actions at home and abroad, was thrust to the forefront anew in debates about institutional balance following the terror attacks on the United States on September 11, 2001 and the subsequent wars in Afghanistan and Iraq and on terrorism more generally. To subscribers of the Satan model, presidents like George W. Bush circumvented Congress through claims of executive privilege,[85] signing statements defying congressional legislative intent,[86] and by continuing military operations beyond the scope of authorizations alongside "extraordinary rendition" of

---

[82] Nelson, "Evaluating the Presidency," p. 6.
[83] See James L. Sundquist, *The Decline and Resurgence of Congress* (Washington, DC: Brookings Institution, 2002).
[84] Andrew Rudalevige, *The New Imperial Presidency: Renewing Presidential Power after Watergate* (Ann Arbor: University of Michigan Press, 2005), p. 8.
[85] Mark J. Rozell, "Executive Privilege Revived: Secrecy and Conflict during the Bush Presidency." *Duke Law Journal* 52 (2002): 403–21.
[86] Phillip J. Cooper, "George W. Bush, Edgar Allan Poe, and the Use and Abuse of Presidential Signing Statements." *Presidential Studies Quarterly* 35, no. 3 (2005): 515–32.

suspected terrorists for interrogations tantamount to torture in the assessment of many.[87]

The specter of autocracy is particularly pronounced among those who take Trump's rhetorical outbursts literally and shudder at his impertinent use of the bully pulpit that is notable for browbeating, bravado, and bluster. His continued rallying cries for Hillary Clinton to be jailed (i.e., "lock her up"), impetuous threats to revoke the credentials of news outlets critical of his actions, petulant behavior toward select reporters deemed to be "fake news,"[88] and ridiculing of foreign leaders on social media (e.g., "Little Rocket Man" for Kim Jong-Un of North Korea), evoke ample fears of a drift toward abuse of power, if not war at the expense of longstanding constitutional principles and norms of the presidential office. But what is more, those who view Trump's presidency through the prism of the Satan model share a view that his penchant for self-absorption, embrace of simplistically dichotomous logic that emphasizes an "us" versus "them" mentality, and engagement in impulsive rhetoric is a case for "personality as a source of presidential pathology."[89]

The late presidential scholar James David Barber contended that presidents' performance could be forecast by understanding the way in which personality, the constituent components of which he considered *character*, *worldview*, and *style*, intersects with situational challenges. Character is "the way the President orients himself toward life"; worldview is the locus of "his primary politically relevant beliefs, particularly his conceptions of social causality, human nature, and the central moral conflicts of the time"; and style is his "habitual way of performing three fundamental political roles that

---

[87] James P. Pfiffner, "The Constitutional Legacy of George W. Bush." *Presidential Studies Quarterly* 45, no. 4 (2015): 727–41.

[88] Sally Persons, "Trump threatens to pull 'fake news' credentials." *Washington Times*, May 9, 2018. https://www.washingtontimes.com/news/2018/may/9/donald-trump-threatens-to-pull-fake-news-credentia/; Bill Goodykoontz, "Donald Trump vs. CNN . . . again. Now on a world stage and with a hint of totalitarianism." *USA Today*, July 15, 2018. https://www.usatoday.com/story/opinion/nation-now/2018/07/15/white-house-cancels-john-bolton-interview-cnn-president-trump-column/786369002/

[89] Nelson, "Evaluating the Presidency," p. 6.

include rhetoric, personal relations, and homework."[90] The typology that Barber constructed emphasizes two essential dimensions: presidents' affect toward the job (positive, negative) and the level of energy they bring to it (activity, passivity). Fashioning a fourfold classification, Barber argued that the most suitable chief executives were the "active-positives" like Franklin Roosevelt, Harry Truman, John F. Kennedy, Gerald Ford, and Jimmy Carter. These presidents exhibited high self-esteem, adaptability, and productivity. They invested high levels of energy into the job from which they derived enjoyment in the exercise of power, guided by the pursuit of well-defined personal goals.

Barber cautioned of the dangers that "active-negative" personality types represent. The examples of failed presidencies, including those of Woodrow Wilson, Lyndon Johnson, and Richard Nixon, highlight the degree to which these leaders expended enormous energy in the job but obtained little emotional reward, and were doomed to self-destruction in the Oval Office. Their downfalls were allegedly rooted in deep-seated psychological dysfunction reflected in the classic formulation of the active-negative character: compulsive behavior, uncompromising rigidity, and the elusive quest for personal power to compensate for low self-esteem. Power is a means to self-actualization rather than for noble pursuits in the interest of the greater good. Their ambition is frustrated by preoccupation with success and failure, and an unceasing struggle to manage aggression toward the external environment they confront.

Predictions abound of Trump's impending demise stemming from similar, if not worse, personality defects of the active-negative variety represented by Johnson and Nixon. Many of the president's detractors focus on his use of social media to articulate his populist messaging, suggesting that the eccentricities of his comportment and direct messaging paint a Francis Bacon tableau of an exasperated, paranoid, and even delusional leader. Former aide to President Nixon, John Dean, cites Barber's analysis and opined that Trump's "Twitter account reveals a man constantly complaining or whining about most everything. His only enjoyment in the job

[90] James David Barber, *The Presidential Character: Predicting Performance in the White House* (Englewood Cliffs, NJ: Prentice-Hall, 1977), pp. 7–8.

is that it feeds his insatiable narcissistic appetite for attention."[91] Moreover, as Michael Kruse posits, "He's impulsive and undisciplined and obsesses with taking shots and settling scores and with the sustenance of an image of success even when it's at utter odds with objective reality."[92] In effect, write Joan Johnson-Freese and Elizabeth Frampton, "Trump has only succeeded in revealing his level of discomfort—negativity—with the job of POTUS. The press, which Trump refers to as 'fake news,' is his adversary, much as it was for Active-Negative Richard Nixon."[93]

Uncertainties about Trump's fitness for office reached a fever pitch as he came to the end of his first year, and concerns scarcely receded as the president reached the midpoint of his term. As liberal commentator Bill Press noted in early 2018,

> Questions about Donald Trump's mental capacity dominate the Capitol. A leading psychiatrist tells congressional Democrats that Trump's mental health is "unraveling." Two dozen Democrats introduced legislation requiring that the president be examined and removed from office if deemed unfit by a commission of physicians and psychiatrists. Republican staffers bone up on the 25th Amendment, while CNN headlines: "Is It Wrong to Question Trump's Mental Fitness for Office?"[94]

Other observers suggested that Trump's speech patterns, remarkable for the failure to articulate full sentences, reflect some sort of

---

[91] John W. Dean, "Active-negative Trump is doomed to follow Nixon." *Newsweek*, May 29, 2017. http://www.newsweek.com/activenegative-trump-doomed-follow-nixon-616641

[92] Michael Kruse, "I found Trump's diary—Hiding in plain sight." *Politico Magazine*, June 25, 2017. https://www.politico.com/magazine/story/2017/06/25/i-found-trumps-diaryhiding-in-plain-sight-215303

[93] Joan Johnson-Freese and Elizabeth Frampton, "The dangers of Donald Trump as an active-negative president." *China US Focus*, July 11, 2017. https://chinausfocus.com/foreign-policy/the-dangers-of-donald-trump-as-an-active-negative-president-to-us-china-policy

[94] Bill Press, "Is Trump mentally fit for office?" *The Hill*, January 18, 2018. http://thehill.com/opinion/white-house/368008-press-is-trump-mentally-fit-for-office

recent cognitive deterioration.[95] Armchair psychologists who made rather scathing evaluations of Trump outside a clinical setting, despite a violation of the so-called "Goldwater Rule" of the American Psychological Association (APA), published a book detailing the connection between the early chaos of the new Trump administration and the president's supposed mental defects.[96] By late summer 2018 the debate was reinvigorated when, after Trump sacked advisor Omarosa Manigault, who had previously appeared on his television show *The Apprentice*, she claimed that the president was in mental decline. The firing coincided with Bob Woodward's book *Fear*, which compared Trump's state of mind with that of Richard Nixon forty-four years earlier. As Jill Abramson submits in her review of Woodward's work, replete with the iconic Watergate investigative journalist's trademark anonymous sources and lack of verifiable references, "[t]hen, as now, the country faced a crisis of leadership caused by a president's fatal flaws and inability to function in the job."[97]

Many outside the Beltway also shared ongoing concerns about Trump's mental health. As Trump reached his one-year anniversary in office, an *ABC/Washington Post* poll in January 2018 found that 47 percent of Americans believed Trump is mentally

[95] John McWhorter, "What Trump's speech says about his mental fitness." *New York Times*, February 6, 2018. https://nytimes.com/interactive/2018/02/06/opinion/trump-speech-mental-capacity

[96] Bandy X. Lee, *The Dangerous Case of Donald Trump: 27 Psychiatrists and Mental Health Experts Assess a President* (New York: Thomas Dunne Books, 2017). The "Goldwater Rule" prohibits professional opinions by psychologists on any president whom they have not examined personally or from whom they have obtained permission to discuss publicly mental health issues. The rule stems from 1964 Republican presidential candidate Barry Goldwater's successful lawsuit (*Goldwater v. Ginsburg*, 1969) for libel against the magazine *Fact*, which polled mental health experts about his fitness for office. See Aaron Levin, "Goldwater rules based on long-ago controversy." *Psychiatric News*, August 25, 2016. https://psychnews.psychiatryonline.org/doi/full/10.1176/appi.pn.2016.9a19

[97] Jill Abramson, "Bob Woodward's meticulous, frightening look inside the Trump White House." *Washington Post*, September 6, 2018. https://www.washingtonpost.com/outlook/bob-woodwards-meticulous-frightening-look-inside-the-trump-white-house/2018/09/06

unstable, with 48 percent disagreeing.[98] The data changed little by September 2018, with a plurality of 48 percent of Americans believing Trump was mentally fit for the job, and 42 percent disagreeing.[99] Trump's most dogged Democratic detractors in Congress seized on the divide in public views to argue on behalf of their partisan constituency that he should be removed from office. Maxine Waters' (D-CA) indefatigable vituperations to "Impeach 45" are in part based on a belief that the president is mentally unfit. Trump, in turn, called Waters "low IQ" and "the face of the Democratic Party." The president and other of her critics charge that she suffers from issues connected to "Trump Derangement Syndrome," another psychological condition missing from the *Diagnostic and Statistical Manual of Mental Disorders* of the APA. The alleged cognitive ailment refers to such a vehement, irrational disdain for the president that the patient borders on insanity or a nervous breakdown.[100]

Only the American social surrealist artists of yesteryear, with their brush strokes depicting hallucinogenic nightmares "pervaded by the unknown"[101] at the depths of the Great Depression, could sketch the madcap moments in contemporary time when psychologists testify before congressional subcommittees

---

[98] Rebecca Morin, "Poll: Almost half of voters question Trump's mental stability." *Politico*, January 22, 2018. https://www.politico.com/story/2018/01/22/poll-trump-mental-health-354902

[99] See Quinnipiac University Poll, September 10, 2018. https://poll.qu.edu/national/release-detail?ReleaseID=2567

[100] Thomas Lifson, "Maxine Waters goes completely unhinged." *American Thinker*, March 17, 2017. https://www.americanthinker.com/blog/2017/03/maxine_waters_goes_completely_unhinged.htm. "Trump Derangement Syndrome" is a term borrowed from late conservative commentator Charles Krauthammer, who described "Bush Derangement Syndrome" as the "the acute onset of paranoia in otherwise normal people in reaction to the policies, the presidency—nay—the very existence of George W. Bush." See Krauthammer, "The delusional dean." *Washington Post*, December 5, 2003. https://www.washingtonpost.com/archive/opinions/2003/12/05/the-delusional-dean/cbc80426-08ee-40fd-97e5-19da55fdc821/?utm_term=.314e37cbee2f

[101] Ilene Susan Fort, "American Social Surrealism." *American Art Journal* 22, no. 3 (1982): 8.

that the president is "going to unravel"[102] under the pressures of the office while the president simultaneously proclaims himself a "stable genius" on Twitter and oddly compares himself to Ronald Reagan, who had Alzheimer's disease.[103] But setting aside the frivolity of diagnosing any politician's psychological stability from afar, Trump's detractors insist he is unqualified and unsuited for the office based on observable behavior that they find offensive. This belief undergirded one vote in the House of Representatives in December 2017 to remove him from office. Texas Democratic Congressman Al Green fashioned articles of impeachment formally focused on allegations of the president's obstruction of justice. A closer reading of Green's indictment of Trump evinces the degree to which president's Twitter attacks on fellow African American Representative Frederica Wilson (D-FL), whom the president called "wacky," and other elements of Trump's public conduct guided Green's charge that Trump had "brought disrepute, contempt, ridicule and disgrace on the presidency," and that he had "sown discord among the people of the United States." Moreover, Green's bill indicted Trump's handling of white supremacists' clashes with protestors in Charlottesville, Virginia in August 2017 and the president's brazen condemnations of black NFL players, commencing with Colin Kaepernick of the San Francisco 49ers, who took to kneeling during the national anthem to protest alleged police brutality.[104] Fifty-eight Democrats in the House supported the doomed measure.

Green's, of course, was not the last effort to oust the president. Immediately after Democrats won back the House of Representatives in the mid-term elections of 2018, California Representative

---

[102] Brett Samuels, "Lawmakers briefed by Yale psychiatrist on Trump's mental health: Report." *The Hill*, January 3, 2018. https://thehill.com/homenews/administration/367362-lawmakers-briefed-by-yale-psychiatrist-on-trumps-mental-health-report

[103] Andrew Restuccia and Craig Howie, "Trump defends mental health: I'm a 'stable genius'." *Politico*, January 7, 2018. https://www.politico.eu/article/donald-trump-slams-media-over-mental-health-reports/

[104] Christina Marcos, "The nearly 60 Democrats who voted for impeachment." *The Hill*, December 6, 2017. http://thehill.com/blogs/floor-action/house/363645-the-nearly-60-dems-who-voted-for-impeachment

Brad Sherman filed H.R. 13 to reintroduce articles of impeachment based on the president's alleged obstruction of justice.[105] Calls for impeachment continued in the wake of the release of the Mueller report in spring 2019 (see Chapter 7). Ultimately in December 2019 the Democratic-controlled House voted two articles of impeachment along party lines, one for abuse of power and another for obstruction of Congress stemming from an unrelated matter: the president's July 25 phone call to Ukrainian President Volodymyr Zelenskiy. House Democrats alleged Trump had engaged in a quid quo pro arrangement for military aid to be released on condition that Ukraine investigate the business dealings of former Vice President Joe Biden's son, Hunter, who received a lucrative board position on Burisma, the country's natural gas company. The president was acquitted by the Senate on both articles on February 5, 2020.

Regardless, public opinion not only among progressives but also among "Never Trumpers" on the right of the political spectrum solidifies that "[t]o critics, Trump represents the sum of all fears: a populist demagogue who preys on voter anger, stokes racism, enacts self-enriching policies, and fans the flames of class division and partisan polarization that have been growing for decades."[106] Trump characterized Hillary Clinton as the devil in the 2016 campaign. But to his opponents he has brought nothing but fire, brimstone, and maleficence—if not psychosis—to the Oval Office as much for his political style as for substantive policy accomplishments.

---

[105] See Brad Sherman, "The case for impeaching Donald Trump." *Huffington Post*, October 5, 2017. https://www.huffingtonpost.com/entry/the-case-for-impeaching-donald-j-trump_us_59a5e4a3e4b08299d89d0a9b; and Sherman, "Why I filed articles of impeachment against Trump." *Washington Post*, January 9, 2019. https://www.washingtonpost.com/opinions/why-i-filed-articles-of-impeachment-against-trump/2019/01/09/aaa59a3c-12c7-11e9-ab79-30cd4f7926f2_story.html?utm_term=.e53ebe4c8297

[106] Linda Feldmann, "Disrupter in chief: How Donald Trump is changing the presidency." *Christian Science Monitor*, January 4, 2018. https://www.csmonitor.com/USA/Politics/2018/0104/Disrupter-in-chief-How-Donald-Trump-is-changing-the-presidency

C. Samson, scapegoating, and the sublimely impossible presidency

Finally, the Samson model posits that the capacity for presidential leadership is in general decline in the contemporary era, regardless of the officeholder. Just as Delilah had betrayed Samson by cutting his Nazarite hair and robbing him of his enormous power, in the immediate post-Watergate era Congress abjured the promising flame of presidential leadership by imposing significant constraints on the exercise of power. Scholars like George Reedy posited that after Watergate the executive was "imperiled" rather than imperial.[107] The travails of one-term Presidents Ford and Carter in a decade of congressional resurgence in the 1970s had arguably hamstrung the Oval Office through enhanced oversight on Capitol Hill, congressional reorganization aimed at strengthening leaders' control of the legislative agenda, and a general lack of followership of the president.[108]

Like Samson's destruction of the temple in Gaza that brought back his strength, Ronald Reagan may well have reinvigorated presidential leadership, at least temporarily, with his policy stances toward the former Soviet Union and stunning legislative victories in 1981 through a combination of oratorical flourish and negotiation behind the scenes.[109] Regardless, many scholars emphasize the endurance of the Samson model by pointing to the continuing and widening "expectations gap" between what the public

---

[107] George Reedy, The Twilight of the Presidency: From Johnson to Reagan (New York: Dutton, 1987).

[108] See Roger H. Davidson, "The Presidency and the Three Eras of the Modern Congress." In James A. Thurber (ed.), Divided Democracy: Cooperation and Conflict Between the President and Congress (Washington, DC: Congressional Quarterly Press, 1991), pp. 61–78; Richard S. Conley, The Presidency, Congress, and Divided Government: A Postwar Assessment (College Station: Texas A&M University Press, 2002); Charles O. Jones, The Trusteeship Presidency: Jimmy Carter and the United States Congress (Baton Rouge: Louisiana State University Press, 1988); Yanek Mieczkowski, Gerald Ford and the Challenges of the 1970s (Lexington: University Press of Kentucky, 2005).

[109] John W. Sloan, "Meeting the Leadership Challenges of the Modern Presidency: The Political Skills and Leadership of Ronald Reagan." Presidential Studies Quarterly 26, no. 3 (1996): 795–804.

anticipates presidents to be able to accomplish and what they really can. From this viewpoint, inflation of expectations is worse than the rising interest rates of the 1970s. "Since the birth of the modern presidency," Richard Waterman, Carol Silva, and Hank Jenkins-Smith assert, "the policy demands on the presidency have expanded exponentially, with presidents currently expected to resolve virtually every societal problem,"[110] from the economy and the national debt to foreign affairs, terrorism, and intractable social issues. In other words, demands on the Oval Office exceed what is likely realizable by any presidential administration.

Trump's supporters and detractors hold diametrically opposite opinions of the Samson model. The president's proponents applaud his major accomplishments, many of which have been implemented through executive action. On this front, the president does not appear to have had his trademark auburn coiffure sheared like Samson's locks. Regardless, when Congress fails to act on issues ranging from immigration reform to "repeal and replace" of the Affordable Care Act (i.e., ACA, or "Obamacare"), Capitol Hill becomes a convenient scapegoat to support the thesis that a cabal of shadowy creatures lurking in a murky slough alongside the Potomac are bent on hindering the will of the people as Trump interprets it. If Trump is Samson, it is *not* the president's lack of prowess in the "art of the deal" that is in question. Rather, it is the fault of lily-livered legislative leaders and pusillanimous political foes with personal vendettas like the late John McCain (R-AZ), whose "thumbs down" on repealing the ACA in the Senate was little more than political theater to humiliate Trump, defy the preferences of the people, and preclude the administration's success. At rambunctious campaign rallies Trump's battle cry to restore presidential power is based on "reform" of Congress by electing Republican candidates who pledge uncompromising fealty to him.

For Trump's critics, many are optimistic that the Samson model can constrain the president and immobilize his policy agenda and

[110] Richard Waterman, Carol L. Silva, and Hank Jenkins-Smith, *The Presidential Expectations Gap: Public Attitudes Concerning the Presidency* (Ann Arbor: University of Michigan Press, 2014), p. 16.

worst populist instincts. Such a model is thus to be celebrated. Whether through the checks and balances of the constitutional system, manipulation of institutional rules by the minority or majority in the bicameral Congress, or judicial review of controversial policies, the "veto points"[111] in the very structure of American government serve as a paramount and *positive* check on an otherwise runaway presidency. Even the president's conservative critics, including the prominent Pulitzer Prize-winning columnist George Will, suggested that one way of containing Trump is to halt the servility the president demands from congressional Republicans by robbing him of legislative majorities in the mid-term elections of 2018. Imposing divided control of the White House and Capitol Hill arguably combines with traditional checks and balances to hamstring the president's legislative agenda. Calling the president a "Vesuvius of mendacities," Will appealed to Republicans to restrain Trump, contending that

> to vote against his party's cowering congressional caucuses is to affirm the nation's honor while quarantining him. A Democratic-controlled Congress would be a basket of deplorables, but there would be enough Republicans to gum up the Senate's machinery, keeping the institution as peripheral as it has been under their control and asphyxiating mischief from a Democratic House.[112]

Will got his wish on November 6, 2018 as Democrats picked up enough seats to gain the majority in the House of Representatives and impose a form of divided government reminiscent of Ronald Reagan's last two years: a Republican-controlled Senate and a Democratic-controlled lower chamber. The legislative stalemate that has since taken hold is to be rejoiced as a central mechanism to curb the excesses of Trump's impulses and his attempt to

---

[111] George Tsebelis, *Veto Players: How Political Institutions Work* (Princeton, NJ: Princeton University Press, 2002).

[112] George Will, "Vote against the GOP this November." *Washington Post*, June 22, 2018. https://www.washingtonpost.com/opinions/vote-against-the-gop-this-november/2018/06/22/a6378306-7575-11e8-b4b7-308400242c2e_story.html

reshape the Grand Old Party (GOP) in his own populist image. With the assistance of Majority Leader Mitch McConnell (R-KY), the president has successfully played off one chamber against the other, from legislation he finds objectionable to impeachment.

IV. Trump, populism, and the theory and exercise of presidential power

The Savior, Satan, and Samson perspectives raise the critical question of how the operationalization of Trump's populist style of leadership challenges or comports with scholars' understanding of, and prescriptions for, the exercise of presidential power in the American system of separated institutions. Trump has deftly employed the levers of the rhetorical presidency to reinforce support among core factions of his successful, if tenuous, electoral coalition in 2016. But substantively, the president has scored few victories in Congress, notwithstanding tax cuts and two Supreme Court appointments.[113] Instead, many of Trump's most consequential policy victories have come through unilateral actions based on existing statutory authority or constitutional prerogative, such as immigration and a border wall, prompting extensive court litigation.

Trump's leadership approach is at variance not only with prescriptive theories of presidential power emphasizing informal persuasion over formal, constitutional authority but also with his campaign assurances of superlative negotiating skill. The mismatch between the president's self-proclaimed perspicacity in negotiation and bargaining and his modus operandi of unilateralism merits scrutiny. A paradoxical feature of Trump's populist

---

[113] Mckay Coppins, "A Faustian bargain pays off for conservative Christians," *The Atlantic*, February 1, 2017. https://www.theatlantic.com/politics/archive/2017/02/conservatives-react-to-trump-scotus-pick/515265/; Julie Zauzmer, "As Trump picks Brett Kavanaugh for the Supreme Court, evangelicals rejoice: 'I will vote for him again'." *Seattle Times*, July 9, 2018. https://www.seattletimes.com/nation-world/nation-politics/wapoas-trump-picks-kavanaugh-for-the-supreme-court-evangelicals-rejoice-i-will-vote-for-him-again/

style is the active alienation of officials in Congress and in the wider executive branch whose support is critical for both negotiation and the implementation of his policies.

A. Neustadt, bargaining, and power as persuasion

By embracing the unilateral model of leadership that stresses the formal, constitutional mechanisms of presidential power, Trump has largely eschewed the bargaining theory advocated by Richard Neustadt six decades ago with the publication of *Presidential Power and the Modern Presidents*. An advisor to Presidents Harry Truman and John F. Kennedy, Neustadt employed his observations to assess the successful practice of personal power in the White House. Like Niccolò Machiavelli's classical work *The Prince*, his focus is on the realities of governing—less on normative theory and more on situating leadership "amid a general context of complex contingencies and conflicting interests" and on "using the realities of power and contingency to educate public and professional opinion about the fitting ends, means, and personal qualities of leaders."[114] As George C. Edwards III notes, "Neustadt's framework highlights the president's operational problem of *self-help* in thinking about influence strategically."[115] Neustadt emphasized persuasion as the central source of presidential power, which is bolstered by the chief executive's prestige, reputation, and unique position atop the political order:

> Effective influence for the man in the White House stems from three related sources: first are the bargaining advantages inherent in his job with which to persuade other men that what he wants of them is what their own responsibilities require them to do. Second are the expectations of those other men regarding his ability and will to

---

[114] Stephen H. Wirls, "Machiavelli and Neustadt on Virtue and the Civil Prince." *Presidential Studies Quarterly* 24, no. 3 (1994): 461.

[115] George C. Edwards III, "Neustadt's Power Approach to the Presidency." In Robert Y. Shapiro, Martha Joynt Kumar, and Lawrence R. Jacobs (eds.), *Presidential Power: Forging the Presidency for the Twenty-First Century* (New York: Columbia University Press, 2000), p. 9.

use the various advantages they think he has. Third are those men's estimates of how his public views him and of how their publics may view them if they do what he wants. In short, his power is the product of his vantage points in government, together with his reputation in the Washington community and his prestige outside.[116]

Bargaining theory emphasizes that the president must take pains to shield his unique resources in the Oval Office from those who would challenge him. First, in terms of reputation, the president must exhibit resoluteness and decisiveness. Convincing others of the certainty of his success reinforces loyalty and underlines the costs they may anticipate by obstructing his goals. The biggest risk to the president's reputation is the perception of successive failures, which strike at the foundation of his reputational advantage by undermining the confidence others have in his ability. Second, popular support is critical to presidential bargaining power. Politicians anticipate the reaction of voters in deciding to favor or oppose the president. If the president suffers from low prestige outside the Beltway, those inside Washington's political institutions have greater latitude to resist his leadership with impunity. Finally, the president must necessarily safeguard his personal power. Sitting at the apex of government, no one else has the unique, global view of the system like the president— and no one has the ability to substitute such an all-encompassing view for him. Others are influenced by narrow, parochial interests, whether electoral (Congress) or institutional (bureaucratic).

Through the midpoint of his term, Trump has clearly defied the tenets of Neustadt's prescriptions with a style of leadership that is more improvisational than farsighted. During the transition in 2017 the White House was notable for chaos, short-lived appointments, and uncertainty surrounding the president's commitment to policy objectives. This dynamic undermined his reputation as an honest broker. Trump earned a certain notoriety for indecision and backtracking on positions that left members

[116] Richard E. Neustadt, *Presidential Power and the Modern Presidents: The Politics of Leadership from Roosevelt to Reagan* (New York: Free Press, 1990), p. 150.

of Congress and many outside Washington flummoxed as to his priorities and doubting any potential detriment to them for failing to support legislation he advocated.

The abortive machinations of Republicans on Capitol Hill to repeal and replace the ACA, and the president's irresolution, are a case in point. During the presidential campaign Trump "repeatedly pointed to the repeal of Obamacare as a top priority and a key reason why he wanted to be president," promising some sixty-eight times that he would rescind the law.[117] However, as the GOP legislative majority got under way in early 2017 and wrestled with constructing a health care reform bill that could attract majority support, Trump grew impatient, claimed "nobody knew that health care could be so complicated," and suggested that Republicans should let Obamacare implode as a means of assigning blame to Democrats.[118] As Doyle McManus maintains, Trump's leadership on the ACA repeal suffered from four primary defects. First, the president did not learn the details of legislative proposals. Second, he "signaled repeatedly that his heart wasn't in the effort—that he'd be just as happy, maybe happier, if the bill didn't pass." Third, he never made any efforts to persuade the public and secure grassroots support at a time when public support for the ACA had strengthened. And finally, he undercut any influence over recalcitrant lawmakers, "most of whom have run more times than the president" and who did not believe him when he contended they would suffer in the next election if they voted against the bill that ultimately failed.[119]

---

[117] Ryan Koronowski, "68 times Trump promised to repeal Obamacare. The White House says it's already moving on." *ThinkProgress*, March 24, 2017. http://www. thinkprogress.org/trump-promised-to-repeal-obamacare-many-times-ab9500dad31e

[118] Madeline Conway, "Trump: 'Nobody knew that health care could be so complicated.' The president appears to nod to the grim political reality around repealing and replacing Obamacare." *Politico*, February 27, 2017. http://www.politico.com/story/2017/02/trump-nobody-knew-that-health-care-could-be-so-complicated-235436

[119] Doyle McManus, "It turns out Donald trump is not an Artist of the Deal." *Los Angeles Times*, March 24, 2017. http://www.latimes.com/opinion/op-ed/la-oe-mcmanus-trump-healthcare-failure-20170324-story.html

Turning Neustadt's theoretical precepts of presidential leadership upside-down, Trump has tacitly accepted the realities of Democratic opposition, equivocation by many in the congressional GOP over following his lead, and possible electoral advantages of "strategic disagreement."[120] The president has recognized that his political rivals have endeavored to destabilize his prestige and political influence by questioning his very legitimacy. "Trump's adversaries," Stephen B. Young highlights,

> consciously or not, have taken Neustadt's analysis to heart. They tirelessly work to deny Trump the power to persuade. They have belittled him, disparaged him, insulted him and, systemically, day in and day out, have challenged his integrity, his intelligence and his ethics—all tending to deny him stature and credibility.[121]

Instinctually, the president returns fire with the anti-elite rhetoric that reassures and enlivens his core electoral base, and promises to fight on in other policy domains like building a wall or securing better bilateral trade deals. But the result legislatively and in electoral terms is halting progress at best, stalemate and a continuation of the status quo at worst: "Trump has secured his base, and the Democratic leadership has held its core support. Neither side has majority backing among the people."[122]

B. Unconventional and unimpeded? The unilateral foundations of presidential power

It is little wonder that Trump has generally exchanged persuasion and bargaining for the unilateral perquisites of the presidency for many of his most important policy successes. The second face of presidential power—the opposite side of the coin to Neustadt's bargaining model—derives from classic analyses of the chief executive's

---

[120] John B. Gilmour, *Strategic Disagreement: Stalemate in American Politics* (Pittsburgh: University of Pittsburgh Press, 1995).

[121] Stephen B. Young, "The power of the presidency: Why Trump can't make it go." *Minneapolis Star-Tribune*, March 31, 2017. http://www.startribune.com/the-power-of-the-presidency-why-trump-can-t-make-it-go/417835453/

[122] Ibid.

constitutional authority, including those of Edward Corwin and Clinton Rossiter.[123] Scholars who question Neustadt's emphasis on behavioralism contend that "the key to an understanding of presidential power is to concentrate on the constitutional authority that the president asserts unilaterally through various rules of constitutional construction and interpretation."[124] As Kenneth Mayer asserts, "A president's ability to effect major policy change on his own is in many instances less dependent on personality or the powers of persuasion than on the office's formal authority and the inherent characteristics of governing institutions."[125] Unquestionably, there are significant benefits to acting alone. "When presidents act unilaterally to set policy," William G. Howell posits,

> they present Congress (and the Courts) with a fait accompli. Rather than proposing legislation and hoping Congress enacts it, or vetoing legislation, and hoping that Congress does not override, here presidents can independently shift policy in any way they wish, and there it will stay, until and unless either Congress or the courts effectively respond.[126]

Presidential prerogative traverses the domestic and foreign policy realms, and flows from constitutional powers outlined in Article II (e.g., the armed forces, treaty negotiation, etc.), congressional delegations of authority through legislative statutes in the administration of laws, and broad interpretations of inherent powers (i.e., war powers, emergency powers, etc.) that are subject to intense debate in scholarly and legal circles.[127] Unilateral actions may include executive orders, memoranda, proclamations, national

[123] See Raymond Tatalovich and Byron Daynes, "Towards a Paradigm to Explain Presidential Power." *Presidential Studies Quarterly* 9, no. 4 (1979): 428–41.

[124] Richard Pious, *The American Presidency* (New York: Basic Books, 1979), p. 16.

[125] Kenneth R. Mayer, *With the Stroke of a Pen: Executive Orders and Presidential Power* (Princeton, NJ: Princeton University Press, 2001), p. 224.

[126] William G. Howell, *Power without Persuasion: The Politics of Direct Presidential Action* (Princeton, NJ: Princeton University Press, 2003), p. 26.

[127] Examples include Franklin Roosevelt's internment of Japanese-Americans during World War II and Harry Truman's seizure of the steel mills during the Korean War.

security and homeland security directives, and signing statements. As Philip J. Cooper maintains, presidents can employ their prerogative power to accomplish a number of policy *and* political goals with these instruments. These include, inter alia, implementing swift changes in foreign policy, generating publicity, circumventing Congress, controlling the executive branch, responding to emergencies and directing disaster aid, and rewarding supporters.[128]

Trump's unilateral actions line up unmistakably with rational choice theories of unilateralism. William G. Howell hypothesizes that presidents will utilize the independent levers of the office when Congress is unable to enact legislation, there is alternation in party control of the White House, and during unified control of the presidency and Congress when presidents are less likely to confront a coalition capable of overturning executive actions.[129] In the latter scenario, if a consensus existed on Capitol Hill, legislation would likely be the result and consequently restrict the president's discretion. All three conditions apply to Trump's first two years in office, and there is ample empirical evidence to support the thesis that political and institutional context in addition to the president's criticism of, and fractious relationship with, elites in Congress, the executive branch, and the courts has contributed to his preference for independent action.

The president has been able to rescind his predecessor's regulatory rules and push forth his own vision for the economy, deregulation, and international affairs in ways that are reminiscent of Reagan's first year.[130] From border security and immigration to

---

[128] Philip J. Cooper, *By Order of the President: The Use and Abuse of Executive Direct Action* (Lawrence: University Press of Kansas, 2002), p. 239.

[129] Howell, *Power without Persuasion*.

[130] Reagan signed forty-nine executive orders in 1981; Trump signed fifty-five in 2017, and thirty through mid-September 2018. Reagan also set his sights on institutionalizing regulatory reform with the establishment of the Presidential Task Force on Regulatory Relief in January 1981 and by ordering the Office of Information and Regulatory Affairs (OIRA) in the Office of Management and Budget (OMB) to undertake cost–benefit analyses of new regulations. See George C. Eads and Michael Fix (eds.), *The Reagan Regulatory Strategy: An Assessment* (Washington, DC: The Urban Institute, 1984); Barry D. Friedman, "A Case-Study Analysis of the Reagan Regulatory Review Program." *Politics and Policy* 21, no. 4 (1993): 705–20.

the reduction of tax and regulatory burdens and approval of the Keystone XL and the Dakota Access Pipelines, Trump's executive actions quickly reaffirmed his promises to overturn significant components of President Obama's policy legacy. Additionally, the president drew upon his constitutional authority to withdraw the United States from the Paris Climate Accord, the Trans-Pacific Partnership, and the Joint Comprehensive Plan of Action (JCPOA), better known as the "Iran Nuclear deal," while boldly moving the U.S. embassy from Tel Aviv to Jerusalem—a promise that was not kept by any of his predecessors dating back to Clinton. Finally, some proclamations, like those dramatically reducing the size of federal monuments in Utah to enable natural resource extraction by oil and mining companies, rewarded a core business constituency of his 2016 campaign.[131]

Yet executive orders and independent actions are scarcely a panacea for any president. They are subject to congressional scrutiny and judicial review. As Howell puts it, the other two co-equal branches of the government "define what the president can accomplish on his own . . . Congress's ability and the courts' willingness to overturn them remain the final arbitrators of what presidents can accomplish should they decide to act unilaterally."[132] On the legal front, Trump has faced numerous court challenges, including the highly publicized travel ban on certain Muslim countries, the "two for one" reduction for every

---

[131] On December 4, 2017, Trump signed two proclamations. The first reduced the Bear's Ears National Monument by an astounding 1.3 million acres, or 85 percent; the second reduced the Grand Staircase-Escalante National Monument by nearly 876,000 acres, or 47 percent. Environmentalists and Native American tribes have launched legal challenges. See Gregory Korte, "Trump shrinks Bears Ears, Grand Staircase-Escalante monuments in historic proclamations." *USA Today*, December 5, 2017. https://www.usatoday.com/story/news/politics/2017/12/04/trump-travels-utah-historic-rollback-national-monuments/919209001/; Michelle L. Price and Brady McCombs, "Native American tribes sue over Trump's decision to shrink Utah national monument." *Chicago Tribune*, December 5, 2017. http://www.chicagotribune.com/news/nationworld/politics/ct-trump-national-monuments-20171205-story.html

[132] Howell, *Power without Persuasion*, p. 99.

new agency rule (E.O. 13771),[133] the termination of Deferred Action on Childhood Arrivals (DACA) for the children of illegal immigrants, and the attempt to reorient congressional appropriations to a border wall with Mexico, just to highlight a few. These latter examples suggest that Trump has been unable to bypass structural constraints that have at a minimum delayed his policy objectives, at least in terms of the judiciary. Whether the Democratic House majority that was seated in 2019 seeks to limit the president's authority is an open question at the time of writing. Regardless, the most important lesson in the longer view of history is that circumventing Congress with the stroke of a pen has its potential hazards. A Democratic successor to Trump could quickly dismantle his immigration, regulatory, and foreign policy changes absent congressional legislation. One of the central lessons of the Obama foreign policy inheritance, for example, is that his use of executive agreements and failure to enshrine his priorities in treaties approved by the Senate left his legacy to be disassembled with relative ease by his successor.[134]

Trump's reliance on the unilateral prerogatives of the presidency befits a populist style that is founded upon impatience with, and indignity toward, elites and mediated institutions like Congress. The controversies his actions stir and even his defeats can be manipulated for rhetorical consumption. His supporters applaud his executive actions and tout them as "promises made, promises kept" and blame others for his defeats at the hands of judges.[135]

---

[133] Lydia Wheeler, "Court tosses challenge to Trump's two-for-one regulatory order." *The Hill*, February 26, 2017. http://thehill.com/regulation/court-battles/ 375617-court-tosses-challenge-to-trumps-two-for-one-regulatory-order

[134] See Jeffrey Peake, "Obama, Unilateral Diplomacy, and Iran: Treaties, Executive Agreements, and Political Commitments." In Richard S. Conley (ed.), *Presidential Leadership and National Security Policy: The Obama Legacy and Trump Trajectory* (New York: Routledge, 2018), pp. 142–71.

[135] Dan Merica, "Trump turns to once-mocked executive orders to tout wins." *CNN*, April 27, 2017. https://www.cnn.com/2017/04/27/politics/ trump-executive-orders/index.html; Christopher Buskirk, "While Trump's critics keep talking, our president is fulfilling his promises." *USA Today*, January 18, 2018. https://www.usatoday.com/story/opinion/2018/01/18/ while-trumps-critics-keep-talking-our-president-fulfilling-his-promises-christopher-buskirk-column/1041117001/

The president's detractors, on the other hand, suggest that his reliance on executive orders and other unilateral instruments of the presidency is a plot to undermine the Constitution and a sign of fundamental weakness.[136]

The penultimate question is the long-term sustainability of Trump's dependence on a strategy of independent action combined with an anti-elite narrative that threatens to destabilize his own administration's policy implementation. His most controversial policies implemented at the outset of his term, including the travel ban on select Muslim countries and unilateral foreign policy initiatives connected to his "America First" agenda, provoked the resistance of his own civil service.[137] Trump rejoiced in firing Acting Attorney General Sally Yates for refusing to defend the travel ban in court and suggested she was part of the "deep state" bias he confronted in the Department of Justice. When 900 State Department employees signed a letter condemning the travel ban, White House Press Secretary Sean Spicer bluntly stated that dissenting career bureaucrats should "get with the program or they should go."[138] In response to the mêlée, the president tweeted: "There is nothing nice about searching for terrorists before they can enter our country. This was a big part of my campaign. Study the world!"[139] If he is manipulating the unilateral levers of the presidency for rhetorical consumption, "Trump," as Howell suggests,

> may be playing to a base that cares less about policy than about waging an existential war on Washington. The dustups caused by these unilateral directives may not productively change policy, but in

[136] David M. Driesen, "President Trump's Executive Orders and the Rule of Law." Syracuse University. *Social Science Research Network* (SSRN Papers, 2018). https://papers.ssrn.com/sol3/papers.cfm?abstract_id=3114381

[137] "America first and last; Donald Trump's foreign policy." *The Economist*, February 4, 2017, p. 17.

[138] Oren Dorrell, "Nearly 1,000 State Department staffers condemn Trump's travel ban." *USA* Today, January 31, 2017. https://www.usatoday.com/story/news/world/2017/01/31/nearly-1000-state-department-staffers-condem-trumps-travel-ban/97306024/

[139] @realDonaldTrump. "There is nothing nice about searching for terrorists before they can enter our country. This was a big part of my campaign. Study the world!" *Twitter*, January 30, 2017, 4:27 a.m.

the eyes of Trump's supporters, they may serve as proof positive that their man is righteously renouncing the discredited rules of a broken political system.[140]

V. The Trump presidency, populism, and American political development

The objective of this book is to analyze Trump's populist leadership style from a political development perspective, with a particular focus on his first two years in office. In the subfield of American political science, political development focuses on "the causes, nature, and consequences of key transformative periods and central patterns in American political history"[141] as a means of building theories about political change through case-study analysis. The goal is to place the presidency of Donald Trump and his populist style of governance within the broad scholarly dialogue on the sinuous historical evolution of the nation's highest political office, and where his populist style is potentially situated in "political time" or cycles of history.[142] A central thread of inquiry that runs through this study addresses whether Trump may be a *reconstructive* president who is transforming the institution of the presidency and the political order, whether he is a *disjunctive* president signifying the dying embers of the Reagan "regime" and imminent defeat in 2020, or whether his presidency represents a "punctuated equilibrium"[143] of change to the status quo that is based more on style than substance in a period of cyclical ambiguity.

This book develops a framework to explicate Trump's leadership style that draws from a historical, comparative perspective.

[140] William G. Howell, "Unilateral politics revisited (and revised) under Trump." *Princeton University Press Blog*, February 6, 2017. http://blog. press.princeton.edu/2017/02/06/william-g-howell-unilateral-politics- revisited-and-revised-under-trump/

[141] Rogan Kersh, "The Growth of American Political Development: The View from the Classroom." *Perspectives on Politics* 3, no. 2 (2005): 335.

[142] Stephen Skowronek, *The Politics Presidents Make* (Cambridge, MA: Harvard University Press, 1997).

[143] Frank R. Baumgartner and Bryan D. Jones, *Agendas and Instability in American Politics*, 2nd edition (Chicago: University of Chicago Press, 2010).

A common feature of the populist flare across time in the American experience is the articulation of unconventional, emotionally charged, and frequently quixotic appeals. The rhetoric of populism is distinctive for its recurring themes: reproach of elites, emphasis on the needs and desires of "ordinary people," support of majoritarianism over pluralism, simplification of issues, and romanticization of the past with frequent nativist overtones. The particular argumentative frames employed by populists highlight the intersection of, and variable disjuncture between, *rhetorical style, symbolism*, and *substantive policy*.

Trump's exercise of the populist leadership style can be juxtaposed with prior presidents and failed candidates with similar impulses and rhetorical bravado. Key examples include Andrew Jackson, William Jennings Bryan, Barry Goldwater, George Wallace, and H. Ross Perot. How does Trump's populist brand variably connect to his predecessors? One central argument of the book is that although the *vessel* for Trump's direct communication (social media) appears much different than previous candidates and presidents with populist platforms (e.g., speeches, newspapers, electronic townhalls), he shares, inter alia, with his populist forerunners a style that reflects a disdain for a political class of privileged elites, a focus on allegedly threatened social values, indifference toward co-equal institutions, and an anti-intellectual discourse often infused with conspiracy theory.

The broader question this analysis considers is the relative sustainability of Trump's populist style vis-à-vis the integrity of formal and informal institutions of American democracy and the perils that style may portend in the long term. The contradictions of Trump's 2016 campaign victory with the 2018 mid-term election backlash that handed Democrats control of the House of Representatives underscore a profoundly ambivalent electorate, an anxious citizenry, and profound polarization. Trump prevailed in the 2016 election despite strong majorities reporting that he was untrustworthy, was unqualified to be president, and lacked the temperament to serve as chief executive. Yet he surpassed 2012 Republican standard-bearer Mitt Romney's share of the vote among evangelical Christians and

Hispanics.[144] And about a third of 650 counties that voted for
Barack Obama twice (2008, 2012) flipped to support him in
2016, even though voters interviewed in fourteen states "said
they did not like Mr. Trump as a person and did not consider
themselves die-hard supporters. Some were even embarrassed
by him."[145] "Affectively polarized" in the present climate of
mounting civil discord and factual relativism, "Americans fear
the other party more than they like their own, not merely disagreeing with but actively disliking each other."[146] One of the
most disquieting legacies of Trump's presidency, in terms of his
own comportment and his detractors' reactions to his populist juggernaut, may be the exacerbation of incivility in a polity
increasingly defined by a loss of communicative norms in the
age of social media and an absence of "universal pragmatics"[147]
necessary to a healthy civic discourse.

VI. *Plan of the book*

The scope of this book extends to Trump's early forays into
politics and the shaping of his populist style, including the con-
spiracy-theory tactic of igniting the "birther" controversy surrounding President Barack Obama's national origin as a prelude
to running for the presidency. Subsequent chapters analyze his
behavior during the 2016 election cycle, his rabble-rousing post-
election rallies, and his governing strategy through the midpoint
of his term.

Chapter 2 provides a theoretical conceptualization of populism
to analyze Trump's leadership style comparatively and appraise

[144] Chris Cilizza, "The 13 most amazing findings in the 2016 exit poll."
Washington Post, November 10, 2016. https://www.washingtonpost.com/
news/the-fix/wp/2016/11/10/the-13-most-amazing-things-in-the-2016-exit-
poll/?utm_term=.82f37b291451

[145] Sabrina Tavernise and Robert Gebeloff, "They voted for Obama, then went
for Trump. Can Democrats win them back?" *New York Times*, May 14, 2018.
https://www.nytimes.com/2018/05/04/us/obama-trump-swing-voters.html

[146] Singh, "'I the People'," p. 19.

[147] Jürgen Habermas, "Some Distinctions in Universal Pragmatics." *Theory and
Society* 3, no. 2 (1976): 155–67.

the implications for campaigning and governing. The chapter identifies essential components of populist approaches to leadership and clarifies the definition of populism, per se. One key notion in American populism is the presidency as the "tribune" of the people—a better representative of the popular will than Congress—and the legitimization of presidential action through popular authority conveyed upon the president by the electorate's endorsement of his policy stances. A second component is the rejection of consensual politics and instead "the use of an antagonistic appeal that pits the people as represented by the president against a special interest."[148] Finally, a common characteristic of the populist style is the accent on a "corrupt elite" against which only a mass political movement can prevail.[149] It is this leitmotif of anti-elitism and exaltation of the "common man," the "little man," or the "people" broadly defined that connects Trump to a historical tradition of populism and the development of the plebiscitary presidency in bygone eras. Yet the apparent paradoxes of the Trump presidency—and indeed populist movements of yesteryear—include the oscillation "between a desire to transform, and so create a new order of things, and a desire to restore a yearned-for (or imagined) old order."[150]

Chapter 3 considers the origins of Trump's populism. The chapter reviews his controversial business career and his gravitation toward a brand of populism that was shaped by political forays in the 1980s. The chapter outlines the origins of his political views alongside his apparent and interminable quest for self-aggrandizement and the rise of his populist rhetoric.

Chapter 4 analyzes the dynamics of the 2016 electoral cycle in terms of populist messaging by Trump and Bernie Sanders, in particular. The analysis considers the psycho-social dynamics of

[148] Terri Bimes and Quinn Mulroy, "The Rise and Decline of Presidential Populism." *Studies in American Political Development* 18, no. 2 (2004): 139.
[149] Michael Kazin, *The Populist Persuasion: An American History* (Ithaca, NY: Cornell University Press, 1998).
[150] Steve Fraser and Joshua B. Freeman, "In the Rearview Mirror: History's Mad Hatters—The Strange Career of Tea Party Populism." *New Labor Forum* 19, no. 1 (2010): 76.

Trump's populist spectacles and narratives during the 2016 election and the differences and similarities to Sanders' appeal. The chapter also highlights how the populist insurgencies on the Left and Right transformed the framework of the 2020 presidential contest.

Chapter 5 examines Trump's singular comportment in the immediate aftermath of the 2016 election. Emphasis is placed on his post-election and post-inaugural rallies. The analysis emphasizes that Trump's primary goal was not to persuade voters or policymakers on Capitol Hill, but rather to consolidate his base of support in furtherance of a new form of permanent campaign.

Chapter 6 considers briefly Trump's governing approach through the midpoint of his term. Exchanging bargaining theory for the unilateral levers of the presidency, Trump's most significant policy victories have come through executive action, including regulatory reform. The chapter accentuates the risks associated in bypassing Congress for Trump's potential legacy.

Chapter 7 considers briefly how Trump's populist approach to leadership may jeopardize his presidency. The major perils to his legacy include constitutional, criminal, and political liabilities. The more profound question is how the populist style has impacted civic dialogue in ways that conflict with the Founders' vision of the nation's highest office and where the nation goes in the post-Trump era.

Chapter 8 provides a brief epilogue on the state of Trump's populist presidency a little less than a year from the 2020 election. Of critical importance is the future fate of the Republican Party whether he is re-elected, removed, or defeated. Ideological consistency and conviction politics are not the staple of Trump's populist style—and his eventual exit from politics raises more questions than answers about the Republican brand in the future.

The populist precedent

History repeats itself, first as tragedy, second as farce.

—Karl Marx

You are a den of vipers and thieves. I have determined to rout you out, and by the Eternal, (bringing his fist down on the table) I will rout you out!

—Andrew Jackson

Never forget that the press is the enemy. The establishment is the enemy. The professors are the enemy. Professors are the enemy. Write that on a blackboard 100 times and never forget it.

—Richard Nixon

I. Introduction: conceptualizing populism

The ontology of populism seems as elusive as the futile effort to hold a moonbeam in the palm of one's hand. Operationalization of the term in the scholarly literature is as ambiguous as it is diverse in struggling to capture the essence of a phenomenon that resembles the fabled phoenix, rising inexplicably from the cinders to disrupt the political environment periodically and then vanishing into obscurity. Ironically, as Ernesto Laclau suggests, "We know to what we are referring when we call a movement or an ideology populist, but we have the greatest difficulty in translating the intuition into concepts."[1] It follows, as one scholar noted, that it is "a cliché to start writing on populism by lamenting the lack of

---

[1] Ernesto Laclau, *Politics and Ideology in Marxist Theory: Capitalism—Fascism—Populism* (London: New Left Books, 1977), p. 143.

clarity about the concept and casting doubts about its usefulness for political analysis."[2]

The central problem is that theoretical constructs of populism tend to be "comprehensive but too vague, or else they are clear but too narrow."[3] The term has been used to different ends with definitions so broad that they fail to distinguish between types of movements that may be democratic or anti-democratic in nature. Populism has been utilized as a pejorative term to disparage some movements, particularly on the Right, and sound the alarm of authoritarianism, bigotry, and xenophobia.[4] At the same time, populist leadership has been acclaimed for the potential to restore civic virtue, inclusion, and equality as a fundamental component of American political culture that accentuates vigilance against powerful elites.[5] The discordant understandings of the essence of populism reflect the dilemma of cobbling together a definition from rather different academic literatures that span time, space, and geography from Europe and Latin America to the United States.[6]

Scholars have taken numerous approaches to the phenomenon in the hopes of finding cross-national linkages and fashioning a unified theory. Cas Mudde views populism as a "thin-skinned ideology that considers society to be ultimately separated into two homogenous and antagonistic groups, 'the pure people' and

[2] Francisco Panizza, "Introduction: Populism and the Mirror of Democracy." In Francisco Panizza (ed.), *Populism and the Mirror of Democracy* (London: Verso, 2005), p. 1.

[3] Margaret Canovan, "Two Strategies for the Study of Populism." *Political Studies* 30 (1982): 546.

[4] James Pierson, "Why Populism Fails." *The New Criterion* 37, no. 9 (January 2018): 18.

[5] See Harry Boyte, *We the People Politics: The Populist Promise of Deliberative Public Work* (Dayton, OH: Kettering Foundation, 2011).

[6] See Cristóbal Rovira Kaltwasser, "The Ambivalence of Populism: Threat and Corrective for Democracy." *Democratization* 19, no. 2 (2014): 184–208; Cas Mudde and Cristóbal Rovira Kaltwasser, "Exclusionary vs. Inclusionary Populism: Comparing Contemporary Europe and Latin America." *Government and Opposition* 48, no. 2 (2013): 147–74; Ghita Ionescu and Ernest Gellner (eds.), *Populism: Its Meaning and National Characteristics* (New York: Macmillan, 1969).

the 'corrupt elite'."[7] Laclau contends that populism is the logic of all politics itself insofar as the emergence of the "people" as a collective actor is key to the *process* of radical change.[8] Emphasizing the necessity of "a relation of equivalence between a plurality of social demands," Laclau asserts that "[p]opulism is not an ideology but a way of constructing the political based in interpellating the underdog against those in power."[9] Others, like Jan-Werner Müller, maintain that populism is strategic. For Müller, populist leaders emphasize a "moralized antipluralism" by arguing that they alone represent the people. Further, populists adhere to a noninstitutionalized notion of the "people 'out there'—in existential opposition to officeholders who have been authorized by an actual election, or even just opinion polls, which fail to reflect what populists see as the true popular will."[10] The implication is that elections, representative institutions, and procedural dynamics are of negligible importance to governance and democratic outcomes if the populist leader discerns the will of the people.[11]

Scholars will certainly continue to search for the holy grail of a comprehensive and comparatively inclusive paradigm of populism that can solidify a theoretical and empirical nexus between leaders with styles and policy objectives as dissimilar as Jean-Marie Le Pen in France, Juan Péron in Argentina, Evo Morales in Bolivia, and Jair Bolsonaro in Brazil. The more modest goal of this chapter is to fashion a conceptualization of the populist style capable of placing Donald Trump's leadership style in context with his American forerunners, assessing his potential legacy in the broader sweep of

[7] Cas Mudde, *Populist Radical Right Parties in Europe* (Cambridge: Cambridge University Press), p. 23.
[8] See Ernesto Laclau, *On Populist Reason* (London: Verso, 2005).
[9] Ernesto Laclau, "Why Populism?" In *New Populisms and the European Right and Far Right Parties* (Milan: Edizioni Punto Rosso, 2012), pp. 13–14. http://www.rivistaprogettolavoro.com/uploads/1/7/0/3/17033228/i_nuovi_pupulismi_in_eu.pdf#page=13
[10] Jan-Werner Müller, *What Is Populism?* (Philadelphia: University of Pennsylvania Press, 2016), p. 27.
[11] See Aziz Z. Huq, "The People against the Constitution." *Michigan Law Review* 116 (2018): 1133; also, Nadia Urbinati, "The Populist Phenomenon." *Raisons Politiques* 137, no. 3 (2013): 145–6.

history, and evaluating the implications of that style for our understanding of presidential power. The common thread in American
populism is the expression of anti-elitism bolstered by the belief
in what Richard Nixon called a "great silent majority"[12] of voters
whose concerns have gone unaddressed by elected officials. Grasp-
ing the themes populists emphasize and the style they utilize to
take aim at elites is the first piece of the definitional puzzle this
chapter unravels as a means of undertaking a broader, comparative
analysis.

John Judis's definition of populism as a conflictual relationship between an elite and a people is a basic and indispensable
starting point to understand the populist style.[13] In the American
tradition, the geography of populist reverie is located in a figura-
tive and frequently romanticized *patria* of some variety, "an ideal
society of the past and of the heart."[14] The redemptive vision of
American populism, as Michael J. Lee suggests, is its collectiv-
ization of the "people," described as "ordinary, hard-working,
God-fearing, and patriotic Americans."[15] Put another way, "Populism is thus a grand form of rhetorical optimism; once mobi-
lized, there is nothing ordinary Americans cannot accomplish."[16]
As Linda Schulte-Sasse notes of Ross Perot's populist symbolism,
"the American People are the 'owners' of the country and need to
keep their 'servants' from grabbing the booty. Perot's reversal of
a hierarchical conception in which one presumes that Congress
and others of influence in Washington are of a higher rank than

[12] Nixon's "Great Silent Majority" speech on Vietnam policy was broadcast
on November 3, 1969. See http://www.americanrhetoric.com/speeches/
richardnixongreatsilentmajority.html
[13] John B. Judis, *The Populist Explosion: How the Great Recession Transformed American and European Politics* (New York: Columbia World
Reports, 2016), p. 15.
[14] Tjitske Akkerman, "Populism and Democracy: Challenge or Pathology?"
Acta Politica 38, no. 2 (2003): 151.
[15] M. J. Lee, "The Populist Chameleon: The People's Party, Huey Long, George
Wallace, and the Populist Argumentative Frame." *Quarterly Journal of
Speech* 92, no. 4 (2006): 358.
[16] Michael Kazin, *The Populist Persuasion: An American History* (Ithaca, NY:
Cornell University Press, 1998), p. 2.

ordinary people gives his rhetoric a revolutionary ring,"[17] even if specific policy propositions lack detail and substance on how to right the wayward ship of state.

Defining the parameters of populism requires an understanding that the phenomenon

> is not really a "thing" at all. It is, rather, an "effect," a style, a syndrome, a device—or series of devices—involving, to varying degrees and intensities, the myth of direct popular power—a component of politics of different shades.[18]

As a consequence, efforts to reduce the expression of populist tactics in the arenas of campaigning or governing to politics on the left or right of the political spectrum cannot reconcile the apparent void of "inner logic"[19] that often characterizes idiosyncratic leaders and ephemeral movements with significant internal contradictions. "This is why," Martin Eiermann argues, "any attempt to associate populism with a particular conservative or progressive tradition—and thus to condemn it in partisan fashion—is bound to falter: The logic and rhetoric of populism have been harnessed by diverse groups for different ends."[20]

The first objective of this chapter is to delineate a framework of populism as political style. A reckoning of Trump's brand of populism within the broader sweep of history requires setting forth a working definition of a set of characteristics of the populist style that is inclusive enough to connect him to his populist antecedents and contemporaries, and still sufficiently nuanced to account both for contextual differences across time and the unique expressions of Trump's populist ethos. Moreover, demarcating the populist style necessitates analyzing the tendencies of

---

[17] Linda Schulte-Sasse, "Meet Ross Perot: The Lasting Legacy of Capraesque Populism." *Cultural Critique* 25 (1993): 99.

[18] Maxine Molyneux and Thomas Osborne, "Populism: A Deflationary View." *Economy and Society* 46, no. 1 (2017): 2.

[19] Müller, *What Is Populism?*, p. 10.

[20] Martin Eiermann, "How Donald Trump Fits into the History of American Populism." *New Perspectives Quarterly* 33, no. 2 (2016): 33.

American populism vis-à-vis the ancient philosophers' interpretation of the dangers of demagoguery, and surveying whether American political culture acts as a hedge against the excesses of populist rhetoric.

The second goal of this chapter is to juxtapose Trump's stylistic bonds with American populists of previous eras. It is beyond the scope of this book to recount the rich details of Andrew Jackson's transformative presidency or the failed campaigns of William Jennings Bryan, George Wallace, Barry Goldwater, or H. Ross Perot. Rather, the objective is to grasp the implications of the populist campaigning and governing style for political party cohesion and institutional stability, and what the recurring constituent characteristics of populist narratives imply in terms of conceptualizing the "people," majoritarian tendencies vis-à-vis pluralism, issue simplification, and nostalgia for the past that often morphs into nativism of various colors.

The third goal of the chapter is to situate Trump's potential legacy within the conceptual framework of "political time," articulated by Stephen Skowronek as repeating cycles of history.[21] A definitive resolution to the question of Trump's prospects—in spite of, or due to, his populist approach—as a reconstructive president, an orthodox innovator wedded to maintenance of the status quo, or a tragically disjunctive and ill-fated figure like James Buchanan or Herbert Hoover, is admittedly precarious. Conclusions are necessarily circumspect, based as they are on limited observation to date. But the tenets of regime theory may be employed as a baseline to chart conceivable outcomes.

II. American populism: a style in search of a definition

In the era of Donald Trump, populism is now a widely used catchphrase, and even fodder for cable television programs. *The Next Revolution*, a Sunday evening show on Fox News, purports to provide an intellectual distillation of "positive populism." According

---

[21] Stephen Skowronek, *Presidential Leadership in Political Time: Reprise and Reappraisal* (Lawrence: University Press of Kansas, 2008).

to the host Steve Hilton, former advisor to British Prime Minister David Cameron, showcasing positive populism entails accenting the ways in which elites have *victimized* people in the hopes of creating a working-class coalition that unifies supporters of President Trump and socialist Vermont Senator Bernie Sanders.[22]

Such a perspective may appear incredible to many. The 2018 elections in Florida are a case in point. In late summer 2018 the Sunshine State's Democratic and Republican primary electorates set up a November governor's race between Bernie Sanders-backed Andrew Gillum (mayor of Tallahassee) and Trump acolyte Ron DeSantis (three-term member of Congress). The contest was widely billed as a proxy war between two diametrically opposed populist camps with entirely different visions of America on the socio-economic front.[23] Upon his surprise primary upset of Gwen Graham, daughter of former Florida Governor Bob Graham, Gillum contended that

> We're going to make clear to the rest of the world that the dark days that we've been under, coming out of Washington, that the derision and the division that has been coming out of our White House, that right here in the state of Florida we are going to remind this nation of what is truly the American way.[24]

For his part, DeSantis posited on election night that Gillum

> wants to abolish ICE [Immigration and Customs Enforcement]. He wants a billion-dollar tax increase. He wants a single-payer health-care system in Florida, which would bankrupt the state . . . He wants

---

[22] Nellie Bowles, "Silicon Valley now has its own populist pundit." *New York Times*, August 12, 2017. https://www.nytimes.com/2017/08/12/style/steve-hilton-fox-news-silicon-valley-populist-pundit.html

[23] Max Greenwood, "Gillum to face tougher road in Florida after primary stunner." *The Hill*, August 29, 2018. http://thehill.com/homenews/campaign/404269-gillum-to-face-tougher-road-in-florida-after-primary-stunner

[24] Quoted in Patricia Mazzei and Jonathan Martin, "A black progressive and a Trump acolyte win Florida governor primaries." *New York Times*, August 28, 2018. https://www.nytimes.com/2018/08/28/us/politics/florida-arizona-election-results.html

to make Florida Venezuela. But he also combines a far-left ideology with managerial incompetence.[25]

In his reference to Florida's economic progress under Republican Governor Rick Scott, another devotee of the president who ran successfully for the U.S. Senate in the 2018 mid-term elections, DeSantis' warning to voters not to "monkey this up" was considered by many a racist slur against Gillum, an African American. Gillum responded in kind, suggesting that such allegedly bigoted comments were directly out of the "the handbook of Donald Trump" and that "they no longer do whistle calls. They're now using full bullhorns."[26]

If the Florida governor's race, which DeSantis won narrowly, represented a microcosm of a larger, epic battle between the primary voting bases of the Democratic and Republican parties, how can Sanders and Trump, who effectively galvanized opposite poles of the existing party structure, be lumped together simultaneously as representatives of populism? The answer is that their crusades and their surrogates share a cohesiveness insofar as the core messaging is directed at a mutual ensemble of casualties, the "increasing numbers of citizens [who] believe that the economic and political systems of the country are rigged against them."[27] The dynamic is surely compounded by the decline of so-called "mainstream" politics and increasing alienation of voters from traditional party politics.[28] Defying conventional understandings

---

[25] Ian Hanchett, "DeSantis: Gillum 'wants to make Florida Venezuela'." *Breitbart*, August 28, 2018. https://www.breitbart.com/video/2018/08/28/desantis-gillum-wants-to-make-florida-venezuela/

[26] William Cummings, "Andrew Gillum says Ron DeSantis 'monkey' comment is straight out of Trump handbook." *USA Today*, August 29, 2018. https://www.usatoday.com/story/news/politics/onpolitics/2018/08/29/andrew-gillum-ron-desantis-monkey-comment-out-trump-playbook/1139968002/

[27] Geoffrey Kabaservice, "Wild populism has a long history in US politics, but Trump is surely unique." *The Guardian*, January 14, 2017. https://www.theguardian.com/commentisfree/2017/jan/15/wild-populism-long-history-us-politics-trump-surely-unique

[28] Peter Mair, "Ruling the Void: The Hollowing of Western Democracy." *New Left Review* 42 (November–December 2006).

of voters in the two-party system, "Trump," for his part, "has complicated the traditional calculus of left and right in interesting ways, winning over many union members who feel threatened by free trade and globalisation."[29]

The critical argument is that the language of populism can be at once impulsive, flexible, vague, simplistic, and targeted—regardless of any dogmatic precepts or partisan inclinations that guide the message. With its exaltation of the virtue of the common man against elites, "populist rhetoric is compatible with all kinds of different social bases and economic interests, with ideologies of different kinds or with lack of ideology altogether."[30] As Julian Baggini notes, the term can embrace rather unflappably the declamations of both Trump and Sanders because "this kind of populism sees mainstream politics as, at best, bankrupt and at worst, corrupt. Political power has been seized by vested interests and elites, robbing the ordinary people of their entitlements."[31] For Trump the culprit includes a cabal of liberal Democrats and "establishment" Republicans in Washington, DC that has for too long ignored voters.[32] For Sanders, like his Senate colleague Elizabeth Warren, it is the millionaires and corporations who have inflicted inequality on the masses.[33] Both politicians' insurgent bombast variably embraces conspiracy theory to explicate the fate of the downtrodden.

The unlikely linkages between Trump and Sanders emphasize the degree to which populism must be understood as a *mode of persuasion*[34] connected to *political style* rather than an ideology.[35] How may we define political style? Moffit and Tormey provide

---

[29] Kabaservice, "Wild populism has a long history in US politics."

[30] Margaret Canovan, "Two Strategies for the Study of Populism." *Political Studies* 30 (1982): 552.

[31] Julian Baggini, "How Rising Trump and Sanders Parallel Rising Populism in Europe." *New Perspectives Quarterly* 33, no. 2 (2016): 22.

[32] Raynard Jackson, "The monsters Washington created." *Charlotte Post* (NC), November 17, 2016, p. 5A.

[33] Jason Horowitz, "With palpable sense of conviction, Sanders presses economic message." *New York Times*, October 11, 2015, p. A26.

[34] Kazin, *The Populist Persuasion*, p. 3.

[35] Cas Mudde, "The Populist Zeitgeist." *Government and Opposition* 39, no. 4 (2004): 542–63.

a simple explication of the concept as "the repertoires of performance that are used to create political relations."[36] Performance,
understood as spectacle, imagery, and the accompanying oratory,
is central to understanding the populist ethos and the construction of leaders' rapport with the citizenry. The populist style, as
Shogan asserts, hinges on spectacles that "lend themselves to the
portrayal of presidents as energetic, dynamic, hyper-masculine
individuals who defeat evil in the name of American democracy."
Politics-as-usual, or "the intellectual process of deliberation cannot constitute a spectacle."[37] The notion harkens back to Erving
Goffman's "presentation of self."[38] Pretense, posturing, emotion,
and personality are part and parcel of contextualized performative politics in which the politician is judged in the public arena
on the basis of honesty, authenticity, and "character."[39] The fer-
tile ground for stylized populism emerges across the eras of the
American Republic in the search to mobilize the "people" in the
midst of some real or perceived crisis in which elites are unable
to solve the problems of ordinary citizens, or worse, allegedly do
not care about the people they feign to represent.

If American populism is more zeitgeist than coherent doctrine,
a common thread of the style includes normative assumptions
about the nature of the polity that contravene most poignantly
the pluralist or Madisonian precepts on which the American
Republic was founded. As Huq contends, "Populism hence is less
a matter of policy preferences and more a question of the guiding assumptions about how democracy can and should work and
how leaders can and should relate to the people."[40] Schoor argues
convincingly that five core traits differentiate the populist style
along five dimensions that focus on the nature of the "people,"

---

[36] Benjamin Moffitt and Simon Tormey, "Rethinking Populism: Politics, Mediatisation and Political Style." *Political Studies* 62, no. 2 (2014): 387.

[37] Colleen Shogan, "Anti-Intellectualism in the Modern Presidency: A Republican
Populism." *Perspectives on Politics* 5, no. 2 (2007): 296.

[38] Erving Goffman, *The Presentation of Self in Everyday Life* (New York:
Doubleday Anchor, 1959).

[39] John Corner and Dick Pels (eds.), *Media and the Restyling of Politics* (London:
Sage, 2003), p. 10.

[40] Huq, "The People against the Constitution," p. 1132.

politicians, democracy, politics, and the contextual situation.[41] Populists take a decidedly negative perspective toward politicians, simultaneously celebrate those who qualify as the "people" while placing limits on the definition, and see politics through the lens of Manichean conflict between ordinary folks and "elites" in a crisis setting.

III. The populist style and demagoguery: classical linkages and American exceptionalism

The term "populism" is a comparatively recent formulation in the lexicon of American politics. It was coined in the early 1890s with the emergence of the People's Party in the United States. More general use of the expression in everyday parlance did not take place until the 1970s.[42] Yet the sages of old would easily recognize the political style, now labeled populist, that has variably impacted political dynamics in the United States dating back to the presidency of Andrew Jackson. The classical understanding of populism is most closely associated with *demagoguery*, which troubled ancient philosophers. The pivotal question is the degree to which the American variant of populism, and the inherent dangers the Founders believed the stylistic inclination might pose, differs from the Hellenic analysis generally and with reference to Donald Trump and his American predecessors specifically.

From classical texts a demagogue may be defined as a provocateur that employs fiery rhetoric to fan the flames of popular passions, not by reasoned argument and measured persuasion, but rather by prejudice and ignorance. The etymology of "demagogue" derives from the Greek *demos* (the people) and *agogos* (leader). Today the word presumably offends the objective ear, connoting a term that is "slightly gentler than 'fascist' and

---

[41] Carola Schoor, "In the Theater of Political Style: Touches of Populism, Pluralism, and Elitism in the Speeches of Politicians." *Discourse & Society* 28, no. 6 (2017): 664–5.

[42] W. Robert Connor, "A Vacuum at the Center." *The American Scholar* (Spring 2018): 22.

slightly more dignified than 'buffoon'."[43] It may well be that a milder designation such as populism "appeals to our preference for an unprejudiced way to bring to light what lurks below the surface of these forms of politics: feelings of neglect, disappointment, frustration, demoralization; distrust of elites; fear and even hatred of differences."[44]

Greek philosophers correlated demagoguery with mob rule. Aristotle noted that the interconnection between the people and such leaders is

> the mutual support they give to each other, the flatterer to the tyrant, the demagogue to the people: and to them it is owing that the supreme power is lodged in the votes of the people, and not in the laws.[45]

Through rhetorical exhortations aimed at inciting envy and resentment, demagogues prey upon the darker traits of the human spirit. Demagogues are frequently men of great ambition, who "by acting as popular leaders bring things to the point of the people's being sovereign even over the laws."[46] Aristotle identified Pericles' successor, Cleon, as the wellspring of an anti-intellectual oratory that defied the mores of the day and set the city-state on a path to self-destruction. In *The Athenian Constitution* he writes that Cleon

> seems, more than any one else, to have been the cause of the corruption of the democracy by his wild undertakings; and he was the

---

[43] Megan Garber, "What we talk about when we talk about 'demagogues'." *The Atlantic*, December 10, 2015. https://www.theatlantic.com/entertainment/archive/2015/12/what-we-talk-about-when-we-talk-about-demagogues/419514/

[44] Connor, "A Vacuum at the Center," pp. 22–3.

[45] Aristotle, *Aristotle's Politics: A Treatise on Government* (New York: G. Routledge, 1895), p. 133.

[46] Aristotle, *Aristotle in 23 Volumes*, vol. 21. Translated by H. Rackham (Cambridge, MA: Harvard University Press; London: William Heinemann Ltd., 1944), Book 5, Section 1305(a) [1]. http://www.perseus.tufts.edu/hopper/text?doc=Perseus:abo:tlg,0086,035:5

first to use unseemly shouting and coarse abuse on the Bema, and to harangue the people with his cloak girt short about him, whereas all his predecessors had spoken decently and in order.[47]

The demagogue lacks self-control and judgment, and is the harbinger of despotism and the demise of democracy. Drawing on the "assumed wisdom of ordinary people . . . [h]e trusts his impulses, lets them well up, doesn't turn them over in his mind searching for unintended consequences or pause to contemplate complexity."[48] In the *Republic*, Plato considered the implications of the demagogue's rhetoric and the servility of the mob:

> the people [are] always accustomed to set up one man as their spe-cial leader and to foster him and make him grow great . . . It is plain therefore, that when a tyrant grows naturally, he sprouts from a root of leadership and from nowhere else . . . [T]he leader of the people who, taking over a particularly obedient mob, does not hold back from shedding the blood of his tribe but unjustly brings charges against a man . . . bringing him before the court, murders him . . . and hints at cancellations of debts and redistributions of land . . . if he's exiled and comes back in spite of his enemies, . . . he come back a complete tyrant.[49]

Such classical arguments were scarcely lost on the American Founders in Philadelphia in 1787. In Federalist #1 Alexander Hamilton, one of the key proponents of a strong executive in debates about the American constitutional structure, recognized candidly the danger of demagoguery, opining that

> To judge from the conduct of the opposite parties, we shall be led to conclude that they will mutually hope to evince the justness of their opinions, and to increase the number of their converts by the loud-ness of their declamations and the bitterness of their invectives . . .

---

[47] Aristotle, *The Athenian Constitution* (Cambridge, MA: Charles River Editors, 2018), p. 28.

[48] Connor, "The Vacuum at the Center," p. 28.

[49] Plato, *The Republic*. Translated by Alan Bloom (New York: Harper Collins, 1968), 565c–565e, pp. 244–5.

An over-scrupulous jealousy of danger to the rights of the people, which is more commonly the fault of the head than of the heart, will be represented as mere pretense and artifice, the stale bait for popularity at the expense of the public good. It will be forgotten . . . that a dangerous ambition more often lurks behind the specious mask of zeal for the rights of the people than under the forbidden appearance of zeal for the firmness and efficiency of government. History will teach us that the former has been found a much more certain road to the introduction of despotism than the latter, and that of those men who have overturned the liberties of republics, the greatest number have begun their career by paying an obsequious court to the people; commencing demagogues, and ending tyrants.[50]

James Madison similarly acknowledged the allure of the demagogue in Federalist #10, noting that "[m]en of factious tempers, of local prejudices, or of sinister designs, may, by intrigue, by corruption, or by other means, first obtain the suffrages, and then betray the interests, of the people."[51] What concerned Madison most was that anti-intellectualism would prevail: that passion would supplant reason, just as the Greeks worried.[52] The architect of the Constitution parted ways with the ancients insofar as his blueprint for a new governmental charter included a *large* and diverse Republic with a division of power between levels of government as well as within the institutional structure, as a bulwark against demagogues who might be tempted to incite a "rage for paper money, for an abolition of debts, for an equal division of property, or for any other improper or wicked project."[53]

Donald Trump's detractors fear that the 45th president has all the attributes of a classical demagogue bent on upending the Constitution—and who may prove the disastrous exception to the Founders' genius.[54] Such trepidations are not new: the same

[50] Federalist #1. http://avalon.law.yale.edu/18th_century/fed01.asp
[51] Federalist #10. http://avalon.law.yale.edu/18th_century/fed10.asp
[52] Federalist #49. http://avalon.law.yale.edu/18th_century/fed49.asp
[53] Federalist #10. http://avalon.law.yale.edu/18th_century/fed10.asp
[54] See Robert Kuttner, "Donald Trump's Constitution." *The American Prospect* (Summer 2016): 5–7.

allegations were hurled against Andrew Jackson nearly two centuries ago. To be sure, Trump's hyperbolic oratory, even when juxtaposed with Jackson's disdain for Nicholas Biddle and the Bank of the United States, appears exceptional. But is he a classic demagogue capable of unraveling the nation's foundational charter or overturning longstanding notions of essential freedoms cherished by generations of Americans? As Robert Singh asserts, "[t]he Founders would recognize the seductive power of a dilettante digital demagogue, but the failure of their design to prevent Trump's rise does not imply its inability to contain a disruptive presidency."[55] If mere "parchment barriers,"[56] as Madison argued, are insufficient to preclude tyranny, American political culture as it has evolved may be one of the most vital elements in containing the most potentially sinister impulses of the populist ethos.

Populist republicanism in the American tradition, as Thomas Goebel typecasts it, is a "complex amalgam of ideas, attitudes, rhetorical strategies, and reform demands" that center specifically on eradicating public officials' corrupt practice of abusing public power for their own gain.[57] Historically populist movements in the United States have been subsumed within the larger party system and constitutional checks and balances have precluded their leaders from running roughshod over fundamental liberties. Moreover, "American populism," writes Henry Olsen, "as it has taken shape again and again throughout our history, has not yielded the demagogic figures that so worried the classical philosophers."[58] The reason may be located in essential components of American political culture.[59] First, Olsen emphasizes the

---

[55] Singh, "'I, the People'," p. 21.

[56] Federalist #48. http://avalon.law.yale.edu/18th_century/fed48.asp

[57] Thomas Goebel, "The Political Economy of American Populism from Jackson to the New Deal." *Studies in American Political Development* 11, no. 1 (1997): 109–48.

[58] Henry Olsen, "Populism, American Style." *National Affairs* 36 (Summer 2018). https://nationalaffairs.com/publications/detail/populism-american-style

[59] See also Kazin, *The Populist Persuasion*. The author emphasizes complementary elements of the American creed, including equality and self-reliance, as part of a "shared language": "In this unique nation, all men were created

degree to which populist movements focus less on the centrality of a charismatic leader and more on the populist's message of a deficit of opportunity for upward mobility among hard-working, ordinary people. In this way, the populist acts as a mouthpiece for the forgotten man—not a supreme leader whose appeal is a cult of personality. Second, however much elites are maligned rhetorically for interfering in the individual's effort to improve his lot,

> the "other" tends not to be vilified as an implacable enemy without rights. Instead, he is an adversary: one who might be corrupt or acting unjustly at the moment, but still a fellow citizen who retains his basic American goodness, is capable of redemption, and is secure in his rights.[60]

Finally, Olsen highlights the absence of the redistribution of property in the American populist experience. American populists' agenda is "typically a case for using government to advance self-reliance or enable prosperity and growth."[61]

Donald Trump's populist rhetoric shares much in terms of the philistine grandiloquence that vexed the ancients. His improvident calls for political adversaries to be jailed, relentless attacks on the media including the rescinding of the White House press pass of a prominent CNN reporter, and the claim that he could pardon himself raise significant questions about a commitment to constitutional norms.[62] Yet there is evidence in line with Olsen's view that American political culture remains a vital, extra-constitutional safeguard against the excess of Trump's populist rhetoric

equal, deserved the same change to improve their lot, and were citizens of a self-governing republic that enshrined the liberty of the individual. It was also proudly defensive: America was an isolated land of virtue whose people were on constant guard against the depredations of aristocrats, empire builders, and self-aggrandizing officeholders within and outside its borders" (p. 12).

[60] Olsen, "Populism, American Style."
[61] Ibid.
[62] Jonah Goldberg, "Can President Trump pardon himself? It's complicated." *Los Angeles Times*, June 5, 2018. http://www.latimes.com/opinion/op-ed/la-oe-goldberg-trump-pardon-20180605-story.html

and shoot-from-the-hip policy impulses. It is critical to under-score that the president's most controversial and polarizing poli-cies have been met with substantial, majority disapproval. The travel ban on certain foreign nationals in 2017 and his handling of illegal immigrant families at the southern border in 2018 are cases in point.[63] In summer 2018 even Trump's daughter Ivanka and First Lady Melania urged him to halt the policy of sepa-rating families detained by authorities in Texas and elsewhere, and public opposition was so intense the president had to reverse course via executive action.[64] Similarly, despite Trump's quotid-ian harangues against the "fake news" press that bring crowds at campaign rallies to their feet, a General Social Survey poll found that only 13 percent of those surveyed believed that "President Trump should close down mainstream news outlets, like CNN, the Washington Post and the New York Times."[65] Finally, in 2018, nearly three-quarters of Americans insisted that the media should utilize First Amendment guarantees of a free press to serve as a watchdog on the government, an *increase* of 6 percent from 2017. Such polls are bad news for a despot seeking to overthrow the "Fourth Estate's" role in holding public officials accountable or for a would-be dictator who arrogantly believes that Ameri-cans will countenance abrogation of the freedoms guaranteed in the Bill of Rights.

The point is that despite Trump's fervid rhetoric and the con-tentious policies he has undertaken, the president has neither

[63] Pew Research Center, U.S. Politics & Policy, "Views of Trump's executive order on travel restrictions." February 16, 2017. http://www.people-press.org/2017/02/16/2-views-of-trumps-executive-order-on-travel-restrictions/

[64] Ben Kamisar, "Poll: 88 percent of voters don't want families separated at border." *The Hill*, June 27, 2018. http://thehill.com/homenews/administration/394480-poll-88-percent-of-voters-dont-want-families-separated-at-border; John Wagner, Nick Miroff, and Mike DeBonis, "Trump reverses course, signs order ending his policy of separating families at the border." *Washington Post*, June 20, 2018. https://www.washingtonpost.com/powerpost/gop-leaders-voice-hope-that-bill-addressing-family-separations-will-pass-thursday/2018/06/20/cc79db9a-7480-11e8-b4b7-308400242c2e_story.html?utm_term=.2342240925d0

[65] IPSOS News & Polls, "Americans views on the media." August 7, 2018. https://www.ipsos.com/en-us/news-polls/americans-views-media-2018-08-07

been able to undermine the attachment to axiomatic civil liberties which Americans cherish nor successfully surmounted essential constitutional checks including judicial review, notwithstanding his efforts to delegitimize an independent counsel investigation into alleged collusion with Russia during the 2016 campaign (see below). Moreover, Congress has scarcely been goaded into passing unconstitutional bills of attainder for Hillary Clinton or former FBI Director James Comey. Neither individual has been indicted in a court of law, let alone imprisoned. There have been no suspensions of habeas corpus, and members of the news media have not been imprisoned. Most critically, it is apparent that many Americans, unlike some in the media or the Democratic Party, do not take Trump's hyperbole literally and at face value. As media analyst Howard Kurtz suggests, "[m]any voters shrug off his provocations and exaggerations because they think he is delivering for them on kitchen-table issues" and "[a]fter more than 16 months in office, despite the media's hair-on-fire approach, the country is growing more accustomed to his reality-show style."[66]

If there is any ideological coherence in that style, it is in part the seizure of salient cultural issues such as the national anthem or flag burning that galvanize the emotion of the president's core supporters. On the economic front it is Trump's exchange of multinational trade for bilateralism, an emphasis on restoring fairness to international commerce practices, and renovation of American power on the global stage. Some commentators argue that apart from immigration issues, the president "lacks any deeply held conservative beliefs."[67] However, as James Pierson asserts, "Donald Trump does

[66] Howard Kurtz, "A Trump jump in the polls despite the media's gloom-and-doom portrayal." *Fox News*, June 8, 2017. http://www.foxnews.com/politics/2018/06/08/trump-jump-in-polls-despite-medias-gloom-and-doom-portrayal.html

[67] Chris Cillizza, "Donald Trump isn't the next Barry Goldwater. It'd be easier for Republicans if he was." *Washington Post*, May 19, 2016. https://www.washingtonpost.com/news/the-fix/wp/2016/05/09/donald-trump-isnt-the-next-barry-goldwater-itd-be-easier-for-republicans-if-he-was/?utm_term=.5ad1317189ec

in fact stand for one of the great conservative causes of the present era—namely the preservation of the traditional nation state as the framework for our security, prosperity, and liberties."[68] Whether ongoing conflicts with NATO allies and trading partners in North America or China and outreach to North Korea will restore the nation-state as Trump envisions remains an open question. But ultimately the electorate's trepidations about the president, as evidenced by his inability to top 50 percent approval through the midpoint of his term, suggest the limits of his demagogic appeal in the long term, and the confines of his attraction based on personality. In sum, the message may well be feted more than the performative extravagances of the messenger. But the broad implications of Trump's style merit a thorough comparative assessment.

IV. Trump and the populist style in comparative perspective

How does Trump's populist style connect to his predecessors across the eras of American history? Thoughtful comparison mandates a systematic approach that distills the common features of the populist mode of messaging. On a general level, American populists, including movements such as the Know Nothing Party of the 1850s and the Progressive Party of the 1890s, failed candidates for the White House as diverse as William Jennings Bryan in 1896 and George Wallace in 1968, and successful presidential victors such as Andrew Jackson in 1828 and Donald Trump in 2016 variably share constituent elements of a worldview that shapes their narrative and approach to the political environment. Donald Trump is in many ways less unique as a populist candidate (and now president) than suggested by the media, sharing as he does essential commonalities with his forerunners.

Michael Federici sketches a set of characteristics that are frequently attached to the populist frame of mind. These attributes include: 1) suspicion of elites, including bureaucrats, intellectuals, and business leaders; 2) faith in the virtue and common sense of ordinary people; 3) preference for simplicity

---

[68] Pierson, "Why Populism Fails," p. 22.

in lieu of complexity; 4) reverence for religion; 5) conspiracy theory; 6) anti-intellectualism; 7) sectarianism; 8) mistrust of science and technology; and, 9) a belief in majoritarian democracy.[69] Several other of Federici's traits correspond to notions dating to the nineteenth century, comprising 1) nostalgia for agrarian society; 2) obsession with economic panaceas; 3) emphasis on formal and informal equality of the "people" as a homogeneous, moral community; and, 4) enthusiasm for various forms of direct democracy.[70]

Populists have sought the presidency successfully and unsuccessfully with particular convictions about the nature of executive power. Such assumptions about the presidential office intersect with the stylistic messaging foci elaborated by Federici and others. As Terry Bimes and Quinn Mulroy assert, there are two fundamental components of populist thought about the presidential office, specifically. First, popular authority legitimizes presidential action because the president is a better representative of the people than Congress, a mediated institution, or appointive institutions such as the judiciary. "The president," Bimes and Mulroy argue, "identifies himself as the representative of the people, attempts to rally popular support for his position, and uses that claim of popular support as a weapon in political battles."[71] Second, populist presidents and candidates frame political conflict by setting the "people" in opposition to some elite.

> In order to be considered a populist leader, the president must consider himself to be a tribune of the people and employ antagonistic appeals that pit the people against a special interest. Popular authority is thus a *necessary* but not *sufficient* condition of presidential populism.[72]

[69] Michael P. Federici, The Challenge of Populism: The Rise of Right-Wing Democratism in Postwar America (New York: Praeger, 1991), pp. 35–6.
[70] Michael Lind, "Power to the People." *New Republic*, September 4, 1995, pp. 37–8.
[71] Terry Bimes and Quinn Mulroy, "The Rise and Decline of Presidential Populism." *Studies in American Political Development* 18 (2004): 138.
[72] Ibid., p. 140.

Objective   Conceptual Commonalities   Argumentative Frames & Expressions   Example

Anti-Elitism
- Anti-incumbency
- Party structure/stability → Internal dissension
- Institutions → Formal/informal

Goldwater
Trump
Jackson
Trump

Ordinary People
- Popular support → Legitimacy > Congress, Courts
- Grassroots movement
- Organic protest

Bryan
Goldwater
Wallace
Perot
Trump

Majoritarianism
- Direct democracy
- Unmediated communication

Perot
Trump

Issue Simplification
- Anti-Intellectualism
- Conspiracy theory

Bryan
H. Long
Wallace
Perot
Trump

Nostalgia for Past
- Nativism ← → Race/ethnicity
- → Nationalism
- Religiosity → Sectarianism

Wallace
Goldwater
Trump
Bryan
Know-Nothings
Fr. Coughlin

Restoration v. Redistribution

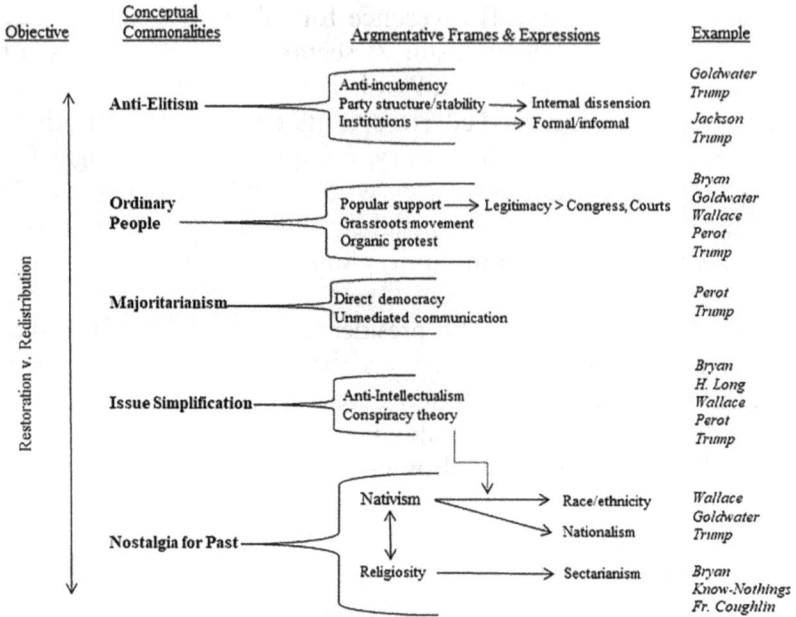

Figure 2.1 Conceptualizing and Comparing Populist Candidates, Presidents, and Movements

Figure 2.1 is a heuristic that separates out characteristic components of the American populist style as a means of comparing populist candidates, presidents, and movements and their relative impact on the political system. The graphic highlights three essential cogs in the wheel of message articulation, communication, and legitimization: 1) the philosophical and policy objectives; 2) conceptual commonalities; and 3) argumentative frames, expressions, and possible implications. The five conceptual commonalities represent a precis of Federici's longer list of populist attributes to highlight the operationalization of the populist style. The two center columns in Figure 2.1 join conceptual configurations of populism to the argumentative frames and expressions employed by candidates and movements. These fundamental rhetorical themes that populists emphasize include narratives focused on anti-elitism, an emphasis on ordinary people and the legitimizing effect of popular support, majoritarianism, issue simplification, and nostalgia for the past. How these dimensions coalesce under particular contexts enables a more thorough comparative analysis of populist candidates, presidents, and in some cases, ephemeral political movements.

Commencing from the left-hand side of the graphic, it is vital to underscore that the objective of populist messaging may be theoretically *redistributive* or *restorative* in the quest for political reform and a return to some equilibrium. The notion of property, wealth, or income redistribution, however, has rarely been as strong a staple of progressive populism in the United States as one might find in other parts of the globe. Some may consider Vermont Senator Bernie Sanders' 2016 presidential campaign an exception to the general rule. But upon closer inspection Sanders' stances represent a modern incarnation of progressive populist tendencies dating back to the nineteenth century. As detailed later in Chapter 4, Sanders called for expanded access to governmental medical programs and paid child care, increases in the minimum wage, and free college education that would presumably be accomplished through the mechanisms of progressive taxation and corporate regulatory reform.[73] It is the allegedly lopsided distribution of wealth and disproportionate power wielded by corporations that must be redressed from Sanders' perspective in order to restore some semblance of economic balance and opportunity for the ordinary, middle-class American.

The People's Party of the 1890s and William Jennings Bryan in his 1896 presidential campaign emphasized similar themes in the crisis that beset farmers. Monopolistic railroads and banks putatively held too much power over the agricultural sector. Regulatory reform of the transportation industry (railroads) and free silver coinage in lieu of adopting the gold standard would rectify economic inequities including the freefall of agricultural prices. In his allegorical recounting of the 1896 presidential election and beyond, L. Frank Baum's *The Wonderful Wizard of Oz*

---

[73] Daniel Marans, "In era of Donald Trump, Bernie Sanders sees 'The beginning of a political revolution'." *Huffington Post*, January 31, 2018. https://www.huffingtonpost.com/entry/bernie-sanders-response-donald-trump-state-of-the-union_us_5a715645e4b0ae29f08c1628

may well have been far more successful long term in the literary world than the People's Party or Bryan's presidential bids. But the fictional narrative remains a potentially important pedagogical tool to grasp how essential debates about monetary policy and the obstacles to economic and regulatory reform influenced the rise and demise of a particular populist movement, immortalized in Bryan's "Cross of Gold Speech" in a bygone era.[74]

This common theme of restoration need not be limited to economics or a particular pole along the progressive–conservative continuum in American politics. Indeed, populist movements and presidential candidates have been just as disposed to level arguments against socio-cultural changes and endeavor to reinstate allegedly vanishing values and Christian mores. Donald Trump often emphasizes patriotism and religiosity in his rhetoric, linking "God and the military in a way that appeals especially with his evangelical supporters."[75] He has bemoaned the use of "happy holidays" in lieu of "Merry Christmas,"[76] established a "faith office" in the White House,[77] and symbolically on the day commemorating national prayer, signed an executive order aimed at extending religious liberty and reversing the ways "the Federal government has used the power of the state as a weapon against people of faith bullying and even punishing Americans

[74] See Hugh Rockoff, "The 'Wizard of Oz' as Monetary Allegory." *Journal of Economic Policy* 98, no. 4 (1990): 739–60; Joshua Keating, "Conspiracy theorists' on-again-off-again relationship with gold." *Foreign Policy*, April 15, 2003. https://foreignpolicy.com/2013/04/15/conspiracy-theorists-on-again-off-again-relationship-with-gold/

[75] Gene Zubovich, "The Christian Nationalism of Donald Trump." *Religion & Society*, July 17, 2018. https://religionandpolitics.org/2018/07/17/the-christian-nationalism-of-donald-trump/

[76] Jonathan Lemire and Ken Thomas, "Trump, unlikely religious favorite, hails Christian values, return of 'Merry Christmas'." *Chicago Tribune*, October 13, 2017. http://www.chicagotribune.com/news/nationworld/politics/ct-trump-values-voter-summit-20171013-story.html

[77] White House, "Executive Order on the Establishment of a White House Faith and Opportunity Initiative." May 3, 2018. https://www.whitehouse.gov/presidential-actions/executive-order-establishment-white-house-faith-opportunity-initiative/

for following their religious beliefs."[78] Further, Trump's torrential criticism of NFL players who refuse to stand for the national anthem (and team owners or League officials who condone the practice) is another example of a socio-cultural populism of restoration, in this case one that targets elites in professional sports for their putative disdain for the flag that Trump interprets as disrespect of military veterans.

It is vital to recall, however, that five decades earlier, amidst the Vietnam War and civil rights movement, George Wallace seized upon a disconsolate mood of social upheaval and analogous concerns about cultural decay as a means of exploiting "the changes that Americans came to know by many names: white backlash, the silent majority, the alienated voters."[79] Wallace took aim at race relations, in particular, as the proximate cause of societal turmoil and couched his support for racial segregation not only by drawing frequently upon Biblical references but also by invoking an artful interpretation of the American Founders' intent regarding liberty and interracial association. As Wallace elaborated in his 1963 inaugural gubernatorial address in Montgomery, Alabama, "Segregation Now, Segregation Forever":

> And so it was meant in our racial lives . . . each race, within its own framework has the freedom to teach . . . to instruct . . . to develop . . . to ask for and receive deserved help from others of separate racial stations. This is the great freedom of our American founding fathers . . . but if we amalgamate into the one unit as advocated by the communist philosophers . . . then the enrichment of our lives . . . the freedom for our development . . . is gone forever. We become, therefore, a mongrel unit of one under a single all powerful government . . . and we stand for everything . . . and for nothing.[80]

[78] Emily Tillett, "Trump signs 'religious liberty' executive order." *CBS News*, May 4, 2017. https://www.cbsnews.com/news/trump-signs-religious-liberty-order-to-defend-freedom-of-religion/

[79] Dan T. Carter, "Legacy of Rage: George Wallace and the Transformation of American Politics." *Journal of Southern History* 62, no. 1 (1996): 12.

[80] George Wallace, "Segregation Now, Segregation Forever." Inaugural Address as Alabama Governor, January 14, 1963. Full text available at http://www.blackpast.org/1963-george-wallace-segregation-now-segregation-forever

Re-establishing social harmony and dispelling collective discord, as Wallace so divisively argued in the 1968 campaign, depended quintessentially upon a return to racial *inequality* that cultural elites—intellectuals, judges, academics, and progressive politicians, and others whom he disdained—flatly rejected. It is as myopic as it is facile, perhaps, to overlook the appeal of Wallace's populist rhetoric in some quarters a half-century ago lest the contemporary focus on Trump's melodramas on social media or at post-election campaign events supplant historical memory. Wallace's oratorical acumen was every bit as stinging and raucous as Trump's rallies and tweets in terms of his social populism. And the classical understanding of the relationship between the people and demagogue was as distinct for Wallace as it is for Trump. As Dan T. Carter maintains,

> A wild energy seemed to flow back and forth between Mr. Wallace and his audience as he called out their mutual enemies: bearded hippies, pornographers, sophisticated intellectuals who mocked God, traitorous anti-Vietnam War protesters, welfare bums, cowardly politicians and "pointy-head college professors who can't even park a bicycle straight".[81]

Moving to the argumentative frames and expressions in Figure 2.1, populist candidates' anti-elite narratives generally take aim at incumbent politicians and can precipitate significant internal dissension in the two major parties. Moreover, populist presidents like Jackson and Trump have called into question the legitimacy of formal and informal institutions like the Bank of the United States or the media, respectively, arguably occasioning a sense of crisis and instability. Populists justify their tactics by cultivating storylines focused on "ordinary Americans," and seek to cement the authenticity of their message through claims that they represent grassroots activism that is organic in

---

[81] Dan T. Carter, "What Donald Trump owes George Wallace." *New York Times*, January 8, 2016. https://www.nytimes.com/2016/01/10/opinion/campaign-stops/what-donald-trump-owes-george-wallace.html

nature. Moreover, as proponents of majoritarian rule, populists clamor for direct democracy and search for means of unmediated communication with their supporters through the available technology of the day—whether newspapers, electronic town hall meetings, campaign rallies, or social media. Another important propensity of the populist style is issue simplification, or the quest to reduce complex socio-economic and political challenges to the least common denominator. Generalizations that are often exceedingly broad, factually inaccurate, and even untruthful may be tinged not only with anti-intellectualism, understood as a scorn for expert opinion and scientific knowledge, but also with conspiracy theories constructed upon paranoid ideation. Finally, populists of all varieties share some sense of nostalgia for the past—a longing for some type of homecoming to some better place in time, the past as prologue for a brighter future. A return to religious values, recapturing the essence of a pastoral life of the family farmer, the renaissance of the glory days of industrial enterprise, and the nativist yearning to reconstruct American greatness with an emphasis on exceptionalism that excludes the "other" in racial or ethnic terms, or on the world stage, are versatile (if sometimes time-bound) components of the populist argumentative frame. The implications for democratic stability, the legitimacy of democratic institutions, accountability of American chief executives, and broader social relations vary by degree according to context as the next sections clarify.

A. Anti-elitism and party instability: Trump and Goldwater as contrasts in the populist style

As Figure 2.1 emphasizes, the most important tie that binds populists across political time is anti-elitism. Although anti-elite sentiment is a dominant leitmotif of the populist style, the definition of what or who exactly constitutes an elite may span elected officials in formal political institutions (e.g., incumbent politicians) to leaders of informal institutions (e.g., media, business, sports). Regardless, there are two distinct patterns of potential instability that may arise from the populist narrative. The first is the rhetorical assault on incumbent politicians by populist presidential candidates *outside the governing structure* that can prompt significant internal party dissension. On this account, Barry Goldwater and Donald Trump provide contrasting examples based on their mode of messaging.

It is scarcely uncommon for modern presidential candidates—especially populists—to run *for* the nation's highest political office by running *against* the "mess in Washington" created by unprincipled, self-serving incumbent scoundrels determined to maintain the status quo. But at what cost to party unity? In announcing his candidacy for the presidency in 1964, Republican Barry Goldwater stated "I will not change my beliefs to win votes. I will offer a choice, not an echo." Wresting power from the Eastern Establishment wing of the party, the dissenters from moderate GOP orthodoxy who backed Goldwater's nomination in 1964—like Trump's in 2016—represented a "party aligned with a movement" and a repudiation of career politicians.[82] What commenced as a "draft Goldwater" campaign in 1962 resulted in a frontal assault on the party elite at the Cow Palace in Daly City, California two years later at the Republican convention.[83] As Kilgore explains,

> The energy of Goldwater's movement was directed against compromised members of the GOP—the RINOs [Republicans in Name Only] of their time. According to Goldwater, President Dwight Eisenhower had embraced "the siren song of socialism." Goldwaterites accused the Republican establishment of "me-tooism" and advocating a "dime store New Deal."[84]

The fundamental tenets of Goldwater's brand of populist conservatism included fiscal restraint, an opposition to federal

[82] Sam Tennenhaus, "The GOP, or Goldwater's Old Party." *The New Republic*, June 11, 2001, p. 33. See also Rick Perlstein, *Before the Storm: Barry Goldwater and the Unmaking of the American Consensus* (New York: Nation Books, 2009).

[83] See F. Clifton White, *Suite 3505: The Story of the Draft Goldwater Movement* (New Rochelle, NY: Arlington House, 1967).

[84] Ed Kilgore, "The Spirit of Goldwaterism." *Washington Monthly*, April 18, 2014. https://washingtonmonthly.com/2014/04/18/the-spirit-of-goldwaterism/

power, and militant anti-communism. Regarding federal over-reach, Goldwater may have opposed the 1964 Civil Rights Act on libertarian and not racist principles, objecting to "the extension of federal power over private enterprise" in terms of forced integration and employment quotas.[85] But the Ku Klux Klan's endorsement of his candidacy alienated and offended not only African Americans but affronted many voters on both sides of the aisle while culling support in the South. With respect to the threat of internal subversion that so consumed McCarthyites a decade earlier, "[t]he hard core of Goldwater's support," Rovere maintains, "has always come from people whose alarm centers on Communists in the United States and who tend to relate, and subordinate, all other issues to this one."[86]

Goldwater's "constitutive rhetoric" was aimed at creating a particular grassroots, conservative identity.[87] In his moral and ethical critiques not only of the New Deal but also the moderates in his own party who eschewed his reading of the Constitution and downplayed the Soviet threat, Goldwater sought to differentiate conservatism from liberalism and *his vision* of conservatism from other varieties in order to construct a narrative capable of mobilizing voters. As Thurber notes, "[t]he image of Goldwater delegates at the 1964 Republican convention booing Governor Nelson Rockefeller (New York) as he called for a more progressive stand on race and other matters symbolizes to many the death of liberal Republicanism."[88]

Goldwater's declaration in his 1964 nomination acceptance speech that "extremism in the defense of liberty is no vice" was

---

[85] Michael Gerson, "Barry Goldwater's warning to the GOP." *Washington Post*, April 14, 2017. https://www.washingtonpost.com/opinions/michael-gerson-barry-goldwaters-warning-to-the-gop/2014/04/17/9e8993ec-c651-11e3-bf7a-be01a9b69cf1_story.html?utm_term=.bd537957feca

[86] Richard H. Rovere, "The campaign: Goldwater." *The New Yorker*, October 3, 1964. https://www.newyorker.com/magazine/1964/10/03/the-campaign-goldwater

[87] Andrew Taylor, "Barry Goldwater: Insurgent Conservatism as Constitutive Rhetoric." *Journal of Political Ideologies* 21, no. 3 (2016): 242–60.

[88] Timothy N. Thurber, "Goldwaterism Triumphant? Race and the Republican Party, 1965–1968." *The Journal of the Historical Society* 7, no. 3 (2007): 350.

for the media "proof positive that [he] was crazy."[89] His opponents cast him as a nuclear trigger-happy, unhinged insurgent. From comments that appeared to advocate the use of atomic weapons in Vietnam to making Social Security voluntary, Goldwater "proved so gifted at exposing his most alarming instincts that it was practically unnecessary for his opponent to attack him."[90] But the Johnson campaign did seize on moderate Republicans' disdain of the unflappable Arizonan's policy positions to highlight the degree to which Goldwater's candidacy had cleaved the GOP into warring factions. As one Johnson campaign advertisement underscored:

> Back in July in San Francisco, the Republicans held a convention. Remember him? He was there, Governor Rockefeller. Before the convention he said Barry Goldwater's positions can "spell disaster for the party and for the country." Or him? Governor Scranton. The day before the convention he called Goldwaterism a "crazy quilt collection of absurd and dangerous positions." Or this man, Governor Romney. In June, he said Goldwater's nomination would lead to the "suicidal destruction of the Republican Party." So, even if you're a Republican with serious doubts about Barry Goldwater, you're in good company. Vote for President Johnson on November 3rd. The stakes are too high for you to stay home.[91]

In the final analysis the rift in the Republican Party led to Goldwater's electoral demise and the most stunning defeat of a GOP presidential candidate in the post-World War II era. But the fissure was temporary, and did *not* condemn the party of Lincoln to permanent oblivion in future presidential contests. As Tom Wicker posits, Goldwater

---

[89] John Dean, "Don't compare Trump's presidential campaign to Barry Goldwater's." *Verdict*, May 27, 2016. https://verdict.justia.com/2016/05/27/dont-compare-trumps-presidential-campaign-barry-goldwaters

[90] Louis Menand, "He knew he was right." *The New Yorker*, March 26, 2001. https://www.newyorker.com/magazine/2001/03/26/he-knew-he-was-right

[91] "Republican Convention," 1964. Lyndon Johnson television campaign advertisement. Transcript and video available at the Museum of the Living Image, http://www.livingroomcandidate.org/commercials/1964/republican-convention#3991

was the most ideological and factionist candidate of either major party since William Jennings Bryan ran on a free silver platform in 1896. As the candidate of a faction that had captured the Republican party, rather than the overwhelming choice of that party's consensus, Mr. Goldwater suffered sharp defections that amounted almost to a party split.[92]

Goldwater lost to Johnson in a landslide, winning just 38.7 percent of the popular vote. He won six states in the Electoral College, all in the South save for his home state of Arizona—which he carried by a single percentage point thanks to a narrow edge in Maricopa County. Nationally 80 percent of Republicans who cast ballots supported Goldwater, a figure 15 percent lower than for Richard Nixon in 1960 and 1972.[93] Exact figures for Republican abstentions are not available, but voter turnout models suggest that moderate GOP voters were most likely to abandon Goldwater, just as moderate party leaders had.[94]

While Goldwater employed an ultimately abortive populist message against the liberal-to-moderate GOP establishment, he did so primarily on the basis of principle. Politics, South Dakota Democratic Senator and 1972 presidential nominee George McGovern noted, "suffers when politicians of differing views permit those differences to degenerate into personal, mean-spirited attacks on each other's integrity. Barry Goldwater never did that."[95] Indeed, Goldwater returned to the Senate and remained until 1987. He happily continued to politely exasperate his Republican colleagues

---

[92] Tom Wicker, "Johnson swamps Goldwater." *New York Times*, November 4, 1964. https://archive.nytimes.com/www.nytimes.com/books/98/04/12/specials/johnson-goldwater.html

[93] Gallup Poll, "Election Polls, Vote by Groups, 1960–1964." https://news.gallup.com/poll/9454/election-polls-vote-groups-19601964.aspx; "Election Polls—Vote by Groups, 1968–1972." https://news.gallup.com/poll/9457/election-polls-vote-groups-19681972.aspx

[94] Michael D. Martinez and Jeff Gill, "The Effects of Turnout on Partisan Outcomes in U.S. Presidential Elections 1960–2000." *Journal of Politics* 67, no. 4 (2005): 1271.

[95] George McGovern, "Goldwater: A good friend." *Washington Post*, June 4, 1998. https://www.washingtonpost.com/wp-srv/politics/daily/june98/mcgovern4.htm

who pursued a social agenda antithetical to his libertarian convictions on issues such as discrimination against homosexuals in the military, even after his retirement.[96] He earned the respect of many who opposed his candidacy in 1964, including Democratic Oregon Governor Barbara Roberts, who co-chaired Goldwater's campaign for gay rights. Roberts suggested "[h]e's the kind of spokesman who makes people focus on this issue through new eyes."[97]

Alas, herein lies a fundamental distinction between the strains of populism along the dimension of anti-elite rhetoric employed by Goldwater and Donald Trump as outsiders, separated as they are by a half-century: Goldwater's defeat, and the disunity it caused, was ephemeral and his resentment of the "establishment" was more principled than personal. Richard Nixon was elected four years later, again in 1972, and Ronald Reagan was swept to victory in 1980 despite the culmination of the Watergate fiasco six years earlier. The feisty senator from the Grand Canyon State played an important role outside the White House and even after he left the Senate as a leading and respected intellectual in debates about the direction of American politics. By contrast, it remains entirely unclear if Donald Trump's excessive personalization of anti-elite antipathy has done irreparable harm to GOP unity in the future—or whether such unity depends on the president's ability to reshape the Republican Party in his own populist image.

Donald Trump's denunciation of the GOP establishment in his 2016 election bid was intensely personal and his invectives and vulgarities at times were beyond the bounds of decency. The insolent

---

[96] As one example, on Republican efforts to ban homosexuals in the military in 1993, Goldwater opined that "[y]ou don't need to be 'straight' to fight and die for your country. You just need to shoot straight" and that "[t]o see the party that fought communism and big government now fighting the gays, well, that's just plain dumb." Quoted in "Goldwater calls opposition to gays in military 'dumb'. *Deseret News* (Salt Lake City), August 22, 1993. https://www. deseretnews.com/article/306128/GOLDWATER-CALLS-OPPOSITION-TO-GAYS-IN-MILITARY-DUMB.html

[97] Quoted in Lloyd Grove, "Goldwater's left turn." *Washington Post*, July 24, 1994. https://www.washingtonpost.com/wp-srv/politics/daily/may98/goldwater072894.htm

attacks he leveled against fellow primary candidates during debates and on social media—"low energy" Jeb Bush, "lyin' Ted" Cruz, "little Marco" Rubio and his supposed diminutive masculinity, not to mention his disrespectful comments about the physical features of Carly Fiorina or Cruz's wife—as much or more than his controversial policy stands, were met with a fervent chorus of disapproval and disbelief from incensed Republicans. The essential purpose for the moment is to highlight the degree to which Trump's visceral and malicious defamation of his opponents' character proved turning points that fueled an internecine battle in the GOP that continues to foment intermittently well in advance of 2020.

One watershed was the Twitter assault Trump initiated in early March 2016 during the primary season as groups backing his opponents launched attack ads in Florida and elsewhere. Trump called Senator Lindsay Graham (SC) and former presidential nominee Mitt Romney "nasty, angry, jealous failures" with "ZERO credibility!" and lambasted the "REPUBLICAN ESTABLISHMENT" (without defining its membership) for allegedly failing to halt Obama's two successful runs for the White House.[98] Another crossroads was reached sinuously, as NBC News documented, in the run-up to the 2016 general election campaign as

> [s]ome party stalwarts rejected him [Trump] after his initial refusal to denounce former KKK [Ku Klux Klan] grand wizard David Duke's endorsement. Still more had reached a breaking point after Trump attacked the Hispanic judge presiding over lawsuits against his failed business venture, Trump University. Others cited Trump's personal attack on a Gold Star military family as the limit.[99]

[98] @realDonaldTrump, "Lindsey Graham is all over T.V., much like failed 47% candidate Mitt Romney. These nasty, angry, jealous failures have ZERO credibility!" *Twitter*, March 6, 2016, 8:03 a.m. https://twitter.com/realdonaldtrump/status/706812638215303168?lang=en; "We cannot let the failing REPUBLICAN ESTABLISHMENT, who could not stop Obama (twice), ruin the MOVEMENT with millions of $'s in false ads!" *Twitter*, March 7, 2016, 9:03 a.m. https://twitter.com/realdonaldtrump/status/706827555622547456?lang=da

[99] *NBC News*, "The Republicans opposing Donald Trump—and voting for Hillary Clinton." November 6, 2016. https://www.nbcnews.com/politics/2016-election/meet-republicans-speaking-out-against-trump-n530696

By August 2016 fifty former national security officials, many of whom had served in the administration of George W. Bush, signed a letter condemning Trump and charging that he "lacks the character, values and experience" to be president and "would put at risk our country's national security and well-being."[100] Finally, the surfacing of an *Access Hollywood* video tape in early October 2016, in which Trump crudely rejoiced in his sexual objectification of women and carnal pursuits, cemented many die-hard Republicans' antipathy toward his candidacy.[101] As Ronald Brownstein asserts, on the weekend that the video made its way to front-page news,

> more Republican leaders had renounced their party's nominee than in any 24-hour period since the day in June 1912 when Theodore Roosevelt's supporters bolted from the GOP convention after the re-nomination of President William Howard Taft . . . nearly one-third of Republican senators and almost one-third of Republican governors had declared they would not vote for Trump.[102]

The result was the birth of the "Never Trump" movement, which nevertheless failed to militate against the president's grass-roots appeal on Election Day 2016.[103] Still, reinvigorated by a plethora of controversies in the president's first year in office, including his intemperate comments about the Muslim travel ban, the clash between white supremacists and protestors in

---

[100] David E. Sanger and Maggie Haberman, "50 G.O.P. officials warn Donald Trump would put nation's security 'at risk'." *New York Times*, August 8, 2016. https://www.nytimes.com/2016/08/09/us/politics/national-security-gop-donald-trump.html

[101] *Los Angeles Times*, "Transcripts: What the mics caught Donald Trump saying in 2005 and what he said in his taped apology." http://www.latimes.com/politics/la-na-pol-trump-bush-transcript-20161007-snap-htmlstory.html#

[102] Ronald Brownstein, "Trump may be finished—but Trumpism is just getting started." *The Atlantic*, October 13, 2016. https://www.theatlantic.com/politics/archive/2016/10/trump-legacy-gop/503813/

[103] Lauren R. Johnson, Deon McCray, and Jordan M. Ragusa, "#NeverTrump: Why Republican Members of Congress Refused to Support Their Party's Nominee in the 2016 Presidential Election." *Research & Politics* (January–March 2018): 1–10. http://journals.sagepub.com/doi/pdf/10.1177/2053168017749383

Charlottesville, Virginia in August 2017, veneration for Vladimir Putin, and unprecedented criticism of his own attorney general Jeff Sessions, Trump's detractors in the loose coalition of malcontents remain steadfastly opposed to his presidency and his plans for a re-election bid. While some analysts contend the movement is moribund without a clear leadership alternative to Trump in the short term, undercurrents of opposition to Trump's quest for a second term by prominent Republicans remain palpable.[104] In the lead-up to the mid-term elections of 2018, few GOP members of Congress appeared willing to pledge support for Trump's re-election bid in 2020 despite welcoming his support for their re-election in all but a few cases.[105]

The president's shots across the bow at so-called establishment figures in his own party who oppose him, including scurrilous indictments of the late Senator John McCain (R-AZ) and former President George H. W. Bush, both in poor health at the time before their passing, were complemented by scathing critiques of retiring senators like Bob Corker (TN) and Jeff Flake (AZ).[106]

---

[104] See John Cassidy, "The problem with the 'Never Trump' movement." *The New Yorker*, March 3, 2016. https://www.newyorker.com/news/john-cassidy/the-problem-with-the-never-trump-movement; Emerald Robinson, "The collapse of the Never-Trump conservatives." *American Spectator*, June 29, 2018. https://spectator.org/the-collapse-of-the-never-trump-conservatives/

[105] Manu Raju, "Trump declared he's running again. Many Republicans aren't ready to back him." *CNN*, April 19, 2018. https://www.cnn.com/2018/04/19/politics/congress-republicans-trump-second-term/index.html

[106] See Greg Price, "Donald Trump mocked both John McCain, who is dying, and George H. W. Bush, who just lost his wife, at Montana rally." *Newsweek*, July 6, 2018. https://www.newsweek.com/donald-trump-mccain-bush-dying-1010966; @realDonaldTrump, "How could Jeff Flake, who is setting record low polling numbers in Arizona and was therefore humiliatingly forced out of his own Senate seat without even a fight (and who doesn't have a clue), think about running for office, even a lower one, again? Let's face it, he's a Flake!" *Twitter*, June 7, 2018. https://twitter.com/realdonaldtrump/status/1004722061808427008; @realDonaldTrump, "Bob Corker, who helped President O give us the bad Iran Deal & couldn't get elected dog catcher in Tennessee, is now fighting Tax Cuts. . ." *Twitter*, October 24, 2017, 5:13 a.m. https://twitter.com/realdonaldtrump/status/922798321739161600?lang=en

But the president seemingly turned establishment resentment against him on its head. The power with which Trump's diatribes resonated with a core base of Republican voters scarcely went unnoticed by incumbents or neophyte candidates seeking office in the 2018 mid-term elections. Many reckoned that any criticism of the president could provoke an electoral backlash in the GOP base, while securing his backing was a Midas touch for victory.[107] Some analysts contend that Trump, as kingmaker, doggedly pursued a relatively successful "purge" of his opponents in the GOP, particularly via endorsements of special election and primary candidates in battleground states.[108] Through early September 2018 sixteen of eighteen candidates endorsed by Trump won primary or special election battles in advance of the mid-term elections.[109]

In the final analysis, Goldwater shared with Donald Trump a "take no prisoners," impromptu style that more than perturbed his GOP opponents who, in turn, called into question his fitness for office. But Barry Goldwater did not have Twitter, and

[107] Arizona Senate candidate Martha McSally is an exemplar in this regard. Having refused to endorse Trump's presidential candidacy in 2016, McSally actively sought to praise him and emulate his political style in the August 2018 primary so he would not endorse her rivals, Dr. Kelly Ward and former Maricopa County Sheriff Joe Arpaio, whom Trump pardoned after being convicted for criminal contempt. McSally prevailed with 55 percent of the vote, and Trump subsequently endorsed her candidacy against Democrat Kyrsten Sinema. See Philip Elliott, "Martha McSally, who learned to love Donald Trump, wins Arizona primary." *Time*, August 29, 2018. http://time.com/5381225/martha-mcsally-arizona-donald-trump/; Joe Ferguson, "McSally opens up on her relationship with Trump in new interview." *Arizona Daily Star*, June 1, 2018. https://tucson.com/news/local/mcsally-opens-up-on-her-relationship-with-trump-in-new/article_5e071168-65ef-11e8-8d43-1f72f837631a.html

[108] Alex Isenstadt, "Trump purges enemy and reshapes party in his own image." *Politico*, October 24, 2017. https://www.politico.com/story/2017/10/24/trump-republicans-corker-flake-purge-244139

[109] *Ballotpedia*, September 4, 2018. https://ballotpedia.org/Endorsements_by_Donald_Trump

[f]or all the vitriol that came his way, no one ever accused Barry Goldwater of being a liar or otherwise lacking in honor; and his implacable conservative libertarianism was not only beyond question but the very reason so many despised and feared him.[110]

Many of Goldwater's critics, including Governors George Romney (Michigan) and Nelson Rockefeller (New York), in addition to Dwight Eisenhower and Richard Nixon, ultimately came around to support the Goldwater–Miller ticket in 1964.[111]

The same may not be said for the backlash against Trump in Republican circles. During the 2016 campaign and beyond, Trump's public and private conduct became a focal point for a significant number of members of Congress, prominent officials in previous GOP presidential administrations, and renowned conservative pundits. Trump's continual castigation of the Republican establishment simply left few of the party elite and those dubious of his conservative credentials—at least those not running for re-election on Capitol Hill—with any rationale to support him or otherwise come to his defense, but instead to call for his ouster. The final *pièce de théâtre* on Donald Trump's legacy to reshape the Republican Party is a work in progress. The opera of GOP disunity remains a cacophony of voices in search of a director capable of articulating a coherent musical score to Trump's populist juggernaut, but internal discord in some quarters continues at the moment in a way that it did not following Goldwater's presidential bid in 1964.

B. Anti-elitism and institutional delegitimization: Jackson and Trump

A second dynamic of anti-elitism is the narrative of allegedly corrupt institutions against which *elected* populist presidents

---

[110] Harry Stein, "The Goldwater takedown." *City Journal*, April 2016. https://www.city-journal.org/html/goldwater-takedown-14787.html

[111] Stuart Rothenberg, "Comparing the GOP divides, 1964 and 2016." *Inside Elections*, May 24, 2016. https://www.insideelections.com/news/article/comparing-the-gop-divides-1964-and-2016

take aim. The situation is obviously rare in the sense that only two populist candidates have prevailed in presidential elections in two centuries. Regardless, having won the White House, populist presidents may attack elites from atop their position in the political order, setting up inter-institutional conflict that may either disrupt policymaking and administration or unsettle the political system by challenging the legitimacy of co-equal branches of government (or agencies within the executive branch). Andrew Jackson's successful challenge to the Bank of the United States and Donald Trump's recriminations of seditious, "deep state" actors in the Justice Department and Federal Bureau of Investigation (FBI) are instructive as exemplars of this phenomenon. The key commonality of the populist assaults undertaken by Jackson and Trump is the destabilizing effect in the institutional realm.

A brief synopsis of Andrew Jackson's successful effort to destroy the Bank of the United States cannot do justice to the subtleties and complexities of his political combat with Henry Clay, Congress, and Nicholas Biddle, president of the Second Bank from 1823 to 1836. But the essentials of the ordeal underscore how the populist approach operated, albeit much differently in the nineteenth century, and left an important legacy at a formative juncture in presidential politics. Jackson's veto of a bill to recharter the Second Bank of the United States was part of a

> political philosophy that has rippled through the American political firmament for nearly 200 years. Call it conservative populism—and aversion to bigness in all of its forms, including big government, and a faith in the capacity of ordinary folks to understand and to act upon their own interests. Conservative populism includes a natural aversion to entrenched elites, who always fight back against conservative populists whenever they challenge elite power.[112]

The First Bank of the United States was chartered by Congress in 1791 at the behest of Treasury Secretary Alexander Hamilton.

---

[112] Robert W. Merry, "Andrew Jackson's populism: It started with a hatred of crony capitalism." *The American Conservative*, May–June 2017, p. 23.

President George Washington signed the bill somewhat reluctantly and only after he was convinced that the Constitution authorized the measure. James Madison and Thomas Jefferson vehemently opposed the idea on grounds that the Bank would benefit primarily investors and those in industry to the detriment of most ordinary Americans. The purpose of the Bank was to pay off debts associated with the Revolutionary War, raise money for the inchoate national government, create public credit, and solidify a common currency.[113] The Bank's charter expired in 1811 when Vice President George Clinton broke a Senate tie and opposed the measure. French-born banker Stephen Girard then purchased the Bank and its building in Philadelphia, and was a major private creditor for the government's financing of the War of 1812 with Great Britain.

As the nation once again reeled from post-war debts in the aftermath of the conflict that left the White House in flames, Congress rechartered a Second Bank of the United States in 1816. John C. Calhoun of South Carolina and Henry Clay of Kentucky led the successful effort over the objections of Jeffersonians. By the time that James Monroe appointed Nicholas Biddle as president of the Bank in 1823, the Bank's inept handling of the Panic of 1819, which included a quick expansion and then contraction of credit, had brought opprobrium from Americans who were skeptical about paper money. Biddle managed to turn the Bank around by the mid-1820s but ultimately became a central protagonist in the acrimonious political drama that ended the "Era of Good Feelings."

Though perhaps not immediately apparent at the time, the election of 1824 proved a crucial turning point for the eventual demise of the Bank. In the three-way race between Andrew Jackson, Henry Clay, and John Quincy Adams, no candidate secured a majority in the Electoral College and the election was thrown to the House of Representatives. Despite Jackson's winning a plurality of the popular vote, Clay, Speaker of the House, maneuvered to fasten support from enough state delegations to hand the presidency to Quincy Adams. Jackson and his supporters called the process a "corrupt

---

[113] See *Digital History*, "Alexander Hamilton's financial program." http://www
.digitalhistory.uh.edu/disp_textbook.cfm?smtID=2&psid=2973

bargain," rife with conspiracy, to undermine the will of the people. As one Philadelphia newspaper suggested, based on an anonymous letter from a congressman, "a brief account of such a BARGAIN as can only be equaled by the famous Burr conspiracy of 1801." The author claimed that

> Adams supporters had sent a message to Clay supporters offering an appointment to secretary of state in exchange for Clay's support in the House vote. Allegedly, Clay's friends then took this offer to Jackson's men, seeking a counteroffer. "But none of the friends of Jackson would descend to such mean banter and sale".[114]

Adams' appointment of Clay as secretary of state seemingly confirmed the crooked sausage-making that took place behind the scenes.

The narrative of the "corrupt bargain" became the rallying cry of Jackson and his supporters in the election of 1828, in which Old Hickory defeated the incumbent Adams handily. But it did not put rivalries to rest. "Jackson," Daniel Feller writes,

> came to the presidency with a deep sense of grievance against his enemies, real and imagined, in the existing political establishment and with a conviction that the government had fallen from Jeffersonian austerity into profligacy and corruption. This he was determined to reverse. The Bank was barely mentioned in Jackson's 1828 successful campaign against incumbent John Quincy Adams. But, after assuming office, Jackson learned of branch officers using the Bank as what one Jackson partisan called "an engine of political oppression" against his followers.[115]

By 1829 the president argued, inter alia, that the Bank had failed to produce a stable currency system.[116]

---

[114] Christopher Marquis, "Andrew Jackson: Winner and loser in 1824." *American History*, April 2008, p. 56.

[115] Daniel Feller, "King Andrew and the Bank." *Humanities*, January–February 2008, p. 30.

[116] See Bray Hammond, "Jackson, Biddle, and the Bank of the United States." *Journal of Economic History* 7, no. 1 (1947): 1–23.

Jackson broke with tradition in his use of the veto power to lay the groundwork for destroying the Bank. In contrast to his predecessors who had used the veto to block bills on constitutional grounds, Jackson employed the power to thwart legislation with which he disagreed in terms of policy. The president first challenged internal improvements in the so-called Maysville Road Bill in 1830 by arguing that the costs exceeded the capacity of the Treasury to make payments on the national debt. Moreover, the president called the bill "irregular, improvident, and unequal appropriations of the public funds" and argued that the bill

> has no connection with any established system of improvements; is exclusively within the limits of a State, starting at a point on the Ohio River and running out 60 miles to an interior town, and even as far as the State is interested conferring partial instead of general advantages.[117]

But in reality, while "Jackson sought to justify his actions through the Constitution and national expediency . . . a personal grudge against Henry Clay probably had as much to do with it as anything else."[118]

Clay's quest to recharter the Bank became a central issue in the 1832 presidential campaign and Jackson stood ready for a veto showdown. Nicholas Biddle had requested the legislation in January 1832, a full four years before the Bank's commission was set to expire, and Clay delivered with a plan that would cement the Bank's status for fifteen years. Both Biddle and Clay believed that they could force Jackson's hand in a gambit to chase him from the White House later that year. One of Jackson's key allies in Congress, Thomas Hart Benson, undertook a hurried investigation into the president's complaints about the Bank but failed to halt the legislation. The bill subsequently passed by wide margins in both the House and Senate. When it arrived on his desk

---

[117] Andrew Jackson, "Veto Message Regarding Funding of Infrastructure Development." May 27, 1830. https://millercenter.org/the-presidency/presidential-speeches/may-27-1830-veto-message-regarding-funding-infrastructure
[118] Clayton Jackson, "The Internal Improvement Vetoes of Andrew Jackson." *Tennessee Historical Quarterly* 25, no. 3 (1966): 262.

rather symbolically on the Fourth of July, an undeterred Jackson turned to his Vice President, Martin van Buren, and exclaimed resolutely, "The bank is trying to kill me, *but I will kill it.*"[119] Although historians dispute the authorship of the lengthy veto message,[120] it was skillfully fashioned to place Jackson squarely on the side of the common man against the elite classes to which the president tied Clay and Biddle.

Jackson returned the measure to Congress with his objections on July 10. The veto message commenced with the basic contours of his criticism of the Bank and the larger implications. The president wrote:

> Entertaining this opinion, and deeply impressed with the belief that some of the powers and privileges possessed by the existing bank are unauthorized by the Constitution, subversive of the rights of the States, and dangerous to the liberties of the people, I felt it my duty at an early period of my Administration to call the attention of Congress to the practicability of organizing an institution combining all its advantages and obviating these objections.[121]

The text, as Sean Wilentz asserts, was

> a powerful call to arms. Jackson and his advisors clearly designed it to reach over the heads of Congress and build public support. Discrete sections reached out to the disparate elements in Jackson's coalition, each with different reasons for opposing the Bank. For eastern workingmen and western radicals, the message contained ripsnorting polemics against the "opulent" Bank as a tyrannical monopoly ... Southerners drawn to Calhoun would, Jackson's advisors hoped, approve the message's assertions that the bill violated the "rights of the States," and the "liberties of the people." For patriotic Americans everywhere, there were the complaints,

[119] Quoted in John Clement Fitzpatrick (ed.), *The Autobiography of Martin Van Buren.* Annual Report of the American Historical Association for the Year 1918 (Washington, DC: Government Printing Office, 1920), vol. 2, p. 625.

[120] See Lynn L. Marshall, "The Authorship of Jackson's Bank Veto Message." *Mississippi Valley Historical Review* 50, no. 3 (1963): 466–77.

[121] "President Jackson's Veto Message Regarding the Bank of the United States; July 10, 1832." http://avalon.law.yale.edu/19th_century/ajveto01.asp

verging on demagogy, about how foreigners, especially British investors, owned a large portion of the Bank's stock and siphoned off American prosperity.[122]

After the Senate sustained Jackson's veto on July 13 by a margin of 22–19, five votes short of an override, the matter moved front and center to the presidential campaign. The issue galvanized Jackson's grassroots supporters who took to the streets in support of the president's position as a deadly cholera epidemic swept across the country that summer. As Robert Remini recounts,

> Democrats were old hands at election tricks themselves, in fact better at them than the National Republicans. In a colorful campaign of noise and nonsense, they tried to screen the unpleasant talk about banks and panics and cholera behind an organized diversion of parades, illuminations, songs, hickory pole raisings, barbecues and rallies. Parades and barbecues were the favorites. Near Philadelphia, for example, gigantic hickory poles were marched through town and planted in the public square on election eve … At another city, some 5,000 persons attended a rally for the President. "A splendid band of music enlivened the scene, and a piece of artillery was employed in giving salutes." Then came several long addresses extolling the virtues of the President, followed by six cheers and shouts of "Huzza for Old Hickory," "Democracy against Aristocracy," "Victory." The rally ended with the singing of "The Hickory Tree," a tuneful little ditty that cheered on the electorate:

> > "Hurra for the Hickory Tree!
> > Hurrah for the Hickory Tree!
> > Its branches will wave o'er tyranny's grave.
> > And bloom for the brave and free."[123]

Jackson's critics portrayed him as "King Andrew the First," as memorialized by a cartoon widely circulated in newspapers of the era, and chastised him for an alleged abuse of power and

[122] Sean Wilentz, *Andrew Jackson*. American Presidents Series (New York: Henry Holt & Co., 2005), pp. 81–2.

[123] Robert V. Remini, *Andrew Jackson and the Bank War: A Study in the Growth of Presidential Power* (New York: W. W. Norton, 1967), pp. 103–4.

a trampling of the Constitution.[124] The president's close advisor, frontier journalist Amos Kendall, carefully depicted Jackson as savior of the American people in his "Review" campaign pamphlet that was widely circulated and reprinted in newspapers.[125] Jackson prevailed in 1832 in the three-way election contest over rivals Henry Clay and Anti-Mason candidate William Wirt, though his popular vote total dropped somewhat compared his victory in 1828. Regardless, the president subsequently ordered that deposits be removed from the Bank.[126] A short-term financial crisis spearheaded by Biddle was subsequently unsuccessful in resurrecting attempts to recharter the Bank.[127] In 1834, Clay introduced a resolution of censure against Jackson's moves. The Senate passed the resolution, while the House expressed a resolution of support for the president. Turning again to Kendall for advice, Jackson filed a "Protest" with the Senate. The document, which outlined Jackson's devotion to the common man and made reference to his military service, was aimed more at his voting base than at Congress itself.[128] For his part, Henry Clay sought to organize a more effective opposition to Jackson, an alleged would-be king, and "reached into English history for the anti-royalist label 'Whig.' A new party was born, and named."[129] By early 1836 the Bank became a private holding and functioned no longer in the national interest.

Jackson's termination of the Bank combined with his "Specie Circular" in 1836 to contribute to the Panic of 1837, which doomed his successor, Martin van Buren, to a single term in office. The executive order mandated that land be purchased in gold or silver and reflected his skepticism of paper currency. The devaluation of paper money yielded runaway inflation and speculation that sent

---

[124] See Library of Congress, "King Andrew the First." https://www.archives.gov/exhibits/treasures_of_congress/Images/page_9/30a.html

[125] Fred F. Endres, "Public Relations in the Jackson White House." *Public Relations Review* 2, no. 3 (1976): 9.

[126] Arthur M. Schlesinger, *The Age of Jackson* (Boston: Little, Brown, 1945), p. 98.

[127] Ibid., p. 103.

[128] Endres, "Public Relations in the Jackson White House," 8.

[129] Richard Brookhiser, "Whigged out." *American History*, September 2016, p. 18.

the national economy into a tailspin. "Had the Bank of the United States still been operating in 1837," argues Jeff Nilsson,

> it might have been a steadying influence in the financial sector. It might have helped in the distribution of specie instead of letting it collect mostly in eastern banks. And it might have reassured the country that a strong, well-regulated, central bank was still conducting business.[130]

Jackson cemented his legacy as a champion of the common man by delegitimizing and destroying an allegedly plutocratic institution, but at what cost? As Phil Davies suggests,

> Banking booms followed by busts would occur roughly every decade for the rest of the 19th century and into the 20th. Without a bona fide central bank to exercise control over currency and access to credit, the monetary system was susceptible to periodic banking disruptions.[131]

Scholars suggest that the Bank was needlessly abolished thanks to missed opportunities for compromise between the stubborn personalities and maneuverings of Biddle, Clay, and the president.[132] Regardless, Jackson's populist crusade against the Bank was critical in expanding the powers of the president and transforming the relationship between the executive and the people, as well as between the president and Congress. He set a new

---

[130] Jeff Nilsson, "How one executive order devastated the country." *Saturday Evening Post*, May 10, 2017. https://www.saturdayeveningpost.com/2017/05/one-executive-order-devastated-country/

[131] Phil Davies, "The 'Monster' of Chesnut Street." *The Region*, September 2008, p. 45. http://www.minneapolisfed.org/publications_papers/pub_display.cfm?id=4046

[132] See Edwin J. Perkins, "Lost Opportunities for Compromise in the Bank War: A Reassessment of Jackson's Veto Message." *Business History Review* 61, no. 4 (1987): 531–50. For a game-theoretic review, see James A. Morrison, "This Means War! Corruption and Credible Commitments in the Collapse of the Second Bank of the United States." *Journal of the History of Economic Thought* 37, no. 2 (2017): 221–45.

precedent for the use of the veto and employed electoral politics to bypass Congress and take issues directly to the people. And "he advanced the concept that the President is the direct (and sole) representative of the people, a revolutionary concept for its time."[133] To his enemies, Jackson ran roughshod over the Constitution and was a treacherous demagogue. As R. Seymour Long maintains, he acted with a

> kind of tribunician power to protect the people against their own elected representatives, and which might be interpreted as conveying a doctrine which almost partook of the nature of Caesarism. It might, however, be contended on his behalf that the framers of the constitution, by so carefully separating the executive from the legislative power, rendered such a view of the functions of the president one which might at least plausibly be held. If Jackson had belonged to the Hamiltonian school of large construction, his temper might well have rendered him dangerous to the proper balance of the constitution. As it was, he at least believed himself to be acting as a faithful of Jefferson in all his public career.[134]

The essence of Donald Trump's crusade against actors in the Department of Justice and FBI dovetails in many ways with Jackson's tactics to destroy the Bank by delegitimizing it. Although Trump did not set out to abolish these critical executive departments, his unending criticism of the organizations' political appointees and civil service employees challenged their legitimacy and intentions, and caused a crisis of confidence in them in the public view while undermining internal moral. Convinced that cabals of "holdovers" from President Obama's two terms and politically motivated operators were bent on subverting his presidency, Trump took the issue directly to the people via social media. Like Jackson, he regarded key actors as political enemies and framed conflict in personal terms.

At the heart of Trump's rhetorical war with allegedly entrenched bureaucrats plotting his ultimate downfall is the supposition that

---

[133] Remini, *Andrew Jackson and the Bank War*, pp. 177–8.
[134] R. Seymour Long, "Andrew Jackson and the National Bank." *English Historical Review* 12, no. 45 (1897): 86–7.

"the government is actually controlled by hidden hands that ignore the law without compunction. It assumes these government actors wantonly ignore the law."[135] The controversy about a "shadow government" composed of "deep state" actors commenced in early 2017 with allegations that Obama operatives had wiretapped his election headquarters at Trump Tower in New York City during the 2016 election. The apparent objective was to uncover Russian meddling in the election and potential collusion between Trump's campaign staff and Russian operatives. In a barrage of Twitter messages in March 2017 the president contended that Obama had engaged in a "Nixon/Watergate" conspiracy and tied the unsubstantiated assertion to a new McCarthyism.[136]

Later that month, Trump's allegations appeared to some as at least partially vindicated. FBI Director James Comey told House Intelligence Committee members that although the president had not been the focus of wiretapping, the agency had in fact been investigating the president's campaign and possible Russian influence in the 2016 election. More than a year later it was revealed that agents at the FBI had used an opposition research dossier connected with the Hillary Clinton campaign, written by former British intelligence operative Christopher Steele, to secure a warrant from the Foreign Intelligence Surveillance Act (FISA) Court, and the primary target was a low-level advisor to Trump, Carter Page. As of early fall 2019, the matter of possible criminality in the procurement of the warrant has not been resolved despite protracted hearings and investigations by congressional Republicans and the firings or demotions of a half-dozen FBI employees.

Still, the fallout was significant and fit Trump's continuing narrative of "deep state" conspiracies and witch hunts that were aimed at his ouster. Notable was the firing of FBI Deputy Director

---

[135] Z. Byron Wolf, "How Donald Trump could delegitimize his own government." *CNN*, March 11, 2017. https://www.cnn.com/2017/03/11/politics/trump-deep-state/index.html

[136] Chris Johnston, "'This is McCarthyism': Trump accuses Obama of 'wiretapping' his office before election." *The Guardian*, March 4, 2017. https://www.theguardian.com/us-news/2017/mar/04/donald-trump-accuses-obama-of-wire-tapping-his-office-before-election

Andrew McCabe, whose wife ran as a Democrat for a state senate seat in Virginia and had received campaign contributions from the sitting governor, Terry McAuliffe. Trump regularly lambasted McCabe on Twitter as an example of political corruption in the Washington swamp. McCabe was fired in March 2018 for leaking unauthorized information to the media and was referred to the Justice Department for criminal prosecution. Similarly, the revelation of thousands of derogatory text messages about the president between Peter Strzok and his lover and fellow agent Lisa Page only confirmed for the president that the FBI was out to destroy him.[137] Strzok had led the investigation into Russian meddling and the Trump campaign dating to 2015, and had procured a guilty plea from former National Security Advisor Michael Flynn for lying about contacts with the Russian ambassador. Flynn was advised not to have an attorney present during his questioning and the president and his supporters contended that the "process crime" was tantamount to a form of entrapment. Strzok was ultimately fired in August 2018.

The firings of McCabe and Strzok followed the president's decision to dismiss FBI Director James Comey, who became an implacable foe of Trump, in early May 2017. In effect, the firings of McCabe, Strzok, and Comey represented a "purge" of the key individuals who commenced the Russia investigation.[138] The president's suspicions about Comey dated to July 2016 when the director broke with agency precedent and provided a public soliloquy regarding Hillary Clinton's use of a private email server as secretary of state in which he declared she would not be prosecuted but then proceeded to detail a litany of possible chargeable offenses. Critics of Comey's handling of the matter, including Trump, alleged

---

[137] Philip Bump, "A complete timeline of the events behind the memo that threatens to rip D.C. in two." *Washington Post*, February 2, 2018. https://www.washingtonpost.com/news/politics/wp/2018/01/30/a-complete-timeline-of-the-events-behind-the-memo-that-threatens-to-rip-d-c-in-two/?noredirect=on&utm_term=.2878d49a9a25

[138] Bradley P. Moss, "Trump's purge of the FBI is complete." *Politico*, August 13, 2018. https://www.politico.com/magazine/story/2018/08/13/peter-strzok-fired-donald-trump-fbi-219355

that the FBI had come to the conclusion to exonerate Mrs. Clinton before the investigation had concluded and that a double standard existed regarding the Russia inquiry.

Trump became steadfastly critical of Comey's handling of the counterintelligence investigation of Russian influence in the 2016 campaign and accused the FBI director of grandstanding and politicizing the matter. Trump met with Comey in February 2017 and allegedly asked if he were directly under investigation, something Comey refused to say publicly until later testimony before Congress. Moreover, the president (according to Comey) asked him about his loyalty to him and requested that he "let go" charges against National Security Advisor General Michael Flynn for lying to the vice president and the FBI about his contacts with Russian Ambassador Sergei Kislyak. Ultimately Trump fired Comey on May 9, 2017. On social media the president had repeatedly pointed to what he believed was an abject contradiction: evidence of Clinton's wrongdoings were verifiable, while notions of collusion with Russia were unsubstantiated and fictitious. In the termination letter Trump cited the alleged opinions of the Attorney General and Deputy Director of the FBI that Comey was no longer able to "effectively lead the Bureau. It is essential that we find new leadership that restores public trust and confidence in its vital law enforcement mission." But Trump's protracted conflict with Comey, and the latter's successor, Robert Mueller, would do anything but accomplish that goal.

Within days of his firing, Comey leaked a memo detailing his private meeting with Trump to a law school friend that was widely published in May 2017. The next month he told the Senate Intelligence Committee that "I didn't do it myself for a variety of reasons but I asked him to because I thought that might prompt the appointment of a special counsel."[139] Comey got his wish shortly after his dismissal. Deputy Attorney General Rod Rosenstein authorized former FBI Director Robert Mueller to

---

[139] Quoted in Katie Bo Williams, "Comey leaked memos to prompt special counsel." *The Hill*, June 8, 2017. https://thehill.com/policy/national-security/336932-comey-leaked-memo-to-prompt-special-counsel

head a special counsel investigation with the broad mandate of identifying "any links and/or coordination between the Russian government and individuals associated with the campaign of President Donald Trump; and any matters that arose or may arise directly from the investigation."[140] During his Senate testimony,

> [w]hile Comey may not have expressed an overt opinion about whether Trump is guilty of obstruction of justice, the careful former prosecutor certainly laid out a set of facts that any prosecutor could use to try to prove just that.[141]

The convolutions of the special counsel's investigation into the matter of potential collusion between the Trump campaign and Russia are too many to detail. Mueller procured several plea deals or indictments of Trump associates, including attorney Michael Cohen, George Papadopoulos, and Paul Manafort—yet none had relevance to Russia collusion directly. Nonetheless, what *is* most remarkable is Trump's direct and unyielding criticism of the special counsel specifically, and the FBI more generally, when compared to the way in which his predecessors handled such matters. Independent counsel or special counsel investigations into the executive have been numerous, and every president dating to Gerald Ford—save Barack Obama—confronted some type of special investigation.[142] Investigations ranged from Carter's personal finances, the Iran–Contra affair under Reagan and H. W. Bush, Bill Clinton's land dealings in Arkansas that morphed into impeachment for attempts to cover up an affair with a White House intern, and

[140] *New York Times*, "Rod Rosenstein's letter appointing Mueller Special Counsel." May 17, 2017. https://www.nytimes.com/interactive/2017/05/17/us/politics/document-Robert-Mueller-Special-Counsel-Russia.html
[141] Domenico Montanaro, "Is Trump guilty of obstruction of justice? Comey laid out the case." *NPR*, June 10, 2017. https://www.npr.org/2017/06/10/532321287/is-trump-guilty-of-obstruction-of-justice-comey-laid-out-the-case
[142] Sonam Sheth, "Obama is the only president since Nixon who didn't face an independent investigation." *Business Insider*, October 23, 2017. https://www.businessinsider.com/obama-nixon-trump-russia-independent-investigation-2017-10

leaked information that "outed" CIA operative Valerie Plame under George W. Bush. In each of these cases, chief executives took pains to avoid attacking the independence or legitimacy of those conducting the inquiries. Not so for Donald Trump.

A global perspective on Trump's social media activity provides important insights into his campaign to delegitimize not only Mueller's probe specifically but also to counter the broader dynamics of the Russia collusion narrative by delegitimizing the leadership of the FBI and Justice Department. From June 2018 through December 2018 Trump called the Russia investigation a "witch hunt" on social media more than ninety times. From December 2017 through December 2018 he referred to the matter as a "hoax" more than three dozen times. During the same period, he chastised Robert Mueller by name sixty-nine times, contending that the special counsel had severe conflicts of interest and was bent on destroying people's lives unnecessarily. Trump posited that the investigatory staff was a shill for Hillary Clinton and the "resistance" on the Left. He tweeted that the staff included "13 hardened Democrats, some big Crooked Hillary supporters, and Zero Republicans." Although Mueller is a registered Republican and was FBI director under George W. Bush, independent research did verify that thirteen of seventeen members of the staff were registered as Democrats at some point, nine made donations to Democrats, and six donated to Hillary Clinton's presidential campaign.[143] Trump apparently became convinced by some close advisors of "mounting evidence of pro-Clinton bias among senior FBI officials" that only reinforced his war of words against the special counsel's investigation.[144]

James Comey was also the brunt of Trump's Twitter diatribes, despite his exit from the FBI. The president gave him the sobriquet "Leakin' James" and "Slippery James" and chastised the former FBI director ninety-nine times on Twitter from May 2017 through

[143] Matt Zapotosky, "Trump said Mueller's team has '13 hardened Democrats.' Here are the facts." *Washington Post Blogs*, March 18, 2018.
[144] Philip Rucker, Matt Zapotosky, and Carol D. Leonnig, "Trump escalates attacks on FBI." *Washington Post*, March 18, 2018, p. A21.

December 2018 for allegedly lying, leaking information, and making false statements as part of a political agenda and personal vendetta. Trump's objective was to turn the premise of the Russia collusion investigation on its head by declaring his innocence and indicting the investigators for wrongdoing themselves based on political motives. One tweet from the president encapsulates the strategy: "Comey drafted the Crooked Hillary exoneration long before he talked to her (lied in Congress to Senator G), then based his decisions on her poll numbers. Disgruntled, he, McCabe, and the others, committed many crimes!"[145]

Trump also took aim at his own attorney general, Jeff Sessions. The former Alabama Senator made a fateful decision to recuse himself from the Russia matter in March 2017 when he revealed he had had conversations with Ambassador Kislyak several times during the campaign. The disclosure appeared to contradict his confirmation hearing testimony, and Democrats were quick to call for Sessions' resignation. Instead, the attorney general said on March 3 that "I have decided to recuse myself from any existing or future investigations of any matters related in any way to the campaigns for president of the United States"[146] as a means of extricating himself from further controversy. The president considered the move "very unfair," if not a personal rebuke, amidst consideration of firing Mueller. In an interview with the *Los Angeles Times* Trump asserted of Sessions:

> How do you take a job and then recuse yourself? If he would have recused himself before the job, I would have said, "Thanks, Jeff, but I'm not going to take you." It's extremely unfair—and that's a mild word—to the president.[147]

[145] @realDonaldTrump, "Comey drafted the Crooked Hillary exoneration long before he talked to her (lied in Congress to Senator G), then based his decisions on her poll numbers. Disgruntled, he, McCabe, and the others, committed many crimes!" *Twitter*, April 16, 2018, 5:25 a.m. https://twitter.com/realdonaldtrump/status/985856662866202624

[146] Quoted in Meaghan Keneally, "Timeline leading up to Jeff Sessions' recusal and the fallout." *ABC News*, July 26, 2017. https://abcnews.go.com/Politics/timeline-leading-jeff-sessions-recusal-fallout/story?id=45855918

[147] Noah Bierman, "Trump criticizes Sessions and vents frustration at Russia investigation and leaders of the Justice Department and FBI." *Los Angeles*

Angry that Sessions had placed him in an untenable situation, Trump's frustration mounted over the next year. On Twitter the president said in early August 2018:

> This is a terrible situation and Attorney General Jeff Sessions should stop this Rigged Witch Hunt right now, before it continues to stain our country any further. Bob Mueller is totally conflicted, and his 17 Angry Democrats that are doing his dirty work are a disgrace to USA![148]

The president questioned Sessions' competence and political acumen three weeks later when he tweeted:

> Jeff Sessions said he wouldn't allow politics to influence him only because he doesn't understand what is happening underneath his command position. Highly conflicted Bob Mueller and his gang of 17 Angry Dems are having a field day as real corruption goes untouched. No Collusion![149]

Presidents' discrediting of their cabinet appointees is not without precedent, but rather unusual when undertaken in such a public way. One might point to Andrew Johnson's disdain for Lincoln's Secretary of War, Edwin Stanton, or Jimmy Carter's dismissal of Joseph Califano, whom he considered disloyal.[150]

[   ] *Times*, July 19, 2017. https://www.latimes.com/politics/washington/la-na-essential-washington-updates-trump-attacks-attorney-general-sessions-1500514853-htmlstory.html

[148] @realDonaldTrump, "This is a terrible situation and Attorney General Jeff Sessions should stop this Rigged Witch Hunt right now, before it continues to stain our country any further. Bob Mueller is totally conflicted, and his 17 Angry Democrats that are doing his dirty work are a disgrace to USA!" *Twitter*, August 1, 2018, 6:24 a.m. https://twitter.com/realdonaldtrump/status/1024646945640525826

[149] @realDonald Trump, "Jeff Sessions said he wouldn't allow politics to influence him only because he doesn't understand what is happening underneath his command position. Highly conflicted Bob Mueller and his gang of 17 Angry Dems are having a field day as real corruption goes untouched. No Collusion!" *Twitter*, August 25, 2018, 5:36 a.m. https://twitter.com/realdonaldtrump/status/1033332301579661312

[150] See Edward Walsh, "A serene Carter." *Washington Post*, July 22, 1979.

But Trump's antipathy toward Sessions went beyond questioning the attorney general's integrity to deepen the narrative that the broader Department of Justice could not be trusted as a politically neutral agency. As one critic put it, Trump's social media barrages

> violate norms of law-enforcement independence from presidential influence. Their proximate aim is to discredit the Justice Department and FBI, probably in order to delegitimize it as the investigation of Robert Mueller gets ever closer to the president. And they appear to be part of an effort to weaken public confidence in American institutions more generally—not just DOJ, but also the "so-called" courts, the "fake news" media, the supposedly lying, incompetent intelligence community, and others.[151]

Trump fired Sessions within days of the 2018 mid-term elections. His nominee to replace Sessions as attorney general, William Barr, had opined that the Mueller investigation's premise about presidential obstruction of justice is "fatally misconceived."[152] The final chapter of the post-investigation dust-up remains unwritten after the release of the Mueller report in spring 2019 and Mueller's bumbling testimony before Congress. But what are the potential short- and long-term consequences of Trump's quest to delegitimize the broader Justice establishment?

Public opinion data and internal polling within the FBI underscore the implications. A Reuters/IPSOS survey in February 2018 found that 73 percent of Republicans believed that the Mueller investigation was politically motivated against the president, while three-quarters of Democrats believed the president was seeking to

[151] Jack Goldsmith, "The cost of Trump's attacks on the FBI." *The Atlantic*, December 4, 2017. https://www.theatlantic.com/politics/archive/2017/12/the-high-price-of-sessionss-failure-to-defend-the-justice-department/547382/

[152] Sadie Gurman and Aruna Viswanatha, "Trump's Attorney General pick criticized an aspect of Mueller Probe in memo to Justice Department." *Wall Street Journal*, December 19, 2018. https://www.wsj.com/articles/trumps-attorney-general-pick-criticized-an-aspect-of-mueller-probe-in-memo-to-justice-department-11545275973

delegitimize the FBI and Justice.[153] Another poll several months later indicated a similar partisan split, as

> Democrats have largely remained supportive of the FBI and its work. Republicans and politically independent individuals increasingly think the nation's top law enforcement agency is skewed in its treatment of the Trump administration as allegations of wrongdoing ensnare a growing number of the president's staff.[154]

A Pew Research Center poll in July 2018 accentuated the relative toll of Trump's rhetoric, at least among his supporters. Republican confidence in the FBI fell 16 points over the span of a year to 49 percent, with negative views of the agency doubling to 44 percent.[155] Within the FBI itself, an internal "climate study" evidenced falling confidence among the rank-and-file in the director, Christopher Wray, after Comey's firing as well as in the honesty and integrity of senior leaders. The sense of alienation, Scott R. Anderson and Benjamin Wittes suggest, may be reactions to

> the firing of James Comey as FBI director, the removal of Deputy Director Andrew McCabe, countless attacks by President Trump on federal law enforcement, the controversy over text exchanges between counterintelligence agent Peter Strzok and former FBI lawyer Lisa Page, and the proliferation of a conservative media narrative that portrays the FBI as ground zero in a "Deep State" conspiracy.[156]

[153] Chris Kahn, "Most Republicans believe FBI, Justice Dept. trying to 'delegitimize' Trump: Reuters/Ipsos poll." *Reuters*, February 5, 2018. https://www.reuters.com/article/us-usa-trump-russia-poll/most-republicans-believe-fbi-justice-dept-trying-to-delegitimize-trump-reuters-ipsos-poll-idUSKBN1FP2UH

[154] Laura Santhanam, "FBI support is eroding, but most Americans still back bureau, poll says." *PBS Newshour*, April 17, 2018. https://www.pbs.org/newshour/politics/fbi-support-is-eroding-but-most-americans-still-back-bureau-poll-says

[155] *NBC News*, "Pew poll: GOP sours on FBI." July 24, 2018. https://www.nbcnews.com/card/pew-poll-gop-sours-fbi-n894016

[156] Scott R. Anderson and Benjamin Wittes, "Climate change is real at the FBI—and here is the data to prove it." *Lawfare*, July 15, 2018. https://www.lawfareblog.com/climate-change-real-fbi-and-here-data-prove-it

Trump's attacks on the FBI as "beleaguered" with a reputation "in tatters" were exacerbated by congressional Republicans' allegations of surveillance abuses on the Trump campaign, if not outright corruption. The controversies prompted Director Christopher Wray to undertake a YouTube video for employees in February 2018 in which he urged them to "keep calm and tackle hard" while focusing on process as a hedge against criticism. As one agent reflected, "There's a lot of anger. The irony is it's a conservative-leaning organization, and it's being trashed by conservatives. At first it was just perplexing. Now there's anger, because it's not going away."[157]

The cases of Andrew Jackson and the Bank and Donald Trump and the FBI highlight a curious element of presidential politics that is unique to the populist ethos. Both presidents sought to undermine the legitimacy and authority of extant institutions by portraying them as bastions of corruption. For Jackson, the rallying cry was the way in which the Bank represented elite economic interests to the detriment of the common man. For Trump the staunch criticism of elites within the nation's top law enforcement agency reinforced the narrative of widespread malfeasance and conspiracy in the "swamp" of the capital that he commenced during his campaign. Both presidents personalized conflicts to the point that they embraced notions that their political enemies were determined to destroy them, and by extension, the common Americans who supported them. The objective was, as former Trump advisor Steve Bannon expressed, an indefatigable fight "to deconstruct the administrative state."[158] The costs to the economy under Jackson were palpable. The negative impact of the politicization of the FBI is just as potentially profound for the public's confidence in the rule of law—and all the more precarious if the conspiracy theories Trump articulated so publicly are in whole or in part correct.

---

[157] Quotes from Devlin Barrett and Matt Zapotosky, "Inside the FBI: Anger, worry, work—and fears of lasting damage." *Washington Post Blogs*, February 3, 2018.

[158] Philip Rucker and Robert Costa, "Bannon vows a daily fight for 'deconstruction of the administrative state'; Trump's chief strategist outlines a nationalist agenda and says the president will fulfill his hard-line promises." *Washington Post Blogs*, February 24, 2017.

C. Ordinary people, organic protest, and popular support

The second conceptual commonality in Figure 2.1 emphasizes the populist affection toward ordinary people. The populist style takes a Rousseauian view of the people as inherently righteous, capable, and good. Populists of all stripes emphasize their presumed role as an emissary for the forgotten man and woman in America and variably accentuate their role as protector against elite abuses.

In his farewell address, for example, Andrew Jackson reminded his fellow citizens "that eternal vigilance by the people is the price of liberty, and that you must pay the price if you wish to secure the blessing." Similarly, William Jennings Bryan's political philosophy was intricately linked to an unending belief in the wisdom and honesty of ordinary Americans. As the "Great Commoner" once said, "My place in history will depend on what I can do for the people, and not what the people can do for me." Similarly, in his 1964 acceptance speech as the GOP presidential nominee, Barry Goldwater emphasized that "[i]t is the cause of Republicanism to ensure that power remains in the hands of the people."[159] Finally, George Wallace said it most succinctly: "You're tops. You're the people."[160]

But the populist definition of the "people" can be highly exclusionary in nature in the most extreme rhetoric. Politicians, corporate leaders, academics, the press, immigrants, or foreign powers do not qualify as components of the people and are singled out for ridicule. Müller cites Donald Trump's campaign statement that "the only important thing is the unification of the people—because other people don't mean anything"[161] as a prime example. The "other" is to be shunned, rejected as disingenuous, and legitimately threatened with prosecution (rhetorically or in reality) to alienate him or her from any connection to the "real"

---

[159] "Goldwater's 1964 acceptance speech." *Washington Post.* https://www .washingtonpost.com/wp-srv/politics/daily/may98/goldwaterspeech.htm

[160] Quoted in Richard Lowry, "Their George Wallace—and ours." *National Review*, April 25, 2016, p. 18.

[161] Müller, *What Is Populism?*, p. 22.

people. Capitalizing on Hillary Clinton's imprudent reference to his supporters as a "basket of deplorables" in the 2016 election campaign, Trump called repeatedly for her to be jailed. The president leveled similar condemnations at more than a dozen politicians in both parties, from "deep state" actors in his own Justice Department to those who burn the American flag.[162] The dynamic commenced early in his electoral juggernaut as "Trump sought to attack the very legitimacy of his opponents, deeming protesters 'thugs' and 'paid' activists, and continued into his early term when he challenged a federal judge's authority to oppose a travel ban on Muslims."[163] And of course, just days after assuming office, Trump began borrowing the Stalinist phrase "enemy of the people" to describe the "fake news" media when criticized in the press, a refrain that has since continued on Twitter and at virtually every rally he has held.[164] This latter focus overlaps with conspiracy theory employed by the president (see below), insofar as there is allegedly a broad swath of "others" out to ruin him, including establishment politicians, clandestine cells of his detractors in the federal bureaucracy, and the press who collude to undermine the people's will as he interprets and expresses it.

Trump's excessive rhetoric against elites as corrupt and inferior falls in line with a messaging style that dismisses them as immoral, and therefore justifies their ostracization.[165] Trump began attacks on elites as early as 2015, when he tweeted: "Let's Trump the Establishment! We are no longer silent. We will Make

---

[162] Julia Arciga, "James Comey, welcome to the long list of people Donald Trump wants to jail." *Daily Beast*, April 18, 2018. https://www.thedailybeast.com/james-comey-welcome-to-the-long-list-of-people-trump-wants-to-jail

[163] Ishan Tharoor, "Trump's populism is about creating division, not unity." *Washington Post*, February 6, 2017. https://www.washingtonpost.com/news/worldviews/wp/2017/02/06/trumps-populism-is-about-creating-division-not-unity/?utm_term=.5e2d19318d5e

[164] William P. Davis, "'Enemy of the People': Trump breaks out this phrase during moments of peak criticism." *New York Times*, July 19, 2018. https://www.nytimes.com/2018/07/19/business/media/trump-media-enemy-of-the-people.html

[165] Müller, *What Is Populism?* pp. 3, 19–20.

America Great Again!"[166] As a campaign foil and rallying cry, the president frequently references elites' arrogance without defining specifically their ranks, but rather by implying the cadre includes anyone who opposes him and his supporters. As Eugene Scott suggests, references to the abhorrent elite is "often used as a slur to suggest that those who disagree with conservative values on guns, marriage, abortion and immigration are out of touch and have little in common with the average American."[167] At a stop in Duluth, Minnesota, in 2018 Trump opined that "[t]hey always call the other side 'the elite.' Why are they elite? I have a much better apartment than they do." He continued by stating that "I'm smarter than they are. I'm richer than they are. I became president and they didn't. And I'm representing the greatest, smartest, most loyal best people on Earth—the deplorables, remember that?"[168] Indeed, the president often references *his* supporters as more intelligent, more capable, and more hard-working than the "stone cold losers" who comprise the "establishment." In 2018 in Fargo, North Dakota, Trump asserted: "We got more money, we got more brains, we got better houses and apartments, we got nicer boats, we're smarter than they are and they say they're the elite. You're the elite, we're the elite."[169]

[166] @realDonaldTrump, "Let's Trump the Establishment! We are no longer silent. We will Make America Great Again!" *Twitter*, July 22, 2015, 12:03 p.m. https://twitter.com/realdonaldtrump/status/623931297698705408

[167] Eugene Scott, "Trump's dislike of—and desire to be a part of—the 'elite'." *Washington Post*, June 21, 2018. https://www.washingtonpost.com/news/the-fix/wp/2018/06/21/trumps-dislike-of-and-desire-to-be-a-part-of-the-elites/?utm_term=.15d5f1e5f8a1

[168] Quoted in Harriet Agerholm, "Donald Trump asks why other people are called the elite when 'I have a much better apartment and I'm richer than they are'." *The Independent* (UK), June 21, 2018. https://www.independent.co.uk/news/world/americas/donald-trump-elite-better-apartment-richer-minnesota-rally-a8409621.html

[169] Quoted in Jacqueline Thomsen, "Trump: My supporters should be called the 'super elite'." *The Hill*, June 27, 2018. http://thehill.com/homenews/administration/394551-trump-my-supporters-should-be-called-the-super-elite

D. Majoritarian tendencies

Whereas the pluralist perspective emphasizes negotiation, minority rights, and institutional arbitration in conflict resolution to reach compromise within the context of majority rule, populists perceive democratic politics as a binary conflict between irreconcilable forces: the pure and virtuous people against unscrupulous elites. There is no question of resolving competing interests through representative institutions that mediate popular will. Such a perspective emphasizes majoritarian rule and privileges conflict over conciliation. As Pierson notes, "[p]opulist campaigns tend to reject coalitional politics as one of the vices of modern politics that should be overcome rather than accommodated."[170] There is egocentricity in this regard, as populist appeals focus more on self-interest than the collective good. As Gary C. Woodward posits, "[t]he Populist style encourages the audience to consider public policy largely in terms of the collective impact it has on personal economic welfare rather than on the national welfare."[171] One danger is that minority groups may be singled out and identified as the cause of contemporary angst and subjected to discriminatory policy, particularly in times of emergencies—whether real, imagined, or contrived.[172] The current debate over immigration, and Trump's blaming of crime on illegals, justifies policies that run counter to traditional constitutional protections of due process.

Another straightforward expression of majoritarianism in the populist mindset is the emphasis on direct democracy and unmediated, direct communication with the people. In this regard, populists have made use of the prevailing technology of the time. In the early nineteenth century, "going public"[173]—appealing over the heads of members of Congress directly to grassroots

---

[170] Pierson, "Why Populism Fails," p. 19.
[171] Gary C. Woodward, "Reagan as Roosevelt: The Elasticity of Pseudo-Populist Appeals." *Central States Speech Journal* 54, no. 1 (Spring 1983): 48.
[172] Huq, "The People against the Constitution," p. 1143.
[173] Samuel Kernell, *Going Public: New Strategies of Presidential Leadership* (Washington, DC: CQ Press, 2006).

constituencies—violated the mores of the day.[174] In Andrew Jackson's case, his supporters therefore utilized newspapers, or the "penny press," to criticize the president's opponents and promote his policies.[175] William Jennings Bryan's fiery oratory at the turn of the century, by contrast, was legendary. Transcripts of his speeches were reprinted in the partisan press of the day for his supporters to take delight in, and his detractors to rue. In 1901 Bryan started his own newspaper in Lincoln, Nebraska, as a platform to embrace his supportive audience.

In the more contemporary period, while stump speeches continue as a form of primary outreach, technological advances have played a central role in shaping notions of direct communication that bypasses the traditional media. Ross Perot utilized informal town hall meetings to communicate with "ordinary Americans." Seizing on emerging technologies, he promised, as president, that he would "augment the people's direct expression of their will—through instant plebiscites via interactive television and tele-polling—with conventional opinion polls."[176] Such a policy certainly would have given new meaning to the idea of "machine politics" by circumventing the norms of democratic deliberation.[177] Donald Trump, of course, has employed social media in conjunction with raucous post-election rallies as a means of solidifying unfettered interaction with his supporters and circumventing media filtering. These rallies, like those of his contemporary predecessors, provide the aura of spontaneity and organic protest that is the bread and butter of the populist style.

[174] On this point, see Jeffrey K. Tulis, *The Rhetorical Presidency* (Princeton, NJ: Princeton University Press, 2017), in particular the discussion of the impeachment of Andrew Johnson and the president's "Swing around the Circle" speaking campaign against Radical Republicans.

[175] Joseph P. McKerns, "The Limits of Progressive Journalism History." *Journalism History* 4, no. 3 (1977): 88–92.

[176] Jean Bethke Elshtain, "A parody of true democracy." *Christian Science Monitor*, August 13, 1992. https://www.csmonitor.com/1992/0813/13181.html

[177] Carl M. Cannon, "Machine politics." *Forbes*, July 2, 1997. https://www.forbes.com/1997/07/02/voting.html#3746835dab69

E. Issue simplification: the desultory path to anti-intellectualism and conspiracy theory

The fourth conceptual commonality in the populist style noted in Figure 2.1, and which deserves ample comparative attention, is the penchant for facile and often unidimensional explanations of complex socio-political and economic problems. The hazard is that the populist's tendency to over-simplify increases the probability of irrationality and illiberalism vis-à-vis democratic norms of deliberation, especially when conspiracy theory enters into the mix. Civility, diversity, tolerance, reason, and truth are critical to "a public space for discussion and negotiation across social and power differences."[178] Trump's penchant for anti-intellectual discourse that includes the rejection of facts and snubbing so-called experts is lengthy. Invoking conspiracy theory, the president has questioned everything from climate change and environmentally friendly light bulbs to polling tactics allegedly bent on sabotaging his 2016 presidential bid.[179] In foreign affairs, critics contend he engages in *argumentum ad baculum*, "an overtly aggressive and presumptively illegitimate reliance upon personal defamation, shallow threats and persistent intimidation,"[180] whether in his unilateral action to withdraw the United States from the Iran nuclear deal or in his personal invectives against leaders as different as Kim Jong-Un of North Korea, Angela Merkel of Germany, and Justin Trudeau of Canada.

But Trump is scarcely the first populist to reject intellectual discourse. The solutions proffered by populists are often simplified, reactionary, and lack specifics. Examples abound: Bernie Sanders' pleas for universal health (i.e., Medicare for All) and child care based on higher taxes on corporations without serious empirical

[178] Silvio Waisbord, "Why Populism Is Troubling for Democratic Communication." *Communication, Culture & Critique* 11, no. 1 (2018): 23.
[179] Matthew Motta, "The Dynamics and Political Implications of Anti-Intellectualism in the United States." *American Politics Research* 46, no. 3 (2018): 466.
[180] Louis René Beres, "Trump and the triumph of anti-reason." *U.S. News & World Report*, July 13, 2017. https://www.usnews.com/opinion/op-ed/articles/2017-07-13/donald-trump-and-the-triumph-of-anti-reason-in-america

investigation of the economic implications;[181] Ross Perot's conviction that experts and technocrats could solve the nation's financial ills and run the country like a business;[182] George Wallace's bigoted pleas to return to the era of Jim Crow to restore an old order to social relations; the Know-Nothing Party's belief that the solution to economic dislocation was generally a matter of halting Irish Catholic immigration (e.g., "no Irish need apply" as the signs read on New York City storefronts).

Anti-intellectualism has repeatedly been a hallmark of the populist style, understood as the "attainment of knowledge through instincts, character, moral sensibilities and emotion."[183] Perhaps the most disconcerting dynamic that can animate the populist spirit is the proclivity to locate a convenient scapegoat to blame for the country's tribulations. In that effort, the populist style is prone not only to reject facts but also to embrace conspiracy theories grounded in suppositions of subversion, suspicion, or contrived theses that are empirically unverifiable and even irrational.

Reinforcing anti-elite rhetoric, conspiracy theory, as operationalized by populists, is essentially the belief that some covert group of actors, or an individual, is secretly engaged in a malicious plot to attain some goal at odds with the interest of the people. Psychologists posit that conspiratorial messaging is appealing when randomness and coincidence are easier to explain through intuition, symbols, and metaphors rather than by analytical reasoning. Three mental currents may subtend one's disposition to accept the tenets of conspiracy theories. The first is confirmation bias, or people's "willingness to accept explanations that fit what they already believe." The second is proportionality bias, or "the inclination to believe that big events must have big causes." The

---

[181] Lisa Kennedy Montgomery, "Bernie Sanders' 'Medicare for All' plan would blow up the economy." *Fox Business*, July 31, 2018. https://www.foxbusiness.com/politics/bernie-sanders-medicare-for-all-plan-would-blow-up-the-economy-kennedy

[182] On this point, see Harold Loeb, *Life in a Technocracy: What It Might Be Like* (Syracuse, NY: Syracuse University Press, 1996).

[183] Colleen Shogan, "Anti-Intellectualism in the Modern Presidency: A Republican Populism." *Perspectives on Politics* 5, no. 3 (2007): 295.

third is an illusory pattern perception, or the "tendency to see causal relations where there may not be any."[184]

Conspiracy theories are scarcely novel in American politics, as historian Richard Hofstadter documents extensively.[185] From the Conway Cabal during the Revolutionary War to conjectures that Lyndon Johnson was complicit in John F. Kennedy's assassination, belief in cover-ups has frequently supplanted logic and evidence in political narratives.[186] Far-fetched conspiracy theories have even occasionally been lampooned in popular culture, as the abstruse stanzas of Diamond Rio's 1996 music video "It's All in Your Head" underscore with a comedic flair. The clip features actor Martin Sheen as an apocalyptic preacher instigating brawls with the denizens of smoky pool halls. In his dying words to his son, amidst images of President Kennedy in Dallas in 1963, Elvis Presley posters, and Neil Armstrong strolling on a barren lunar landscape, Sheen admonishes the boy: "don't ever trust what the government say . . . We never walked on the moon, Elvis ain't dead, you ain't going crazy, it's all in your head." Reflecting on his father's soap-box sermons, the boy declares: "it revealed to me down in my soul, there were two shooters on the grassy knoll."[187] If, as the song suggests, "it's all interpretation" and "to find the truth, you have to read between the lines," Donald Trump's infusion of paranoia into a reading of the lyrics

---

[184] William Cummings, "Conspiracy theories: Here's what drives people to them, no matter how wacky." *USA Today*, December 23, 2017. https://www.usatoday.com/story/news/nation/2017/12/23/conspiracy-theory-psychology/815121001/

[185] Richard Hofstadter, *The Paranoid Style in American Politics* (New York: Vintage, 2012).

[186] See Bernhard Knollenberg, *Washington and the Revolution, a Reappraisal: Gates, Conway, and the Continental Congress* (New York: Macmillan Company, 1940); Albert A. Harrison and James Moulton Thomas, "The Kennedy Assassination, Unidentified Flying Objects, and Other Conspiracies: Psychological and Organizational Factors in the Perception of 'Cover-up'." *Systems Research and Behavioral Science: The Official Journal of the International Federation for Systems Research* 14, no. 2 (1997): 113–28.

[187] https://www.youtube.com/watch?v=p8Otmhv6YOI

of American politics is in a league whose roster includes a long line of prominent players.

William Jennings Bryan, for example, held that a monopoly of eastern bankers who supported the gold standard did so to increase substantially the amount of money that debtors would have to repay them. But what is more, Bryan injected conspiracy theory into the argument to explain the nature of the cabal responsible for the impact on farmers. As Knight asserts,

> antisemitism was widespread in the Populist Party, from which Bryan drew much of his support. Concerns over "Jewish moneyed interests" in New York had aligned many antisemites against the gold standard, and Bryan used what some conspiracy theorists see as coded language to speak to those concerns.[188]

Indeed, Bryan's exhortation in his 1896 Democratic Convention "Cross of Gold Speech" that "[y]ou shall not press down upon the brow of labor this crown of thorns. You shall not crucify mankind upon a cross of gold" has been interpreted, correctly or incorrectly, as a recrimination of Jews not only for the death of Christ but also for the plight of the agrarian class at the hands of Hebrew bankers.[189] Bryan took aim more directly at a wealthy, Jewish banking family when he argued that the United States "shall be administered on behalf of the American people and not on behalf of the Rothschilds and other foreign bankers."

Bryan's narrative is consistent with the scapegoating of a foreign "other" built upon irrationality rather than reason. "The Rothschilds," Chad Weisman notes,

> were a prominent and powerful Jewish banking family with a presence in a handful of European countries . . . Later, those who escaped the Holocaust would move to the United States. Given their prestige, they have, for more than two centuries, been the subject of a number

---

[188] Peter Knight, *Conspiracy Theories in American History: An Encyclopedia* (Santa Barbara, CA: ABC-CLIO, 2003), p. 141.

[189] James Ledbetter, "Has the Famous Populist 'Cross of Gold' Speech Been Unfairly Tarred by Anti-Semitism?" *JSTOR Daily* (Business and Economics), July 6, 2016. https://daily.jstor.org/william-jennings-bryan-cross-of-gold/

of conspiracy theories including one that asserts that they control the world's central banks.[190]

Bryan's legacy may well be one of enduring distrust of Jews in international monetary affairs. The suspicion has morphed into an illogicality by which some have held the sons of Abraham accountable for everything from Kennedy's assassination to bad weather.[191]

In the modern era, populist presidential candidates have been similarly susceptible to such *déraisonnement*. For Barry Goldwater in 1964, the proponents of conspiracy theories posed a significant dilemma for his campaign, which was already troubled by his brash commentaries and all-too-candid, boorish, and off-putting personal engagement of supporters.[192] Goldwater was indubitably an ardent anti-communist, but his presidential campaign became intertwined with grassroots activists and organizations that actively promoted the notion of colossal communist collusion in the U.S. government, a plot that even supposedly involved former President Dwight Eisenhower. The problem for Goldwater was that however much he sought to cast off the most eccentric of such conjectures, those activists had been central in securing his presidential nomination.

Richard Stormer, an evangelical Christian conservative, published *None Dare Call It Treason* to coincide with Goldwater's 1964 presidential bid. Following the tack of Joseph McCarthy, Stormer posited that the Warren Commission on Kennedy's assassination was directed by a communist newspaper and argued that

---

[190] Chad Weisman, "In US elections, a history of anti-Semitism." *Times of Israel*, August 30, 2016. https://www.timesofisrael.com/the-specter-of-anti-semitism-is-nothing-new-in-us-elections/

[191] See Yair Rosenberg, "Conspiracy theories about the Rothschilds are a symptom. The problem is deeper." *Washington Post*, March 21, 2018. https://www.washingtonpost.com/news/posteverything/wp/2018/03/21/conspiracy-theories-about-the-rothschilds-are-a-symptom-the-problem-is-deeper/?utm_term=.cb77a6388fcd

[192] On Goldwater's campaign style, see Rich Perlstein, *Before the Storm: Barry Goldwater and the Unmaking of the American Consensus* (New York: Nation Books, 2009), particularly chapter 16.

subversives in the State Department had been responsible for the Soviet seizure of Central and Eastern Europe after World War II. Stormer's work was complemented Phyllis Schlafly's *A Choice Not an Echo*, in which the firebrand anti-feminist contended that "establishment" Republicans had sold out conservatives by rigging presidential nominations behind the scenes to support moderates from Wendell Wilkie to Dwight Eisenhower. Further, Robert Welch, head of the John Birch Society, spearheaded a grassroots effort composed of tens of thousands who believed that

> [t]he federal government, the deep state, was "50–70 percent" Communist and was "under operational control of the Communist party" . . . Obviously academia and the news media were infiltrated, but the U.S. Chamber of Commerce also consisted of fellow travelers, and former Republican President Dwight Eisenhower had been an agent of the Kremlin.[193]

Clearly, had Eisenhower been a Soviet patsy, it is doubtful he would have ordered the last aerial spy mission of the U2 program in 1960 over the Soviet Union. That mission led to the capture of Francis Gary Powers and the embarrassing show-trial that was used by Khrushchev as a pretext to walk out of peace talks in Paris. But those stubborn things called facts, as John Adams once noted, were no matter for the Birchers, who simply "didn't like Ike."

On the advice and efforts of conservative intellectual William F. Buckley, Goldwater strove to distance his campaign from Welch and the John Birch Society. As Matthew Dallek notes,

> Buckley understood the problem: conservatism, he explained, had to bring "into our ranks those people who are, at the moment, on our immediate left—the moderate, wishy-washy conservatives . . . I am talking . . . about 20 to 30 million people . . . If they are being asked to join a movement whose leadership believes the drivel of Robert Welch, they will pass by crackpot alley, and will not pause

---

[193] Kurt Anderson, "How the GOP went crazy." *Slate*, February 2, 2018. https://slate.com/news-and-politics/2018/02/right-wing-conspiracy-theories-from-the-1960s-to-today.html

until they feel the warm embrace of those way over on the other side, the Liberals".[194]

Goldwater heeded Buckley's advice. To disentangle his campaign from the Birchers he even penned a letter in *National Review* condemning Welch's "views far removed from reality."[195] Yet conspiracy theory-laden publications "resonated with conservatives who believed that for more than a decade liberal elites had conspired to keep them out of mainstream institutions: universities, media, the two main parties" and supporters of Goldwater "treated them as campaign literature: handing them out at rallies, distributing them at the convention, mailing them to Republican delegates."[196]

While certainly not the only reason for his massive defeat in 1964, Goldwater's connection to conspiracy theorists clearly complicated his bid for the White House. The Birchers continued to wreak havoc on the conservative movement in the 1960s, nearly sinking Ronald Reagan's initial rise in the GOP beginning with his California gubernatorial bid in 1967. Reagan's key advisors, Stu Spencer and Bill Roberts, were more successful in extricating the "Great Communicator" from the excess and idiosyncrasies of Welch and his ilk.[197] Still, while Buckley's influence was instrumental in that period, the Birchers' views on history and politics, infused by soupçon and resentment, have proven remarkably resilient in Republican spheres in recent decades, punctuated by the rise of the Tea Party and ultimately Donald Trump.[198]

---

[194] Matthew Dallek, "The conservative 1960s." *The Atlantic*, December 1995. https://www.theatlantic.com/magazine/archive/1995/12/the-conservative-1960s/376506/

[195] Quoted in Anderson, "How the GOP went crazy."

[196] Nicole Hemmer, "How the right became addicted to conspiracies." *Washington Post Blogs*, July 18, 2018.

[197] Matthew Dallek, *The Right Moment: Ronald Reagan's First Victory and the Decisive Turning Point in American Politics* (New York: Free Press, 2000).

[198] See Sean Wilentz, "Confounding fathers: The Tea Party's Cold War roots." *The New Yorker*, October 18, 2008. https://www.newyorker.com/magazine/2010/10/18/confounding-fathers

The two independent populist candidates for the White House, George Wallace in 1968 and Ross Perot in 1992, also shared an appreciation for conspiracy narratives. Both candidates made the case that subversives were actively undermining the American democracy. In addition, each discerned plots that were aimed at them personally, including assassination. Each relied on impression rather than evidence to make his case.

As Dan T. Carter avers, Wallace's rhetoric was gauged to evoke a "nonanalytical emotional response" by "probing his audiences' deepest fears and passions and articulating those emotions in a language and style they could understand."[199] One of those fears was collusion by governmental officials sympathetic to communists and criminals. "Wallace," Michael Lee writes, "invoked signs of the apocalypse with his narrative of a crisis-ridden nation where 'thugs roamed the streets with impunity' and 'cowardly politicians, bureaucrats, and distant federal judges capitulated to these loathsome forces'."[200] One of Wallace's favorite targets was the judiciary generally and the U.S. Supreme Court specifically. He routinely contended that the High Court "refuses to recognize the Communist conspiracy and their intent to 'bury us'."[201] Easily identifiable in their black robes, the justices were prime targets for Wallace's denunciations as the branch of government subject to the least popular control.[202] Citing decisions on civil rights, law and order, and religion, Wallace contended that the Court was bent on upending democratic rule:

---

[199] Dan T. Carter, *The Politics of Rage: George Wallace, the Origins of the New Conservatism, and the Transformation of American Politics* (Baton Rouge: Louisiana State University Press, 2000), pp. 345–6.

[200] Michael J. Lee, "The Populist Chameleon: The People's Party, Huey Long, George Wallace, and the Populist Argumentative Frame." *Quarterly Journal of Speech* 92, no. 4 (2006): 372.

[201] George Wallace, "The Civil Rights Movement: Fraud, sham, and hoax." Address, July 4, 1964. http://www.blackpast.org/1964-george-c-wallace-civil-rights-movement-fraud-sham-and-hoax

[202] Lloyd Rohler, "Conservative Appeals to the People: George Wallace's Populist Rhetoric." *Southern Communication Journal* 64, no. 4 (1999): 318.

they don't like our form of government. They think they can establish a better one. In order to do so it is necessary that they overthrow
our existing form, destroy the democratic institutions created by the
people, change the outlook, religion, and philosophy, and bring the
whole area of human thought, aspiration, action and organization,
under the absolute control of the court.[203]

Wallace also believed that the 1972 assassination attempt on
him at a Laurel, Maryland rally was the product of some type of
conspiracy. Although he publicly ruled out the idea that President Nixon was directly responsible, Wallace questioned how the
would-be assassin, Arthur Bremer, availed himself of the money,
resources, and intelligence necessary to firing off the bullets that
left him in a wheelchair permanently.[204] He ultimately came to
believe that perhaps one of Nixon's aides was culpable, a speculation taken up by authors such as Richard Sprague, who maintained that Bremer, a busboy from Milwaukee, was a pawn in an
elaborate, clandestine operation headed by a Central Intelligence
Agency (CIA) operative under the direction of G. Gordon Liddy.[205]
Adding fuel to such speculation was Gore Vidal's suggestion that
E. Howard Hunt, an advisor in Nixon's White House, might have
penned Bremer's disjointed memoir, *An Assassin's Diary*, in order
to cover up such a plot against Wallace spearheaded by the president's "Plumbers."[206] Such conjectures resurfaced upon Bremer's
release from prison in 2007 after serving a forty-year sentence for
attempted murder, despite the former convict's refusal to discuss
the events four decades ago.[207]

---

[203] Wallace, Address, July 4, 1964. http://www.blackpast.org/1964-george-c-
wallace-civil-rights-movement-fraud-sham-and-hoax

[204] "George Wallace suggests shooter was part of a conspiracy." YouTube, published
February 15, 2015. https://www.youtube.com/watch?v=FAxB9WYJN_Q

[205] Richard E. Sprague, *The Taking of America, 1-2-3* (self-published, 1976).
http://www.denkmalnach.org/download/ToA.pdf

[206] Gore Vidal, "The art and arts of E. Howard Hunt." *The New York Review*,
December 13, 1973. Available from the Harold Weisberg Archive, Hood Col-
lege at http://jfk.hood.edu/Collection/Weisberg%20Subject%20Index%20
Files/V%20Disk/Vidal%20Gore/Item%2001.pdf

[207] Joel McNally, "Release of Wallace shooter rekindles conspiracy talk." *The
Capital Times* (Madison, WI), September 1, 2007, p. A8.

H. Ross Perot's United We Stand presidential campaign in 1992 was steeped in even more lavish intrigue and conspiracy theory drama. Perot, writes Michael Kelly, did not discriminate on the left or right of the political spectrum with his embrace of conspiracies from "secret global cabals, to Byzantine tales of vast criminal enterprises undertaken with secret Government approval, to talk of organized evil that stretches across continents and over decades, or even centuries."[208] The implausibility of the snappish Texan's vividly imaginative and fanciful accounts of history prompted many newspapers to portray his condition as "Perot-noia."[209]

Some of Perot's far-fetched claims of scheming derived from his interest in locating and freeing prisoners of war (POWs) who had gone missing in action (MIA) during the Vietnam War. He contended that the CIA had used covert operations in Laos in the 1970s as shields for heroin trafficking by groups with which the U.S. government had allied, and then-CIA director George H. W. Bush—against whom he was running on the GOP side of the aisle in 1992—had failed to take action when the Vietnam War ended in 1975.[210] Perot, who believed in the 1980s that the CIA might "ghost" him if he continued to pursue the release of POWs, became furious with Bush (then-vice president) and the Reagan White House when he was spurned in his efforts to chair a committee on the matter. The problem, as Bob Woodward and John Mintz affirm, is that

> a number of government officials who have dealt with Perot on the MIA issue have found him unwilling to accept any report or evidence that undermines his belief that U.S. servicemen are alive in Southeast Asia. "He becomes a repository for all the crazy theories,"

---

[208] Michael Kelly, "The 1992 Campaign: Candidate's record; Perot shows penchant for seeing conspiracy." *New York Times*, October 26, 1992. https://www.nytimes.com/1992/10/26/us/the-1992-campaign-candidate-s-record-perot-shows-penchant-for-seeing-conspiracy.html

[209] "Perot-noia." *St. Petersburg Times*, October 27, 1992, p. 8A.

[210] B. Duffy, "Perot points the finger at the CIA." *Sunday Herald Sun* (Melbourne, Australia), May 31, 1992.

said one former National Security Council official who worked with Perot on the issue.[211]

Perot's wrath was manifest in his subsequent investigations of Bush and his extended family, on which he spent tens of thousands of his funds in an attempt to uncover financial scandal, corruption, and a linkage between Vice President Bush and the Iran–Contra affair that never emerged. President Bush, seeking re-election in 1992, called the investigations not very "American" and his press secretary, Marlin Fitzwater, said of Perot's investigative crusade, which included the president's children, "I think it's shocking and frightening to see that kind of bizarre behavior on the part of a presidential candidate."[212]

Perot was particularly predisposed to believe that conspirators were actively attempting to assassinate him. In the third presidential debate in October 1992, he recounted how he had survived several purported attempts on his life, the motives of which hinged on his commitment to public service:

> When I was asked by our Government to do the P.O.W. project, within the year the Vietnamese had sent people into Canada to make arrangements to have me and my family killed—and I had five small children—and my family and I decided we would stay the course. And we lived with that problem for three years. Then I got into the Texans' War on Drug program and big-time drug dealers got all upset.[213]

Perot alleged that the Vietnamese had hired members of the Black Panthers to assassinate him, and his dog had bit one of the five intruders on his lawn in Dallas, Texas in 1969. But the

---

[211] Bob Woodward and John Mintz, "Perot launched investigations of Bush; billionaire considered then-vice president, weak, indecisive and possibly corrupt." *Washington Post*, June 21, 1992, p. A1.

[212] Ann Devroy, "Perot investigations not very 'American,' Bush says." *Washington Post*, June 23, 1991, p. A12.

[213] "The 1992 Campaign; Transcript of 3d TV debate between Bush, Clinton and Perot." *New York Times*, October 20, 1992. https://www.nytimes.com/1992/10/20/us/the-1992-campaign-transcript-of-3d-tv-debate-between-bush-clinton-and-perot.html

incident was never reported to local authorities or the FBI. Paul McCaghren, head of Dallas police intelligence, bluntly said "it did not happen."[214] Police also confirmed that there was no credible evidence of the Texas drug dealer allegation or other plots.[215] But Perot persisted in such fabrications. He even suggested just prior to his 1993 televised debate with Vice President Al Gore on the North American Free Trade Agreement (NAFTA) that Cubans, hired by Mexicans, had planned to kill him for his opposition to the accord. Perot explained that the assassination "would take place in Tampa or at the debate in Washington . . . The organization is a Mafia-like group in favor of the North American Free Trade Agreement."[216] Fortunately, the debate occurred without incident—other than Perot's obvious frustration with Gore's elegantly erudite presentation of facts that left the Texan's visage red with anger on CNN.

Perot lodged frequent, unsubstantiated allegations that the Republican Party and George H. W. Bush were "out to get" him and his family during the 1992 presidential campaign. At one point, Perot believed that his office phones were being wiretapped by Bush's campaign. For the vice president's part, his campaign staffers suggested someone had contacted them with an offer to provide damaging information on Perot, which they categorically rebuffed.[217] Perot nevertheless continued publicly with a narrative that the Opposition Research Unit of the Republican National Committee, under the direction of Bush, was a dirty-tricks operation focused on smearing him.[218] In fact, Perot quit

[214] *Chicago Tribune*, "Perot has charged plotting before; proof lacking." October 26, 1992. http://www.chicagotribune.com/news/ct-xpm-1992-10-26-9204070126-story.html

[215] Rupert Cornwell, "Perot's dirty tricks paranoia rekindles doubts." *Ottawa Citizen*, October 27, 1992, p. A3.

[216] Michael Isikoff, "Perot tells large rally of death threat; 'mafia-like' group backing NAFTA cited." *Washington Post*, November 8, 1993, p. A4.

[217] Michael Isikoff, "FBI investigates alleged wiretapping, attempted sale of Perot phone tapes." *Washington Post*, August 14, 1992, p. A20.

[218] Mary McGrory, "Ross Perot: folksy and frightening." *St. Petersburg Times*, June 29, 1992, p. A7.

his campaign in July after he claimed that he had received numerous reports that the GOP planned to publish altered photographs of his daughter Carolyn, along with claims she was a lesbian, in order to disrupt her wedding the following month.[219] Perot had previously stated that he suspended his campaign because rival Bill Clinton's support had become "revitalized." Appearing to be magnanimous, Perot charged that support for him would precipitate a crisis if the presidential election were to be decided in the House of Representatives.[220]

Perot's allegations against Bush were as baseless as those regarding assassination plots. As he noted in a *60 Minutes* interview on the Columbia Broadcasting System (CBS), the wily Texan said "I can't prove any of it today."[221] Perot's ire at those in the media who questioned his lack of evidence was routinely on display during his helter-skelter campaign. Just prior to Election Day, he told reporters "I am sick and tired of you all questioning my integrity without a basis for it."[222] The FBI never uncovered any evidence that Bush had been responsible for any dirty-tricks operations against Perot. Ironically, Scott Barnes, a Perot supporter, contended that he and a producer for the British Broadcasting Corporation (BBC) had inadvertently convinced the business tycoon of such a conspiracy in a deceitful bid to embarrass Bush. Perot was a true believer.

Donald Trump's belief in widespread conspiracies rivals the fantastic yarns spun by Perot, notwithstanding claims of assassins lurking in the shadows. As elaborated in the next chapter, Trump

---

[219] Norma Greenway, "Perot's conspiracy allegations just raving of paranoid, Bush camp says." *Montreal Gazette*, October 27, 1992, p. A15.

[220] Ben Smith III, "Perot drops out; he asserts election in House 'would be disruptive' to the country, cites 'revitalized' Democratic Party; says he realized it wasn't possible to win three-way presidential race." *Atlanta Journal and Constitution*, July 16, 1992, p. A1.

[221] Richard L. Burke, "The 1992 campaign: The overview; Perot says he quit in July to thwart G.O.P. 'dirty tricks'." *New York Times*, October 26, 1992. https://www.nytimes.com/1992/10/26/us/1992-campaign-overview-perot-says-he-quit-july-thwart-gop-dirty-tricks.html

[222] Quoted in Evan Ramstad, Associated Press, "Perot not new to cries of conspiracy." *Kitsap Sun* (WA), October 28, 1992. https://products.kitsapsun.com/archive/1992/10-28/249220_perot_not_new_to_cries_of_consp.html

gained significant traction in his first flirtation with a White House bid in 2012 by raising the unsubstantiated accusation that President Barack Obama was not born in the United States. Trump rode an ephemeral wave of popular support in some GOP circles in 2011 with the notion that Obama was somehow a Manchurian candidate straight out of a plot from Richard Condon's 1959 conspiracy novel. Indeed, a PPP poll in 2011 showed that 23 percent of Republican voters "say they would not be willing to vote for a candidate who stated clearly that Obama was born in the U.S." and Trump's support among those subscribing to the birther conjecture was at one point three times more than other GOP candidates who had thrown their hats in the ring.[223] In 2016 Trump ultimately, if reluctantly, accepted that Obama was born in the United States after he produced a birth certificate from Hawaii, but then shifted blame to the Hillary Clinton campaign for stirring the controversy originally.[224] Many view Trump's shenanigans as tinged with the coded language of racism.[225]

As president, Trump is beyond compare to any of his predecessors in the White House with respect to the overlay of conspiracy theories articulated to explain his travails, rally his supporters, or rebuff criticism. In 2016,

> Trump's campaign turned the conspiratorial mind-set into something like a governing philosophy. It posited suspicion of outsiders, accusations of elite interference in his affairs, and deliberate campaigns of misinformation by his opponents as the rationale for his own candidacy.[226]

---

[223] See Tom Monkovic, "Donald Trump and conspiracy theories: A signal from 2012." *New York Times*, May 18, 2016. https://www.nytimes.com/2016/05/19/upshot/donald-trump-and-conspiracy-theories-what-a-poll-in-2011-signaled.html

[224] Maggie Haberman and Alan Rappeport, "Trump drops false 'birther' claim but offers new one: Clinton started it." *New York Times*, September 17, 2016, p. A10.

[225] Brad Knickerbocker, "Are Donald Trump and his fellow 'birthers' racist?" *Christian Science Monitor*, April 30, 2011. https://www.csmonitor.com/USA/Politics/2011/0430/Are-Donald-Trump-and-his-fellow-birthers-racist

[226] David Runciman, "The plots against America." *Chronicle of Higher Education*, January 15, 2017.

Subsequent chapters explore such implications including Trump's campaign for the Oval Office and his unswerving attacks on the "fake news" media and belief in "deep state" actors in the Department of Justice, FBI, and State Department that are putatively determined to remove him from office.

Conspiracy theory during Donald Trump's presidency has arguably become an artifact of political life in the United States, and both the president and his detractors bear responsibility. But as Professor Paul Musgrave posited, Trump and his contributions to the contemporary political culture have rendered conspiracy thinking mainstream. The normative quandary is that "[c]onspiracy theories, rumor and outright lies now drive the news cycle . . . In the long term, the damage done to trust by the normalization of untruth may threaten the social contract on which democracy itself rests."[227] It remains a curious dynamic that populism of the past and present is rooted in a "style of mind, not always right-wing in its affiliations, that has a long and varied history" and that Richard Hofstadter described as the "paranoid style simply because no other word adequately evokes the qualities of heated exaggeration, suspiciousness, and conspiratorial fantasy."[228] The question for Trump's legacy is the degree to which the line between irrational suspicion and legitimate mistrust has been breached in an irreversible way.[229]

F. Nostalgia for the past, nativism, and nationalism

Finally, the fifth conceptual commonality in Figure 2.1 is the populist nostalgia for the past. The yearning to return to a romanticized place in time can assume numerous forms and the

---

[227] Paul Musgrave, "Democracy requires trust. But Trump is making us all into conspiracy theorists." *Washington Post*, March 7, 2017. https://www.washingtonpost.com/posteverything/wp/2017/03/07/democracy-requires-trust-but-trump-is-making-us-all-into-conspiracy-theorists/?utm_term=.7829b95f127a

[228] Scott Horton, "The paranoid style in American politics." *Harper's*, February 28, 2019. https://harpers.org/blog/2007/08/the-paranoid-style-in-american-politics/

[229] Ibid.

implications are far-ranging, from domestic to foreign affairs. Like a page out of Marcel Proust's oeuvre *À la recherche du temps perdu*, populists have a tendency to idealize recapturing a simpler time associated with America's formative years or periods of pre-eminence, all rooted in an allegedly more virtuous epoch—while often overlooking or dismissing the hardships endured by many. Populists, George Packer writes, are "people with a sense of violated ownership, holding a vision of an earlier, better America that has come under threat."[230] William Jennings Bryan, for example, waxed lyrical about the agricultural life as pure and wholesome, which set him against progressives focused on issues surrounding urbanization.[231] Donald Trump, on the other hand, sentimentalizes America's eras of industrial prowess and economic growth. Hearkening back to the splendor of the nineteenth century, the president noted that "[t]he industrial revolution was certainly in terms of economically [*sic*]—that was when we started to grow." Moreover, he reminisced that he "liked the Ronald Reagan years. I thought the country had a wonderful, strong image."[232] In Trump's case, there is no consideration of progressives' struggle against child labor or monopolies in the early twentieth century, or the socio-economic pain associated with Reagan's austerity that brought about the 1981–2 recession.

Religiosity may infuse populist messaging by portraying an idyllic vision of the future based on moral values and the glory days of the past. Here again, William Jennings Bryan combined a form of economic populism with traditional religious values in his unique style. Yet the darker side of populists' nostalgia may include a retreat into sectarianism and the fostering of a

---

[230] George Packer, "The populists." *The New Yorker*, September 7, 2015. https://www.newyorker.com/magazine/2015/09/07/the-populists

[231] Paul W. Glad, "Bryan and the Progressives." In Paul W. Glad (ed.), *William Jennings Bryan: A Profile* (New York: Hill and Wang, 1968), p. 111.

[232] Quoted in Chris Hubbuch, "Donald Trump: 'Temperament is one of my greatest assets'." *LaCrosse Tribune*, August 16, 2016. https://lacrossetribune.com/community/vernonbroadcaster/news/local/donald-trump-temperament-is-one-of-my-greatest-assets/article_0d8deb40-48b9-5777-bcb2-739036d76fb9.html

nativism that targets certain races or ethnicities. As one example, the Know-Nothings of the 1850s embraced conspiracy theory to argue that a Catholic plot against Protestants in America was under way. According to the Know-Nothings (and the American Party as it was known by 1855), the Papist scheme to subvert American democracy, emanating from Europe, was clearly visible in the mass Irish and German immigration that was a threat to socio-cultural norms. The strength of anti-Catholic hysteria often eclipsed even the slavery issue prior to the election of 1860.[233] As another example, Father Charles Coughlin, a critic of Franklin Roosevelt during the Great Depression, amalgamated anti-capitalist, social justice perspectives based on elements of Catholic doctrine with pro-fascist, anti-internationalist, and anti-Semitic stances in advance of World War II to articulate a largely incoherent populist message heard nationwide via radio until he was shut down.[234]

The messaging of Barry Goldwater, George Wallace, and Donald Trump represents rather interesting cases of comparison and contrast on the question of race, nativism, and nationalism. While racism clearly guided Wallace's messaging, Goldwater and Trump have been fairly or unfairly associated with white nationalism. Goldwater's crusade against the Civil Rights Act of 1964 has had a lasting impact on blacks' generally negative views of Republicans, populist or otherwise. As Michael Gerson notes, Goldwater "had been a founding member of the Arizona NAACP. He helped integrate the Phoenix public schools. His problems with the Civil Rights Act were theoretical and libertarian—an objection to the extension of federal power over private enterprise."[235] Nonetheless, upon Goldwater's nomination, Rev. Martin Luther King asserted that "[w]hile not himself a

---

[233] See Michael F. Holt, "The Politics of Impatience: The Origins of Know-Nothingism." *Journal of American History* 6, no. 2 (1973): 309–31.

[234] See Kazin, *The Populist Persuasion*, ch. 5.

[235] Michael Gerson, "Barry Goldwater's warning to the GOP." *Washington Post*, April 17, 2014. https://www.washingtonpost.com/opinions/michael-gerson-barry-goldwaters-warning-to-the-gop/2014/04/17/9e8993ec-c651-11e3-bf7a-be01a9b69cf1_story.html?utm_term=.5de85e577c5a

racist, Mr. Goldwater articulates a philosophy which gives aid and comfort to the racists."[236] The empirical proof was both the Ku Klux Klan's (KKK) open backing of Goldwater and his electoral victories in five states of the South amidst the turmoil of the Civil Rights Movement. His elegant libertarian arguments on the dangers of the excesses of federal power fell short of convincing many that segregation could be eradicated voluntarily and without governmental intervention.

It is understandable why some view a linkage between the populist messaging of Wallace and Trump. Is it merely coincidence that the campaign slogans "Stand Up for America" in 1968 and "Make America Great Again" in 2016 appear so similar? Does Trump share the same idealized view of "white" America as Wallace did? As Michael Lind suggests,

> Wallace was an outspoken white supremacist, while Trump tends to speak in a kind of code, starting with his "birther" campaign against President Obama, and his criticism of illegal immigrants and proposed ban on Muslims may appeal to fringe white nationalists even if it has offended many if not most Latinos.[237]

Many critics identify Trump's descriptions of Mexican illegals as "bad hombres" and rapists, his comment that the United States should have more immigrants from Norway than from "shithole countries" like Haiti and El Salvador, and his reproach of African American athletes in the NFL with the racism and fearmongering of George Wallace five decades earlier. Moreover, the optics of Trump's reaction to the unsolicited endorsement by KKK grand wizard David Duke raised serious questions about the president's understanding of, or sensitivities to, issues of race.

---

[236] Quoted in Zeba Blay, "This MLK quote sums up the rise of white supremacy post-Trump." *Huffington Post*, January 15, 2017. https://www.huffington-post.com/entry/this-mlk-quote-sums-up-the-rise-of-white-supremacy-post-trump_us_5875426de4b099cdb1000431

[237] Michael Lind, "Donald Trump, the perfect populist." *Politico Magazine*, March 9, 2016. https://www.politico.com/magazine/story/2016/03/donald-trump-the-perfect-populist-213697

Trump stumbled in his initial response to the endorsement, suggesting that he did not know who Duke was and blaming a bad earpiece for his answer to a CNN journalist on the question.[238] Three days later the president, on MSNBC's *Morning Joe*, clarified his opinion that

> David Duke is a bad person, who [*sic*] I disavowed on numerous occasions over the years . . . I disavowed him. I disavowed the KKK . . . Do you want me to do it again for the 12th time? I disavowed him in the past, I disavow him now.[239]

The disavowal was too little, too late for Trump's critics, who found it difficult to square with perceived *sous-entendus* of racism in his campaign and beyond. Using the president's overtures to grassroots evangelical groups about restoring Judeo-Christian values as the basis for his backing, Duke claimed that

> [w]hile Trump wants to make America great again, we have to ask ourselves, "What made America great in the first place?" The short answer to that is simple. America was great not because of what our forefathers did—but because of who our forefathers were. America was founded as a White Christian Republic. And as a White Christian Republic it became great.[240]

Trump's clumsy error in judgment—unless it is something more sinister as his critics suggest—is reminiscent of another populist's blunder a quarter-century earlier. Ross Perot's appearance before the National Association for the Advancement of

---

[238] Eric Bradner, "Trump stumbles on David Duke, KKK." *CNN Politics*, February 29, 2016. https://www.cnn.com/2016/02/28/politics/donald-trump-white-supremacists/index.html

[239] Quoted in Eugene Scott, "Trump denounces Duke, KKK." *CNN Politics*, March 3, 2016. https://www.cnn.com/2016/03/03/politics/donald-trump-disavows-david-duke-kkk/index.html

[240] Quoted in Peter Holley, "KKK's official newspaper supports Donald Trump for president." *Washington Post*, November 2, 2016. https://www.washington-post.com/news/post-politics/wp/2016/11/01/the-kkks-official-newspaper-has-endorsed-donald-trump-for-president/?utm_term=.3a55ea1a6e18

Colored Persons (NAACP) in Nashville in 1992 raised the similar specter of racism at worst, insensitivity at best. While calling for voting rights in the District of Columbia and economic development, Perot referred to crime and other social problems in the black community by using the phrase "you people" in front of the African American audience of prominent leaders. Some immediately interpreted the comments as pejorative and patronizing, including one attendee who asserted that

> [w]hen he said "you people" or "your people," it was like waving a red flag in front of a bull. It's something white folks have used when they don't want to call you nigger, but they don't want to treat you like an equal.[241]

As the *New York Times* noted, Perot "further jolted his listeners by preaching about how his mother fed black hobos during the Depression, and how kindly his cotton-broker father treated the blacks who worked for him. That's volatile stuff, awkwardly handled."[242] Perot's generally evasive answers on affirmative action and civil rights legislation, and the defensiveness he displayed, did not make him a racist. Rather, it reflected an essential problem he shared with Trump's uneven handling of attempts at outreach to African Americans: the degree to which he underestimated the racial divide in America.[243]

Trump's refusal to dismiss Duke immediately for the racism he propounds must be understood within the context of other controversies that have led critics to question his commitment to civil rights. In the clash between protestors and white supremacists

---

[241] Will Clark, president of the San Bernardino, California NAACP, quoted in Peter Applebome, "THE 1992 Campaign: Racial politics; Perot speech gets cool reception at N.A.A.C.P." *New York Times*, July 12, 1992. https://www.nytimes.com/1992/07/12/us/the-1992-campaign-racial-politics-perot-speech-gets-cool-reception-at-naacp.html

[242] *New York Times*, "Ross Perot's 'People'." July 14, 1992. https://www.nytimes.com/1992/07/14/opinion/ross-perot-s-people.html

[243] See Clarence Page, "'You people' gaffe shows Perot the perils of populism." *Chicago Tribune*, July 15, 1992. http://www.chicagotribune.com/news/ct-xpm-1992-07-15-9203030818-story.html

in Charlottesville, Virginia opposed to the removal of a statue of Confederate General Robert E. Lee, Trump appeared to sympathize with white nationalists, asserting that there were "some fine people on both sides" and indicting the "alt-left" protestors for inciting violence.[244] Moreover, his denunciation of black NFL players' protests and refusal to stand for the national anthem, as detailed in Chapter 6, exacerbated the view of coded messages aimed at white Americans. It may well be that contemporary populists' inability to connect with minorities is a product of their narrow, nativist-oriented messaging aimed at "ordinary" people that excludes a community that has had a very different collective experience historically, and for which the narrative of returning to a glorious past ignores the ugly legacy of slavery and its consequences.

Still, tying Trump's contradictory comments on race to the legacy of George Wallace remains a stretch, however confusing the president's positions appear. Wallace's "opposition to federal power," Richard Lowry asserts, "was clearly driven by his hatred of civil-rights legislation"[245] and opposition to federal power. By contrast, Trump is *not* a segregationist, made overt efforts to reach out to African American voters in the 2016 election by indicting Democrats' lack of success in advancing black economic progress (i.e., "What do you have to lose?"), and dismisses arguments about "states' rights," at least vis-à-vis so-called sanctuary cities that seek to protect illegal immigrants from federal enforcement policies. On civil rights, Trump made a pilgrimage to the opening of the new Civil Rights Museum in Jackson, Mississippi in December 2017, despite calls by some African Americans for him to steer clear of the event. In his prepared remarks, Trump said:

> The civil rights museum records oppression, cruelty and injustice inflicted on the African-American community . . . The fight to end

[244] Rosie Gray, "Trump defends white-nationalist protesters: 'Some very fine people on both sides'." *The Atlantic*, August 14, 2017. https://www.theatlantic.com/politics/archive/2017/08/trump-defends-white-nationalist-protesters-some-very-fine-people-on-both-sides/537012/
[245] Lowry, "Their George Wallace and ours," p. 18.

slavery, to break down Jim Crow, to end segregation, to gain the right to vote, and to achieve the sacred birthright of equality—that's big stuff. Those are very big phrases, very big words.[246]

Such words certainly would never have been uttered by Wallace—at least until after his Christian "conversion" following his assassination attempt.

Finally, nativism and nationalism have been part and parcel of populists' rhetoric in the realm of foreign affairs. For Goldwater, Wallace, and Trump there is an inexorable, internal tension in the search for a relative balance between isolationism and exercise of American might expressed by casting aspersions on elites for alleged failures. As Hofstadter explains:

> The circumstances of our historical development have encouraged a complex which D. W. Brogan once called "the illusion of American omnipotence"—the notion that we are all-powerful in the world, and that failure to achieve our ends arises only from unforgivable weakness of will or from treason in high places.[247]

Contemporary populists on the right have hearkened back to George Washington's admonishment to avoid foreign entanglements, have advocated quick and decisive victory when conflict is necessary, have emphasized the squandering of foreign aid to unfriendly countries, and have complained that foreign powers take advantage of the United States. These are the leitmotifs of the populist nationalism in foreign affairs. As Jesse Walker suggests, a Wallace speech on the Vietnam War sums up the core themes, and could just have easily come from the lips of Goldwater or Trump:

> There's the declaration that he wouldn't have gotten us into this mess in the first place. There's the focus on foreign aid, and there's

---

[246] Quoted in Michael D. Shear and Ellen Ann Fentress, "Trump, rejecting calls to stay away, speaks at civil rights museum." *New York Times*, December 9, 2017. https://www.nytimes.com/2017/12/09/us/politics/trump-mississippi-civil-rights-museum.html

[247] Richard Hofstadter, "A long view: Goldwater in history." *New York Review of Books*, October 8, 1964. https://www.nybooks.com/articles/1964/10/08/a-long-view-goldwater-in-history/

the idea that the U.S. is being ripped off by its alleged allies. There's the hand-waving promise to consult the best experts. There's the double reference to flexing Washington's military muscle ("make full use of the country's conventional weapons") and achieving peace ("to quickly end this war and bring our boys home"). And of course, there's the disdain for radical protesters. There were reasons here to believe the speaker might be more dovish in practice than his internationalist opponents, and there were reasons not to be sure. It wasn't a speech for doves, and it wasn't a speech for global crusaders either. It was a speech for nationalists.[248]

For populist nationalists notions of the limited exercise of power on the world stage are difficult to accept and victory is the only option. Goldwater's and Wallace's (most particularly his running-mate Curtis Lemay's) advocacy of overwhelming force and potentially the use of nuclear weapons to halt the Vietnam War quickly are matched by Trump's condemnation of the Obama administration's limited air strikes on Libya and by his decisive action against the Assad regime in Syria in 2017 for the use of chemical weapons on the civilian population. Yet it is difficult to square Trump's opposition to the war in Iraq, strong sanctions on Iran, and defense of "enhanced interrogation" of terror suspects with his admiration for Russian President Vladimir Putin while censuring NATO allies for not paying their "fair share" for collective defense arrangements.

Regardless, the thread that ties Trump to Wallace and Goldwater, in particular, is the approach to conflict resolution:

> You try to stay out, but if provoked, you go in with maximum force and kill everything in sight. Then you go home. It's a way of looking at the world that's just as intrinsic to white working-class Americans as hostility to minority-group "takers" or hypocritical and supercilious elites.[249]

---

[248] Jesse Walker, quoted in Ed Kilgore, "Trump and the George Wallace tradition of foreign policy." *New York Magazine*, August 30, 2016. http://nymag.com/daily/intelligencer/2016/08/trump-and-the-george-wallace-tradition-of-foreign-policy.html

[249] Kilgore, "Trump and the George Wallace tradition of foreign policy."

If there is no unifying ideological or philosophical basis to Trump's positions, "his mix of militaristic and anti-interventionist opinions is as good a demonstration as you can find of the ways nationalism can be pulled in different directions."[250]

Recriminations of elites' profligate squandering of taxpayer money on foreign aid are another populist linkage. Although foreign aid represents 1 percent or less of the federal budget historically, populists have seized on the public's perennially incorrect belief that a quarter or more of the budget is directed abroad. As one example, a 2015 survey by the Kaiser Family Foundation discovered that the average respondent believed that 28 percent of the budget was spent on foreign aid.[251] Capitalizing on this erroneous impression, Goldwater, Wallace, and Trump all called into question the degree to which foreign aid bolsters U.S. adversaries. As Harry Stein notes, "[t]he Goldwater movement represents a mass protest by conservative minded people against foreign aid" in addition to "excessive welfare, high taxes, foreign policy and the concentration of power in the federal government."[252] During his ten years in the Senate Goldwater never backed one final foreign aid authorization or appropriations bill.[253] For his part, Wallace called for "[t]he discontinuance of foreign aid programs except where determined to be in our national interest. No foreign aid to Communist countries or those countries who aid Communists."[254] One Wallace campaign ad in 1968 featured a

---

[250] Jesse Walker, "One candidate had a foreign policy that anticipated Trump." *Reason*, August 30, 2016. https://reason.com/blog/2016/08/30/trump-wallace-foreign-policy

[251] Poncie Rutsch, "Guess how much of Uncle Sam's money goes to foreign aid. Guess again!" *National Public Radio*, February 10, 2015. https://www.npr.org/sections/goatsandsoda/2015/02/10/383875581/guess-how-much-of-uncle-sams-money-goes-to-foreign-aid-guess-again

[252] Harry Stein, "The Goldwater takedown." *City Journal* (Autumn 2016). https://www.city-journal.org/html/goldwater-takedown-14787.html

[253] Ben W. Heineman, Jr., "Goldwater: The record." *Harvard Crimson*, October 9, 1963. https://www.thecrimson.com/article/1963/10/9/goldwater-the-record-pbarry-goldwater-is/

[254] George Wallace for President 1976 Campaign Brochure, "George C. Wallace has the courage America needs now." http://www.4president.org/brochures/1976/wallace1976brochure.htm

large cargo ship headed out to sea, while the narrator declared: "Watch your hard-earned tax dollars sail away to anti-American countries." Wallace picks up the narration, affirming that "[a]s president, I will halt the giveaway of your American dollars and products to those nations that aid our enemies."[255]

Reproach of foreign aid and unfair trade animates Trump's "America First" doctrine, with similar refrains to those of Goldwater and Wallace as a means of tapping grassroots political support. In his 2018 State of the Union Address, the president indicted countries that voted in favor of a United Nations (UN) resolution opposing his plan to move the U.S. embassy in Israel from Tel Aviv to Jerusalem. Trump opined that

> In 2016, American taxpayers generously sent those same countries more than $20 billion in aid. That is why, tonight, I am asking Congress to pass legislation to help ensure American foreign assistance dollars always serve American interests and only go to friends of America, not enemies of America.[256]

The president doubled down on his antipathy to sending aid to perceived adversaries in his September 2018 speech before the UN General Assembly, maintaining that, "[m]oving forward, we are only going to give foreign aid to those who respect us and, frankly, are our friends. And we expect other countries to pay their fair share for the cost of their defense."[257] On foreign trade, the president similarly complains incessantly about unfair treatment by other countries—and has taken steadfast aim at traditional allies. In June 2018 Trump accused the G7 of imposing "massive" tariffs on American products and unfair practices leveled

[255] 1968 Wallace Campaign advertisement. https://www.youtube.com/watch?v=4RZ4G251WR4

[256] "President Donald J. Trump's State of the Union Address," January 30, 2018. https://www.whitehouse.gov/briefings-statements/president-donald-j-trumps-state-union-address/

[257] "Remarks by President Trump to the 73rd Session of the United Nations General Assembly," New York, September 25, 2018. https://www.whitehouse.gov/briefings-statements/remarks-president-trump-73rd-session-united-nations-general-assembly-new-york-ny/

at farmers.[258] Negotiating more equitable trade deals, chastising trade partners, and blaming former presidential administrations for putatively conceding American economic interests to foreign governments transforms trade, like aid, into an identity issue in the populist messaging frame. As Danielle Kurtzleben posits,

> That doesn't mean it's overtly a race or gender issue, as the phrase "identity politics" tends to evoke—rather, it taps into a specific idea of what it means to be American. That identity is loaded with nostalgia and emotion, which together have been at the core of Trump's message since Day 1 and appealed to millions of white, working-class voters who supported his campaign.[259]

G. Reprise

Trump's linkages to his populist predecessors are evident on the five conceptual commonalities elaborated in this review. Indeed, what is most striking is the degree to which Trump's populist style integrates each of the five commonalities, while his predecessors borrowed variably from the traits. Still, the fundamental connection between Trump and his populist inspirations of yesteryear redounds to what Michael Kazin asserts is the

> most basic and telling definition of populism: a language whose speakers conceive of ordinary people as a noble assemblage not bounded narrowly by class, view their elite opponents as self-serving and undemocratic, and seek to mobilize the former against the latter.[260]

The emphases on ordinary folks, majoritarian instincts, conspiracy theory, and nostalgia for the past are common features in the

[258] Delphine Strauss, "Economists reject Trump claims of unfair trade system." *Financial Times*, June 18, 2018. https://www.ft.com/content/2edf26f8-6b28-11e8-b6eb-4acfcfb08c11

[259] Danielle Kurtzleben, "Trade is an identity issue, and Trump knows it." *NPR*, March 10, 2018. https://www.npr.org/2018/03/10/592450875/trade-is-an-identity-issue-and-trump-knows-it

[260] Kazin, *The Populist Persuasion*, p. 1.

argumentative frames and expressions of the populist ethos in the American experience. As the preceding narrative underlines, the implications are far-reaching, from internal party dissension, a rejection of the Madisonian precepts of institutional balance and minority protections, the delegitimization of formal and informal institutions, and the blending of artful anti-intellectual narratives with the search for a return to an idealized, glorious past to which many minorities take exception.

It is important to accentuate, at least briefly, other symbolic connections and contradictions in the populist character. It is difficult to square, for example, the paradox of rich business tycoons like Trump and Perot taking up the mantle of the average, working-class American with hyperbole against establishment politicians, who otherwise facilitated their corporate success in real estate and information technology, respectively. Similarly, although Trump and Goldwater both took aim at the media and expressed controversial policy stances adjudged by the dominant Republican political class as extreme, Goldwater's lifelong crusade for a particular form of principled conservatism stands in stark contrast to Trump's chameleonic political maturation elucidated in the next chapter. Finally, apart from his rabble-rousing oratory and biting critiques of elites, Trump's nexus to William Jennings Bryan is tenuous, notwithstanding Steve Bannon's arguments to the contrary.[261] Bryan was a transformative figure within the Democratic Party who had a substantive grasp of economic issues, supported labor unions and progressive taxation, held deep religious convictions, and carefully cultivated relations with the press in his crusade against the gold standard in the 1896 election.[262]

Yet it is scarcely coincidental that Trump has shown great reverence and affection for Andrew Jackson, the last successful populist presidential candidate, albeit nearly two centuries ago.

---

[261] *The Economist*, "The big switchover—William Jennings Trump and the monetary elite," February 27, 2017.

[262] Michael Kazin, "Donald Trump is no William Jennings Bryan." *Politico*, February 27, 2017. https://www.politico.com/magazine/story/2017/02/william-jennings-bryan-steve-bannon-donald-trump-populist-214822

As Douglas Brinkley notes, "it's a conscious move for Trump to embrace Jackson. In American political lore, Jackson represents the forgotten rural America while Trump won by bringing out that rural vote and the blue collar vote."[263] The 45th president made a pilgrimage to the Hermitage in Tennessee just two months into his term, laid a wreath upon Jackson's grave, and called him "a people's president."[264] He hung a portrait of Jackson conspicuously in the Oval Office to encourage comparisons to the nation's embattled seventh president, suggesting the degree to which he "has embraced the idea that he's a modern-day Old Hickory, a populist outsider and scourge of Washington elites."[265]

Trump's comparisons of himself to Jackson as a man of action wittingly or unwittingly disregard the Tennessean's personal history as a slave owner, his penchant for violence in solving disputes, and his brutal treatment of Indigenous peoples. The specter of anti-intellectualism merges with nativist sentimentalization of the past in Trump's appropriation of Jackson's heritage. As historian H. Lee Cheek avers, Trump "has no knowledge of the misdeeds of Jackson that are central to a complete understanding of his political career."[266] Perhaps most strikingly, Trump has eagerly drawn upon the imagery of the Hero of New Orleans' anti-Native American legacy to denigrate one of his most dogged political foes, Democratic Senator Elizabeth Warren of Massachusetts (whom he mockingly calls "Pocahontas" for her claims of Cherokee ancestry). And in November 2017, the optics of Trump's presentation of medals to octogenarian Navajo code-talkers from World War II, standing stoically as they did in the Oval Office near the prominently positioned painting of Jackson—who declared war on the Seminoles and forced the Cherokee and four other tribes on the

---

[263] Cited in Jonathan Lemire, "Trump embraces legacy of Andrew Jackson." *Associated Press: Worldstream*, February 19, 2017.

[264] Dave Boyer, "Donald Trump to visit home of hero Andrew Jackson." *Washington Times*, March 15, 2017.

[265] Peter Grier, "The (semi) secret history of Trump's Andrew Jackson portrait." *Christian Science Monitor*, February 9, 2017.

[266] Quoted in Louis Jacobson and Sara Waychoff, "PolitiFact: What's up with Donald Trump and Andrew Jackson?" *Tampa Bay Times*, May 3, 2017.

Trail of Tears[267]—was a spectacularly grotesque display of cultural insensitivity compounded by the president's extemporaneous harangue against Warren.[268] Only in the myopic, self-absorbed province of Trump's populist politics could an opportunity to honor and celebrate the sacrifice of military veterans of the nation's First Peoples be transformed into an occasion to berate a political opponent. The occasion was handled in as perfidious a manner as Jackson's supposed magnanimity toward Native Americans with the implementation of the Indian Removal Act of 1830 by forcing them off ancestral homelands to secure their well-being. The egocentrism and ethnocentrism on display nevertheless confirms another component in the comparative nativism that animates Trump's populist style. The exceptional Diné warriors at the White House event were clearly *not* the "ordinary" Americans and grassroots supporters of Trump to whom the messaging was targeted.[269] Many would call them extraordinary for a patriotism that defied the president's understanding of their historical plight.

V. The Trump presidency in political time

At the midpoint of Trump's term, political pundits have wrestled relentlessly with the question of the president's prospective legacy. Peering into opaque crystal balls filled with the caffeine vapors

---

[267] Estimates of the deaths of Cherokee, Chickasaw, Choctaw, Creek, and Seminole natives from hunger, disease, and mistreatment by soldiers as they were forced into the western lands is estimated at between 4,000 and 8,000. See Russell Thornton, "Cherokee Population Losses during the Trail of Tears: A New Perspective and a New Estimate." *Ethnohistory* 31, no. 4 (1984): 289–300.

[268] "Trump makes Pocahontas crack at Navajo code talkers event." *CNN*, November 17, 2017. https://www.youtube.com/watch?v=YAP9vWl0mAk

[269] Proportionally, the service of Native Americans in the U.S. military, from World War II to Korea and Vietnam, exceeds that of any other group. The statistics are stunning in consideration of the tragedies inflicted upon Natives by the military itself. See Kevin Gover, "American Indians serve in the U.S. military in greater numbers than any ethnic group and have since the Revolution." *Huffington Post*, May 22, 2015. https://www.huffingtonpost.com/national-museum-of-the-american-indian/american-indians-serve-in-the-us-military_b_7417854.html

rising from coffee house speculation, subjective interpretations of Trump's place in history run the gamut from a descent into authoritarianism and a failed presidency to a remarkable renaissance of presidential power, a resurgence of national economic might, and a transformation of American politics. Bringing objectivity to the intensely partisan colloquies on nightly cable news programs mandates an impartial analysis focused on the ways in which Trump's populist governing style intersects with identifiable patterns of change and continuity in the political order across time. A central reference point in the scholarly debate that guides this analysis is Stephen Skowronek's regime theory based on the notion of "political time."

In *The Politics Presidents Make* Skowronek formulates the thesis that presidents come to office at historically demarcated junctures in time and space that are defined by recurrent cycles of sequential patterns in regime construction, deterioration, and reconstruction. These conditions, over which presidents have no control, but to which they must adapt, pose structural constraints on the exercise of leadership. "The presidency," Skowronek argues, "is a governing institution inherently hostile to inherited governing arrangements."[270] As the focal point in a constitutional system of co-equal institutions, the president's quest to legitimize executive action is paradoxical. The presidency is "order-shattering" insofar as the incumbent must make full use of independent prerogative, "order-affirming" in the bid to articulate the constitutional justification for the disruptive effects of the exercise of such prerogative, and "order-creating" in the search to engineer new political arrangements that stand the tests of time and legitimacy within the political order. As Skowronek maintains, "[g]etting these three impulses to work together—the political message and practical effect of each reinforcing the other—is no easy matter. That is why incumbents so often find themselves at cross purposes."[271]

---

[270] Skowronek, *The Politics Presidents Make*, p. 20.
[271] Ibid., p. 21.

Previously established commitments	President's Political Identity	
	Opposed	Affiliated
Vulnerable	Politics of Reconstruction	Politics of Disjunction
Resilient	Politics of Preemption	Politics of Articulation

Figure 2.2 Recurrent Structures in Presidential Authority in Skowronek's Political Time Framework

Source: Adapted from Stephen Skowronek, *The Politics Presidents Make: Leadership from John Adams to Bill Clinton*. (Cambridge, MA: Harvard University Press, 2003), p. 36.

A reproduction of Skowronek's classification of recurrent structures of presidential authority clarifies the key proposition regarding the limits and prospects for presidential innovation. As Figure 2.2 shows, juxtaposing the president's political identity with the previously established commitments of the prevailing regime in which he is located in political time yields four variably different challenges in the legitimization of executive action. The lynchpin of the typology is whether the state of the regime in which the president finds himself is vulnerable or resilient. Vulnerability or resiliency depends on the degree to which previous solutions to contemporary problems are politically, organizationally, and ideologically secure and deemed legitimate.

Opportunities for *reconstruction* exist when the regime is vulnerable and the president is able to convincingly repudiate the failed approach of the old order with the promise of some new solutions to pressing problems. Examples include Thomas Jefferson, Andrew Jackson, Abraham Lincoln, and Franklin Roosevelt. As Skowronek explains:

Opposition to the old regime held sway in the Congress as well as the presidency, and though the election returns did not convey any clear message as to what exactly should be done, they did reflect a

148

general political consensus that something fundamental had gone wrong in the high affairs of state.[272]

At the other end of the spectrum are presidents who confront regime vulnerability and are affiliated with the established set of commitments regarded as irrelevant or unsuccessful. The result is a politics of *disjunction*. The impossibility of presidential leadership stems from the difficulty that the "president can neither affirm the integrity of governmental commitments nor forthrightly repudiate them," and consequently "his authority to control the political definition of the moment is completely eclipsed, and he is consumed by a problem that is really prerequisite to leadership, that of establishing any credibility at all."[273] Skowronek cites the examples of John Adams, John Quincy Adams, Franklin Pierce, James Buchanan, Herbert Hoover, and Jimmy Carter whose conundra ranged, inter alia, from slavery to economic decline that doomed them to political oblivion.

In the case of resilient regime circumstances, presidents face a different set of challenges. Those affiliated with established commitments are most likely to engage in the politics of *articulation*, in which "orthodox innovation" is the standard. Though constrained by partisan divisions in government, presidents draw legitimacy by galvanizing "political action with promises to continue the good work of the past and demonstrate the vitality of the established order in changing times."[274] As reaffirmations of the majority party, James Monroe, James Polk, Theodore Roosevelt, Harry Truman, and Lyndon Johnson are the exemplars of this scenario. On the other hand, presidents who enter the White House opposed to the prevailing regime are most likely to engage in the politics of *pre-emption*. The major constraint of this unique governing context for presidents is that "their repudiative authority is manifestly limited by the political, institutional, and ideological supports that the old establishment maintains."[275] The strategy of pre-emptive

---

[272] Ibid., p. 37.
[273] Ibid., p. 39.
[274] Ibid., p. 49.
[275] Ibid., p. 43.

presidents is to manipulate divisions within the dominant governing coalition in the bid to enlarge their own base of support—a
divide and conquer strategy. But prospects for success are dim if
history serves as a guide. "These presidents," Skowronek asserts,
"will in effect be probing for reconstructive possibilities without
clear warrant for breaking clearly with the past, and when they
probe too deeply, they get caught in a showdown crisis of constitutional proportions."[276] Paragons of pre-emption include John
Tyler, Andrew Johnson, Woodrow Wilson, and Richard Nixon.

In recent scholarship, Skowronek revisited his earlier work
to place recent presidents within his typology.[277] With Ronald
Reagan considered a reconstructive president whose regime
remains dominant, George H. W. Bush and George W. Bush
are considered orthodox innovators who engaged in the politics of articulation. As opposition presidents, Bill Clinton and
(presumably) Barack Obama fall into the category of presidents
occupied by the politics of pre-emption. Alas, the central question today is where Donald Trump potentially fits within the
framework of regime theory.

It is vital to underscore that Skowronek's concept is neither prescriptive nor aimed at prediction, per se. The theory of
political time is constructed with hindsight in the long sweep
of history dating to the early Republic. Trump's presidency is
a work in progress, indeed a moving target, which complicates
the effort to make informed judgments on his place in political time based on limited observation at the midpoint of his
term. Moreover, critics of Skowronek's theory contend that "[a]
s a probabilistic theory with no specified set of reconstructive
tasks deemed necessary for success, regime theory appears vulnerable to charges of nonfalsifiability."[278] Such difficulties and

---

[276] Ibid., p. 45.
[277] Stephen Skowronek, *Presidential Leadership in Political Time: Reprise and Reappraisal* (Lawrence: University Press of Kansas, 2008).
[278] Curt Nichols and Adam S. Myers, "Exploiting the Opportunity for Recon-
structive Leadership: Presidential Responses to Enervated Political Regimes."
American Politics Quarterly 38, no. 5 (2010): 812.

critiques notwithstanding, Skowronek's framework, which has been hailed as one of the most important conceptual innovations in scholarship by transcending the traditional divide in studies of the modern and historical presidency,[279] can be utilized as a roadmap to navigate possible conclusions.

Figure 2.3 sketches Trump's potential placement in political time and how we may understand the junction of his populist political style with regime cycles. Two of the three classifications are contingent upon the explicit notion that Trump is affiliated with the dominant regime constructed by Reagan in the 1980s. If we surmise that the Reagan legacy is *not* at its imminent conclusion, then Trump is most likely an orthodox innovator engaged in the politics of articulation consistent with this dominant regime. Trump's political style may be unorthodox but is carrying out the policy canons of the Reagan legacy at the margins. Trump's broad focus on economic growth, including the championing of tax cuts and deregulation, as well as his appointment of conservative Supreme Court justices and emphasis on American military strength, is consonant with Reagan's stances, even if his trade policy centered on economic nationalism differs from that of the "Great Communicator."

If Trump's presidency is an inheritance of the Reagan regime, a wholesale reconstruction is unlikely. But a second possibility is a middling category, one in which Trump can "reconstruct-from-within." Skowronek reluctantly admits that Trump might be able

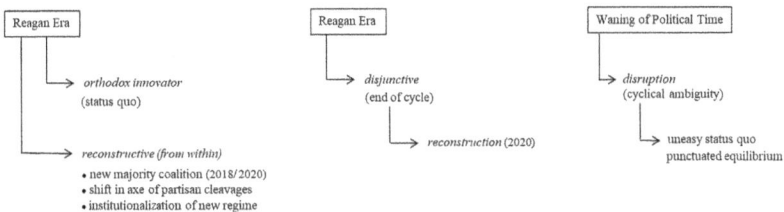

Figure 2.3 Trump's Potential Placement in "Political Time"

[279] Douglas J. Hoekstra, "The Politics of Politics: Skowronek and Presidential Research." *Presidential Studies Quarterly* 29, no. 3 (1999): 657–71.

to reconstruct the disjointed conservative regime in place currently. The thesis is consistent with Trump's emphasis on electing Republicans who support him rather than longstanding party positions and "uniting a coalition around this much more virulent orthodoxy." Skowronek remains skeptical, though, because Trump

> wasn't endorsed in the election even by his own party, he was rejected by half of American voters, and now he's going to be a great repudiator, the forger of a new coalition and inspiration for some new, long-lasting orthodoxy? That doesn't make any sense to me. It's never happened before.[280]

Nonetheless House Republicans who managed to win seats in the 2018 mid-term elections, despite retiring to the minority, have united universally behind the president's opposition to the investigations and impeachment proceedings undertaken by Speaker Nancy Pelosi and her cadre of Democratic leaders.

Skowronek argues that the establishment of a new, majority coalition in support of Trump would violate two essential rules of cycles. First, as government "becomes more inclusive and interdependent in its interests, the Jacksonian standard (for reconstruction) becomes increasingly irrelevant and irrational." Second, the condition that is absent is evidence that no viable alternative exists to the present regime.

> Without a prior disjunction—essentially, a crisis in the reigning orthodoxy of government—demonstrating that the old order is beyond repair, the president won't be able to seize control of the meaning of his changes. You can't reconstruct politics if there is not more or less a consensus that what came before was a complete and systemic failure. Trump won the 2016 election by talking up this fabricated image of the Obama presidency as a failure, but it had very little foundation in reality.[281]

---

[280] Stephen Skowronek, quoted in Richard Kreitner, "What Time Is It? Here's What the 2016 Election Tells Us about Obama, Trump, and What Comes Next." *The Nation*, November 22, 2016. https://www.thenation.com/article/what-time-is-it-heres-what-the-2016-election-tells-us-about-obama-trump-and-what-comes-next/

[281] Ibid.

A third, alternative thesis strongly supported by progressives, Never-Trumpers, and the president's most ardent detractors (though more cautiously by Skowronek himself) is that Trump is a disjunctive president. In this scenario, the fundamental interpretation of political time, noted in the middle graphic of Figure 2.3, assumes that the Reagan cycle is at its end. If so, regime deterioration foreshadows the president's demise at the hands of one of many Democratic presidential aspirants in 2020. Regardless of the eventual Democratic nominee, from this perspective, like Carter before him in the most immediate preceding period, Trump is destined to be a one-term president. In the dialectic of regime reconstruction, degeneration, and collapse, a disjunctive Trump presidency marks the breakdown of state–social relations and an obsolete *ancien régime* of unsustainable, discredited commitments that will logically result in the Reagan cycle's imminent demise and the incumbent's ouster.

If Trump is a disjunctive president like Quincy Adams, Buchanan, Hoover, and Carter before him, this path of historical determinism suggests he will fail regardless of his populist appeals. As Christopher Baylor of Holy Cross College noted in the *Washington Post*:

> Here's one sign that the Reagan revolution is now ending. At the end of its cycle, a dominant party can't agree on new policies for changing times. And so its last gasp in the White House comes to symbolize outmoded politics.[282]

There is some evidence to support the thesis, insofar as Republicans failed to enact health care reform, public support for the ACA has increased, the GOP is divided over the national budget, debt, and deficits, internal dissension over the Trump's "America First" trade policy is palpable, and the president's immigration stances, including the construction of a border wall with Mexico,

---

[282] Christopher Baylor, "Is Trump the last gasp in Reagan's Republican Party?" *Washington Post*, May 11, 2016. https://www.washingtonpost.com/news/monkey-cage/wp/2016/05/11/is-trump-the-last-gasp-of-reagans-republican-party/?utm_term=.8fefbcdfb155

are as unpopular with the public as they are with many stalwarts of his party in Congress.

Citing progressive theorist Corey Robin, Damon Linker posits that

> [i]f Trump's entire presidency amounts to a series of performative contradictions over domestic and foreign policy, it will be a strong indication that he's following in Carter's footsteps in attempting to hold a crumbling regime together while gesturing in the direction of a new regime he's incapable of founding and consolidating for himself.[283]

Indeed, Trump's post-election campaign rallies and tactics, as Chapter 5 explores, have been targeted at consolidating his base of support, not extending it despite tax cuts and economic growth. Thus, if the precise keys to success in reconstructive regime change include (a) shifting the main axis of partisan cleavage, (b) assembling a new majority coalition, and (c) institutionalizing a new political regime,[284] Trump may indeed find himself on the disjunctive end of the historical continuum.

A fourth possibility is that political time as a concept is less relevant in the current era, whether defined as the Reagan regime or something else. Curt Nichols notes that

> Skowronek locates the problem of reconstruction for the contemporary period within the institutional domain. In fact, he suggests that political time may now be "waning" because the modern proliferation of institutions, organized interests, and independent authorities makes resistance to reconstructive efforts more formidable. This is to say that the growth and thickening of the welfare state has created an institutional environment that affords defenders of the status quo strong veto possibilities, making it hard to alter the political regime's path-dependent course of development. Skowronek argues that were

---

[283] Damon Linker, "Donald Trump's presidency is upon us. But who will President Trump be?" *The Week*, January 17, 2017. http://theweek.com/articles/673549/donald-trumps-presidency-upon-but-who-president-trump

[284] Curt Nichols, "Modern Reconstructive Presidential Leadership: Reordering Institutions in a Constrained Environment." *The Forum* (August 2014): 284.

it not for the fact that the scope of presidential power has also been expanding over time, increasing the formal and informal resources the chief executive possesses (e.g., signing statements and communication technologies), successful reconstructive leadership might have already become impossible.[285]

If presidents have less opportunity for innovation, reconstruction, and institution-building, more profound ideological and partisan divides afford fewer possibilities for critical electoral realignments to empower them in reconstructive leadership. Even the appointment process to the U.S. Supreme Court, as evidenced by the Senate's theatrical maelstrom of the closely contested confirmation of Brett Kavanaugh in fall 2018, suggests another way in which political time may have faded. Kevin McMahon makes a compelling argument that prior nomination failures occurred at the end of cycles of articulation, in the midst of a disjunctive presidency, or by pre-emptive presidents attempting to shift the ideological trajectory of the High Court. Citing Harriet Miers' miscarried appointment under George W. Bush, McMahon contends that today "any candidate chosen by a president of the opposing party will garner a significant degree of instant opposition" and that "presidents will have a difficult time choosing a 'compromise' candidate if they desire to do so . . . and it is likely that all nominees—especially those cast as transformative thinkers—will be contested with the waning of political time."[286]

Still, Skowronek's framework may ultimately fail to account in many ways for an *unorthodox innovator* like Trump whose populism intersects with an uncertain place in political time. As disruptor-in-chief, Trump's presidency may reflect the Republic's uneasy status quo marked by uncompromising hyperpartisanship, the scarcity of consensus on the basic direction of socio-economic

---

[285] Curt Nichols, "Reagan Reorders the Political Regime: A Historical–Institutional Approach to Analysis of Change." *Presidential Studies Quarterly* 45, no. 4 (2015): 703–26.

[286] Kevin J. McMahon, "Presidents, Political Regimes, and Contentious Supreme Court Nominations: A Historical Institutional Model." *Law & Social Inquiry* 32, no. 4 (2007): 949.

policy, and disagreement even on the fundamental meaning of the Constitution. Moreover, Trump's populist attacks on members of Congress and the courts in his unbridled quest to "Drain the Swamp" suggest a path toward the *deconstruction* and delegitimization of institutional norms (e.g., fraudulent electoral processes, "deep state" obduracy to his policies, personal attacks on politicians and journalists, destabilization of international commitments, etc.) that could very well undermine his own administration.[287] As such, Trump's presidency might come to represent a form of "punctuated equilibrium"[288] if this style of politics becomes the norm. By acting as a pre-emptive president vis-à-vis what *he* regards as the dominant regime—a host of self-interested, insider elites—Trump's construction of the narrative of politics is as consequential and divisive as any time since the upheavals of the 1960s. As Stuart Shapiro notes,

> From the perspective of his supporters, Trump is an outsider who will change the culture of Washington. His tumultuous first year is merely evidence of the tectonic changes he is bringing to the presidency. From his detractors' perspective, unlike both his immediate Republican predecessors and other disjunctive presidents, Trump is dangerously clueless, disrespectful of American institutions, uninterested in a legacy beyond personal aggrandizement. Although his presidency may bring huge changes, the nature of those changes is highly unpredictable and potentially dangerous (nuclear war, long-term damage to the rule of law and to American supremacy).[289]

* * * * *

Trump's legacy in the annals of American populist history remains an open question, just as his potential place in political time is

---

[287] Z. Byron Wolf, "How Trump could delegitimize his own government." *CNN*, March 11, 2017. https://www.cnn.com/2017/03/11/politics/trump-deep-state/index.html

[288] Frank R. Baumgartner and Bryan D. Jones. *Agendas and Instability in American Politics*, 2nd edition (Chicago: University of Chicago Press, 2010).

[289] Stuart Shapiro, "Three views of Trump." *The Hill*, January 6, 2018. http://thehill.com/opinion/white-house/367600-three-views-of-trump

indeterminate at present. In the final analysis, much depends on the 45th president's ability to maneuver through the minefields of potential peril that define his ongoing political struggles. The possible threats to his presidency—from impeachment, congressional and independent investigations of his 2016 campaign and personal business affairs, and inability to expand his electoral coalition—are taken up in greater detail in Chapter 7. But to understand these dynamics as well as his populist approach to governance, as the next chapter elucidates, it is critical to examine Trump's past forays into politics and the evolution of his populist style.

The roots of Trump's populism

You know, wealthy people don't like me.
—Donald Trump, at the Republican National Convention, 1988

If I ever ran for office, I'd do better as a Democrat than as a Republican—and that's not because I'd be more liberal, because I'm conservative. But the working guy would elect me. He likes me. When I walk down the street, those cabbies start yelling out their windows.
—Donald Trump, *Playboy*, 1990

How stupid are our leaders?
—Donald Trump, Trump Tower, June 16, 2015

I. Introduction

Donald Trump delights in keeping people guessing. As he expressed on Twitter, "I love watching these poor, pathetic people (pundits) on television working so hard and so seriously to try and figure me out. They can't!"[1] Any astute observer of the president's political style, from the journalist to the scholar, confronts an irony as remarkably grand as the tycoon's real estate holdings. With a net worth of $3.1 billion, the president declares himself a protector and champion of working-class Americans against elites of all stripes.[2] Throughout his private-sector career and now as president, he takes pains to disassociate himself from, if not consciously rebel against

---

[1] @realDonaldTrump, "I love watching these poor, pathetic people (pundits) on television working so hard and so seriously to try and figure me out. They can't!" *Twitter*, August 12, 2016, 4:43 a.m. https://twitter.com/realdonaldtrump/status/764064821000056832

[2] *Forbes*, "The definitive net worth of Donald Trump." https://www.forbes.com/donald-trump/#721d32028992

and antagonize, the economically well-to-do, insisting that he is an outcast among their ranks. Such rhetoric dates to three decades ago. When CNN's Larry King asked him if he were a George H. W. "Bush Republican" at the 1988 GOP Convention in Houston, Texas, Trump sanguinely replied "no" and maintained that

> The people that I do best with drive the taxis. You know, wealthy people don't like me because I'm competing with them all the time. And I like to win. I go down the streets of New York and the people that really like me are the workers.[3]

His perspective has changed little since. As he flirted with a run for the White House in 1999, Trump said, "Rich people who know me love me. Rich people who don't know me hate me. The working man loves me."[4]

During the 2016 presidential campaign and well into his first two years in office, Trump vigorously celebrated ordinary Americans—the middle class, blue-collar workers, manual laborers, and farmers. Pledging an economic renewal that included the return of manufacturing jobs, he found receptive audiences in key swing states like Iowa, where his double-digit victory over Hillary Clinton was in no small part connected to voters' "shared distaste for the elites the president spent his campaign scorning."[5] As president he couched tax cuts and tough bilateral trade renegotiations repeatedly as mechanisms to restore fairness to these forgotten voters.[6] "It is time," the

---

[3] Quoted in Connie Friedersdorf, "When Donald Trump became a celebrity." *The Atlantic*, January 6, 2016. https://www.theatlantic.com/politics/archive/2016/01/the-decade-when-donald-trump-became-a-celebrity/422838/

[4] Quoted in Maureen Dowd, "Trump l'oeil tease." *New York Times*, September 19, 1999, p. WK17.

[5] Iowa Republican Party Chairman Jeff Kauffman, quoted in Cathleen Decker, "Trump's war against elites and expertise." *Los Angeles Times*, July 27, 2017. http://www.latimes.com/politics/la-na-pol-trump-elites-20170725-story.html

[6] For example, the president wrote @realDonaldTrump, "Our Steel and Aluminum industries (and many others) have been decimated by decades of unfair trade and bad policy with countries from around the world. We must not let our country, companies and workers be taken advantage of any longer. We want free, fair and SMART TRADE!" *Twitter*, March 1, 2018, 7:12 a.m. https://twitter.com/realdonaldtrump/status/969183644756660224

president contended, "to take care of OUR people, to rebuild OUR NATION, and to fight for OUR GREAT AMERICAN WORKERS!"[7]

Scholars, journalists, and commentators, understandably engrossed in quotidian White House palace intrigue and spell-bound by Trump's tangled tweets in the wee hours of the morning, have paid scant attention to the questions that guide this chapter: How is the president's embrace of populism connected to the evolution of his political views and his shrewd politicking dating to the 1980s, and with what significance in the search to understand the roots of his political style? There is no particular consensus, only informed speculation, regarding the underlying sources of Trump's self-anointed populist persona. At one level, his anti-elitism appears at times to reflect a profound resentment of those who stood in the way of his business success or otherwise crossed him—and the *Schadenfreude* cultural elites and the press expressed when his ventures failed to the tune of approximately $9 billion and his marriage to Ivana collapsed. At another level, psychologists might argue that his admiration for working-class Americans, on whose labor he built his empire, is paternalism masking some repressed guilt. As intriguing as such theses might be, they are summarily dismissed by the president's most ardent critics, who reject the authenticity of his populism and insist instead that his rhetoric is little more than a ruse for a "plutocratic course that betrays the very people he tricked into voting against themselves . . . from opposing an increase in the minimum wage to calling for draconian cutbacks in college loan programs for hard-pressed middle and working-class students."[8]

---

[7] @realDonald Trump, "It is time to take care of OUR people, to rebuild OUR NATION, and to fight for OUR GREAT AMERICAN WORKERS!" *Twitter*, September 27, 2017, 6:55 p.m. https://twitter.com/realdonaldtrump/status/913220484640182272

[8] Robert Shrum, "Donald Trump is not a populist. To be him, Democrats will have to show what real populism is all about." *Politico*, August 29, 2017. https://www.politico.com/magazine/story/2017/08/29/donald-trump-not-a-populist-215552

The objective of this chapter is not to provide a comprehensive biography of the business mogul's cradle-to-Oval Office odyssey. Rather, the goal is to delineate constituent elements of Trump's mindset toward the realm of politics prior to his 2016 electoral juggernaut by analyzing the mosaic of his attitudes and relationships. This analysis reveals distinct patterns of past behavior and intertwining rhetoric that are exceptionally consonant with the central elements of the populist style elaborated in Chapter 2. His penchant for conspiracy theory, however, emerged only in the years immediately before his run for the presidency in 2016. As Dylan Matthew writes:

> On the core issues he cares about the most—international trade, immigration, foreign policy—he's strikingly consistent. He's always been anti-immigrant, always been protectionist, always been fiercely nationalistic on matters of war and peace. More generally, he's always believed in the fundamental zero-sum nature of the world.[9]

Careful observation underscores that Trump's halting ventures into the political world and his demeanor as a businessman are variably marked by the essential dimensions of populism elaborated in the last chapter: anti-elitism, advocacy of the ordinary citizen, issue simplification buttressed by nativism, and conspiracy theory. Although a self-proclaimed conservative, the president's anti-elitist worldview is largely non-ideological, and more stylistic than doctrinaire. As a businessman, he gave prodigiously to *both* mainstream political parties as a hedge to curry favor with elected officials who could aid his commercial enterprises. In return, both parties courted him, largely to no avail as his self-proclaimed affinity with the ordinary working American steered rhetoric that took aim at both Democrats and Republicans. Moreover, Trump's penchant for holding grudges against politicians regardless of partisan affiliation, deriding competitors, and disparaging the press commenced long ago. His legendary disdain for Mayor Ed Koch (which was reciprocal),

---

[9] Dylan Matthews, "Zero-sum Trump." *Vox*, January 19, 2017. https://www
.vox.com/a/donald-trump-books

controversies surrounding his involvement with the United States Football League (USFL), and picayune squabbling with newspapers over reviews of his books or less than flattering pictures of his physique foreshadowed his condescension toward politicians, haughtiness toward cultural elites, and superciliousness toward the media that would flourish to unprecedented heights during and after the 2016 presidential campaign. Furthermore, his nativist instincts and anti-intellectual discourse are notable in his Manichean framing of international trade disputes. He frequently assailed political leaders for allegedly selling out U.S. interests abroad, branding such rhetoric with the Trump name. Today it may be China, Mexico, or Canada, but in the 1980s it was Japan and Saudi Arabia most prominently in his crosshairs. Finally, his engagement of conspiracy theory following the 2008 election is a more contemporary development that emerged with assertions that Barack Obama was possibly a Manchurian candidate as a Muslim born outside the United States. The effort to delegitimize Obama was a purely strategic calculus by Trump in the run-up to his effort to secure the GOP nomination in 2016.

II. Trumping ideology? The road to populist politics

With his meteoric rise in real estate and other ventures in the 1980s, youth, and name recognition, it is scarcely coincidence that Donald Trump was wooed by both mainstream political parties. He routinely denied having aspirations for public office of any kind, yet slyly encouraged speculation by expressing fascination with politics. As he told CNN in 1988, "I enjoy it, I enjoy the system. I doubt I'll ever be involved with politics beyond what I do right now, but I do enjoy the system. I find it, a really, really beautiful thing to watch."[10] Incredulous that Trump had no political ambition, figures in both parties pursued his support and dangled opportunities before him. As Michael Kilian noted in 1987, "[p]ractically every Republican and Democratic presidential candidate has sought Trump's endorsement and financial

[10] Interview with Larry King at the Republican National Convention, August 1988. https://www.youtube.com/watch?v=Usb0iE5WiZI

162

backing, and people in both parties have expressed an interest in his becoming a candidate—for the Senate if not the presidency."[11]

Although registered as a Republican by 1987, Trump walked a fine line and, until his first bid for the presidency in 1999, sought to avoid alienating either mainstream party. He supported the "Campaign for Prosperity," a political action committee established in support of Republican Jack Kemp's abortive presidential bid in 1988.[12] When prominent Democrats, including House Speaker Jim Wright, invited him to host a dinner in advance of the 1988 election, Trump politely demurred, underscoring that he was conflicted because he had already pledged to do so for Republican friends. Striking a non-partisan tone uncharacteristic of his comportment today, he promised that he would continue "supporting the candidates I consider the best in both parties."[13] Some Democratic critics were indignant at the mere thought of recruiting the tycoon to their ranks. "Mr. Trump as the master of ceremonies at a function to boost the Democrats' fortunes," declared Ross K. Baker sardonically, "is like the Sheriff of Nottingham presiding over a fund-raiser for Robin Hood" and a petty attempt by some in the party to be "associated with a more upscale clientele."[14]

Some Republicans, however, viewed Trump as a possible unifying figure to make in-roads in the otherwise dyed-in-the-blue Empire State. Others expressed a little buyer's remorse for his endorsements. Nonetheless, Trump remained largely non-committal in his partisan gamesmanship as he focused on building his business empire. New York State GOP Party Chairman Anthony Colavita placed Trump at the top of a list of Republican leaders capable of heading a "fusion" ticket alongside disaffected Democrats in the bid to defeat Mayor Ed Koch in 1988.[15] Trump

[11] Michael Kilian, "Ace of Trump: an artful dealer, usually with the best hand." *Chicago Tribune*, November 22, 1987, p. D1.

[12] *New York Times*, "Scouting." August 5, 1986, p. A20.

[13] Fox Butterfield, "Trump turns down Democrats' dinner." *New York Times*, November 24, 1987, p. A18.

[14] Ross K. Baker, "Dump Trump." *New York Times*, November 24, 1987, p. A23.

[15] *New York Times*, "G.O.P. to ask Trump about mayoral bid." June 16, 1987, p. B2.

openly broke with Koch in 1987, calling him a "moron,"[16] but did not run for office. That same year Trump was the master of ceremonies for a fundraising event on behalf of George H. W. Bush. The lavish setting at the Plaza Hotel, owned by Trump, featured an ice sculpture with the inscription "B.U.S.H." and a parade of flamboyant invitees including boxing promoter Don King, whose hairstyle is among the few to ever rival the real estate dynast's signature coiffure. Trump said of the vice president, "He's a *great* man. He's a man I support."[17] The patrician Bush family was supposedly taken aback by the extravagantly tawdry event that attendees called "utterly chaotic."[18] The relationship between Trump and Bush became more strained when, in the 1990 budget debacle, Reagan's successor reneged on his 1988 pledge not to raise taxes.[19] At the depth of his financial crisis in the 1990s, Trump would rupture publicly, at least half-heartedly, with Poppy, claiming that as president Bush had "done nothing to save" the real estate industry. Though he would not say for whom he planned to vote in 1992, Trump surmised that Bill Clinton "couldn't do any worse."[20] In the 1989 New York City mayoral race, he had similarly played both sides of the fence by supporting Democrat David Dinkins *and* Republican Rudy Giuliani in the primaries. In effect he won no matter which candidate prevailed in the final tally in November. Trump said he "had been too preoccupied with celebrating Mr. Koch's defeat to choose between the winners."[21] But supporting candidates of

[16] Fox Butterfield, "Trump hints at dreams beyond building." *New York Times*, October 5, 1987, p. B1.

[17] Sidney Blumenthal, "Election '88 and the Wall Street bypass." *Washington Post*, April 21, 1988, p. C1.

[18] Michael Kilian, "Power shift: D.C. won't stand for dreadfully chic anymore, with Poppy and Bar at the helm." *Chicago Tribune*, December 28, 1988, p. F5.

[19] Brett Barrouquere, "How a fundraiser brought George H. W. Bush, Donald Trump and Don King together." *Chron*, September 16, 2016. https://www.chron.com/news/politics/us/article/A-Bush-a-Trump-and-a-King-How-a-fundraiser-9227763.php

[20] Rick Wartzman and Dana Milbank, "Clinton's strengths with business leaders is rare for a Democrat." *Wall Street Journal*, September 24, 1992, p. A1.

[21] Sam Roberts, "Dinkins gaining support among business executives." *New York Times*, September 26, 1989, p. B1.

both parties across the local and national political landscape was a clear strategic calculation.

Trump's campaign contributions followed a similar tack. The political reality of Democrats' grip on city politics in New York vis-à-vis his business interests placed him in conflict with his Republican leanings, however deep or wide they flowed. As a result Trump underwrote candidates of both parties, depending on context. In 1988 he was one of just a couple of dozen $100,000 "soft money" contributors to George H. W. Bush's election effort while also supporting Democrats at the local level.[22] One way Trump was able to shroud some of his divergent contributions from scrutiny was to use multiple corporations under his control to circumvent legal limits—a practice that caught the eye of the State of New York in 1988.[23] Regardless, he continued to support different candidates for the same office, and of both parties, in primary and general elections to hedge his bets on politicians of any stripe who could facilitate his real estate and casino ventures.[24]

In 1999 Trump changed his party affiliation to Independent as he eyed a run for the White House under the Reform Party banner. Ross Perot's populist legacy as founder of the inchoate and shambolic organization, which included rallying cries against elites, calling for term limits on members of Congress, eliminating the federal budget deficit, and indicting foreign trade policy, clearly appealed to Trump's political instincts. Charging that the Republican Party had moved too far to the right of the political spectrum, he formed a presidential exploratory committee in 1999 and embarked on a short-lived campaign that terminated on Valentine's Day, February 14, 2000.

Trump's detractors argued that his ephemeral bid for the Reform Party nomination was tantamount to "a salesman's pitch—a string

---

[22] Frank Lynn, "A closer look at the gorillas of G.O.P. finance." *New York Times*, January 26, 1989, p. B1.

[23] Frank Lynn, "Investigations will expand in New York." *New York Times*, March 17, 1988, p. B1.

[24] Jack Anderson and Dale van Atta, "Trump's art of political giving." *Washington Post*, October 20, 1989, p. E5.

of semi-articulated views construed [as] semi-political policy posi-tions."[25] During television interviews Trump appeared moderate to progressive on social issues. He professed he was in favor of univer-sal health care, abortion rights for women, and the right of gays to serve openly in the military—all while simultaneously singing the praises of tax cuts and Oprah Winfrey as a potential running-mate. Many critics suggested that the media blitz was little more than a ruse to prop up his book sales and his business empire. As Gail Collins blithely opined while citing his acrimonious divorce from his first wife Ivana and his pledge to wed (a third time) the daz-zling Slovenian model Melania Knauss if he were elected, Trump's ideology "seems firm only in regard to the virtues of tax incentives for real estate development and the evils of alimony."[26] As another observer commented,

> Politicians, at least, pretend to talk about issues. They may not offer nuts-and-bolts policy information, but they are happy to expound theories, sweeping philosophies and the wonderful country that is America. But Trump quickly seems bored by his own rhetoric. Strike that. Trump has no discernible rhetoric. He seems bored by issues. Still, the attention has been nice.[27]

A closer examination of Trump's book *The America We Deserve*, published in January 2000, contravenes critiques that he failed to articulate coherent policy views even if details were less than abundant. In the opening pages he delved straight away into a stinging censure of his political rivals, contending that Pat Buchanan of the Reform Party had "lost it" by venerating Adolph Hitler, that Al Gore was "confused" and had to pay progressive Naomi Wolf, author of *The Beauty Myth*, to learn how to be an alpha male, and that Senator Bill Bradley (D-NJ) was a "disaster"

---

[25] Edward Helmore, "How Trump's political playbook evolved since he first ran for president in 2000." *The Guardian*, February 5, 2017. https://www.theguardian.com/us-news/2017/feb/05/donald-trump-reform-party-2000-president

[26] Gail Collins, "Reform Party 101." *New York Times*, September 17, 1999, p. A23.

[27] Robert Givhan, "On a different plane." *Washington Post*, December 23, 1999, p. C1.

for tax policy. Embellishing his outsider status, Trump promised to be a straight-talker who was not "prepackaged," "plastic," or "handled" like other career politicians. The balance of his short book emphasized a host of issue foci, albeit with vague policy outlines that were short on specifics but consistent with the populist message he sought to develop. These included issues such as 1) the importance of business to America's prosperity while forecasting an impending crash worse than 1929; 2) education, teaching citizenship in schools and improving school choice; 3) crime, support of the death penalty, criticisms of judges' sentencing practices, and enhanced immigration control; 4) foreign policy, adapting to the post-Cold War era by stressing deal-making and trade relationships, getting tough on China, and cooperating with Russia with skepticism; 5) saving Social Security by paying off the national debt by levying a tax on the wealthy; and 6) implementing universal health care.

Ultimately the internecine battles to cement control of the Reform Party chased Trump from the nomination race. He described the underbelly of the party as a "fringe element" that was in favor of repealing the income tax and believed his candidacy was a sham: "When I held a reception for Reform Party leaders in California, the room was crowded with Elvis look-alikes, resplendent in various campaign buttons and anxious to give me a pamphlet explaining the Swiss-Zionist conspiracy to control America."[28] Calling Pat Buchanan "Attila the Hun," he justified his withdrawal by stating that "the Reform Party now includes a Klansman, Mr. Duke, a neo-Nazi, Mr. Buchanan, and a communist, Ms. Fulani. This is not company I wish to keep." Oddly, a decade-and-a-half later, Trump stirred ample controversy by refusing to immediately reject the endorsement of the head of the Ku Klux Klan, one of the unsavory figures he cited as a rationale for his decision to exit the Reform Party. In March 2016 Trump stated: "I don't know anything about David Duke. I don't know anything about what you're even

[28] Donald J. Trump, "What I saw at the revolution." *New York Times*, February 19, 2000, p. A15.

talking about with white supremacy or white supremacists. So, I don't know."[29]

What is nevertheless striking is the degree to which Trump's abortive bid for the Reform Party nomination helped to fashion a coherent, populist messaging style he would fine-tune and carry on to victory in the Republican Party in 2016. But the sojourn was sinuous across Bill Clinton's metaphorical "Bridge to the 21st Century." Seemingly disaffected with politics after the 2000 fiasco during which the Reform Party imploded, Trump registered as a Democrat in 2001 and switched back to the Republican Party in 2009. While wandering in the political wilderness in the first decade of the new millennium, he supported George W. Bush's successful re-election bid in 2004 and endorsed Arizona Senator John McCain's candidacy for the White House in 2008. Settling on a home in the GOP, he halted campaign contributions to Democrats in 2010 and focused solely on supporting Republican candidates.

Trump's speech at the Conservative Political Action Conference (CPAC) in February 2011 was a watershed insofar as it galvanized conservative activists in the GOP (while drawing scathing rebukes from libertarians supportive of Texas Congressman Ron Paul). After the O'Jays song *For the Love of Money*—the theme song to his television show *The Apprentice*—stopped, Trump launched into a heated criticism of President Obama, called him a president without a record, and posited that China, India, Mexico, South Korea, and the Organization for Petroleum Exporting Countries (OPEC) had made the United States a "whipping post for the rest of the world. The world is treating us without respect; they [*sic*] are not treating us properly."[30] Two years later, in March 2013, Trump returned to CPAC with variations on the same populist themes, though his rhetoric was more caustic and accentuated his vision of conservativism based more on pragmatic politics than anything

---

[29] Quoted in German Lopez, "We need to stop acting like Trump isn't pandering to white supremacists." *Vox*, August 14, 2017. https://www.vox.com/policy-and-politics/2017/8/13/16140504/trump-charlottesville-white-supremacists

[30] Donald Trump, Speech to CPAC, February 10, 2011. http://www.p2012.org/photos11/cpac11/trump021011spt.html

else. He emphasized the perils of illegal immigration while suggesting more legal immigrants from Europe come to the United States.
He warned Republicans not to harm social safety-net programs
like Medicare, suggested that Iraqi oil revenues be used to pay the
families of fallen veterans in that conflict that commenced in 2003,
and complained of President Obama's "unprecedented media protection." Focusing on situations in Syria and Afghanistan, not to
mention trade, Trump ranted that "[t]he fact is we're run by either
very foolish or very stupid people."[31] Following CPAC the business
magnate invested more than $1 million to investigate a run for the
White House as President Obama finished out his second term.

Trump's winding route to the GOP presidential nomination
in 2016 was preceded by his support of Republican standard-
bearer Mitt Romney in 2012, and his decision to decline a run
for the governorship of New York in 2014 against incumbent
Democrat Andrew Cuomo. Polls showed he had little support in
the Empire State against Mario Cuomo's son. But also looming
over his political calculation was the degree to which his populist
messaging as an outsider would have likely rung hollow had he
pursued other political opportunities at the state level—and if
successful, he would have become part of the very political elite
he decried in advance of his ultimate presidential run in the GOP
he was planning. Others contend that it was a profound dislike
of President Obama, who caricatured Trump at the White House
Correspondents' Dinner in April 2011, and "[t]hat evening of
public abasement, rather than sending Mr. Trump away, accel-
erated his ferocious efforts to gain stature within the political
world."[32] Obama's scathing lampoon of Trump took place the
very week that the president produced his birth certificate amidst
the "birther" campaign that the real estate tycoon had kindled
(see below).

Whatever Trump's ultimate motivations to seek the highest
office in the land, the threads of his populist style were sewn over

[31] Donald Trump, Speech to CPAC, March 15, 2013. http://www.p2016.org/photos13/cpac13/trump031513spt.html
[32] Maggie Haberman and Alexander Burns, "Trump 2016 bid began in effort to gain stature." *New York Times*, March 13, 2016, p. A1.

the course of three decades as he drifted toward, away from, and back to the Republican Party. His approach to politics may be more *ideational* than ideological. But there is a particular consistency in the evolution of his populist appeals and issue emphases across time. As discussed next, often personality, petty disputes, and over-the-top responses to criticism play as much if not more of a role than policy in defining his style.

III. Champion of the working man, equal opportunity offender, winner at all costs

Trump articulates a particular conception of the ordinary American—the blue-collar worker, manual laborer, the taxi driver—and proclaims himself as the advocate of the forgotten man. This narrative is reinforced by rhetoric that denigrates politicians on a personal level, maligns competitors, and vilifies cultural elites and the media. Such a storyline was a cornerstone of Trump's pre-presidential career.

The origins of Trump's affection for "ordinary Americans" and the working man may never be fully grasped. The president himself cannot explicate the dynamic with any precision. "He relates to the common man, to middle-class workers," but says "'I don't know why. It's a group of people I respect'."[33] Regardless, it may well be that Trump's prosaic oratory of political and cultural elites' blocking the way of the common man's potential for achievement captures a sense of yearning among many to emulate the lifestyle that can accompany an embarrassment of riches on the scale that Trump has adduced. As Robert Givhan suggests, "[i]f the average Joe suddenly found himself swimming in dough and had no hang-ups about how he would be judged he would indulge in the level of magnificent excess of which Trump is a master."[34] Moreover, there is a case to be made by his supporters that when

---

[33] Givhan, "On a different plane," p. C1.
[34] Ibid.

Trump mocks the weak, when he spews bigotry, when he dispar-
ages people in African and Hispanic countries and says he's tired of
immigrants coming into this country, taking our jobs and raping our
women, he's speaking for millions of Americans . . . Trump is talking the way Americans do in barrooms, restaurants, at kitchen tables
and family barbecues.[35]

If Bill Clinton's byzantine doublespeak (e.g., "it depends on what
the meaning of *is* is") offends those without a law degree who are
unable to decipher the subtleties of grand jury testimony, surely
Trump's candid if sometimes vulgar outbursts appeal to a sense
of authenticity to which many Americans can relate. The messaging employed by Trump as a tribune of the people is analogous to
populist French National Front leader Jean-Marie Le Pen's quip
that *"il dit tout haut ce que les autres pensent tout bas"*—he says
out loud what everyone thinks to himself.[36]

Trump appears an unlikely candidate to identify with average
Americans from any objective measure of wealth, and the notion
that his success is a story of rags to riches belies his family history
and the influential role of his father, Fred. Still, he has consistently used the imagery and mythology of the self-made man who
is "above politics," and who wins at any cost, to attract a curious
devotion among his supporters. He laid bare the notion best in
his 2000 book, noted earlier, *The America We Deserve*. Trump
writes at some length of Wendell Willkie, to whom he attempts to
compare himself implicitly. Willkie overcame his humble begin-
nings to become a highly successful lawyer and corporate executive. He switched from the Democratic to the Republican Party
in 1939, successfully challenged the titans of the GOP at the time,

---

[35] Phil Kadner, "Trump's greatest strength: He speaks 'American'." *Chicago Sun-
Times*, August 28, 2018. https://chicago.suntimes.com/columnists/trump-speaks-
american-greatest-strength/

[36] See Laurent Pinsolle, "Celui qui oserait dire tout haut ce que les électeurs
penseraient tout bas: Jean-Marie Le Pen a-t-il raison de penser que les Français
ne croient plus à l'étiquette de fasciste qui lui est collée?" *Atlantico*, July 26,
2013. http://www.atlantico.fr/decryptage/celui-qui-oserait-dire-tout-haut-que-
electeurs-penseraient-tout-bas-jean-marie-pen-t-raison-penser-que-francais-
ne-croient-plus-797623.html. Translation by author.

Robert Taft and Thomas Dewey, and won the Republican presidential nomination in 1940. According to Trump, Willkie came within a whisker of defeating incumbent Franklin Roosevelt, though he actually lost the popular vote by 9.9 percent nationally. Regardless, Trump asks the question:

> How did Willkie do it? It seems he had the common touch. Even though he was a millionaire businessman he had a way of relating to the common man. He criticized the platforms of both Democrats and Republicans for "double talk, weasel words, and evasion".[37]

Later in his political manifesto Trump puts his own political courage—and money—where his mouth is by proposing a one-time tax on the wealthy to pay off the $5 trillion national debt that loomed large over the economy. As Adam Nagourney asserts, the simple concept, framed in populist terms,

> also had the advantage of lessening any liability Mr. Trump might believe he could suffer because of his own reputation as a man of wealth. The developer put his own net worth at $5 billion, and said that under his plan, he would owe $750 million in taxes.[38]

Whether Trump identifies with the common man is of perhaps far less significance than if ordinary Americans *identify with him* and link their daily struggles to the anti-elite narrative that is congruent with their frustrations. Trump connects middle- and working-class Americans to a worldview that is easily understandable—that political, economic, and social relationships revolve around conflict that can be overcome through bravado, assertiveness, and, if necessary, intimidation. As Herbert Muschamp submits, Trump's real estate empire "plays the role of Midas in the popular imagination" and he "knows that conflict is a cultural asset."[39] As Howard Kurtz

---

[37] Donald J. Trump and Dave Shiflett, *The America We Deserve* (New York: Renaissance Books, 2000), pp. 8–9.

[38] Adam Nagourney, "Trump proposes clearing nation's debt at expense of the rich." *New York Times*, November 10, 1999, p. A19.

[39] Herbert Muschamp, "A Midas of the gold (yes I do mean gold) cudgel." *New York Times*, November 5, 1997, p. E2.

describes it, Trump's "is a narrative filled with superlatives and triumph over adversity."[40] And many Americans are able to relate to the tales of woe, resilience, and unflappable determination if only the shackles of etiquette are stripped away. Were the common man to speak his mind unreservedly to his boss or his spouse he would indubitably end up jobless and divorced. Trump's extraordinary success, despite his transparent disregard for the norms of decorum in business and personal relationships, provides a curiously vicarious means to defy the rules that apply to most other Americans.

Long before his entry into politics per se, Trump's clashes with the New York political class, disagreements with business rivals, rows with cultural elites, and quarrels with the print media presaged his proclivity, as chief executive, to call into question the character of anyone who engaged in the least perceived slight and take a no-holds-barred approach to prevailing, rhetorically or otherwise, over his rivals. In the political realm, Trump's confrontational relationship with former New York City Mayor Ed Koch in the 1980s is legendary. It is an exemplar of the president's penchant to personalize disagreements and call into question the integrity, aptitude, and even veracity of those who might oppose him.

The dispute between Trump and Koch originated in 1980 when the mayor and other city leaders opposed a tax abatement for the development of Trump Tower in Midtown Manhattan. The New York State Supreme Court ultimately ruled in Trump's favor four years later. Koch argued nonetheless that "some of the most expensive and luxurious accommodations, not only the in the United States but in the world, are entitled to a tax break. Does that make sense? Not to me."[41]

The feud between Trump and Koch escalated in the following years. In 1985 when Trump purchased a controlling stake in the redevelopment of a subway site and refused to comply with the city's mandate to pay the former owners $30 million,

---

[40] Howard Kurtz, "Donald Trump." *Washington Post*, November 22, 1987, p. 133.

[41] David Margolick, "Top state court rules Trump is entitled to tax break for midtown tower." *New York Times*, July 6, 1984, p. B1.

he provoked the mayor's ire.[42] When Koch later led the charge against providing Trump with city tax breaks to construct an Upper West Side Manhattan television center for the National Broadcasting Corporation (NBC) in 1987, the Donald said the mayor had "absolutely no sense of economic development" and called the city under Koch's leadership "a disaster."[43] Trump and Koch engaged subsequently in a flurry of letters to one another in which they traded insults. Despite a truce he declared briefly, Trump took to television on the Public Broadcasting System (PBS) *McNeil-Lehrer* program and proclaimed of the mayor that "I would say he's got no talent and only moderate intelligence."[44] A year later, in 1988, as Trump contemplated selling the seventy-six-acre railroad yards tract along the Hudson River, he said "Ed Koch is an incompetent who would support this project if it were smaller, even though that would mean substantially less tax revenue for the city."[45] By the end of 1988 Trump considered spending $2 million in television advertisements in an effort to oust Koch, whom he had called by such names as "jerk," "loser," "idiot," a "piece of garbage," "moron," and "bully."[46]

Trump's comportment foreshadowed his feuding relationships with legislative leaders in Washington as president. The case of the "Yards" project, as it was known, illustrates his predilection to exchange the need for patience, compromise, and the cultivation of allies in a quest to defeat his adversaries, foster his celebrity, and be perceived as a winner. As Timothy O'Brien argues, "[h]e

---

[42] Josh Barbanel, "Trump and city dispute part of $1 billion project." *New York Times*, May 19, 1985, p. 36.

[43] Alan Finder, "Koch rejects tax break for Trump TV city site." *New York Times*, May 29, 1987, p. B3.

[44] Max J. Rosenthal, "The Trump files: Witness Donald's epic insult fight with the Mayor of New York." *Mother Jones*, August 11, 2016. https://www.mother-jones.com/politics/2016/08/trump-files-donalds-epic-battle-with-ed-koch/

[45] Thomas Lueck, "Trump City site may be sold, developer says." *New York Times*, October 13, 1988, p. B1.

[46] Howard Kurtz, "Trump weights $2 million ad blitz to defeat Koch." *Washington Post*, December 6, 1988, p. A8; Howard Kurtz, "Trump: The book on the tycoon with the towering ambition." *Washington Post*, November 22, 1987, p. F1.

antagonized local residents, planning boards and Koch, raising the ante every time he didn't get exactly what he wanted and publicly accusing Koch of 'ludicrous and disgraceful behavior'."[47]

It was with Koch's death in February 2017 and the discovery of previously unpublished letters by the mayor that the depth of the ill-will between the two leviathan figures of New York City life in the 1980s was revealed. Koch opined that "Donald Trump is one of the least likable people I have met during the 12 years that I served as mayor," and wrote that "[i]t is incomprehensible to me that for some people he has become a folk hero." Considering the developer to be "greedy, greedy, greedy," he reflected that

> Trump obviously considered himself to be my friend at one time, and because of that, or because he gave or raised $70,000 for one of my mayoral campaigns, he expected something in return. He never got it. And he thought that was disloyal.[48]

Other conflicts in which Trump was embroiled during his business career are instructive. One set of incidents involved his casino gambling empire. In the 1980s Trump had chastised the Atlantic City, New Jersey Casino Association because the organization failed to move quickly enough, in his view, to approve twenty-four-hour gambling.[49] He subsequently withdrew from the association, taking his approximately $250,000 annual contribution with him. The implications were clear: if Trump did not get his way on his terms, he would retaliate. In the 1990s, as Congress and the Supreme Court began to struggle with the question of regulating Native-owned casinos, he clashed with Connecticut Governor Lowell Weicker. Weicker had previously reached an agreement with local Native tribes, without legislative approval, that gave them a monopoly on casino gambling

---

[47] Timothy L. O'Brien, "Mitch McConnell is Trump's latter-day Ed Koch." *Bloomberg Opinion*, August 24, 2017. https://www.bloomberg.com/opinion/articles/2017-08-24/mitch-mcconnell-is-trump-s-latter-day-ed-koch

[48] Sam Roberts, "Ed Koch's epic feud with Trump survives the mayor's death." *New York Times*, February 27, 2017.

[49] Albert J. Parisi, "Trump withdrawal laid to impatience." *New York Times*, August 17, 1986, p. NJ10.

in the Constitution State. The Pequot Tribe threatened to halt all tax payments to Connecticut if other gambling facilities were approved by the state legislature. The feud began when Trump testified before Congress in 1993 and said the operators "did not look like Indians." Weicker considered the comments racist, and called Trump a "dirtbag." Trump retaliated by attacking Weicker as a "fat slob."[50]

As another example, Trump's relationship with figures in the sports world as owner of the New Jersey Generals in the now-defunct United States Football League (USFL) was as acrimonious as his row with National Football League (NFL) players and team proprietors over the national anthem as president. Trump testified at a 1986 anti-trust lawsuit trial worth over $1 billion, brought about by the USFL with charges that the NFL had conspired to put the fledgling league out of business. During a meeting at the Pierre Hotel in New York two years earlier, he claimed that NFL Commissioner Pete Rozelle had promised him a franchise should he convince the USFL to drop the matter and halt attempts to implement a spring schedule. Rozelle, on the other hand, is reported to have said, "Mr. Trump, as long as I or my heirs are involved with the NFL, you will never be a franchise owner in the league."[51] The lead attorney for the NFL upbraided Trump's testimony in court, characterizing him "as the worst kind of snake who was selling his colleagues down the river so he could affect a merger of a few rich teams."[52] At issue were memoranda Trump had penned alluding to a potential merger between the USFL and NFL that undermined his credibility with the jury. Sports writer Jeff Pearlman held that "[i]t wasn't Trump's words, so much as his swagger and irritability. The USFL was the little

[50] Jonathan Rabinowitz, "Indians issue threats over new casinos." *New York Times*, January 25, 1995, p. B4.
[51] Richard Ryman, "'Gunslinger' author breaks down USFL." September 26, 2018. https://www.greenbaypressgazette.com/story/news/2018/09/26/usfl-jeff-pearlman-book-football-buck-recounts-wild-ride/1223195002/
[52] Richard Hoffer, "USFL awarded only $3 in antitrust decision: Jury finds NFL guilty on one of nine counts." *Los Angeles Times*, July 30, 1986. http://articles.latimes.com/1986-07-30/sports/sp-18643_1_jury-finds-nfl-guilty/2

league trying to be big, but Trump didn't seem little. Or sympathetic. Or, for that matter, believable."[53] The USFL won only three dollars in damages in the lawsuit, plus attorneys' fees. The debacle prompts some observers to suggest that Trump's crusade against the NFL regarding players' kneeling for the national anthem as president is a longstanding grudge for the embarrassment, which sealed the fate of the USFL's demise.[54]

Whatever Trump's role in the USFL lawsuit, he nonetheless displayed lofty contempt for the owners he purportedly supported. And several reported incidents buttress allegations that his interest in football was primarily for self-aggrandizement. General Manager of the Pittsburgh Maulers described the scene of one owners' meeting as Trump walked in:

> he's bombastic from the start. He's loud, he clearly wants to be noticed. Just a jerk, and a jerk on purpose. He sits down, and the meeting starts and he's reading the *New York Times*. We're meeting, voting on things and he's reading the newspaper. Finally, we get ready to hold a vote and Donald holds open the *New York Times*, stands to get attention, talks over whoever's speaking and says, "Look at this! Look at this! I build a skyscraper and nobody cares! I sign some obscure defensive back and I get three paragraphs in the *Times. That's* why I bought the Generals!"

Another USFL official recounted a similar event, at which Trump attempted to exert domination over the owners through verbal and other crafty means. Fox Butterfield writes that the official, who did not wish to be named, maintained that

> "Donald is a man who doesn't know when he's won" . . . The official recalled that at league meetings Mr. Trump usually remained

[53] Jeff Pearlman, "The day Donald Trump's narcissism killed the USFL." *The Guardian*, September 11, 2018. https://www.theguardian.com/sport/2018/sep/11/the-day-donald-trumps-narcissism-killed-the-usfl

[54] Adam Lusher, "Donald Trump's troubled history with the NFL and why his 'take a knee' fight may stem from a grudge held since the 1980s." *The Independent* (UK), September 28, 2017. https://www.independent.co.uk/news/world/americas/us-politics/donald-trump-take-a-knee-nfl-protest-con-man-huckster-scumbag-american-football-usfl-john-bassett-a7972281.html

silent until the other owners were moving toward a decision. "Then he would begin his little speech ... Hey, look, I'm only 39 years old, I've made some bucks, so I know what I am talking about." After that, the official related, Mr. Trump would "blast everyone else off the face of the earth." Once, as the number of teams in the league had begun to shrink through financial insolvency, the seating arrangements at the meeting room table had to be changed, the official said. Mr. Trump, who by chance of the alphabet had normally been seated opposite the league commissioner, a position of power, found himself consigned to a lesser spot farther away. "So he went in and rearranged the placards personally."[55]

In his pre-presidential career Trump also relished eviscerating cultural elites, castigating everyone from rock stars and comedians to journalists along the way. He attributed negative press coverage and the relative delight that some of his detractors expressed during his financial calamities and divorce from Ivana to a dark psychology. In retrospect he might have pointed to James Barron's reporting of one "ordinary American"—an administrative assistant interviewed near the Trump Plaza Hotel in New York—who mused, "Everyone wants to see him fail ... It's a perverse kind of pleasure."[56] Trump captured the dynamic for all to read in an op-ed in the *New York Times* in 1995 titled "I'm Back," to celebrate his return to financial ascendancy. He posited that "[t]here is a statement commonly used, that 'everyone loves a winner.' But this is really not true. The jealousies, inadequacies and weaknesses of other people more often would lead to the statement 'everyone loves to see a winner fail'."[57] Trump's lavish lifestyle, immodesty, and pugnacity certainly made him a target of ridicule. As Richard Cohen suggested, "the misfortunes of Trump will not enhance our own fortunes and to think otherwise is immature but—it has to be

---

[55] Fox Butterfield, "Trump hints of dreams beyond building." *New York Times*, October 5, 1987, p. B1.

[56] James Barron, "Almost everyone's playing stomp-the-Trump." *New York Times*, June 30, 1990, p. 27.

[57] Donald J. Trump, "I'm back. I'm soaring once again. But enough about you." *New York Times*, November 19, 1995, p. SM58.

said—so satisfying."[58] But Trump would scarcely let anyone have fun at his expense. Alas, he rebuilt his fortune and more by the mid-1990s. And he redoubled efforts to shame his detractors and take aim at anyone who he felt disparaged him or did not accord him the praise he believed he deserved.

Trump has always demonstrated scorn for anyone who discredits him or robs him of attention to which he believes he is entitled. Several examples from his 1990 book, *Surviving at the Top*, are particularly noteworthy. In his review of the manuscript, Floyd Norris of the *New York Times* captures the essence of Trump's quest to put others in their place. Norris asks what *Forbes Magazine*, Trump's real estate competitor Leona Helmsley, cartoonist Garry Trudeau, and the rock group Rolling Stones have in common. The answer for Trump is a particular animus based on the belief that others resented his success:

> Mr. Trump says he did not get along well with Malcolm Forbes; he says that Forbes was envious because Mr. Trump had a larger yacht and that Forbes did not like him because he did not buy many advertisements in Forbes magazine . . . While he says he has no love for the press, he seems to delight in describing the ways he used reporters by getting them to write stories that damaged the financial reputation of those who were opposed to him in deal after deal. Among the other objects of Mr. Trump's scorn in his second book . . . are Leona Helmsley, a "Jekyll-and-Hyde personality" on whom he says he was able to take "sweet revenge" by blocking a land deal, and the Rolling Stones, "a bunch of major jerks," who, he says, were envious of all the attention the press gave to Mr. Trump when his marital difficulties were in the news.[59]

Perhaps one of the few who ever challenged Trump, albeit more often satirically than not (until recently),[60] and did not bear

---

[58] Richard Cohen, "Duck, Donald!" *Washington Post*, July 22, 1990, p. J7.

[59] Floyd Norris, "Whom Trump likes (himself) and hates (many)." *New York Times*, August 22, 1990, p. C15.

[60] See Lisa Respers France, "David Letterman wants to put Donald Trump in a home." *CNN*, July 12, 2017. https://www.cnn.com/2017/07/12/entertainment/david-letterman-donald-trump/index.html

the brunt of his wrath was David Letterman. Trump was a frequent guest on the veteran comedian's *Late Night* on the Columbia Broadcasting System (CBS). Their thirty-year relationship is too complex to detail here. But even Letterman's best "takedowns" of Trump, from questioning his neckties made in China and insinuating he was a racist to unflattering photos of his hair, revealed a cool and collected interviewee who often left the studio unscathed.[61] It may well be that a unique reciprocity existed between the two men. Trump's appearances boosted Letterman's ratings while providing a sounding board for his political views. As Jason Zinoman asserts,

> Mr. Trump test drove his current brand of populism to crowd-pleasing success in front of a blue-state audience, and Mr. Letterman was one of the first mainstream figures on television to regularly treat Trump as a serious political thinker, not just a joke of a rich guy (although he did that, too).[62]

Other celebrities fared less well with Trump. The case of Sacha Baron Cohen illustrates a prime example of Trump's proclivity to harbor resentment of a perceived past transgression that can resurface with a vengeance some years later like a bolt out of the blue. Cohen, a British comedian and actor, is notorious for his social satire *Borat: Cultural Learnings of America for Make Benefit Glorious Nation of Kazakhstan*. The 2006 film might best be described as a humorously absurd if equally offensive and insightful "mockumentary" of American stereotypes and prejudices as a bigoted, chauvinist, anti-Semite Kazakh national embarks on a cross-country road-trip to locate model Pamela Sue Anderson, for whom he wishes to proclaim his love.[63] The inspiration for

[61] Ian Goldstein, "Five of David Letterman's best late night Donald Trump takedowns." *Vulture*, March 28, 2017. http://www.vulture.com/2017/03/five-of-david-lettermans-best-late-night-donald-trump-takedowns.html

[62] Jason Zinoman, "The misunderstood history of Trump on Letterman." *New York Times*, August 15, 2017. https://www.nytimes.com/2017/08/15/arts/television/trump-letterman-misunderstood-history.html

[63] Dan Jolin, "Borat review." *Empire Online*, September 29, 2006. https://www.empireonline.com/movies/borat/review/

the central character emerged from Cohen's production of the *Da Ali G Show* from 2000 to 2004, which featured skits of the character Borat Sagdiyev as well as a fake journalist named Ali G and a gay Austrian fashion designer called Brüno Gehard. In that show that aired variably in the United States, United Kingdom, and Australia, the trifecta of characters lured unsuspecting celebrities and politicians into bogus interviews and asked ridiculous and boundlessly discomfiting questions of the gullible victim. In 2003 Ali G arranged for an interview with Donald Trump at his New York headquarters and posed as a journalist/entrepreneur who sought to sell the tycoon on an invention of ice cream gloves that prevent the frozen treat from dripping onto people's hands. After about sixty seconds of listening to the farcical idea, Trump seemingly discerned the pretense and exited the interview abruptly without engaging further.[64]

The ordeal seemed rather inconsequential until nine years later, when Cohen appeared at the 2012 Academy Awards. He emerged on the red carpet as the character of General Ali Aladeen from his new film, *The Dictator*. Cohen spilled an urn of ashes his character claimed to be from his deceased friend Kim Jong-Il of North Korea onto host Ryan Seacrest's tuxedo. Trump's reaction is significant insofar as it marks an important foray into the use of social media to take aim at those who he felt had treated him unfairly in the past.

Trump took to YouTube in his "From the Desk of . . ." series of clips, all told some eighty-three he produced from 2011 to 2013 in which he expounded upon his political views alongside movie reviews and social critiques.[65] As Matt Willstein notes, Trump recorded a video calling out "'this third-rate character' Sacha Baron Cohen as one of Oscar night's 'biggest losers.' According to Trump, Cohen 'thought he was being cute and funny' when in reality, the whole episode was 'disgraceful'." Trump added ominously that "if

---

[64] "Sacha Baron Cohen recalls the Ali G–Donald Trump interview." https://www.youtube.com/watch?v=W_ref_Xly7Y

[65] Olivia Nuzzi, "Inside Trump's make believe presidential addresses." *Daily Beast*, February 29, 2016. https://www.thedailybeast.com/inside-trumps-make-believe-presidential-addresses

Seacrest had 'real security,' Cohen 'would not be in good shape right now, he would in the hospital, he would have been punched in the face so many times he wouldn't have known what happened'."[66]

Trump employed Twitter to lambast Cohen. First, the day after the awards show he tweeted that

> @SachaBaronCohen is a moron who should have been pummeled by the weak and pathetic security person who stood watching as he poured ashes over @RyanSeacrest, a wonderful guy, at the Academy Award's red carpet. The security person totally froze—he should be fired.[67]

Several months later Trump wrote: "Glad to see that Sacha Baron Cohen's new movie is not only a dud but not too good at the box office. He is talentless. @Sacha_B_Cohen."[68] And finally, in fall 2012 Trump touted his matchless ability to sniff out the poseur, contending "I never fall for scams. I am the only person who immediately walked out of my 'Ali G' interview."[69] Responses to Trump's attacks on social media ranged from supportive and mildly critical to charges he was a humorless boor. Yet the incident was directly out of the playbook he would utilize as president to belittle his real or perceived adversaries and find common cause with many in certain circles skeptical of cultural elites like Cohen, whom they found offensive. As one observer contended,

[66] Matt Willstein, "Inside Sacha Baron Cohen's 13-year feud with Donald Trump, from Ali G to 'Brothers Grimsby'." *Daily Beast*, March 19, 2016. https://www.thedailybeast.com/inside-sacha-baron-cohens-13-year-feud-with-donald-trump-from-ali-g-to-brothers-grimsby

[67] @realDonaldTrump, "@SachaBaronCohen is a moron who should have been pummeled by the weak and pathetic security person who stood watching as he poured ashes over @RyanSeacrest, a wonderful guy, at the Academy Award's red carpet. The security person totally froze—he should be fired." February 27, 2012, 6:58 a.m.

[68] @realDonaldTrump, "Glad to see that Sacha Baron Cohen's new movie is not only a dud but not too good at the box office. He is talentless. @Sacha_B_Cohen." May 22, 2012, 12:31 p.m.

[69] @realDonaldTrump, "I never fall for scams. I am the only person who immediately walked out of my 'Ali G' interview." October 22, 2012, 10:44 a.m.

Donald Trump was the first American businessman to stand up to Cohen's bullying and tell him to take a hike. He was also one of the first Americans to state on record that he hated Borat. If he ever runs for president, he's got my vote.[70]

Finally, Trump's feuds with the print media scarcely commenced with the 2016 presidential election cycle and his use of Twitter to fight back against the purveyors of supposedly "fake news." His relationship with the press dating to the 1980s can only be described as adversarial from the start, with a particular inclination to interpret any negative commentary as a personal assault on his character, intelligence, or dignity or as an attempt to belittle his accomplishments. As M. A. Farber avers, Trump "has always been sensitive to criticism and in the past, was said to have had newspapers with unfavorable articles removed from the gift shops of his casinos."[71]

Trump often chastised the *New York Times*, and occasionally other newspapers, in op-eds or letters to the editor. No matter of controversy seemed to escape his attention, from book reviews to the print media's alleged oversight of his accomplishments and other perceived slights. When the *Times* favorably reviewed Jack O'Donnell's book *Trumped!*, in which the former vice president of Trump's Plaza Casino in Atlantic City, New Jersey criticized the real estate magnate on numerous fronts, Trump penned a letter to the editor. With typical bravado, he discredited the reviewer, Susan Lee, by contending that she

> is an economist. I only hope her review is as inaccurate as her economic forecasts have been. Donald Trump is doing very well—except in the press. Both books by me, "Trump: The Art of the Deal" and "Trump: Surviving at the Top" went to No. 1 on the New York Times best-seller list. Jack O'Donnell's book is a dud.[72]

[70] Joe Queenan, "No More Mr. Nice Guy." *Chief Executive* 222 (December 2006): 63.

[71] M. A. Farber with Diana B. Henriques, "Backstage at the 'Trump-bashing': Despite problems, Donald Trump is as irrepressible as always." *New York Times*, June 10, 1990, p. F6.

[72] Donald J. Trump, "Trumped!" *New York Times*, September 1, 1991, p. BR4.

In 2005, when Trump was cited in Jeff MacGregor's "Character Studies" he said the author "writes poorly. His painterly turn with nasturtiums sounds like a junior high school yearbook entry." Trump also made reference to Mark Singer, whom he disliked for a profile interview in the *New Yorker*. He wrote "Singer's and MacGregor's books will do badly—they just don't have what it takes. Maybe someday they'll astonish us by writing something of consequence."[73]

In other cases Trump felt compelled to correct alleged inaccuracies or oversights in the print media's reporting. In 1991 he reproved the *Wall Street Journal* for writing that he was not planning to engage in the management of his Atlantic City casinos. Trump asserted, "I consider management to be one of my strongest assets, and I will be totally involved in the management of my casinos."[74] In 1993 he chastised the *New York Times* for reporting a story on the Mirage Hotel in Las Vegas. Trump was miffed that the "puff piece" on one of Sin City's premier resorts overlooked the fact that his casinos in Atlantic City were rated four stars by Mobil Travel Guide, while the Mirage obtained only three.[75]

Finally, Trump was particularly indignant at any print story that putatively cast his image in a negative light. In 1997 he composed a response to the "Reliable Source" column of the *Washington Post* in which it was alleged that he took a seat at the funeral of Pamela Harriman, socialite and former ambassador to France, designated for congressional officials only. Refuting the charge, Trump seethed as he wrote:

> I am surprised that your illustrious paper would sink to scandal sheet mentality! I am also surprised that the New York Post covered the story accurately while you were just looking to do your typical bashing of New Yorkers in general.[76]

[73] Donald Trump, "Letters: Character Studies." *New York Times*, September 11, 2005, p. F6.
[74] Donald Trump, "Downside to upside, all around town." *Wall Street Journal*, September 27, 1991, p. A11.
[75] Donald J. Trump, "Counting stars." *New York Times*, July 18, 1993, p. V7.
[76] Donald J. Trump, "Trump bashing." *Washington Post*, March 8, 1997, p. A21.

When the *New York Times* published an article about him in 1996, Trump was apparently offended by a picture that made him look rotund. He reflected that

> If the picture was correct—which fortunately, it was not—then my weight gain should have been mentioned, much as Catherine Deneuve's figure was cited in your article on her. In addition, you would have had a bigger story than the phenomenal success of Trump International Hotel and Tower: a story of a man who gained 250 pounds in one week, which should have been covered as a medical rather than a financial story.[77]

In 1999, he took mild offense to a *Times* story entitled "The Anti-Trump" that featured developer Jerry Speyer. Trump concluded that the title of the story "was the best and only way you could get people to read it." As a means of implicitly belittling Speyer's success, he then devoted an entire paragraph to listing the vast holdings associated with the Trump real estate empire, from the General Motors Building on Fifth Avenue to a new tower opposite the United Nations in New York City.[78]

As a presidential candidate and as chief executive, Trump has taken extensively to Twitter to criticize the media, lay into his political opponents, and convey his views. If the limitations of 140 or 280 characters on a social media platform scarcely restrict his ability to articulate his message, it is a skill he developed over several decades by challenging the print media. His alacrity to "set the record straight" according to the Donald's perspective is matched only by the succinct yet barbed writing style that put his critics on notice years ago.

IV. Jingoism, Japan, and jilted America

A centerpiece of Donald Trump's 2016 presidential campaign was the visceral claim that the United States was getting a raw

---

[77] Donald J. Trump, "Trump's waistline, from Trump's perspective." *New York Times*, May 2, 1996, p. A22.

[78] Donald J. Trump, "The anti-Trump." *New York Times*, January 17, 1999, p. SM10.

deal from its trading partners and allies. He routinely indicted (and continues to accuse) China for unfair commerce practices, currency manipulation, and trade deficits, demanded that NATO allies pay their "fair share," and targeted Mexico and Canada for a renegotiation of NAFTA, an agreement he called one of the worst deals ever.[79] Trump's incredulity about America's "friends" did not, however, emerge out of the ether as he waged his grass-roots electoral campaign in states of the Rust Belt in 2016: he preached a remarkably similar sermon three decades earlier from his New York City business headquarters.

In the 1980s fears abounded that Japan was overtaking the United States as a global economic powerhouse. Trump was one of many voices raising concerns over that country's restrictive trade policies. The trade deficit between the United States and Japan expanded fourfold from 1979 to 1984 from $9 billion to $36 billion. The imbalance in the number of automobiles Japan exported to the United States, numbering close to two million, compared to American exports of fewer than 5,000, prompted Congress to contemplate protectionist policies.[80] "The Japan of the 1980s," Ken Moskowitz contends, "was a confident, some would say an overweening, trade colossus. Today, we've passed through the bubble, the stock market collapse, and 'Japan passing' to a period of tepid growth and doubts about Japan's economic strength."[81] Yet Trump is remarkably consistent in his conviction that the United States is still getting the short end of

[79] @realDonaldTrump, "Remember, NAFTA was one of the WORST Trade Deals ever made. The U.S. lost thousands of businesses and millions of jobs. We were far better off before NAFTA—should never have been signed. Even the Vat Tax was not accounted for. We make new deal or go back to pre-NAFTA!" *Twitter*, September 1, 2018, 8:12 a.m. https://twitter.com/realdonald trump/status/1035908242277376001

[80] See I. M. Destler, "U.S. Trade Policy-making in the 1980s." In Alberto Alesina and Geoffrey Carliner (eds.), *Politics and Economics in the Eighties* (Chicago: University of Chicago Press, 1990), pp. 251–84.

[81] Quoted in Eric Johnston, "Echoes of 1980s trade war seen in Trump comments on Japan." *Japan Times*, January 20, 2017. https://www.japantimes. co.jp/news/2017/01/20/national/politics-diplomacy/echoes-1980s-trade-war-seen-trump-comments-japan/#.W8eYxWhKiyI

the stick on trade with the Land of the Rising Sun. As president, he has continued to denounce Japan for non-trade barriers, such as strict environmental standards that are allegedly responsible for a $70 billion deficit in U.S. automobile exports. As the president asserted, "[w]e sell a car into Japan, and they do things to us that make it impossible to sell cars in Japan, and yet they sell cars into us."[82]

Although he was a private citizen who did not have the bully pulpit of the presidency, in September 1987 Trump arguably drew widespread attention to his view that Japan and other countries were exploiting the United States in terms of trade and military protection in an open letter published in the *New York Times*, *Boston Globe*, and *Washington Post*. He spent over $94,000 for the newspapers to print the missive, which was developed by advertising executives prominent in Ronald Reagan's 1984 re-election campaign. If the op-ed fell short of Ronald Reagan's eloquent "A Time for Choosing" speech in 1964, the move nevertheless fueled speculation that Trump was considering a presidential bid in 1988 and stirred grassroots enthusiasm.[83] The letter prompted one south Florida real estate mogul, Abe Hirschfeld, to launch a "draft Trump" presidential campaign and reprint the communiqué in Miami newspapers and in other venues such as Chicago.[84] Trump did not run for the White House, but did take part in an event in New Hampshire, the nation's first primary state, after one organizer, Mike Dunbar, circulated petitions for Trump to compete in the 1988 Republican primary.[85] Trump told a gleeful audience supportive of his foreign policy stances that "[t]hey're ripping us off left and right. They knock the hell out of

---

[82] Quoted in Takeshi Kawanami, "The 1980s auto trade wars are back." *Nikkei Asian Review*, February 2, 2017. https://asia.nikkei.com/Economy/The-1980s-auto-trade-wars-are-back

[83] Howard Kurtz, "Between the lines of a millionaire's ad; New Yorker's foreign-policy foray follows political overtures." *Washington Post*, September 2, 1987, p. A4.

[84] Buddy Nevins, "Millionaire pushing 'Trump for President'." *Fort Lauderdale Sun-Sentinel*, September 17, 1987, p. 3A.

[85] *New York Times*, "A presidential bid?" July 14, 1987, p. B3.

the United States. Do they say, 'Thank you'? No. Do they like us? Not particularly."[86]

Close analysis of Trump's letter suggests that the leitmotifs of unfair relationships and deadbeat allies pursuing economic growth at American expense under the aegis of the nation's defense spending are one of the fundamental consistencies of Trump's messaging across time. In examining Trump's open letter, one could easily substitute Germany for Saudi Arabia, or China, Canada, or Mexico for Japan today:

> The saga continues unabated as we defend the Persian Gulf, an area of only marginal significance to the United States for its oil supplies, but one upon which Japan and others are almost entirely dependent. Why are these nations not paying the United States for the human lives and billions of dollars we are losing to protect their interests? Saudi Arabia, a country whose very existence is in the hands of the United States, last week refused to allow us to use their mine sweepers to police the Gulf. The world is laughing at America's politicians as we protect ships carrying oil we don't need, destined for allies who won't help. Over the years, the Japanese, unimpeded by the huge costs of defending themselves (as long as the United States will do it for free), have built a strong and vibrant economy with unprecedented surpluses . . . It's time for us to end our vast deficits by making Japan, pay . . . Make Japan, Saudi Arabia, and others pay for the protection we extend as allies. Let's help our farmers, our sick, our homeless by taking from some of the greatest profit machines ever created—machines crated and nurtured by us. "Tax" these wealthy nations, not America. End our huge deficits, reduce our taxes, and let America's economy grow unencumbered by the cost of defending those who can easily afford to pay us for the defense of their freedom. Let's not let our great country be laughed at anymore.[87]

Trump's op-ed was the debut of a torrent of criticism about contemporary handling of foreign affairs he articulated to anyone

---

[86] Larry Eichel, "'Draft Trump' committee in N.H. gets visit from the non-candidate." *Philadelphia Inquirer*, October 23, 1987, p. A3.

[87] Donald Trump, "There's nothing wrong with America's Foreign Defense Policy that a little backbone can't cure." *Washington Post*, September 2, 1987, p. A9.

who would listen. At a graduation address in 1988, he expressed grief that "[s]o many countries are whipping America . . . I respect the Japanese, but we have to fight back."[88] In 1989 he told television idol Oprah Winfrey that the Japanese "come over here, they sell their cars, their VCRs. They knock the hell out of our companies." The same year, he evoked memories of Japan's imperial past and designs on world domination in World War II by proclaiming to CNN's Morton Downey that they "systematically sucked the blood out of America—sucked the blood out!" Trump contended that "[t]hey have gotten away with murder. They have ended up winning the war."[89] In a *Playboy* interview in 1990 he lamented that "[f]irst they take all our money with their consumer goods, then they put it back in buying all of Manhattan."[90]

Trump's proposed solutions of three decades ago are precisely those he has implemented, or threatened to implement, as president by imposing import fees and pursuing bilateral trade renegotiations. And his criticism of trade deals wove seamlessly into anti-elite narratives. In 1989 he opined that

> They're taking this country for one of the great rides in history . . . Why doesn't somebody say to Japan, "You're ripping us off. We love you, but we're going to put a 20% tax on everything you sell in this country until you open up (Japan to U.S. firms)".[91]

On George H. W. Bush's trade policy, including the move toward NAFTA, Trump suggested that "[i]f we get any kinder and gentler,

---

[88] Tez Clark, "What Donald Trump really means when he hates on Japan." *Vox*, June 23, 2015. https://www.vox.com/2015/6/23/8826245/donald-trump-japan-peril

[89] Patrick Gillespie, "Trump praises Reagan on trade—but saw it differently in 1989." *CNN Business*, October 19, 2016. https://money.cnn.com/2016/10/19/news/economy/trump-reagan-japan-trade-1989/index.html

[90] Jonathan Soble and Keith Bradsher, "Donald Trump laces into Japan with a trade tirade from the '80s." *New York Times*, March 7, 2016. http://www.nytimes.com/2016/03/08/business/international/unease-after-trump-depicts-tokyo-as-an-economic-rival.html?partner=bloomberg

[91] Quoted in Stuart Elliott, "Trump targets: All comers." *USA Today*, May 24, 1989, p. 2B.

we won't have any America left."[92] As Bill Clinton dithered on NAFTA, opposing the trade deal before he ultimately came to support it, Trump traveled to Japan in 1993 and called American trade representatives "morons," underscoring that "the Japanese negotiators have done one of the great tap-tap-taps of all time, keeping the ball rolling, giving absolutely nothing and having the American idiots say 'Thank you'."[93] As he formed a presidential campaign exploratory committee in 1999, he asserted that as president he would personally take responsibility for negotiating trade agreements and underscored his belief that "the president has the authority."[94] By 2008, CNN's Fareed Zakaria suggested that "Mr. Trump might be stuck in a 1980s time warp about Japan" when he criticized President Obama's pick of fellow New Yorker Caroline Kennedy as ambassador to Japan. Once again alluding to Japan's martial history, Trump declared that she was being "wined and dined by [Prime Minister Shinzo] Abe and all of these killers. Wined and dined!"[95]

V. Obama as outlander: Conspiracy theory, the "Birther" controversy, and abjection

In 1998 First Lady Hillary Clinton claimed that a "vast right-wing conspiracy" composed of conservative political operatives was bent on undermining the presidency of her husband, Bill.[96] Her spouse

---

[92] Quoted in John M. Glionna, "Couple urge boycott of goods made in Japan." *Los Angeles Times*, November 28, 1989, p. 1.
[93] Andrew Pollack, "Trump on tour; Japan glimpses art of tough talk." *New York Times*, August 19, 1993, p. D2.
[94] *Washington Post*, "Trump on trade: he'd represent; attacking allies, developer says U.S. needs better negotiator." November 1, 1999, p. A20.
[95] Jethro Mullen, "He said what? A look back at Trump's Japan bashing." *CNN Business*, February 8, 2017. https://money.cnn.com/2017/02/08/news/economy/trump-japan-comments-abe/index.html
[96] Karen Tumulty, "How Hillary Clinton helped create what she later called the 'vast right-wing conspiracy'." *Washington Post*, September 3, 2016. https://www.washingtonpost.com/politics/hillary-clinton-was-right-about-the-vast-right-wing-conspiracy-heres-why-it-exists/2016/09/02/4a5e0fba-6879-11e6-99bf-f0cf3a6449a6_story.html?utm_term=.74d34a5ab15a

ultimately faced a lengthy impeachment ordeal between December 1998 and February 1999 for allegedly lying under oath about his relationship with a young intern, Monica Lewinsky. The origins of her argument stemmed from a 1995 memo penned by opposition strategist Chris Lehane, who headed the "rapid-response team" to counter the narratives involving a growing number of investigations and scandals that rocked the Clinton White House.[97] Artful and unsophisticatedly poignant, Mrs. Clinton's condemnation of invisible forces obsessed with her husband's dalliances (i.e., "bimbo eruptions"), allegations of forcible sexual assault (Juanita Broaddrick), and accusations of murder (Vince Foster's death) nevertheless provided a means for some of Bill Clinton's supporters to come to terms with the barrage of accusations as the racy details of independent counsel Kenneth Starr's final report were made public.

In a twist of historical irony, Donald Trump—who indefatigably sought to differentiate himself from his putatively dishonest Democratic rival in 2016—borrowed a page from the tactical manual of "Crooked" Hillary Clinton from the very moment he took up residence in the White House. Trump has insisted that a corrupt, clandestine cabal of Obama holdovers or "deep state" actors in the Departments of Justice and State are responsible for many of his woes, including complicity with the "fake news" media and the protracted investigation by Robert Mueller's FBI into alleged collusion with Russia and Vladimir Putin by his campaign. The goal of his enemies, he asserts, is to delegitimize his authority and oust him from the nation's highest elected office. Trump's exegesis of his embattled presidency has become a daily artifact of his political communication style.

There is scant evidence, however, that conspiracy theory played a central role in Donald Trump's pre-political career to anywhere near the extent that imagined murderous schemes did for H. Ross Perot. Rather, at least to the midpoint in his term, Trump has utilized conspiracy narratives to make frequently

---

[97] Chris Lehane, "Yeah, I wrote the Vast Right-Wing Conspiracy Memo. I stand by every word of it. And it's even worse today." *Politico*, April 27, 2014. https://www.politico.com/magazine/story/2014/04/chris-lehane-right-wing-conspiracy-memo-106059

unsubstantiated claims that political opponents, institutions, and the media are "out to get him." It is a fatuous if formidable retort to his detractors if for no other reason than arguments that bogeymen in the highest echelons of government and the Fourth Estate are resolved to take him down strike a chord with his supporters. The media paint Trump as a frequent liar. The president pointed not only to the Russia collusion investigation of Robert Mueller that failed to uncover any wrongdoing by him or his campaign, but also to the ongoing dust-up at the FBI over Hillary Clinton's opposition research, FISA warrants obtained by an unverified dossier, and the firing, demotions, and criminal referrals of those in the law enforcement agency and broader Justice Department—and the media's reporting or alleged *failure* to report such stories objectively—as plausible evidence of a vast cabal determined to oust him.

The foundation of Trump's affinity for conspiracy theory emerged around 2010, when, as a purely political calculus in advance of a run for the White House, he jumped on the band-wagon of rumors questioning President Barack Obama's place of birth, citizenship, and religious affiliation. The speculation, how-ever, did *not* originate with Trump, nor did it commence with Hillary Clinton's 2008 campaign. As Ben Smith and Byron Tau explicate, the rumors surfaced in cyberspace years earlier and gained traction as Obama considered a run for the White House in 2007:

> The original smear against Obama was that he was a crypto-Muslim, floated in 2004 by perennial Illinois political candidate and serial lit-igant Andy Martin. Other related versions of this theory alleged that Obama was educated in an Indonesian "madrassa" or steeped in Islamist ideology from a young age, and the theories began to spread virally after Obama appeared on the national stage—to the casual observer, from nowhere—with his early 2007 presidential campaign announcement.[98]

---

[98] Ben Smith and Byron Tau, "Birtherism: Where it all began." *Politico*, April 24, 2011. https://www.politico.com/story/2011/04/birtherism-where-it-all-began-053563?paginate=false

The Obama campaign's initial response was to establish a "clearinghouse" of sorts to dispel the false stories, but to little avail.

> For more than a year, Obama relied on conventional means to confront the blogosphere's superheated rumor mill—to little effect. The "fact-check" feature on his website, for instance, only seemed to spawn more, and wilder, rumors. A mention there of Obama's birth certificate spurred National Review Online to demand that he produce it to dispel groundless reports that Obama was actually born in Kenya and therefore would be constitutionally ineligible to be President.[99]

For its part, Clinton's campaign considered the issue briefly as a potential political weapon. Senior political strategist Mark Penn authored a memo entitled "Lack of American Roots" in March 2007 in which he portrayed Obama as lacking fundamental American heritage from his upbringing in Hawai'i and Indonesia, though he did not question Obama's citizenship. Rather, "his roots to basic American values and culture," Penn reflected, "are at best limited. I cannot imagine electing a president during a time of war who is not at his center fundamentally American in his thinking and in his values."[100] As Gregory Krieg notes,

> Clinton never pursued Penn's notion as a line of attack. Later in the year, the campaign dismissed two staff members in Iowa who passed along an email that cast Obama as a Muslim agent bent on "destroying the US from the inside out".[101]

Ultimately Obama released his short-form birth certificate in 2008, which showed he had been born in Honolulu, Hawai'i.

---

[99] Karen Tumulty, "Will Obama's anti-rumor Plan work? The Democratic candidate is turning to the Web to disprove the rumors about his faith, his family and his patriotism." *Time*, June 12, 2008. http://content.time.com/time/subscriber/article/0,33009,1813978,00.html

[100] Quoted in Kyle Cheney, "No, Clinton didn't start the birther thing. This guy did." *Politico*, September 16, 2016. https://www.politico.com/story/2016/09/birther-movement-founder-trump-clinton-228304

[101] Gregory Krieg, "No, Hillary Clinton did not start the 'birther' movement." *CNN*, September 16, 2017. https://www.cnn.com/2016/09/17/politics/hillary-clinton-birther-conspiracy/index.html

But the story remained alive on the airwaves as it simultaneously continued running through the fiber-optic cables of the Internet's reach. As one example, radio host Rush Limbaugh often mused about Obama's estranged half-brother, Malik, who lives in a hut in Kenya. In September 2009 Limbaugh suggested that villagers

> ought to say to the birthers in this country that they've got Obama's birth certificate and that they will put it on display if somebody donates the money to start the building of the family museum. Would that not be cool? The birthers could build the Obama Family Museum! All the Kenyans would have to do is say, "Hey, the first exhibit will be the birth certificate!" Ha-ha-ha-ha-ha-ha-ha.[102]

For his part, Trump

> nurtured the conspiracy like a poisonous flower, watering and feeding it with an ardor that still baffles and embarrasses many around him. Mr. Trump called up like-minded sowers of the same corrosive rumor, asking them for advice on how to take a falsehood and make it mainstream in 2011, as he weighed his own run for the White House. "What can we do to get to the bottom of this?" Mr. Trump asked Joseph Farah, an author who has long labored on the fringes of political life. "What can we do to turn the tide?"[103]

Farah, publisher of WorldNetDaily, appeared on the Sean Hannity radio show in March 2011 and said:

> I thank Donald Trump for raising this issue. I think it's something that as a potential presidential candidate, it sort of raises the stakes here. And I think it's very appropriate for Americans to begin to question if there's a reason that Obama will not produce this simple document . . . And when the governor of Hawai'i, who claims to

---

[102] Rush Limbaugh, "An update on Barry's hut brother." *Rushlimbaugh.com*, September 9, 2009. https://www.rushlimbaugh.com/daily/2009/09/15/an_update_on_barry_s_hut_brother/

[103] Michael Barbaro, "Donald Trump clung to 'birther' lie for years, and still isn't apologetic." *New York Times*, September 16, 2016. https://www.nytimes.com/2016/09/17/us/politics/donald-trump-obama-birther.html

be a lifelong friend of Obama, cannot find this document, cannot produce it, it's natural that this becomes an increasingly big issue.[104]

A year earlier, in 2010, Trump confidant and attorney Michael Cohen had urged the *National Enquirer* to begin questioning Obama's birthplace and American citizenship.[105] The tacky tabloid, scarcely known for world-class reporting, ran a number of sensational stories on the "birther" notion and was front and center in publicizing Trump's decision to hire a cadre of investigators to flesh out Obama's birth certificate in April 2011.[106] In the meantime, throughout the months of March and April 2011 Trump made the rounds of television news and other shows to peddle the idea that Obama's refusal to release his birth certificate was proof he was a Manchurian president. The premise was that the president had something to hide that would otherwise make him ineligible for the presidency—constitutionally or culturally. As he told Laura Ingraham of Fox News,

> I would like to have him show his birth certificate, and can I be honest with you, I hope he can. Because if he can't, if he can't, if he wasn't born in this country, which is a real possibility . . . then he has pulled one of the great cons in the history of politics.

He told the hosts of NBC's *Today* that "[h]is grandmother in Kenya said, 'Oh, no, he was born in Kenya and I was there and I witnessed the birth.' She's on tape. I think that tape's going to be produced fairly soon." On *Fox News* Trump surmised that

[104] Video, "Hannity defends birthers: 'Why are they crucified and beaten up and smeared and besmirched?'" *Media Matters*, March 24, 2011. https://www.mediamatters.org/video/2011/03/24/hannity-defends-birthers-why-are-they-crucified/177928

[105] Associated Press, "National Enquirer hid Trump secrets in a safe, removed them before inauguration." *NBC News*, August 23, 2018. https://www.nbcnews.com/politics/donald-trump/national-enquirer-hid-trump-secrets-safe-removed-them-inauguration-n903356

[106] D. Siegel, "Trump unleashes birther private eyes." *National Enquirer*, April 8, 2011. https://www.nationalenquirer.com/celebrity/trump-unleashes-birther-private-eyes/

[h]e doesn't have a birth certificate, or if he does, there's something on that certificate that is very bad for him. Now, somebody told me—and I have no idea if this is bad for him or not, but perhaps it would be—that where it says "religion," it might have "Muslim." And if you're a Muslim, you don't change your religion, by the way.[107]

Obama hoped to put a definitive end to the unsubstantiated rumors once and for all by releasing his long-form birth certificate publicly on April 27, 2011. The nation's 44th president commented that "[w]e do not have time for this kind of silliness . . . I've puzzled at the degree to which this (story) just kept on going."[108] Trump, in New Hampshire laying the groundwork for a possible presidential campaign, took full credit for forcing Obama's hand and then returned to his standard populist refrains:

Something that nobody else has been able to accomplish. I was just informed while on the helicopter that our president has finally released a birth certificate. I want to look at it. But I hope it's true . . . He should have done it a long time ago . . . I am really honored, frankly, to have played a big role in hopefully—hopefully getting rid of this issue. We have to look at it. We have to see if it is real. What is on that? I hope it checks out beautifully. I am really proud, I am really honored. Now we can talk about oil, we can talk about gasoline prices, we can talk about China ripping off this country . . . I am taking great credit.[109]

But the issue scarcely vanished. Within weeks of the release of the birth certificate, Jerome Corsi published his book *Where's the Birth Certificate?* in which he argued that Obama was not a natural-born citizen and therefore ineligible to hold the office of the presidency.

---

[107] All quoted in Gregory Krieg, "14 of Trump's most outrageous 'birther' claims—half from after 2011." *CNN*, September 16, 2016. https://www.cnn.com/2016/09/09/politics/donald-trump-birther/index.html

[108] Quoted in Alan Silverleib, "Obama releases long-form birth certificate." *CNN*, April 27, 2011. http://www.cnn.com/2011/POLITICS/04/27/obama.birth.certificate/index.html

[109] "Donald Trump remarks on President Obama's birth certificate." *C-SPAN*, April 27, 2011. https://www.c-span.org/video/?299230-1/donald-trump-remarks-president-obamas-birth-certificate

The book alleges a cover-up and conspiracy by the White House to provide false documents, and Corsi questioned why Obama spent thousands in legal fees to litigate the matter in courts if he had nothing to hide. It would take Trump another five years to state once and for all, in 2016, that "President Barack Obama was born in the United States, period" while then maintaining incorrectly that it was his rival, Hillary Clinton, whose campaign had originally instigated the whole story in the first place.[110] And still the story did not rest in peace. In March 2017, more than a year after Obama left the Oval Office, his half-brother Malik tweeted an apparent forgery of a Kenyan birth certificate and alleged that his sibling Barack had been born in that African country.[111]

However distasteful and false, Trump's embrace of conspiracy theory concerning Obama's place of birth won him attention and fit with his anti-elite narratives. His mantra was that he had taken on the sitting president of the United States and compelled him to do something he did not want to do. He then turned the whole affair on its head and indicted the character of his political rival Hillary Clinton with more falsehoods by arguing her campaign was the source of the original rumors. Even President Obama's scathing mockery of Trump for the "birther" controversy at the White House Correspondents' Dinner in May 2011, just a week after the president released his birth certificate, worked to the tycoon's advantage. Taking shots at the host of the event, Trump argued that Seth Meyers, of NBC's *Late Night*, "has no talent. He fell totally flat. In fact, I thought Seth's delivery was so bad that he hurt himself." Trump mused that he viewed "the rough treatment as a measure of the fear he had struck in the Washington establishment. 'It was like a roast of Donald Trump,' he said, clearly reveling in the attention, if not the content."[112]

---

[110] Lily Rothman, "This is how the whole birther thing actually started." *Time*, September 16, 2016. http://time.com/4496792/birther-rumor-started/

[111] Peter Walker, "Barack Obama's Trump-supporting half-brother Malik tweets Kenya birth certificate." *The Independent* (UK), March 10, 2017. https://www.independent.co.uk/news/world/americas/barack-obama-half-brother-malik-kenya-birth-certificate-tweet-donald-trump-supporter-a7622346.html

[112] Michael Barbaro, "After roasting Trump reacts in character." *New York Times*, May 2, 2011, p. A17.

Trump's maneuvers played upon the irrational fears of many of Obama's critics that the nation's first African American president was somehow an alien by birth at worst, or peddled ideas foreign to American political culture at best. And the fears were embedded in a far-flung conspiracy of vast proportions. As historian Robert Alan Goldberg explains:

> This is far beyond the issue of whether this [Obama] is a legitimate president. The real issue for them is this belief that this is a ploy by this hidden group to get power, to move Americans toward socialism or globalism or multiculturalism using Barack Obama as a pawn.[113]

"Making America Great Again" mandated discrediting a president who promised to transform the country in a direction putatively influenced by the post-colonial critiques and "dreams" of his foreign-born father that appeared to Trump and his supporters as anathema to American political culture.

Alas, the roots of the conspiracy mentality that began with the notion that Obama represented something distinctly aberrant to the American creed and now permeates Trump's presidency and his supporters' views brings to mind Julia Kristeva's conceptualization of *abjection*, a complex psycho-social process of casting off the "other." Kristeva writes in her opening paragraph in *Powers of Horror* that "[t]here looms, within abjection, one of those violent, dark revolts of being, directed against a threat that seems to emanate from an exorbitant outside or inside, ejected beyond the scope of the possible, the tolerable, the thinkable."[114] As Derek Hood elucidates, the phenomenon is as psychical as it is political, affective as it is discursive, and subjective as it is ideological. The symptomatic aspects of avoidance and aversion are

---

[113] Quoted in Kate Zernike, "Conspiracies are us: The endless debate over Obama's birth certificate and the paranoid style in American politics." *New York Times*, May 1, 2011, p. WK1.

[114] Julia Kristeva, *Powers of Horror: An Essay on Abjection*. Translated by Leon S. Roudiez (New York: Columbia University Press, 1982), p. 1.

rooted in both discursive and bodily forms that evoke anxiety and panic.[115] The characteristics of the abject are contrived, *invented* as repugnant and otherworldly. The fabricated depiction justifies efforts to ostracize and castigate the outlander.

Kristeva's insights complement Trump's penchant for conspiracy theory in terms of his (and his supporters') use of abjection not only to portray Obama as the "other" but also to fashion anti-immigrant narratives that evoke fear and fright. Consider first, during the 2016 GOP primary race, that Trump implicated Texas Senator Ted Cruz's father in the assassination of beloved President John F. Kennedy in 1963. The depiction of Rafael Cruz as a supporter of Fidel Castro was based on a questionable photograph in which the senior Cruz was allegedly handing out pamphlets with Lee Harvey Oswald. The stunt was aimed at calling into question Ted Cruz's "foreign roots" as a Cuban American and resurrecting fears of communist totalitarianism and Castro's treachery as a former U.S. ally before the 1957 Revolution. The *National Enquirer* ran with the story on Rafael Cruz featuring the picture in question, while Fox News commentator Sean Hannity enthusiastically provided Trump with a platform to promote the deceitful narrative so it would gain currency and discredit his primary opponent. Trump told Hannity:

> It was a picture put in and [the *Enquirer*] wouldn't put it in if they could be sued, that I can tell you. Ted Cruz, I don't think denied it . . . [and] if that were true, what was [Rafael] doing having breakfast . . . three months before the JFK assassination?[116]

PolitiFact rated the veracity of Trump's claim as a "pants on fire" lie after consulting a host of photograph experts and historians

---

[115] Derek Hood, "Racism as Abjection: A Psychoanalytic Conceptualisation for a Post-Apartheid South Africa." *South African Journal of Psychology* 34, no. 4 (2004): 672–703.

[116] *Daily Beast*, "Hannity encourages Trump's JFK-Cruz theory." https://www.thedailybeast.com/hannity-encourages-trumps-jfk-cruz-theory

familiar with the senior Cruz's history.[117] Expressing no remorse for the hoax, Trump said in 2018, "I don't regret anything."[118]

Second, consider the rhetorical narrative and physiological descriptions of immigrants heading a caravan from Honduras to the United States in fall 2018 by Trump and his supporters. The president readied a military response to illegal crossings but submitted publicly without proof that Middle Easterners and "[m]any Gang Members and some very bad people are mixed into the Caravan heading to our Southern Border . . . This is an invasion of our Country and our Military is waiting for you!"[119] Fears of possible terrorists in the caravan's midst were compounded by allegations of the infirmity of other travelers. Further, following the president's lead and tone, one former Immigration and Customs Enforcement (ICE) official, David Ward, told Fox News—without any evidence whatsoever—that the poor migrants are "coming in with diseases such as smallpox and leprosy and TB (tuberculosis) that are going to infect our people in the United States."[120] What better means to justify a military response than to stoke nightmarish, Kafkaesque mental images of the abject: asylum seekers with grisly, blistered, and ulcerated skin, impoverished peasants coughing up blood, and vomiting criminals overrun with smallpox scabs?

[117] Louis Jacobson and Lind Qiu, "Donald Trump's pants on fire claim linking Ted Cruz's father and JFK assassination." *PolitiFact*, May 3, 2016. https://www.politifact.com/truth-o-meter/statements/2016/may/03/donald-trump/donald-trumps-ridiculous-claim-linking-ted-cruzs-f/

[118] Chris Cillizza, "Trump regrets nothing." *CNN*, October 22, 2018. https://www.cnn.com/2018/10/22/politics/trump-regrets-nothing/index.html

[119] @realDonaldTrump, "Many Gang Members and some very bad people are mixed into the Caravan heading to our Southern Border. Please go back, you will not be admitted into the United States unless you go through the legal process. This is an invasion of our Country and our Military is waiting for you!" *Twitter*, October 29, 2018, 7:41 a.m. https://twitter.com/realDonaldTrump/status/1056919064906469376

[120] Quoted in Jason Le Miere, "Fox News guest claims migrant caravan carries 'leprosy,' 'will infect our people,' offers no evidence." *Newsweek*, November 8, 2018. https://www.newsweek.com/fox-news-migrant-caravan-leprosy-1192605

This chilling scenario was alleged by some to be the product of a conspiracy on the Left hatched by Trump's most implacable political foes. Florida member of the House of Representatives Matt Gaetz, for example, suggested that progressive philanthropist George Soros—himself an immigrant from Hungary and a Jew—had funded the caravan to challenge President Trump's resolve.[121] Chris Farrell, member of Judicial Watch, argued on Fox News's Lou Dobbs' program that

> [t]his is a criminal involvement on the part of these leftist mobs. It's a highly organized, very elaborate sophisticated operation . . . A lot of these folks also have affiliates who are getting money from the Soros-occupied State Department, and that is a great, great concern.[122]

Such conspiracy theories about Soros have been spread far and wide. As Talia Lavin asserts, the accusations are not only mendacious but mask a thinly veiled anti-Semitism.[123] Soros is portrayed as much the foreign conspirator as the supposedly insalubrious immigrants he is unjustifiably suspected of goading into breaking U.S. immigration laws.

Surely such narratives frustrate many Americans across the political spectrum because they distract from any *honest* discussion of national sovereignty and legitimate border security issues that include drug smuggling, human trafficking, and the violent, internal state of affairs in countries such as Guatemala and Honduras. But most importantly, those who take their cues from the president's unfounded claims, or those of his acolytes,

[121] Chris Bell, "Fake news follows migrant caravan's journey north." *BBC News*, October 24, 2018. https://www.bbc.com/news/blogs-trending-45951102

[122] Avery Anapol, "Fox Business drops guest who blamed migrant caravan on 'Soros-occupied State Department'." *The Hill*, October 28, 2018. https://the-hill.com/homenews/media/413542-fox-business-exec-condemns-rhetoric-of-guest-who-blamed-migrant-caravan-on

[123] Talia Lavin, "Conspiracy theories about Soros aren't just false. They're anti-Semitic." *Washington Post*, October 24, 2018. https://www.washingtonpost.com/outlook/2018/10/24/conspiracy-theories-about-soros-arent-just-false-theyre-anti-semitic/?utm_term=.3398ba81953c

perpetuate a sinister dialogue with profound social and political implications. The peril is that

> [f]ear and hatred of immigrants is a theme that can cross ideological boundaries for a lot of different far-right movements—for instance, it can be a vehicle for anti-Muslim views or for white supremacist views, and it can be couched as anti-immigration, when in fact, it's targeting the immigrants themselves.[124]

The curious admixture of conspiracy theory and abjection is perhaps one of the most disconcerting elements of the populist mindset Trump formulated before his 2016 victory and that he has exacerbated while in office. That narrative is comparable to, and reminiscent of, the anti-Semitic and racist storylines reaching back to William Jennings Bryan and George Wallace, respectively.

* * * * *

This preceding synopsis of Trump's pre-presidential business career and political ventures highlights the degree to which key elements of his populist style in the White House are discernible by analyzing his past attitudes and comportment beginning in the 1980s. The conclusions that emerge underscore the foundations of his anti-elitism, championing of the common man, simplification of complex issues such as trade connected to nativist impulses, and conspiracy theory. The conceptual commonalities of populism he embraced from atop his Manhattan headquarters three decades ago presaged his confrontational approach to campaigning and governing. If past is prologue, as Trump stated in 1987, "I'm tired of nice people already in Washington."[125]

---

[124] Daniella Silva, "Synagogue massacre suspect pushed caravan conspiracies far-right has embraced." *NBC News*, October 29, 2018. https://www.nbcnews.com/news/latino/synagogue-massacre-suspect-pushed-caravan-conspiracies-far-right-has-embraced-n925921

[125] Quoted in Fox Butterfield, "New Hampshire speech earns praise for Trump." *New York Times*, October 23, 1987, p. B3.

2016: The year of the populists

This is a rigged economy, which works for the rich and the powerful, and is not working for ordinary Americans ... You know, this country just does not belong to a handful of billionaires.
—Vermont Senator Bernie Sanders, April 2015

We really need a public-interest government that is not taking marching orders from the fossil-fuel industry and the banks and the war profiteers. We really need a government that is acting on our behalf.
—Green Party Candidate Jill Stein, May 2016

I'm afraid the election's going to be rigged, I have to be honest.
—Donald Trump, August 2016

I. Introduction

The script of the 2016 presidential election combined elements of a *Sturm und Drang* yarn that literary wordsmiths past and present might well have dismissed as too fictionally outlandish to be believable. Yet to suspend one's disbelief is to recognize that the consequences of the populist narrative from across the political spectrum were as disruptive as they were far-reaching in challenging the political order well beyond the outcome on November 8. The screenplay continues to unfold without a dénouement in advance of the 2020 presidential contest.

Like Cervantes' self-aggrandizing knight-errant searching for a new adventure—declaring patriotism his suit of armor, donning a volatile temperament from reports of chronic insomnia, and engaging in a series of misadventures aimed at freeing the oppressed—Donald Trump emerged on the political scene in 2015 as a quixotic figure that captivated supporters as much as he confounded opponents. Raising his rhetorical sword at political elites amidst lurid tales of chauvinism conflated with chivalry, the business mogul railed against his "establishment" Republican rivals with unprecedented, personally offensive rhetoric, won the GOP nomination with arguments against "stupid people" in government, demonized illegal immigrants as an existential threat to national sovereignty, and sought to remake the Republican Party in his own image. Accusing Democratic nominee Hillary Clinton in the general election campaign not only of co-founding the Islamic State with former President Obama but also being "the devil," his sexist verbal assaults were best characterized by a deleted re-tweet that rekindled memory of Bill Clinton's dalliances in the White House as a means of indicting the former Secretary of State while deflecting his own record of infidelities: "If [Hillary] Clinton can't satisfy her husband, what makes her think she can satisfy America?"[1]

Enter Vermont Senator and self-declared socialist Bernie Sanders, who played Pollyanna to Trump's Don Quixote. Sanders' idealistic enthusiasm about transforming the United States into a Nordic-style social democracy, defined by a cradle-to-grave welfare state, won him 40 percent of the Democratic primary vote while dismissing the structural realities of shrinking federal coffers and a capitalist political economy tied to world markets. He rhetorically bludgeoned economic elites—bankers, big business, and billionaires—for failing to pay their "fair share" and called for an end to "corporate personhood" by amending the Constitution.[2] He upbraided politicians for putatively cultivating socio-economic inequality but failed to detail how exponential costs associated with his plans of Medicare for all, job guarantees, and free college tuition and student loan debt forgiveness could be adequately funded amidst a national debt surpassing $21 trillion. The answer

[1] Jasmine Taylor-Coleman, "The dark depths of hatred for Hillary Clinton." *BBC News*, October 12, 2016. https://www.bbc.com/news/magazine-36992955

[2] Matthew Rothschild, "L.A. and Bernie Sanders Challenge 'Corporate Personhood'." *The Progressive*, December 9, 2011. https://progressive.org/dispatches/l.a.-bernie-sanders-challenge-corporate-personhood/

that brought millennials and old-guard progressives to their feet was to tax Wall Street speculators and corporations hiding money overseas.

Finally, if Arthur Herzog had chosen a politician instead of an engineer to sound the clarion call of climate change and impending societal doom in his 1970s novel *Heat*, he would have needed to look no further than to Dr. Jill Stein of the Green Party forty years later. Convinced that anthropogenic greenhouse gases are an existential threat to the continuity of life on Earth, Stein called for a "climate state of emergency" in August 2016.[3] A central component of her 2016 campaign platform, as in 2012, was the implementation of a "Green New Deal." Assailing governmental elites' inaction on climate change, she proposed emulating the vast public works projects under Franklin Roosevelt in the 1930s. While Trump pledged to withdraw the United States from the Paris Climate Accord on the basis of comparatively unfair costs to the national economy, Stein contended that it was imperative to replace fossil fuels by converting the United States to an "environmentally sustainable, economically secure and socially just"[4] structure with full employment through public jobs. Stein received only 1 percent of the popular vote nationwide and paralleled Sanders' populist arguments against corporate greed, trade deals, health care, and poverty in similar ways. Public spotlight on her campaign may well have come *after* the election with her challenge to results in Wisconsin, which embarrassingly provided Trump with an additional 131 votes.[5] But if many in the media or voters in the mainstream dismissed her signature "Green New Deal" as a fringe, pie-in-the-sky platform in 2016, the proposal was hijacked in earnest by progressive Democrats in Congress

---

[3] Edward Helmore, "Green Party candidate Jill Stein calls for climate state of emergency." *The Guardian*, August 20, 2016. https://www.theguardian.com/us-news/2016/aug/20/jill-stein-green-party-climate-state-of-emergency

[4] Jill Stein, "The Green New Deal." *Jill Stein 2016*, https://www.jill2016.com/greennewdeal.

[5] *Reuters*, "Jill Stein's election recount ends as Wisconsin finds 131 more Trump votes." *The Guardian*, December 12, 2016. https://www.theguardian.com/us-news/2016/dec/12/pennsylvania-recount-jill-stein-request-denied

(most notably Alexandria Ocasio-Cortez of New York) following the mid-term elections of 2018 as well as by several potential 2020 Democratic presidential contenders including Corey Booker, Kirsten Gilibrand, Kamala Harris, and Elizabeth Warren in early 2019.

The year 2016 was undeniably the Year of the Populists. The goal of this chapter is not to detail the presidential election with a chronological, blow-by-blow account. Rather, the objective is to highlight the ways in which leitmotifs articulated by Trump and Sanders borrowed from various elements of the conceptual commonalities of populism. Critically, the analysis focuses on the intersection of populist rhetoric and the psycho-political sources of the appeal of performative politics. The analysis accentuates the difficulties Hillary Clinton faced in navigating the populist onslaught from both the left and the right of the political spectrum and the ways in which the populist ethos of 2016 continues to mold the political environment as the 2020 election nears.

The campaigns of Trump and Sanders borrowed, albeit unevenly, from the traditional populist playbook, steeped as they were in variable elements of anti-elitism, championing of the ordinary man, majoritarianism, anti-intellectualism, and nostalgia and nativism. Yet the degree to which elements of the populist offensives of the 2016 election were transformational (at least in the short term for political narratives) becomes apparent. The campaigns of Trump and Sanders altered the fundamental discourse within the Republican and Democratic parties, respectively, while Stein's focus on climate change—despite her lackluster performance on the national stage—has been subsumed within the Democratic Party and has now become a prominent platform issue. It is easy to lose sight of the degree to which the populist saga of 2016 continues to call into question the formal and informal institutions in the American polity. Closer analysis also throws into sharp relief how the populist style in the electoral realm is not wedded to any one ideological strain and can be employed in pursuit of very different policy ends. And the centrality of social media takes the populist appeal a step further than just standard overtures to the "common man." Social media provide a platform for disgruntled voters to interact with candidates in a way that television never allowed.

II. Donald Trump: from Trump Tower to the Oval Office on the wings of populism

When Donald Trump descended the escalator in Trump Tower in New York City on June 16, 2015 to declare his bid for the White House with his wife Melania by his side and Neil Young's song "Rockin' in the Free World" playing in the background, few in the media or in the Republican Party took his announcement as a presidential candidate seriously. With 57 percent of Republicans holding an unfavorable view of him, Trump commenced his electoral odyssey as "the first candidate in modern presidential primary history to begin the campaign with a majority of his own party disliking him."[6] His "ad-libbed announcement," one observer suggested, "was widely seen at the time as a joke or publicity stunt."[7] A month later only one of four Americans surveyed believed he was earnest in his bid for the Oval Office.[8]

In retrospect, however, the June 2015 announcement laid out a set of issues that reached back to his initial forays into politics three decades earlier and inexorably galvanized grassroots support for his candidacy. Trump began his speech with a dire warning:

> Our country is in serious trouble. We are not respected by anyone. We are a laughing stock all over the world. ISIS [Islamic State in Syria], China, Mexico are all beating us. Everybody is beating us. Our enemies are getting stronger and we are getting weaker. Politicians are all talk and no action. They will never be able to fix our country. They will never bring us to the Promised Land, and I cannot sit back and watch this incompetence any longer.[9]

[6] Henry Enten, "Why Donald Trump isn't a real candidate, in one chart." *FiveThirtyEight*, June 16, 2015. https://fivethirtyeight.com/features/why-donald-trump-isnt-a-real-candidate-in-one-chart/

[7] Jason Silverstein, "Donald Trump's fateful campaign announcement speech has really not aged well." *New York Daily News*, June 16, 2017. https://www.nydailynews.com/news/politics/trump-fateful-campaign-announcement-not-aged-article-1.3250165

[8] Andrew Duggan, "As in 1999, most do not see Trump as serious candidate." *Gallup Poll*, July 14, 2015. https://news.gallup.com/poll/184115/1999-not-trump-serious-candidate.aspx

[9] Donald Trump, Announcement of Candidacy, Trump Tower, New York, NY, June 16, 2015. http://www.p2016.org/trump/trump061615sp.html

Reminiscent of Ronald Reagan's inaugural address in 1981 in which the "Great Communicator" contended that "[i]n this present crisis, government is not the solution to our problem; government is the problem," Trump blamed political elites for the country's ills and touted his outsider status. He asserted that

> *Politicians* are not the solution to our problems—they are the problem. They are almost completely controlled by lobbyists, donors and the special interests—they do not have the best interests of our people at heart. We will never achieve our full potential if we send yet another politician to the White House.[10]

It was at Trump Tower that fateful June day that the campaign slogan "Make America Great Again" was born. The themes of Trump's initial campaign salvo included harangues against politicians for failure to care for veterans, for the decline of the military, and for crumbling infrastructure alongside promises to repeal the Affordable Care Act, negotiate international trade deals to the nation's benefit, and build a wall at the southern border. The latter two issues—trade and immigration—struck a particular chord among Trump's supporters. The focus was a transparent effort to tap into the frustrations of the forgotten American worker by framing trade and immigration as imminent threats to the continuity of the nation's culture and forward economic progress. He argued that China, Japan, and Mexico were

> laughing at us, at our stupidity. And now they're beating us economically. They are not our friend, believe me, but they're killing us economically . . . Mexico is not our friend. They are beating us at the border and hurting us badly at economic development. They are sending people that they don't want—the United States is becoming a dumping ground for the world. . . When Mexico sends its people, they're not sending their best. They're not sending you. They're not sending you. They're sending people that have lots of problems, and they're bringing those problems with us. They're bringing drugs. They're bringing crime. They're rapists. And some, I assume, are good people.[11]

---

[10] Ibid., emphasis added.
[11] Ibid.

Daughter Ivanka's introduction of her father prior to his announcement foreshadowed the ways in which such themes of impending threats from without and from within would unfold in the coming months of the primary and general election campaigns. As she stated of her father, "He is the opposite of politically correct—he says what he means and means what he says."[12] Indeed, one of the central features of Trump's provocative, anti-elite rhetoric employed at campaign rallies and on Twitter was the construction of narratives of internal and external menaces in absolutist terms. The enemy is so powerful, so corrupt that the intolerable situation cannot be resolved through conciliation or negotiation.[13] "Since what is at stake," writes Richard Hofstadter, "is a conflict between absolute good and evil, the quality needed [in a leader] is not a willingness to compromise but the will to fight things out to a finish."[14] Trump's speeches, "studded with such absolutist terms such as 'losers' and 'complete disasters,' are classic authoritarian statements."[15] Yet as Morgan Marietta and her colleagues contend, as a political tactic

> [a]bsolutist as opposed to consequential rhetoric has been shown to activate political participation as well as to bolster impressions of positive character traits. Simply put, politicians who speak in absolutist ways are perceived to be better people, contrary to the negative impression that Trump's language seems to create.[16]

[12] Ibid.

[13] David Rosen and Aaron Santesso, *The Watchman in Pieces: Surveillance, Literature, and Liberal Personhood* (New Haven, CT: Yale University Press, 2013), p. 195.

[14] Richard Hoftstadter, *The Paranoid Style in American Politics and Other Essays* (Cambridge, MA: Harvard University Press, 1996), p. 31.

[15] Thomas Pettigrew, "Social Psychological Perspectives on Trump Supporters." *Journal of Social and Political Psychology* 5, no. 1 (2017): 108.

[16] Morgan Marietta, Tyler Farley, Tyler Cote, and Paul Murphy, "The Rhetorical Psychology of Trumpism: Threat, Absolutism, and the Absolutist Threat." *The Forum* 15, no. 2 (2017): 314–15.

A. Trump's personal campaign against elites

Some of Trump's most vicious personal broadsides against his GOP primary challengers, as well as Hillary Clinton, were documented in Chapter 2. It is worth reiterating, however, that one of the distinguishing characteristics of Trump's messaging vis-à-vis Sanders' indictment of economic and political elites was his penchant for extreme personalization. While Trump did allude to vague and ill-defined elite forces such as the media and the GOP "establishment" allegedly conspiring to preclude his electoral victory (e.g., the frequent reference to "they" are rigging the system against him and his supporters),[17] he was far more prone than Sanders to hurl personal insults at his political opponents and individuals in the media with little regard for decency in the public domain.

In the electoral realm, Trump often focused on the least common denominator of physical characteristics. He called into question Marco Rubio's masculinity at a primary debate while alluding to his own manhood in the bedroom, insinuated in an interview that Carly Fiorina was less than attractive ("Look at that face! Would anybody vote for that?"),[18] and re-tweeted a less than flattering image of Ted Cruz's wife, Heidi, juxtaposed with an image of an elegant Melania. Trump obliquely promised to "spill the beans" on Mrs. Cruz and asserted that "a picture is worth a thousand words," drawing a sharp rebuke from the Texas Senator.[19] At one Republican primary debate, Trump began his wanton verbal assaults with an unprovoked strike on Kentucky Senator Rand Paul, who he suggested should not be on

---

[17] Cathleen Decker, "Trump's war against elites and expertise." *Los Angeles Times*, July 27, 2017. https://www.latimes.com/politics/la-na-pol-trump-elites-20170725-story.html

[18] Katie Reilly, "Carly Fiorina: Donald Trump should step aside as presidential nominee." *Time*, October 8, 2016. http://time.com/4523922/carly-fiorina-donald-trump-mike-pence/

[19] Josh Hafner, "After insulting tweet, Cruz tells Trump: Leave my wife 'the hell alone'." *USA Today*, March 25, 2016. https://www.usatoday.com/story/news/politics/onpolitics/2016/03/24/donald-trump-posted-photo-ted-heidi-cruz/82210692/

the stage in light of failing polling numbers. Paul contended that Trump's "visceral response to attack people on their personal appearance, short, tall, fat, ugly, my goodness that happened in junior high. Are we not all worried?" Trump retorted that "I never attacked him on his looks and believe me there's plenty of subject matter there—that I can tell you."[20]

The psychology of Trump's personal insults conveys much about his anti-elitist rhetoric and why it resonated with his supporters. His abusive expressions are a means to signify that his opponents not only lack intellect commensurate with his but also to underscore their violation of his values. Trump, Nick Haslam asserts,

> specialises in the language of worthlessness. Enemies are routinely derided as "weak," "ineffective," "incompetent," "failing," "lightweight," "third-rate," "losers," or simply the "worst" at something or other. These insults are belittling, communicating a perspective of power and rank looking downward. Stupidity, depravity and peculiarity are lesser quills in Trump's rhetorical quiver. Opponents are frequently dismissed as "stupid," "dopey," "dumb as rocks" or "clowns." Selected others were singled out for supposed immorality, most famously "crooked Hillary," the rigged electoral system that delivered his victory and the corrupt liberal media. Rare individuals, notably Bernie Sanders, are damned for their rarity, ridiculed as "wacko" and "crazy."[21]

Trump's choleric personal slurs seek to establish his dominance in the pecking-order of politics, as in the business world or the chicken pen.[22] "Anger," writes Dan McAdams,

[20] Quoted from Andrew Rafferty, "Trump begins debate by attacking Rand Paul." *NBC News*, September 16, 2015. https://www.nbcnews.com/politics/2016-election/trump-begins-debate-attacking-rand-paul-n428761

[21] Nick Haslam, "The psychology of insults." *The Conversation*, January 23, 2017. http://theconversation.com/the-psychology-of-insults-71738

[22] Nigel Barber, "The psychology of insults." *Psychology Today*, November 21, 2016. https://www.psychologytoday.com/us/blog/the-human-beast/201611/the-psychology-insults

can fuel malice, but it can also motivate social dominance, stoking a desire to win the adoration of others. Combined with a considerable gift for humor (which may also be aggressive), anger lies at the heart of Trump's charisma. And anger permeates his political rhetoric.[23]

What connects Trump and his supporters in their derision of elites is that the latter purportedly "look down on the heartlanders, either in reality or in the minds of the heartlanders, but Trump looks down on the elites . . . he's better off than these people, so he has special credibility to criticize them."[24]

One may only conjecture why, after verbally eviscerating most of the sixteen GOP challengers over whom he triumphed to secure the nomination and ultimately win the White House, Trump invited a handful to meet with him as president-elect and in the early days of his tenure in the Oval Office. Cruz, Trump's most implacable foe in the nomination fight, met with the president-elect privately just days after the balloting on November 8, despite having withheld his endorsement after exiting the primary race in May 2016. Following the meeting, the Texas senator's spokesperson would only say that he "looks forward to assisting the Trump administration," though there was media speculation that Cruz might be offered a cabinet spot.[25] In December 2017 Fiorina, the former CEO of Hewlett-Packard, met with the president-elect at Trump Tower and was effusive in her praise for his cabinet picks. Rumors circulated that she was being considered for the post of Director of National Intelligence. Critics charged that "despite taking a firm stand for women during the campaign, Fiorina was quick to walk back her criticism" of Trump and had abandoned the fight against

[23] Dan P. McAdams, "The mind of Donald Trump." *The Atlantic*, June 2016. https://www.theatlantic.com/magazine/archive/2016/06/the-mind-of-donald-trump/480771/

[24] David A. Graham, "The paradox of Trump's populism." *The Atlantic*, June 29, 2018. https://www.theatlantic.com/politics/archive/2018/06/the-paradox-of-trumps-populism/564116/

[25] Quoted in Theodore Schleifer, "Ted Cruz meets with Donald Trump." *CNN*, November 16, 2016. https://www.cnn.com/2016/11/15/politics/ted-cruz-donald-trump-meeting/index.html

his vile misogyny.[26] Finally, in April 2017 Trump invited Paul to play golf in Virginia and discuss health care reform. Paul said of the encounter, "[i]t was a good conversation and a chance to be with the President. Just the two of us." As for Trump's three-hole win over Paul and his partner, the Kentucky Senator said, "[t]he President never loses, didn't you know?"[27] In the final analysis, of the sixteen primary contenders Trump defeated in the nomination battle, only Ben Carson—whom the president had suggested was out of the Christian mainstream as a Seventh Day Adventist—landed a cabinet position (Housing and Urban Development).

Informed speculation suggests that Trump may have reached out to his former GOP rivals for a number of reasons, none of which is mutually exclusive. On the one hand, perhaps his rationale was to reconcile internal party conflicts, heal bad feelings and co-opt his former opponents. On the other hand, perhaps the tête-à-têtes were simply to stroke his ego. Some observers perceive a kind of "Corleone" effect, whereby Trump plays a character from Francis Ford Coppola's epic film *The Godfather*. The meetings may thus be interpreted as a means of dominating and putting his friends (and enemies) on notice. "Just as in the movie," writes Richard Cohen, "we are not sure what business the Godfather is in. He is about to be president of the United States . . . and now, during the traditional expressions of loyalties from Republicans who actually went to the mattresses to fight Trump but who now vow loyalty and just plain awe,"[28] they beseech him to kiss his ring, perhaps hoping for future favors. "Never make a request without offering your respect and friendship in return," warns Iris Milanova, "otherwise you will be considered weak, unreliable,

[26] Kristen Bellstrom, "Carly Fiorna abandons her defense of women for possible Trump cabinet post." *Fortune*, December 13, 2016. http://fortune.com/2016/12/13/fiorina-trump-national-intelligence-women/

[27] Bill Speros, "Rand Paul on golfing with Donald Trump: 'The president never loses'." *Golfweek*, October 15, 2017. https://golfweek.com/2017/10/15/rand-paul-on-golfing-with-donald-trump-the-president-never-loses/

[28] Richard Cohen, "Our next president, the Godfather." *RealClearPolitics*, November 22, 2016. https://www.realclearpolitics.com/articles/2016/11/22/our_next_president_the_godfather_132408.html

and untrustworthy."[29] As Don Vito Corleone (Marlon Brando) told Bonasera: "Now you come and say 'Don Corleone, give me justice.' But you don't ask with respect. You don't offer friendship. You don't even think to call me 'Godfather'."[30] Others interpret Trump's actions in a similar vein to the bumbling character of Fredo Corleone whose insatiable if ultimately unsuccessful quest for respect and acceptance led to his own undoing.[31]

Regardless, another set of elites in Trump's campaign crosshairs was the media. At campaign rallies (see below) he brought cheering crowds to their feet by pointing to the back of the room at all the red lights of the cameras and indicting news networks for allegedly mendacious reporting. "At nearly every rally," write Dylan Byers and Jeremy Diamond,

> the brash billionaire reams the press as "dishonest," "disgusting," "slime" and "scum," calling political reporters the worst types of human beings on earth, prompting his crowds of thousands of supporters to turn, without fail, to jeer and sometimes curse at the press.[32]

But Trump's diatribes against the press were not just general. As he did with his GOP primary opponents, he also personalized his disdain for major media figures who dared to question him.

Trump's deeply ingrained contempt for female journalists was on full display following the first Republican primary debate on August 6, 2015. *Fox News* reporter Megyn Kelly questioned his views of

[29] Iris Milanova, "15 life lessons from The Godfather." *Thought Catalogue*, January 5, 2014. https://thoughtcatalog.com/iris-milanova/2014/01/15-life-lessons-from-the-godfather/

[30] "Salvatore Corsitto: Bonasera, The Godfather," 1972. *Internet Movie Data Base* (IMDB). https://www.imdb.com/title/tt0068646/characters/nm0181128

[31] *Hindustan Times*, "Twitter's having a blast comparing Donald Trump to Fredo Corleone, the most dim-witted member of Godfather family." February 14, 2019. https://www.hindustantimes.com/hollywood/twitter-s-having-a-blast-comparing-donald-trump-to-fredo-corleone-the-most-dim-witted-member-of-godfather-family/story-fvl9iXBasqk0pL64YxRkPN.html

[32] Dylan Byers and Jeremy Diamond, "Donald Trump's 'sleaze' attack on reporter hits new level of media animosity." *CNN*, May 31, 2016. https://money.cnn.com/2016/05/31/media/donald-trump-reporter-sleaze/index.html

the opposite gender by noting that "[y]ou've called women you don't like fat pigs, dogs, slobs and disgusting animals."[33] Trump had apparently entered the debate (after threatening to boycott it originally) already agitated with Kelly when she had reported that his first wife, Ivana, had allegedly accused him of rape in their divorce but had later retracted the statement. After the segment aired prior to the Republican debate, Trump called Kelly and stated "I almost unleashed my beautiful Twitter account on you, and I still may."[34] Following the debate, after apparently stewing about Kelly's question, Trump told *CNN* host Don Lemon that "[y]ou could see there was blood coming out of her eyes, blood coming out of her whatever" in a transparent reference to menstruation.[35] Trump then unloaded on Kelly on Twitter, ridiculing her as a "bimbo" and a "lightweight." For months the feud on social media continued unabated. Ultimately Trump agreed to meet with Kelly privately. In May 2016 he appeared on her show *Megyn Kelly Presents* and offered a halfhearted apology at best for characterizing her as a floozy. In their exchange, he said, "Oh, okay excuse me. Not the most horrible thing . . . Over your life Megyn, you've been called a lot worse. Isn't that right? Wouldn't you say?"[36] The ordeal satisfied Trump's desire to make Kelly the news story instead of his own comportment as she originally brought to light.

Yet Trump's fascination with blood in his reference to Kelly was not to be the last in reproving female news figures. In June 2017

[33] Quoted in Paola Chavez, Veronica Stracqualursi, and Meghan Keneally, "A history of the Donald Trump–Megyn Kelly Feud." *ABC News*, October 26, 2016. https://abcnews.go.com/Politics/history-donald-trump-megyn-kelly-feud/story?id=36526503

[34] Rick Hampson, "Fox anchor Megyn Kelly describes scary, bullying 'Year of Trump'." *USA Today*, November 15, 2016. https://www.usatoday.com/story/news/politics/elections/2016/11/15/megyn-kelly-memoir-donald-trump-roger-ailes-president-fox-news/93813154/

[35] Holly Yan, "Donald Trump's 'blood' comment about Megyn Kelly draws outrage." *CNN*, August 8, 2015. https://www.cnn.com/2015/08/08/politics/donald-trump-cnn-megyn-kelly-comment/index.html

[36] Quoted in Eliza Collins, "Trump to Kelly: 'You've been called a lot worse' than bimbo." *USA Today*, May 17, 2016. https://www.usatoday.com/story/news/politics/onpolitics/2016/05/17/trump-kelly-youve-been-called-lot-worse-than-bimbo/84519608/

he made a reference to *MSNBC* host Mika Brzezinski as "crazy" and "low-IQ" and "bleeding badly from her face-lift." As Megan Garber suggests, just as in the case of Kelly, "the accusation calls to mind the long cultural history of delegitimizing women as people because of their biological associations with blood. Blood, again, as weakness. Blood as dirtiness. 'Bloody' as an insult, largely because it suggests unruly femininity."[37]

Of course, male reporters in the elite media were no less subject to Trump's jeremiads on the campaign trail, presaging the combative relationship between the president and the press corps in the White House. Jorgé Ramos, a *Univision* reporter who is diametrically opposed to Trump's immigration stances, was thrown out of the room briefly at a press gaggle in August 2015 when he interrupted another reporter to pose a question to the candidate. Trump said that Ramos behaved like a "madman" and was completely "out of line." Yet Trump holds grudges, and part of his antipathy toward Ramos may well have stemmed from a lawsuit he filed against *Univision* to the tune of $500 million for the network's decision to drop his Miss Universe Pageant.[38] In May 2016 Trump launched into a long-winded diatribe against the "dishonest media" that was a precis of his generalized disdain for major network reporters. He called *ABC News* reporter Tom Llamas a "sleaze" for questioning his fundraising for veterans. When *CNN* reporter Jim Acosta questioned Trump's handling of scrutiny, the business tycoon interrupted him abruptly and said, "Excuse me, excuse me. I've watched you on TV. You're a real beauty."[39] Acosta's aggressive questioning of Trump, as president, would

---

[37] Megan Garber, "Mika Brzezinski and Donald Trump's penchant for blood feuds." *The Atlantic*, June 29, 2017. https://www.theatlantic.com/entertainment/archive/2017/06/mika-brzezinski-and-donald-trumps-penchant-for-blood-feuds/532185/

[38] Nick Gass, "Trump: Ramos was 'like a madman'." *Politico*, August 26, 2015. https://www.politico.com/story/2015/08/donald-trump-jorge-ramos-like-madman-121755

[39] Dylan Byers and Jeremy Diamond, "Donald Trump's 'sleaze' attack on reporter hits new level of media animosity." *CNN*, May 31, 2016. https://money.cnn.com/2016/05/31/media/donald-trump-reporter-sleaze/index.html

ultimately lead to the White House's abortive effort in 2018 to revoke his press credential. A federal judge ruled that the action was inappropriate.[40]

B. The grassroots game and the psychology of Trump's populist attraction

Trump's ability to draw rowdy crowds to his circus-like campaign rallies, like his claim to millions of followers on social media, lent legitimacy to the assertion that his presidential candidacy was a grassroots movement composed of ordinary Americans exasperated by politicians' failures in the nation's capital. His typical stump speech during the general election, like his Twitter rants, was baked with the old-fashioned populist recipe of discontent, cultural anxiety, and economic grievance, coated with patriotic themes and promises to return the country to greatness economically and militarily, and decorated with a very personal connection he cultivated with his base of supporters—in person or via electronic devices. Always sensitive to the optics of crowd size, even Trump's questionable claims of thousands or tens of thousands of supporters clamoring outside full stadiums worked to his advantage. When the press challenged assertions that were clearly false he contended it was simply another example of the "fake news" media's design to undermine his campaign.[41]

Close scrutiny of the dynamics of Trump's campaign rallies accentuates the performative politics at the heart of the spectacles

---

[40] Michael M. Grynbaum and Emily Baumgaertner, "CNN's Jim Acosta returns to the White House after judge's ruling." *New York Times*, November 16, 2018. https://www.nytimes.com/2018/11/16/business/media/cnn-acosta-trump.html

[41] See Max Greenwood, "Trump inaccurately claims size of rally day before election was 32,000 instead of 4,200." *The Hill*, April 28, 2018. https://thehill.com/homenews/administration/385365-trump-inaccurately-claims-size-of-rally-before-election-was-32000; Sean Sullivan and Jenna Johnson, "Yes, Donald Trump's crowds are big—but not quite as 'yuge' as he often claims." *Washington Post*, October 29, 2016. https://www.washingtonpost.com/news/post-politics/wp/2016/10/29/yes-donald-trumps-crowds-are-big-but-not-quite-as-yuge-as-he-often-claims/

and the ways in which he operationalized his populist style on the campaign trail. What is most remarkable is the choreography involved in the Trump rally phenomena. From the musical tunes and his recurrently late arrival at the venues to the sequencing of themes in his speeches, virtually every component of Trump's rallies was carefully staged to maximize the appeal of the message and celebrate the messenger himself. His strategic messaging via social media essentially replicated the same dynamics.

As Stephen Reicher and Alexander Haslam contend:

> In simple terms, a Trump rally was a dramatic enactment of a specific vision of American. It enacted how Trump and his followers would like America to be. In a phrase, it was an identity festival that embodied the politics of hope.[42]

Hours before his arrival, Trump would send out a celebratory tweet to attendees and his image appeared on the big screen.[43] Reproducing the ambiance of a rock concert, the background music playing as the crowds trickled in was aimed at building excitement and anticipation through lyrics and dramatic scores consistent with supporters' disquiet, resentment of elites, and hope for a restoration of economic and social values consonant with Trump's forthcoming act. Despite some recording artists' protests, the verses of Twisted Sister's "We're Not Gonna Take It," R.E.M.'s "It's the End of the World as We Know It," and Journey's "Don't Stop Believin'" were variably interspersed with Pavarotti's inimitable version of "Nessun Dorma" ("no one is sleeping"), dramatic orchestral movements from *Phantom of the Opera*, and "Memory" from the Broadway musical *Cats*. The latter was "a poignant metaphor for Trump's place in the presidential race. The song is about an aging cat who longs to reclaim her place among the more popular cats—who, at this point, are

---

[42] Stephen D. Reicher and S. Alexander Haslam, "How Trump Won." *Scientific American Mind* 28 (2017): 2.

[43] Katie Rogers, "The Trump rally: A play in three acts." *New York Times*, October 14, 2018, p. A20.

pretty embarrassed to be around her."[44] It was not uncommon for attendees to break out in spontaneous exclamations of support for the business mogul as they awaited his private jet to touch down on the tarmac and the melodies bellowed from loudspeakers.

The long wait in advance of Trump's arrival at rallies was purposeful and constituted a central component of the spectacle. At one level the delay established a norm of commitment among the congregation and "a sense of shared identity among the crowd members ('We are joined together in our devotion to this movement')." At another level, organizers took pains to request assistance from attendees to join efforts in providing security. Instead of engaging protestors physically, the crowd was instructed to chant "Trump! Trump! Trump!" when possible dissenters were identified.

> As a result of these various tactics, crowd members were induced to act as if they were under threat—and observing themselves and others behaving in this way only served to reinforce the presumption that they truly were under threat, from enemies without and within.[45]

Of course, some protestors did emerge during rallies and were escorted out with jeers while some others met violence that Trump seemed to condone, including the promise to pay the legal fees of offenders.[46] The Trump campaign blamed political opponents such as Bernie Sanders for "planting" protestors to interrupt the rallies.[47] But organic protests by progressives against Trump's

---

[44] Maxwell Tani, "The songs that Donald Trump rallies blast to pump up supporters." *Business Insider*, January 9, 2016. https://www.businessinsider.com/donald-trump-rally-songs-2015-12

[45] Reicher and Haslam, "How Trump Won," p. 2.

[46] Meghan Keneally, "A look back at Trump comments perceived by some as encouraging violence." *ABC News*, October 19, 2018. https://abcnews.go.com/Politics/back-trump-comments-perceived-encouraging-violence/story?id=48415766

[47] Kyle Cheney, "Trump blames Sanders for chaos at his rallies." *Politico*, March 12, 2016. https://www.politico.com/story/2016/03/donald-trump-blames-bernie-sanders-rally-protests-220671

campaign and the mayhem that ensued, like the one in Chicago in March 2016 outside a planned rally that was canceled, solidified that the Trump operation did not hold a monopoly over the threat of violence in the political realm, no matter how much he had contributed to incivility in politicking.[48]

Once he had made a dramatic entrance into the venue, Trump adeptly used humor at the outset of his rallies to draw in his audience. "Long before he fires up his loyal supporters," argues Ed Pilkington, "before he hits them with outrageous comments that send shockwaves around the world, he makes them laugh" with "the intuition and timing of a standup comedian." He "produces belly-laughs out of the vulnerabilities of others, in a relentless stream of mockery and disparagement."[49] The appearance of spontaneous back-and-forth banter with the crowd is commonplace, though it is carefully planned. "At his rallies," reports Michael Finnegan,

> Trump performs like a professional comedian who has memorized a menu of exhaustively rehearsed jokes. He sticks with a few dozen routines, adjusting them to suit his political needs of the moment. The delivery can vary, but his riffs are punctuated by frequent laughs; his punch lines hit more often than they miss.[50]

Moreover, the language Trump employs is "simple in its construction and sometimes non-standard. It prefers the outspoken opinion to the 'politically wise.' This is the language of casual, unguarded talk, private language used in a public arena."[51]

---

[48] See Noah C. Rothman, "Whose violence is it?" *Commentary*, September 2016. https://www.commentarymagazine.com/articles/whose-violence-is-it/

[49] Ed Pilkington, "How does Trump do it? Understanding the psychology of a demagogue's rally." *The Guardian*, December 8, 2015. https://www.theguardian.com/us-news/2015/dec/08/donald-trump-rally-psychology-humor-fear

[50] Michael Finnegan, "All the campaign is a stage for Donald Trump." *Los Angeles Times*, January 29, 2016. https://www.latimes.com/nation/politics/la-na-trump-entertainer-20160129-story.html

[51] Susan Hunston, "Donald Trump and the language of populism." April 2016. https://www.birmingham.ac.uk/research/perspective/donald-trump-language-of-populism.aspx

Although anti-intellectual according to his critics, Trump's simple, colloquial, and straightforward rhetorical style differentiated him from his rivals and reached a broad audience of Americans who identified with the grievances he elaborated.[52] Further, whether mocking political opponents like "Low Energy Jeb" or "Crooked Hillary," describing immigrants as criminals, or lambasting reporters as fraudulent, "[t]hrough the use of gestural methods [hand and body movements], Trump metonymically reduces others to laughable portrayals while elevating himself." The strategy is

> part of a comedic political style that accrues entertainment value as it opposes the usual habitus associated with US presidential candidates. When used in coordination with verbal strategies similarly designed to lampoon opponents, Trump's enactments craft essentialized characterizations of identity categories that simultaneously cast their members as problematic citizens, whether Democrats, disabled, lower class, Muslim, Mexican, or women.[53]

Of course, one indispensable target was the media in attendance at the rallies. Print and broadcast media "were generally kept segregated from the crowd, positioned as a visible presence to be derided when he maligned them as the voice of a hostile establishment."[54] In fact, "[m]embers of the media get an email ahead of the event telling them they are 'required to remain in designated media area until the event concludes'."[55] Trump frequently connected his own frustration with media coverage of his campaign with his attendees' irritation at the press and egged

[52] See Orly Kayam, "The Readability and Simplicity of Donald Trump's Language." *Political Studies Review* 16, no. 1 (2018): 73–88.
[53] Kira Hall, Donna M. Goldstein, and Matthew Bruce Ingram, "The Hands of Donald Trump: Entertainment, Gesture, Spectacle." *Journal of Ethnographic History* 6, no. 2 (2016): 73–4.
[54] Reicher and Haslam, "How Trump Won," p. 2.
[55] Monica Alba, "Tale of two rallies: How Trump and Clinton events look and sound." *NBC News*, January 25, 2016. https://www.nbcnews.com/politics/2016-election/tale-two-rallies-how-trump-clinton-campaign-n503911

on his supporters' outrage. As he suggested at a rally in Hilton Head, South Carolina,

> there's so much dishonesty in the media. And I like to call it out. And one of the things that's really been amazing to me, and such—it's been so beautiful to watch—the level of genius in the public. They get it, you know? They really get it. They want to marginalize us, they want to do all of this and they want to make everybody look like, "Oh, gee".[56]

The media's alleged dishonesty was also front and center in Trump's indictments of the coverage of crowd size at rallies, with which he obsessed. In Hershey, Pennsylvania he brought the crowd to its feet by contending, "I say, isn't it sad that the most dishonest people there are—the media—don't spin the cameras and show them this crowd?"[57] Alas, such invectives aimed at the media borrowed from Trump's penchant for conspiracy theory. His visceral efforts to discredit news organizations, writes Nick Corasaniti, "painting them as part of a broad conspiracy with the Clinton campaign, have reached an intensity never before seen from a presidential candidate" that prompted the Committee to Protect Journalists to pass a resolution that Trump presented "an unprecedented threat to the rights of journalists" and to First Amendment liberties.[58]

The core of Trump's rally speeches then combined other elements of conspiracy theory complemented by issue simplification, nostalgia, and nativism. In effect, "[t]he world of Donald Trump is a dangerous place where there are threats around every corner, where the country is going to the dogs at high speed, and where

---

[56] Transcript, "Donald Trump campaign rally in Hilton Head, South Carolina." C-SPAN, December 30, 2015. https://www.c-span.org/video/?402610-1/donald-trump-campaign-rally-hilton-head-south-carolina

[57] Transcript, "Donald Trump campaign rally in Hershey, Pennsylvania." C-SPAN, November 4, 2016. https://www.c-span.org/video/?418009-1/donald-trump-campaigns-hershey-pennsylvania

[58] Nick Corasaniti, "Partisan crowds at Trump rallies menace and frighten news media." New York Times, October 15, 2016.

only one man has the strength to avoid disaster."[59] He routinely focused on the unfairness of trade relations with China, the need to re-establish manufacturing jobs, President Obama's putative failure to eradicate ISIS, the imperative of building a wall at the southern border that Mexico would allegedly fund to halt illegal immigration, and the general decline of American power and greatness on the world stage. He explained to his audience that such external threats and enemies

> thrive only because of the actions of many enemies within. Sometimes Trump just labeled these enemies as incompetent . . . sometimes he targeted specific individuals (Barack Obama, Hillary Clinton, his Republican rivals), and sometimes he targeted the political class as a whole.[60]

Many of his supporters believed Republican elites were trying to withhold his nomination because of the threat *he* posed to the establishment.[61] His anti-immigrant, anti-establishment discourse inevitably reached a fever pitch as attendees chanted "Build the Wall!" to stop illegal immigrants and "Lock her up!" in reference to Hillary Clinton.

Trump's appeal may have surprised many political pundits and media figures, but the linkage to populists of the past, like George Wallace, was unmistakable. "During times of insecurity," Dan T. Carter argues, "a sizable minority of Americans has been drawn to forceful figures who confidently promise the destruction of all enemies, real and imagined, allowing Americans to return to a past that never existed."[62] But the imagined narrative of that past that Trump articulated was nonetheless a powerful elixir for his supporters' existential if repressed anger at the "system." As Matthew Dickinson posits, "based on the

---

[59] Pilkington, "How does Trump do it?"
[60] Reicher and Haslam, "How Trump Won," p. 2.
[61] Ashley Parker, "At rallies, a combustible atmosphere of anger and malice." *New York Times*, March 13, 2016, p. A22.
[62] Dan T. Carter, "What Donald Trump owes George Wallace." *New York Times*, January 10, 2016, p. SR6.

audience's positive response to his discussion of trade, immigration, economic inequality, and other issues, he had clearly tapped an underlying anxiety shared by a significant number of people." And the expression of those grievances outweighed any elucidation about how, exactly, to fix them. As Dickinson continues, "in contrast to most of his Republican rivals, Trump focused much more on *identifying* the problems facing the country, and presumably his immediate audience, while largely *avoiding* discussing detailed solutions."[63] Trump's spontaneity and off-the-cuff manner of speaking reinforced the anti-intellectual expressive frame of populism. "It's considered an indication of authenticity," asserts George Saunders,

> that he doesn't generally speak from a teleprompter, but just wings it. (In fact, he brings to the podium a few pages of handwritten bullet points, to which he periodically refers as he, mostly, wings it.) He wings it because winging it serves his purpose. He is not trying to persuade, detail, or prove: he is trying to thrill, agitate, be liked, be loved, here and now.[64]

As a type of Vaudevillian act, Trump's campaign and post-election rallies (see Chapter 5)

> have been compared to Grateful Dead concerts, not just because they attract hard core fans who see themselves as part of a community, but also because they offer a rhetorical playlist that is at once predictable yet apt to surprise.[65]

---

[63] Matthew J. Dickinson, "Explaining Trump's Support: What We Saw and Heard at His Campaign Rallies." *The Forum* 16, no. 2 (2018): 174. Emphasis added.

[64] George Saunders, "Who are all these Trump supporters?" *The New Yorker*, July 11 and 18, 2016. https://www.newyorker.com/magazine/2016/07/11/george-saunders-goes-to-trump-rallies

[65] Noah Bierman, "Anatomy of a Trump rally: The hero (that's him), a jester (also him), villains, damsels, dystopia, and lots of grievances." *Los Angeles Times*, October 10, 2018. https://www.latimes.com/politics/la-na-pol-trump-rally-anatomy-20181010-story.html

Supporters' adulation for Trump was boundless, as he recognized in 2017 when he said it was "incredible" that he could shoot someone in the middle of Fifth Avenue and not lose a single voter.[66] Trump's rallies were quintessentially entertaining, a form of political reality show more dramatic than his television series *The Apprentice*. As Bobby Azarian posits:

> To some it doesn't matter what Trump actually says because he's so amusing to watch. With Donald, you are always wondering what outrageous thing he is going to say or do next. He keeps us on the edge of our seat, and for that reason, some Trump supporters will forgive anything he says.[67]

But equally important was the degree to which Trump's rally antics were undeniably irresistible for the media, even if they were often the brunt of his diatribes. The print and broadcast press was drawn like moths to bright lights as Trump delivered his blinding harangues about alleged collusion between news outlets, the Clinton campaign, and establishment elements of the GOP to undermine his candidacy. As Oscar Winberg notes, "Trump's insulting rhetoric drew wide condemnation from politicians, journalists, celebrities, and institutions, but it also attracted considerable media attention." As one example, "Les Moonves, the chairman of CBS, glibly remarked that '[Trump's candidacy] may not be good for America, but it's damn good for CBS,' alluding to the increased revenue that the higher ratings generated."[68]

[66] Tim Marcin, "Trump voters, Republicans overall, actually don't care if the president shoots someone on Fifth Avenue: Poll." *Newsweek*, July 18, 2017. https://www.newsweek.com/trump-voters-republicans-overall-actually-dont-care-president-shoots-someone-638462

[67] Bobby Azarian, "The psychology behind Donald Trump's unwavering support." *Psychology Today*, September 13, 2016. https://www.psychologytoday.com/us/blog/mind-in-the-machine/201609/the-psychology-behind-donald-trumps-unwavering-support

[68] Oscar Winberg, "Insult Politics: Donald Trump, Right-Wing Populism, and Incendiary Language." *European Journal of American Studies* 12, no. 2 (2017): 18. https://journals.openedition.org/ejas/12132

Trump's strategic use of social media recreated the spectacle of the rally and reiterated the same simplified language and messaging of political incorrectness on display in stadiums and airport hangers. To be sure, the New York tycoon was not the first to weaponize social media for political ends,[69] but he *was* the first presidential candidate to employ Facebook and Twitter to galvanize support for his campaign and effectively knock out his rivals, whether in the GOP primary season or in the general election.[70] The Trump campaign, Todd Essig maintains,

> made him into an Internet meme, a digital candidate . . . The disposable flickering signifiers, like his near daily tweets, lack significant connection to the realities being signified other than the performative message, "I will make you feel great again." No moment of his had to be connected to any other, except for that feeling.[71]

His tirades against opponents featured the correspondingly simple, direct, and biting language employed at rallies to portray his authenticity as a Washington outsider.[72] Social media, like his rallies, acted as an echo chamber that served primarily to reinforce the existing beliefs of his supporters and motivate them to the polls.[73] Reflecting the populist penchant for unmediated messaging, "Trump took

---

[69] P. W. Singer and Emerson T. Brooking, *Like War: The Weaponization of Social Media* (New York: Houghton-Mifflin, 2018).

[70] Sue Halpern, "How he used Facebook to win." *New York Review of Books*, June 8, 2017. http://www.nybooks.com/articles/2017/06/08/how-trump-used-facebook-to-win/

[71] Todd Essig, "How the Trump Campaign Built a Political Porn Site to Sell the Pleasures of Hate: What Do We Do Now?" *Contemporary Psychoanalysis* 53, no. 4 (2017): 520.

[72] See Gunn Enli, "Twitter as an Arena for the Authentic Outsider: Exploring the Social Media Campaigns of Trump and Clinton in the 2016 US Presidential Election." *European Journal of Communication* 32, no. 1 (2017): 50–61; Ramona Kreis, "The 'Tweet Politics' of President Trump." *Journal of Language and Politics* 16, no. 4 (2017): 607–18.

[73] Diana Owens, "Twitter Rants, Press Bashing, and Fake News: The Shameful Legacy of Media in the 2016 Election." In Larry J. Sabato, Kyle Kondik, and Geoffrey Skelley (eds.), *Trumped: The 2016 Election that Broke All the Rules* (Lanham, MD: Rowman and Littlefield, 2017), pp. 167–80.

to social media to communicate to followers in a way that was unfiltered and unspoiled by the traditional press."[74] Even the music branding on YouTube campaign advertisements followed the rally strategy. Background music scores were chosen to elicit emotional responses. On the one hand, the Trump campaign used "low-pitch, low-rhythm, and low intensity melody based on orchestral strings to create the mental image of crisis and depression." On the other hand, acoustic elements of songs like Lee Greenwood's "God Bless the USA" and martial movements evoked patriotism, recalling the savior model of the presidency and painting the mental image of Trump as redeemer of the homeland in ways that are reminiscent of the scores "built by Hollywood films throughout the second half of the past century. The music employed in Trump's campaign is classical orchestral music, with string and wind instruments and drum rolls that closely refer to epic and military genres."[75]

In the end analysis, Trump's performative politics on the campaign trail were sufficient to rouse enough support to carry key swing states, including Florida, Pennsylvania, Ohio, Wisconsin, and Michigan, and secure a narrow victory in the state-wide popular vote and carry the Electoral College. His campaign implemented a savvy geographic strategy that took aim at states Hillary Clinton mistakenly took for granted as longtime Democratic bastions, and ignored to her own detriment, particularly in the Rustbelt. As Denise M. Bostdorff contends,

> One of the persuasive tasks of any rhetor is to put listeners in an emotional frame of mind conducive to the persuasive goal at hand. In this, Trump successfully built on discontent and magnified anger into rage so that enough voters in the right states were willing to take a chance on an outsider with no political experience—a billionaire

[74] Jospeh P. Zompetti, "Rhetorical Incivility in the Twittersphere: A Comparative Thematic Analysis of Clinton and Trump's Tweets during and after the 2016 Presidential Election." *Journal of Contemporary Rhetoric* 9, no. 1/2 (2019): 34.

[75] Lluís Mas, Maria-Rosa Collell, and Jordi Xifra, "The Sound of Music or the History of Trump and Clinton Family Singers: Music Branding as Communication Strategy in the 2016 Campaign." *American Behavioral Scientist* 61, no. 6 (2017): 594.

with a track record in obvious contradiction to his populist claims—
as the means toward political transformation.[76]

Put another way, "Trump's candidacy was built by making some
of his supporters feel good about simmering resentments previously kept under wraps by 'political correctness'."[77]

Scholars continue to debate his surprise victory, offering a
wide range of theories to explain his success. The conspiracy
theory surrounding Trump's arguments that the political system
is "rigged" is closely associated with voter support for his candidacy, and conservatives' views more generally in a comparative context, according to several studies.[78] Some psychologists,
like Thomas Pettigrew, contend that Trump's messaging tapped
into the veins of authoritarianism, social dominance orientation,
and outgroup prejudice, and reflected the absence of intergroup
contact and relative deprivation, particularly among male nativ-
ists with less education than the general population, enabling his
messaging on immigration and economic dislocation to "make
people vulnerable to an intense sense of threat."[79]

Yet other analysts accentuate the intersection of his messaging
with structural factors in the election. Nate Cohn, for example,
suggests that the sheer number of candidates—seventeen—in the
GOP field created a substantial collective action problem. Each
focused on a particular niche within the Republican Party and no
candidate with broad appeal emerged at the outset. Without a
clear front-runner in the primary race, and his opponents' incredulity that Trump was a serious candidate, none had a particular
incentive to attack his candidacy effectively as donors stood on
the sidelines. In other words,

[76] Denise M. Bostdorff, "Obama, Trump, and Reflections on the Rhetoric of
Political Change." *Rhetoric and Public Affairs* 20, no. 4 (2017): 698.

[77] Essig, "How the Trump Campaign Built a Political Porn Site to Sell the Pleasures of Hate," p. 521.

[78] Democracy Fund Voter Study Group, "Views of the electorate research study."
August 28, 2017. https://www.voterstudygroup.org/; Pia K. Lamberty, Jens
H. Hellmann, and Aileen Oeberst, "The Winner Knew It All? Conspiracy
Beliefs and Hindsight Perspective after the 2016 US General Election." *Per-
sonality and Individual Differences* 123 (2018): 236–40.

[79] Pettigrew, "Social Psychological Perspectives on Trump Supporters," p. 112.

Mr. Trump's opposition was always far less organized and under-funded than it would otherwise have been. A candidate like Marco Rubio never had a chance to take advantage of the benefits that usually accompany elite support; he didn't have time.[80]

Finally, political scientist James Campbell and his colleagues point to larger historical dynamics shown to affect presidential elections, such as the difficulty of the incumbent party to win a third term, economic growth, party polarization, and the mood of the country in terms of appetite for governmental activism and views of whether the nation is heading in the "right direction." Based on nine different forecast models in advance of 2016, the median anticipated victory for Hillary Clinton was 1.5 percent. She actually won a plurality of the popular vote by 2.1 percent, an irrelevancy due to the geography of the Electoral College.[81] Thus, both the strategic ground game *and* the populist style employed by Trump were pivotal factors in his campaign's success.

> President Trump's persuasive challenge, however, is whether he can keep supporters in a perpetual state of anger to his benefit. Even when anger is justified, it can be exhausting, and once anger dissipates among the majority who are not dedicated true believers, the thirst for revenge can dissipate, too.[82]

This one of many perils he confronts in advance of the 2020 election (see Chapter 7).

III. Bernie Sanders, Santa Claus, and socialism

In September 2015, as the Democratic primary fight between Bernie Sanders and Hillary Clinton geared up, *Fox News* contributor Tom

---

[80] Nate Cohn, "What I got wrong about Donald Trump." *New York Times*, May 5, 2016, A3.

[81] James E. Campbell, "Introduction." Politics Symposium, Forecasting the 2016 American National Elections. *PS: Political Science and Politics* 49, no. 4 (2016): 649–54.

[82] Bostdorff, "Obama, Trump, and Reflections on the Rhetoric of Political Change," p. 698.

Shillue theorized why the elderly Vermont Senator was profiting from a wellspring of support from millennials on college campuses. Shillue submitted bluntly that

> Bernie Sanders is Santa Claus. Many people know what I found out the hard way. When you go to college Santa stops visiting. But you still need to believe in something. That's why you fill the Santa-shaped hole in your heart with a different old white man who promises to give everyone "free stuff".[83]

Although Sanders was never spotted with reindeer or sporting a long white beard the metaphor began to stick with his detractors and his supporters alike. Four months later, at a winter rally at North High School in Worcester, Massachusetts Sanders addressed an overflow crowd of 3,000 attendees. As Brad Petrishen and Craig Semon recounted, "[p]eople started lining up for the event early, cursing the cold but warmed somewhat by a Santa-suited Cambridge man who dressed up as 'Bernie Claus' and sang songs extolling the senator's virtues."[84]

With Sanders' unyielding appeals to secure universal benefits for voters, including a $15/hour minimum wage, a single-payer health care system or "Medicare for all," expansion of Social Security benefits, free college tuition, free pre-kindergarten care, and paid sick leave among other projects, it is understandable why some may have equated Sanders with St. Nicholas, the fabled Catholic saint and fourth-century gift-giver of Myra. But the wily candidate from the Green Mountain State did not play Dire Straits' "Money for Nothing" at his rallies and took umbrage at his opponents' assertions that he had wrapped up his democratic socialist plans in holiday paper to deliver on a sled to the average American without a plan to pay for expanding social benefits. In response to Hillary Clinton's poignant critique that

---

[83] Tom Shillue, *Red Eye*, Fox News, September 30, 2015. https://archive.org/details/FOXNEWSW_20150930_070000_Red_Eye

[84] Brad Petrishen and Craig S. Semon. "Bernin' love warms rally at North High." *Telegram & Gazette* (Worcester, MA), January 3, 2016, p. A1.

his $1.38 trillion plan for health care and $1 trillion proposal for infrastructure development could not be achieved without significant harm to the middle class, which Sanders purported to represent, he turned to one of the chief populist arguments of his campaign: halting corporate greed, taxing investment banks, and reversing the wealthy elite's grip on the political system. In particular, Sanders took aim at elements of the tax code that permit corporations to avoid income taxes by sheltering profits overseas. As he told an audience at the Politics and Eggs event in Manchester, New Hampshire the day after a debate with Clinton: "What we have documented . . . that in a given year, you have very profitable—I mean very profitable—multinational corporations not paying a nickel in federal income taxes. And that seems to me to be absurd."[85]

A month later, Sanders addressed the "Santa Claus" storyline again. To an audience at the University of Central Florida in Orlando, he asserted

> Now some people say, they say, "Oh Bernie, you're a nice guy and you wanna make public colleges and universities tuition free, and you wanna lower student debt; you're like Santa Claus giving away things. How are you going to pay for that?" And I will tell you how we're going to pay for it. What we are going to do is put a tax on Wall Street speculation.[86]

In Carson, California in May 2016 Sanders further elaborated his disdain for corporate fat cats, noting that

> In 2009, Congress, against my vote, bailed out the crooks on Wall Street. Today, Wall Street is doing just fine, and I think it is appropriate to impose a tax on Wall Street speculations . . . Now, Wall Street does not like that idea, and I say, so what? If we win this

[85] Ben Wolfgang, "Sanders denies he's 'Santa Claus' and wants to 'give away a bunch of free stuff'." *Washington Times*, February 5, 2016. https://www.washingtontimes.com/news/2016/feb/5/bernie-sanders-denies-hes-santa-claus/

[86] Gabby Baquero, "Bernie Sanders pushes for free college, health care at rally." *University Wire*, March 10, 2016.

election, Wall Street and the other people who now run this country, are going to learn a very profound lesson. And that is, *they will not continue to get it all.*[87]

The expressive frame of Sanders' populism was characterized by his generalized attacks on economic elites and the politicians who enable them. In contrast to Trump, Sanders only occasionally called out his targets by name, and rarely with vindictive personal rhetoric. His sweeping condemnations of the billionaire class and disdain for big money in political campaigns intertwined elements of conspiracy theory and simplified solutions amidst a grassroots movement that shared his nostalgia not for "the conservation of the past but fulfillment of past hopes"[88] in terms of the progressive ideal of remedying the inequities of wealth concentration. Most importantly, his campaign reminded "his party of something it often forgets: Government was once popular because it provided tangible benefits to large numbers of Americans."[89] What was most remarkable in Sanders' populist juggernaut was the degree to which the septuagenarian captured the imagination of American youth whose support very nearly cost Hillary Clinton the Democratic nomination—and whose lack of enthusiasm for her may well have figured into her general election loss.

A. Sanders on the stump

The overall structure of a Sanders rally is most comparable to Trump's spectacles not only for the vivacity of attendees but also for the consistency in messaging. And like Trump, Sanders' ability to draw huge crowds to his campaign rallies enabled him to stake a claim to a grassroots movement. Moreover, the

---

[87] "Sen. Bernard Sanders, I-VT, Democratic candidate, holds a rally." *Political Transcript Wire*, May 19, 2016. Emphasis added.

[88] Bryan D. Price, "Material Memory: The Politics of Nostalgia on the Eve of MAGA." *American Studies* 57, no. 1 (2018): 115.

[89] E. J. Dionne, "Bernie Sanders: The new St. Nick—His sack of proposals could reframe the popular debate." *Washington Post*, May 15, 2015.

rapidity with which his crowd sizes increased over the course of the Democratic primary season was impressive, growing from a few thousand in battleground states like Iowa to more than 20,000 in some cases and far surpassing the number of attendees at Hillary Clinton's rallies generally.[90] Though underreported by the news media, events like the one in Boston in which twice as many showed up for Bernie in early October 2015 as for Barack Obama in 2007 accentuated the senator's ability to generate widespread enthusiasm, particularly among younger voters and on college campuses.[91]

Grassroots excitement about his campaign was also reflected in his fundraising through social media, which yielded a staggering number of small donations under $200 (and an average of $27 as Sanders frequently touted on the campaign trail) that constituted nearly two-thirds of all the money he culled to outraise Hillary Clinton through April 2015. One analysis reported that one of out every four dollars came from donors outside the workforce, including the unemployed and retired.[92] "In making a virtue of his campaign hunt for small donations," writes Francis X. Clines, "the senator implicitly invites further comparison with Mrs. Clinton,"[93] who received $11 million for speeches and relied on a super PAC (political action committee) to fundraise. The sheer number of small donations enabled him to paint Hillary Clinton as the very type of political insider who could be controlled by the cabal of wealthy donors such as those on Wall Street to which he ascribed the nation's ills.

[90] John Wagner, "Two days later, Sanders draws five times as many people as Clinton to event at same university in N.H." *Washington Post Blogs*, September 21, 2015.

[91] Chris Cillizza, "20,000 people came to see Bernie Sanders in Boston. Why aren't we talking more about it?: #FeeltheBern." *Washington Post Blogs*, October 5, 2015.

[92] Seema Mehta, Anthony Pesce, Maloy Moore, and Christine Zang, "Election 2016; Who's giving Sanders all those $27 donations?" *Los Angeles Times*, June 4, 2016, p. A1.

[93] Francis X. Clines, "Bernie Sanders comes clean." *New York Times Online*, May 26, 2015.

In similar fashion to Trump, Sanders used rallies to peddle his populist attacks on elites—in his case, economic elites (including Trump) who had putatively sold out the hard-working middle class, the elderly, the poor, minorities, and children. His standard stump speech also included invectives against a broken justice system and corrupt campaign finance laws.[94] Conspiracy theory with a moral flair was at the center of Sanders' chief argument against corporations, the wealthy, and political elites who abet the furtherance of their fortunes. During a speech at Liberty University in September 2015, Sanders asserted that

> In the last two years, 15 people saw $170 billion dollar increase in their wealth, 45 million Americans live in poverty. That in my view is not justice. That is a *rigged economy*, designed by the wealthiest people in this country to benefit the wealthiest people in this country at the expense of everybody else.[95]

The line of argument finds its historical analogue with the populist progressives of William Jennings Bryan's era, insofar as big industry is the culprit of the downtrodden. As Michael Kazin posits:

> The original Populists would probably warm up to Sanders, even if their constituents in places like rural Kansas and Georgia might be puzzled to hear familiar rhetoric spoken by an elderly Jew with a Brooklyn accent. The Populists' 1892 platform thundered: "The fruits of the toil of millions are boldly stolen to build up colossal fortunes for a few." Sanders similarly attacks "the billionaire class," whose supposed grip on the state has led to "an enormous transfer of wealth from the middle class and the poor to the wealthiest people in this country."[96]

---

[94] Rick Pearson and Kim Geiger, "Sanders: 'Tough' foreign policy—Presidential campaign storms into Chicago." *Chicago Tribune*, February 26, 2016, p. 1.

[95] C-SPAN, "Bernie Sanders at Liberty University." September 14, 2015. https://www.c-span.org/video/?c4550942/bernie-sanders-liberty-university. Emphasis added.

[96] Michael Kazin, "How can Donald Trump and Bernie Sanders both be populists?" *New York Times Online*, March 22, 2016. http://www.nytimes.com/2016/03/27/magazine/how-can-donald-trump-and-bernie-sanders-both-be-populist.html

Campaign finance figured prominently in Sanders' indictment of political elites for facilitating wealth inequality. As he asserted in his announcement to seek the Democratic nomination,

> To run a credible campaign in this day and age, you do need a whole lot of money ... Whether the magic number is $200 million, it is $150 million, it is a lot of money, but even with that, you would be enormously outspent by the Koch Brother candidates and the other candidates who will likely spend, in the final analysis, over $1 billion, if not two.[97]

In early August 2015 he pledged to introduce legislation to strengthen public financing of campaigns, suggesting that "the current political campaign finance system is corrupt and amounts to legalized bribery."[98] The question for Sanders, which was resoundingly answered by his campaign supporters, was "whether there really is grass-roots support in terms of people standing up and being prepared to take on the billionaire class."[99] Yet for critics on the Right, "[t]he Sanders view has all the hallmarks of a good conspiracy theory. It finds a common thread in disparate phenomena and attributes them to the workings of a shadowy, nefarious force. It is simplistic, paranoid and seductive."[100]

One important distinction between Trump's rallies, speeches, and general comportment and Sanders' populist style, however,

[97] Dan Merica and Nick Viviani, "Sen. Bernie Sanders is running for president." *WIBW-Channel 13* (Montpelier, VT). https://www.wibw.com/home/headlines/Vermont-independent-Sen-Bernie-Sanders-says-I-am-running-for-president-in-interview-with-AP-301764001.html

[98] Quoted in Jordain Carney, "Bernie Sanders to fight for campaign finance reform." *The Hill*, August 4, 2015. https://thehill.com/blogs/ballot-box/presidential-races/250187-sanders-campaign-finance-system-amounts-to-legalized

[99] Quoted in Erin Kelly, "Bernie Sanders: 'I am running in this election to win'." *USA Today*, April 30, 2015. https://www.usatoday.com/story/news/politics/elections/2015/04/29/bernie-sanders-interview-democratic-presidential-race/26576639/

[100] Rich Lowry, "Bernie's conspiracy theory." *Politico*, October 29, 2015. https://www.politico.com/magazine/story/2015/10/bernies-conspiracy-theory-213307

was the tone. Sanders made a concerted effort to avoid personal attacks even as he denounced the avarice of big money interests. He pledged in his May 26, 2015 campaign announcement that "my campaign will not be driven by political gossip or reckless personal attacks." In a thinly veiled shot across the bow at Donald Trump, who would enter the Republican race a month later, Sanders continued by asserting that "[p]olitics in a democratic society should not be treated as if it were a baseball game, a game show or a soap opera."[101] Even though his criticism of Hillary Clinton became sharper as the primary fight ensued, Sanders questioned her judgment and policy stances rather than her character,[102] though the former Secretary of State "accused Sanders of impugning her personal integrity by citing the money the former New York senator raised in contributions and speech-making fees from Wall Street."[103] Still, Sanders refused to engage her email scandal, much to the chagrin of some supporters, when he said "the American people are sick and tired about hearing about your damn emails . . . Enough of the emails—let's talk about the real issues facing the American people."[104]

While Trump rarely if ever ventured into venues where his policy views had little support, Sanders was more intrepid and maintained his commitment to dialogue in potentially hostile territory. In addressing students at the conservative Christian Liberty University in September 2015, he noted, "I came here today because I believe from the bottom of my heart that it is vitally

[101] C-SPAN, "Senator Bernie Sanders campaign announcement." May 26, 2015. https://www.c-span.org/video/?326214-1/senator-bernie-sanders-i-vt-presidential-campaign-announcement

[102] See Patrick Healy and Amy Chozick, "In Democratic debate, Clinton and Sanders spar over judgment." New York Times, April 14, 2016. https://www.nytimes.com/2016/04/15/us/politics/democratic-debate.html

[103] Mark C. Barabak and Evan Halper, "The real question in the Clinton–Sanders debate? How much change do Democrats want?" Los Angeles Times, February 5, 2016. https://www.latimes.com/nation/politics/la-na-0205-new-hampshire-primary-debate-20160205-story.html

[104] Ben Jacobs and Sabrina Siddiqui, "Bernie Sanders to Clinton: People 'are sick of hearing about your damn emails'." The Guardian, October 5, 2015. https://www.theguardian.com/us-news/2015/oct/13/bernie-sanders-hillary-clinton-damn-email-server

important for those of us who hold different views to be able to engage in a civil discourse."[105] He acknowledged political differences with attendees over issues such as abortion and same-sex marriage, but sought common ground on poverty and health care by appealing to their faith.[106] Moreover, Sanders was quick to condemn violence by his supporters at Trump rallies[107] and made an impassioned plea for unity at the Democratic nominating convention, calling upon his acolytes not to walk out, protest, or interrupt Hillary Clinton's coronation as the party's standard-bearer as a "personal courtesy" to him.[108]

B. Populist authenticity, the millennial marvel, and Sanders' legacy

Sanders' authenticity as a progressive populist was never seriously probed by the media, perhaps because his focus on radical, revolutionary discourse about the wealthy, the forgotten middle class, and the poor overshadowed his personal wealth. But if a billionaire like Trump seemed like an unlikely champion of the average American, the same argument could be leveled

[105] *C-SPAN*, "Sen. Bernie Sanders (I-VT): Opening remarks at Liberty University." September 14, 2015. https://www.c-span.org/video/?c4550988/sen-bernie-sanders-opening-remarks-liberty-university

[106] Ashley McKinless, "Bernies Sanders' speech at conservative Christian college a lesson in civility." *America: The Jesuit Review*, September 16, 2015. https://www.americamagazine.org/content/all-things/what-civility-looks-sanders-liberty-university

[107] David Weigel, "Sanders condemns violence at Trump's San Jose rally." *Washington Post*, June 3, 2016. https://www.washingtonpost.com/news/post-politics/wp/2016/06/03/sanders-condemns-violence-at-trumps-san-jose-rally/; Callum Borchers, "Bernie Sanders tells supporters to knock off the violence." *Washington Post*, June 5, 2016. https://www.washingtonpost.com/news/post-politics/wp/2016/06/05/bernie-sanders-tells-supporters-to-knock-off-the-violence/

[108] See Allison Wisk and Julie Westfall, "Democratic National Convention Day One: Bernie Sanders tells supporters, 'Hillary Clinton must become the next president of the United States'." *Los Angeles Times*, July 25, 2016. https://www.latimes.com/nation/politics/trailguide/la-na-democratic-convention-2016-live-sanders-supporters-shout-chants-1469481165-htmlstory.html

against Sanders. Although he continues to rail against inequality in income and inequality in wealth by contending that "the economy is doing great for the top 1 percent,"[109] Sanders' own affluence places him within the very elite he criticizes. In 2017 he earned more than $1 million for the second year in a row, of which more than $800,000 was generated from book royalties while earning $174,000 from his Senate salary.[110] "Sanders," Bradford Betz avers,

> has long brandished his credentials as one of the "poorest" members of Congress to rally against income inequality, a threat the senator has called "the great moral issue of our time." But the senator's income places him high above the national threshold for qualifying for the so-called "One Percent" . . . According to a 2013 Economic Policy Institute report, a family needs an income of $389,436 to be in the top 1 percent nationally.[111]

Additionally, Sanders owns homes in Washington, DC, and Burlington, Vermont, and recently purchased a $600,000 home on Lake Champlain. The percentage of Americans with two or more homes has been estimated at less than 5 percent in recent decades.[112]

---

[109] Bernie Sanders, "Americans need an economy that supports more than the 1 percent." *The Hill*, January 19, 2019. https://thehill.com/opinion/finance/426153-americans-need-an-economy-that-supports-more-than-the-1-percent

[110] Elizabeth Hewitt and Anne Galloway, "For a second year, Sanders earns more than $1M." *VTDigger*, June 22, 2018. https://vtdigger.org/2018/06/22/second-year-sanders-earns-1m/

[111] Bradford Betz, "Bernie Sanders' income tops $1M for second year in row, reports say." *Fox News*, June 24, 2018. https://www.foxnews.com/politics/bernie-sanders-income-tops-1m-for-second-year-in-row-reports-say

[112] Elizabeth Mehren, "Rich collecting 2nd homes/owning 2, 3, even 4 houses becoming commonplace." *Los Angeles Times*, May 23, 2000. https://www.sfgate.com/business/article/Rich-Collecting-2nd-Homes-Owning-2-3-even-4-2777678.php; *Statista*, "Share of Americans who own a second home in 2018, by age." https://www.statista.com/statistics/228894/people-living-in-households-that-own-a-second-home-usa/

If Donald Trump dismissed critiques about his credibility as a champion of the forgotten American with politically incorrect histrionics, Bernie Sanders surmounted criticism by pointing to his long career in public service that solidified his credentials as a progressive. He has been remarkably consistent and disciplined, if not redundant in his revolutionary messaging since his civil rights and anti-Vietnam War activism in the 1960s, while mayor of Burlington, Vermont, as a member of the House of Representatives beginning in 1990, and as a senator since 2006. Jason Horowitz asserts that "Mr. Sanders has talked with clockwork consistency about an economy rigged against the working class, a campaign finance system that corrupts politicians and a corporate media that obscures the truth. 'You could take one of his speeches from 1981, play it in the campaign this year, and no one would know, except his voice sounds a little bit younger',"[113] argued a Sanders' protégé. Undaunted by media figures who dismiss him derisively as a socialist, "Sanders is impervious, and he stays on message no matter what is being said." His simplified message "is hard to listen to if you're expecting variety, but his is the right message. Bernie Sanders is a true phenomenon."[114] And whatever his relative net worth, Sanders' presentation of self also conveyed the imagery of the working-class man of the people in terms of his dress. His rolled-up sleeves, wire-rimmed glasses, and utilitarian fashion contrasts starkly with most political candidates, including Trump who sports expensive suits. "He's flagrantly uncool," writes Véronique Hyland. "There's something comforting about that, for people our age [millennials]—the fact that he looks like your dad (or your granddad) who's here to set things right, down to the Men's Wearhouse wardrobe."[115]

[113] Jason Horowitz, "Over decades, Sanders has stayed on message." *New York Times*, March 26, 2016, p. A11.
[114] David Russell, "The Bernie Sanders phenomenon." *The Hill*, June 24, 2015. https://thehill.com/blogs/pundits-blog/presidential-campaign/245937-the-bernie-sanders-phenomenon
[115] Véronique Hyland, "An ode to Bernie Sanders' rumpled style." *The Cut*, April 15, 2016. https://www.thecut.com/2016/01/bernie-sanders-fashion-style.html

Indeed, the Sanders sensation resonated particularly with the millennial generation, despite the senator's age difference vis-à-vis younger voters. His status as an independent and the anti-elitist messaging he articulated with a focus on income and wealth inequality may well have resounded with younger Americans more because of their poor economic prospects than "free stuff" they hoped to receive in their Christmas stockings. While Sanders, like Trump, largely failed to address one of the underlying causes for the loss of jobs—automation—the narrative about the alleged unfairness of the economic and political system was consonant with many millennials' existential disgust with their own outlook for social mobility. And millennials have extremely weak ties to either mainstream political party.

Why did Sanders beat Clinton in the primary vote among voters 18–29 years old by a 71–28 percent margin in 25 states?[116] "In reality," writes Conor Lynch,

> millennials are the most educated generation *and* the most indebted generation ... They also face a bleak job market, while average wages have steadily declined for young graduates since 2000 ... For young people who choose *not* to go to college and avoid taking on enormous levels of debt, there is an increasingly widening pay gap.[117]

One the great mysteries of Sanders' ultimate primary defeat to Hillary Clinton was that despite his populist message that brought cheering crowds to their feet and eclipsed the former Secretary of State's rallies, she prevailed in the large key states to wrap up the Democratic nomination with relative ease. The lesson may well be that crowd size is a poor indicator of widespread electoral support, despite the appearance of a massive,

[116] Jeff Stein, "Sanders is beating Obama's 2008 youth vote record. And the primary's not even over." *Vox*, June 2, 2016. https://www.vox.com/2016/6/2/11818320/bernie-sanders-barack-obama-2008

[117] Conor Lynch, "They aren't in it for 'free stuff': What critics get wrong about millennial Bernie Sanders supporters." *Salon*, June 24, 2016. https://www.salon.com/2016/06/24/they_arent_in_it_for_free_stuff_what_critics_get_wrong_about_millennial_bernie_sanders_supporters/

grassroots movement. Sanders' supporters were more vocal than Clinton's and spent more time on social media lauding their candidate. But crowd size can be an optical illusion that suggests a bandwagon effect that is absent. "The people at the rally are not a random or representative sample of the electorate," explains political scientist Lynn Vavreck. "These are strategic and well-planned events,"[118] not simply spontaneous happenings. Choreographed rallies take place in carefully chosen venues to maximize the appearance of widespread enthusiasm.

Still, Sanders won 40 percent of the Democratic primary vote—despite not being a member of the Democratic Party. And revelations of the Clinton campaign's control over the Democratic National Committee in the primary fight left a bitter taste in the mouths of Sanders' supporters and many who begrudgingly backed Clinton.[119] As the 2020 presidential election nears, enthusiasm among Sanders' core of supporters, including younger voters, remains steady. Whether he can prevail in securing the Democratic nomination remains unclear in a crowded field of potentially more than two dozen contenders. But what is more lucid is the ways in which Sanders' populist crusade against wealthy elites and corporations, and his focus on expanding universal benefits, have been embraced enthusiastically and almost across-the-board by an ever-enlarging field of progressives seeking to oust Trump. Todd Gitlin's insight at the close of the 2015 primary season still rings true today: "However unpromising his prospects for electoral victory, Mr. Sanders' campaign is already a force. His supporters may not be happy with the Democratic candidate they will probably get, but their influence will persist."[120]

---

[118] Quoted in Tamara Keith, "Campaign mysteries: Why don't Bernie Sanders' big rallies lead to big wins?" NPR, April 26, 2016. https://www.npr.org/2016/04/26/475681237/campaign-mystery-why-dont-bernie-sanders-big-rallies-lead-to-big-wins

[119] Michael Scherer, David Weigel, and Karen Tumulty, "Democrats express outrage over allegations of early party control for Clinton in 2016." *Washington Post Online*, November 3, 2017.

[120] Todd Gitlin, "The Bernie Sanders moment." *New York Times*, July 12, 2015, p. SR3.

III. A coda on Clinton, the conventionality conundrum, and the crosswinds of populism

Democrats' autopsy of Hillary Clinton's general election loss began in the early morning hours of November 9, 2016. Less than a year later, in her memoir entitled *What Happened*, Mrs. Clinton suggested that James Comey's fall 2016 reopening of the investigation into her use of a private email server, the media's "false equivalency" between that matter and Donald Trump's personal and business scandals, and Russian President Vladimir Putin's alleged meddling in the election contributed to her stunning defeat. Such a loosely connected conspiracy theory was perhaps as close as she came to embracing one core element in the populist style.

In her book-length introspection, Clinton did acknowledge tactical errors of her own. She lamented using the pejorative phrase "basket of deplorables" to describe Trump supporters and regretted her promise to put coal miners out of business. But she also recognized that there was a much larger dynamic at hand that she overlooked in her bid for the Oval Office. Her messaging was simply out of lockstep with many voters on both sides of the political spectrum who were seeking anything but a conventional candidate:

> I do think it's fair to say there was a fundamental mismatch between how I approach politics and what a lot of the country wanted to hear in 2016. I've learned that even the best plans and proposals can land on deaf ears when people are disillusioned by a broken political system and disgusted with politicians. When people are angry and looking for someone to blame, they don't want to hear your ten-point plan to create jobs and raise wages. They want you to be angry, too.[121]

Throughout much of the campaign, whether in person or on social media Clinton made her experience and professionalism the cornerstone of her presentation of self to voters. In an

---

[121] Hillary Clinton, *What Happened* (New York: Simon & Schuster, 2017), p. 398.

increasingly volatile world, she asserted that she had the "steady hand" that could unify the country in contrast to Trump, who she claimed was temperamentally challenged for the job of president.[122] Voters did, in fact, score her much higher on emotional stability than Trump.[123] Yet Trump focused on his authenticity as an outsider and de-professionalization of political leadership and painted Clinton as the consummate elite politician who was at the root of the nation's problems in Washington, and scarcely the solution.[124] During the primary season, Bernie Sanders had made a similar case.

"Fundamentally," write Allen and Parnes,

> she was misreading the mood of the voters. Trump was winning primaries because he was a torch-bearing outsider reader to burn the nation's institutions to the ground. Bernie was offering the same thing on the Democratic side, and he had flown in from off the political radar screen to give Hillary fits . . . with Bernie and Republicans attacking her as an agent of the establishment and an avatar of the status quo, [advisor Stan] Greenberg argued, Hillary had to make political reform a central part of her campaign.[125]

But in essence Clinton's policy proposals ranging from climate change and immigration to gun control and health care reform were an extension of her predecessor's two terms in office and lacked the flair for contempt of the political system that Trump and Sanders made the keystone of their populist arguments.[126]

---

[122] Laura Meckler and Siobhan Hughes, "Hillary Clinton pitches her vision for America in acceptance speech." *Wall Street Journal*, July 29, 2016. https://www.wsj.com/articles/hillary-clinton-to-emphasize-experience-steadiness-in-speech-to-democratic-convention-1469747452

[123] Aessandro Nai and Jürgen Maier, "Perceived Personality and Campaign Style of Hillary Clinton and Donald Trump." *Personality and Individual Differences* 121 (2018): 80–3.

[124] Zompetti, "Rhetorical Incivility in the Twittersphere," p. 32.

[125] Jonathan Allen and Amie Parnes, *Shattered: Inside Hillary Clinton's Doomed Campaign* (New York: Crown, 2017), pp. 235–6.

[126] *Chicago Tribune*, "Hillary Clinton promises steady hand in dangerous world." July 28, 2016. https://www.chicagotribune.com/news/nationworld/ct-democratic-national-convention-hillary-clinton-20160728-story.html

Clinton's top campaign advisors suggested that her loss was due to a "host of uncontrollable headwinds that ultimately felled a well-run campaign that executed a sensible strategy, and a soldier of a candidate who appealed to the broadest coalition of voters in the country."[127] As the *Atlantic* reported in its own post-mortem of her defeat, Clinton's politics-as-usual messaging failed to gain sufficient traction with the electorate to push her over the finish line as she was buffeted from the crosswinds of populism from the Right and the Left. She lost the white working-class vote and could not reassemble the "Obama Coalition" of blacks and minorities. Sanders overshadowed her campaign on social justice issues while Trump made jobs a core issue. Her campaign machine, spearheaded by Robbie Mook, relied on academic, data-driven analytics that ignored voters' fury at the grassroots that computer models could not gauge. And her campaign's arrogance was best visible in the fateful choice to take select states in the Rustbelt for granted.[128]

In the post-World War II era the party holding the presidency for two terms has won a third just once, in 1988. Like Hubert Humphrey in 1968 and Al Gore in 2000, Clinton was tasked with walking a fine line in lauding the accomplishments of her predecessor and differentiating herself from failures and polemics of the *ancien régime* without calling into question the viability of a system within which she had played an important role since her youth. Her moderation and relative "politics-as-usual" fit uncomfortably in the gale of voter discontent she confronted from both Trump and Sanders, whose rhetoric of deconstructing or reorienting the very administrative state of which she had been a part condemned her to a populist purgatory.

* * * * *

[127] Anne Karni, "Clinton aides blame loss on everything but themselves." *Politico*, November 10, 2016. https://www.politico.com/story/2016/11/hillary-clinton-aides-loss-blame-231215

[128] Molly Ball, "Why Hillary Clinton lost." *The Atlantic*, November 15, 2016. https://www.theatlantic.com/politics/archive/2016/11/why-hillary-clinton-lost/507704/

The campaign spectacles that defined the Year of the Populists marked a wholesale challenge to the fundamental legitimacy of the social, political, and economic institutions of the United States. On January 20, 2017, Donald Trump took the reins of the presidency and immediately sought to make good on his promises to "drain the swamp" and return the nation to economic prosperity. As the first populist to take up residence in the White House since Andrew Jackson, prescriptive models of presidential leadership provided little insight into how the 45th president would approach policymaking. As the next chapter elucidates, his first order of business was an unprecedented celebratory tour of the key states he won. The majoritarian themes he expounded in his post-election and post-inaugural rallies coincided, perhaps not unsurprisingly, with a policymaking style heavily weighted toward unilateral action—a subject that is taken up in more detail in Chapter 6.

The populist-elect and the permanent campaign

"We had a lot of fun fighting Hillary, didn't we?"
Crowd: "Lock her up! Lock her up!"
—Donald Trump, Post-Election Rally, Cincinnati,
Ohio, December 1, 2016

The forgotten men and women of this country . . . You're not forgotten any longer. You will never be forgotten again.
—Donald Trump, Post-Election Rally, Mobile,
Alabama, December 17, 2016

I. Introduction

Donald Trump's post-election rallies that began in December 2016 and continued into 2017 were akin to a scene out of Ridley Scott's epic film *Gladiator* (2000), featuring actor Russell Crowe. Standing in a Roman arena before a cheering crowd tossing rose petals to hail his victory, Crowe's character study General Maximus defied all the odds by bringing martial triumph to his rag-tag team of myrmillo-armed combatants over Caesar's mighty warriors who unsuccessfully threw everything but the kitchen sink (and the occasional tiger) at them. Then the battle-hardened conqueror impertinently disregards the customs of the day by refusing to follow Caesar's decree by a thumbs-down signal to snuff the life out of his remaining opponent by a cut of the sword. The gesture—the ultimate insult to the discredited tyrant clad with his laurel wreath who embodies the corruption of Rome—plants the seeds of rebellion in the masses and wins Maximus the loyalty of skeptical legislators who otherwise questioned his commitment to the ideals of popular sovereignty.

Demagogic and unmatched in the history of presidential politics in the United States, Trump's post-election celebrations represent a new form of the "permanent campaign" in the colosseum of U.S. politics. Dismissing the norms established by his predecessors, the president-elect exchanged the typical transition mechanics of a new administration with a celebratory and self-aggrandizing "thank you" tour targeted to his base of supporters who helped his campaign prevail in key swing states and defeat rival Hillary Clinton narrowly. Victory in the Electoral College was scarcely a sufficient condition to leave the anti-elitist narrative that drove the 2016 campaign in the rearview mirror, however. The continuation of the festive and unruly rallies after Trump's inauguration demonstrates the degree to which the lifeblood of the populist leadership style does not flow from theories of "good governance," per se. Rather, a continuing dialogue emphasizing the bankruptcy of his political opponents, and criticism of the formal and informal institutions of the American democracy that otherwise stood in the way of his policy goals, enabled Trump to set expectations for future challenges, pre-emptively rationalize possible defeats, and reinvigorate emotional appeals. The objective was not to extend his electoral base or persuade skeptical voters or legislators of his leadership abilities, but rather to buttress the emotional connection with his supporters through the very spectacles that landed him in the Oval Office.

This chapter considers the dynamics of Trump's post-election behavior and the significance for his style of presidential leadership in the White House. Emphasis is placed on the content of Trump's messaging during his "thank you tour" at the end of 2016 and the seamless continuation of rallies into 2017 after his inauguration. The analysis gives primacy to the purpose of the rallies, the rhetoric employed, and what the events indicated about the president's governing style. The chapter also compares Trump's post-inaugural rallies to the type of rhetoric employed by Andrew Johnson—whose behavior violated the standards of presidential behavior in a different era—and galvanized efforts to impose the ultimate sanction on both presidents: impeachment.

II. *The darkling thrush and midwinter maneuverings*

In his December 1900 poem "The Darkling Thrush," English novelist Thomas Hardy reflected on the dawning of a new era. As the nineteenth century drew to a close, the author contemplates the distant sound of a caroler's ethereal "full-hearted evensong of joy unlimited" but struggles to find optimism amidst the bleak, hibernal landscape.[1] The melancholic moment symbolizes the transition from the end of one epoch to the beginning of another, with little certainty about what the future holds. The imagery in Hardy's poem is an apt analogy for where the United States stood in the waning days of autumn following the 2016 election. Trump, the first populist president elected since Andrew Jackson in 1828, was poised to take office in just a few wintry months. Would he temper his rhetorical impulses as he transitioned to governing and unite the country?

The answer became immediately apparent. If Trump was the Darkling Thrush following his November victory at the ballot box, his tweets from the heights of his Manhattan transition headquarters were more like an owl's screech that included an admixture of cheer and resentment that encouraged his supporters as much as it terrified his political opponents. In the three weeks following the presidential election he took to social media to lambast protestors at the play *Hamilton* for their treatment of Vice President-elect Mike Pence, cancel an interview with the "failing *New York Times*," allege voter fraud in New Hampshire, Virginia, and California while singing the praises of the Electoral College, and argue that anyone who burned the American flag should be subjected to a jail sentence. On Thanksgiving he struck a decidedly more positive tone, writing, "Let us give thanks for all that we have, and let us boldly face the exciting new frontiers that lie ahead."[2]

---

[1] Carol Rumens, "Poem of the week: The Darkling Thrush, by Thomas Hardy." *The Guardian*, December 28, 2009. https://www.theguardian.com/books/booksblog/2009/dec/28/poem-of-the-week-the-darkling-thrush-thomas-hardy

[2] Quoted in Jessica Taylor, "Trump calls for unity, healing in Thanksgiving address." *NPR*, November 23, 2016. https://www.npr.org/2016/11/23/503192654/trump-calls-for-unity-healing-in-thanksgiving-address

Critically, on November 29 the White House Director of Social Media announced the commencement of a series of unprecedented post-election rallies that would take place the following month. The presidential campaign was to continue well beyond election night celebrations. On Twitter, Dan Scavino posted that the president-elect would head back to Cincinnati, Ohio on December 1 and included a hashtag "Thank You Tour 2016" resplendent with a red, white, and blue emblem with the "Make America Great Again" slogan front and center. Hours later, Trump noted he would go to Indianapolis, Indiana in advance of the Cincinnati engagement to tout a deal to save thousands of jobs by convincing air conditioning giant Carrier to remain in the state. Determined to buttress his personal connection to the grassroots constituency that had elected him, "[a] grateful Mr. Trump wants to reach out to the heartland folk who matter to him, and like his campaign, the tour portends to be bodacious and media-friendly."[3] Bodacious perhaps, but the events were anything but amicable toward his old nemesis, the media.

A. The president in perpetual motion: the December rallies

The appropriate musical backdrop to Trump's December 2016 tour could have easily been Johann Strauss's *Perpetuum mobile*, with its rapid tempo of uninterrupted streams of repetitive notes. The composition of the president's populist canon borrowed seamlessly from the sheet music of his campaign spectacles. Over the course of fifteen days, from December 2 to December 17, 2016, Trump engaged in a total of nine lively rallies in states in which he prevailed over rival Hillary Clinton by a hair's breadth. In five—North Carolina, Michigan, Wisconsin, Pennsylvania, and Florida—Trump won the statewide vote with under 50 percent of the ballots. In Ohio and Iowa he won by less than 51.5 percent of the vote. Only in Alabama and Louisiana did Trump triumph with more than 55 percent.

---

[3] Jennifer Harper, "'Classy': Donald Trump to embark on a thank you tour of the heartland." *Washington Times*, November 29, 2016. https://www.washingtontimes.com/news/2016/nov/29/donald-trump-to-embark-on-thank-you-tour-2016/

Table 5.1 Post-Election Rallies, December 2016

Date	Location	House district	Representative's margin (2016) (%)	Trump's statewide margin (2016) (%)
12/2/2016	Cincinnati, OH U.S. Bank Arena	OH-1 Steve Chabot	59.2	51.3
12/6/2016	Fayetteville, NC Crown Coliseum	NC-9 Robert Pittinger	58.2	49.8
12/8/2016	Des Moines, IA Iowa Events Center	IA-3 David Young	53.5	51.1
12/9/2016	Baton Rouge, LA Baton Rouge Airport	LA-2 Cedric Richmond*	69.8	58.1
12/9/2016	Grand Rapids, MI DeltaPlex Arena	MI-2 Bill Huizenga	62.6	47.3
12/13/2016	West Allis, WI Wisconsin Expo Center	WI-5 James Sensenbrenner	66.8	47.2
12/15/2016	Hershey, PA Giant Center	PA-15 Charles Dent	58.4	48.2
12/16/2016	Orlando, FL Central Florida Fairgrounds	FL-10 Val Demings*	64.9	48.6
12/17/2016	Mobile, AL Ladd-Peebles Stadium	AL-1 Bradley Byrne	Unopposed	62.1
Average	–	–	65.9	51.5

Note:
* Democratic member of Congress

Table 5.1 details the precise locations of the two-week rally juggernaut, and juxtaposes Trump's statewide margin with that of the local member of the House of Representatives in which the gatherings took place. The relationship between Trump's margin and that of the representative is strongly negative ($r = -.78$, $p = .01$). In all but one case (David Young, IA-3) the rallies were held in constituencies in which the member of Congress ran in a "safe district" by obtaining more than 55 percent of the vote and whose margin of victory clearly outpaced Trump's. Some members were solidly behind Trump in his presidential bid, including Steve Chabot of Ohio and

James Sensenbrenner of Wisconsin.[4] In other cases Trump's rapport with the congressional incumbents, like Bill Huizenga of Michigan whose support was critical in key counties in the Great Lake State, became strained later.[5]

In two instances, the rallies took place in an urban area represented by a Democrat (Cedric Richmond, LA-2 and Val Demings, FL-10). Neither member of the Congressional Black Caucus attended the rally in their bailiwick. Both districts, drawn under the mandates of the Voting Rights Act, are considered to be among the most gerrymandered in the United States.[6] Richmond would later call Trump a racist in advance of the 2018 State of the Union Address,[7] and when bombs were mailed to prominent

[4] Deidre Shesgreen, "Steve Chabot's wild ride on the Trump train." *Cincinnati Enquirer*, April 28, 2017. https://www.cincinnati.com/story/news/politics/2017/04/27/steve-chabots-wild-ride-trump-train/100974626/; Cassi Pollock, "Where every Republican in Congress stands on Donald Trump." *Washington Examiner*, May 27, 2016. https://www.washingtonexaminer.com/full-list-where-every-republican-in-congress-stands-on-donald-trump

[5] Melissa Nann Burke and Chad Livengood, "Huizenga's west Michigan efforts boosted Trump." *Detroit News*, November 13, 2016. https://www.detroit-news.com/story/news/politics/2016/11/12/rep-huizengas-west-michigan-efforts-boosted-trump/93753514/; Melissa Nann Burke, "'Something is not right here': Michigan pols react to Trump remarks on Russia, 2016 election." *Detroit News*, July 17, 2018. https://www.detroitnews.com/story/news/local/michigan/2018/07/16/trump-putin-election-michigan-reaction/789315002/; *Michigan Radio*, "Some Michigan Republican members of Congress criticize Trump's family separation policy." June 19, 2018. http://www.michiganradio.org/post/some-michigan-republican-members-congress-criticize-trumps-family-separation-policy

[6] See Ben Jacobs, "Florida has to redraw congressional districts because, Florida." *Daily Beast*, July 10, 2014. https://www.thedailybeast.com/florida-has-to-redraw-its-congressional-districts-because-florida?ref=scroll; Christopher Ingraham, "America's most gerrymandered congressional districts." *Washington Post*, May 15, 2014. https://www.washingtonpost.com/news/wonk/wp/2014/05/15/americas-most-gerrymandered-congressional-districts/?utm_term=.5b58516379af

[7] Bryn Stole, "Ahead of Trump's State of the Union, Cedric Richmond and the Congressional Black Caucus blast his 'racist rhetoric'." *Baton Rouge Advocate*, January 30, 2018. https://www.theadvocate.com/baton_rouge/news/politics/article_50276bf8-05e9-11e8-afbd-7344421633a8.html

Democrats in fall 2018 Demings opined that "President Trump has encouraged, excused, and alluded to violence repeatedly" and that his "refusal to take responsibility or stop the use of violent rhetoric is inexcusable and dangerous."[8] Both Richmond and Demings ultimately supported Al Green's (D-TX) failed bid to impeach Trump in late 2017.[9]

Analysis of rally video and transcripts underscores elements of the central dimensions of the populist argumentative frame Trump utilized to cement an emotional linkage with his core supporters in advance of moving into the Oval Office. His tactics were in many ways a page out of George Wallace's playbook a half-century earlier, replete with crowds beyond the venue's capacity and considerable anticipation by the audience that included symbols of patriotism and nostalgia in addition to folk music.[10] One of the essential ways in which the president drew in his audience at the rallies—just as he did during the 2016 campaign—was the frequent use of the first person plural "we." While taking his victory lap, Trump took pains to portray his victory and prospective agenda as a collective effort that mandated continuing cohesion while accentuating that the movement was a grassroots success. He portrayed himself simply as a mouthpiece for taking aim at recalcitrant establishment figures in Washington. He was the instrument for insuring the average American's interests would come before self-serving politicians' wellbeing. Complex economic and foreign policy issues were simplified for the layman. Trump's refrain was simple: "Buy American, hire American." To put the polishing touches on the populist layer-cake presented as a political dessert to his cadre of diehard voters, the rallies were sprinkled with criticism of the media, adorned with

---

[8] Kevin Derby, "Val Demings: President Trump has encouraged, excused, and alluded to violence repeatedly." *Florida Daily*, October 28, 2018. https://www.floridadaily.com/val-demings-president-trump-has-encouraged-excused-and-alluded-to-violence-repeatedly/

[9] Christina Marcos, "The nearly 60 Democrats who voted for impeachment." *The Hill*, December 6, 2017. https://thehill.com/blogs/floor-action/house/363645-the-nearly-60-dems-who-voted-for-impeachment

[10] See Richard D. Raum and James S. Measell, "Wallace and His Ways: A Study of the Rhetorical Genre of Polarization." *Communications Studies* 25, no. 1 (1974): 33–4.

nostalgia for the military and veterans, decorated with attacks on flag-burning, and frosted with occasional conspiracy theory of his critics' efforts to preclude the realization of his and *our* success. The venues also provided an opportunity for the president to introduce several cabinet nominees who embodied his plans to revive the armed forces and make good on promises to restore fairness to international trade.

Trump launched his first rally in Cincinnati, Ohio on the evening of December 2, 2016. The event showcased the basic populist chorus that the president would sing throughout his two-week thank-you tour. First, the president quickly established a synergy with the audience by emphasizing his reverence for hard-working supporters, who had achieved a victory that the "dishonest" press deemed impossible. He told the cheering crowd, "Thank you, I love you, too" and pointed to one supporter who was anything but a millionaire, saying, "Some guy, look at this guy. And I do love him. He's a rough looking cookie, though, I'll tell you." Referencing his vote tallies in Ohio, North Carolina, and Pennsylvania, Trump declared:

> we won it big. But then the people back there, the extremely dishonest press said—right? Very dishonest people. (Boos) . . . How about—how about—I mean, how dishonest. How about when a major anchor who hosted a debate started crying when she realized that we won? How about that?

Second, Trump took aim at the elites who had refused to support his campaign, like outgoing Ohio Governor John Kasich, noting that "Hey, in the great state of Ohio we didn't have the upper echelon of politicians, either, did we?" Third, he went through a litany of policy areas he would address—taxes, energy regulations, trade, health care reform, veterans, and ethics reform—without providing too many details. He interspersed his discussion with a celebration of his support among women and Hispanics while casting aspersions against those who would burn the American flag, bringing the crowd to its feet with chants of "USA, USA, USA!" Finally, as the event came to a close, Trump emphasized how all of his efforts required a steadfast, collective determination to make

America great again. He emphasized his status as a representative of the ordinary American, an expression of a crusade much larger than himself: "You know I talk about our great movement and you are the movement. I'm the messenger. I'm just really the messenger. Although I've been a very good messenger, let's face it, right? I've been a pretty good messenger."[11]

Subsequent rallies were variations on these general themes on the stump, with a few twists. In Fayetteville, NC, Trump used the occasion primarily to praise the military. Standing in the shadow of the Army base of Fort Bragg, and with the Marine Corps base at Camp Lejeune just 100 miles away, the president-elect thanked his supporters by noting that "[y]ou went out and pounded the pavement. You organized your fellow citizens and propelled to victory a grassroots movement the likes of which nobody—nobody has ever seen before, and that's beyond our conscience." The balance of the rally lauded veterans and their families, with occasional appeals to patriotism that brought thunderous applause:

> We love our flag, and we don't like it when we see people ripping up our flag and burning our flag. We don't like it. We don't like it. And we'll see what we're going to do about that, OK!

The rally was the perfect venue to introduce his choice of General James "Mad Dog" Mattis as Secretary of Defense. As Trump presented him to the audience, he asserted that

> General Mattis is the living embodiment of the Marine Corps motto semper fidelis, always faithful. And the American people are fortunate that a man of this character and integrity will now be the civilian leader atop the Department of Defense under his leadership, right?

Mattis, in turn, extolled Trump's electoral victories and reinforced his intention to aid the president in rebuilding the military.

---

[11] Quoted in CNN *Transcripts, Anderson Cooper 360 Degrees*. "Trump holds Ohio rally." December 1, 2016. http://transcripts.cnn.com/TRANSCRIPTS/1612/01/acd.01.html

Closing his speech, Mattis took a page out of Trump's playbook by alluding to the media, suggesting that "[t]he script to what we're doing is not yet written. Remember, this has been a great, great movement, the likes of which they have never seen before, the likes of which those folks back there that write the stories . . . [Booing]."[12]

As Trump took center stage in Des Moines, Iowa on December 8 he told his supporters

> I'm here today for one main reason—to say thank you to the great, great people of Iowa . . . You organized your fellow citizens and propelled us to victories at a grassroots and every other level. We have a movement the likes of which this world has never seen before— never seen before.

With Senator Charles Grassley, Representative Jodi Ernst, and Governor Terry Branstad in attendance—the latter of whom he announced would be his nominee as ambassador to China— Trump thanked them for their steady support and took a shot across the bow at those who doubted his resilience in the campaign: "You know, we had some people they would waiver, right, waiver not as long as they came back sometime prior to the vote. They're all right, but we don't like people that waiver, right?" Firing criticism at those in the GOP who failed to support his presidential campaign, Trump said "you know they have the never Trumps right, the never Trumpers, never Trumpers. By the way, they're on respirator right now." Outlining his position on trade and job-creation, the president-elect hearkened back to his outsider status and blamed politicians for forgetting the ordinary American: "to accomplish our goals, we must reject the failed approaches of the past. Government must stop listening to the special interests, and start delivering. . ." He continued: "The American worker built this country, and now it is time for American workers to have a government that, for the first time

[12] *C-SPAN*, "President-elect Donald Trump victory rally in North Carolina." December 6, 2016. https://www.c-span.org/video/?419634-1/president-elect-trump-holds-victory-rally-fayetteville-north-carolina

in decades answers to them. We're going to answer to them." Taking aim at trade policy, he promised that "[w]e're not going to be the stupid people anymore, folks. We're not going to be the stupid people." Finally, ridiculing the "political correctness" of media elites, Trump launched into a criticism of *Time Magazine* for changing the title of its annual publication of the most influential "man" to most influential "person." The president-elect noted that

> You know, I was lucky enough to receive the Time Person of the Year. They use to call it "Man of the Year" . . . but they can't do that anymore, so they call it Person. They want to be politically correct. That's OK. And they talked about—heads up—a divided nation on the cover. They gave me this other, then they have to go a little bit of this stuff—a divided. I said, "I haven't been president, what are you saying that for?" But you know what we're going to bring the nation together. We're going to bring the nation together.[13]

Trump held two rallies on December 9, one in Baton Rouge, Louisiana followed by another in Grand Rapids, Michigan. The event at the airport in Baton Rouge is notable not only for Trump's celebration of the sheer number of those in attendance but also for forays into conspiracy theory. Despite his statewide victory in Louisiana with more than 60 percent of the vote, he lamented that the system was "rigged" because his number of delegates was smaller relative to the popular vote outcome.[14] In Grand Rapids, Michigan, he made controversial comments on African American voters that drew criticism for allegedly using black supporters as tokens to "dispel the idea that he is racist," part of a larger pattern according to the *Huffington Post*.[15]

[13] *C-SPAN*, "President-elect Donald Trump victory rally in Des Moines, Iowa." December 8, 2016. https://www.c-span.org/video/?419792-1/president-elect-donald-trump-holds-rally-des-moines-iowa

[14] *Factbase*, "Donald Trump in Baton Rouge, LA, December 9, 2016." https://factba.se/transcript/donald-trump-speech-baton-rouge-la-december-9-2016

[15] Lydia O'Connor and Daniel Marans, "Here are 16 examples of Trump being racist." *Huffington Post*, December 13, 2016. https://www.huffingtonpost.com/entry/president-donald-trump-racist-examples_us_584f2ccae4b0bd9c3dfe5566

Trump rejoiced in exit poll data that underscored he had done better with black voters by several percentage points compared to Mitt Romney, the GOP presidential candidate in 2012.

> The African-American community was great to us. They came through, big league. Big league. And frankly if they had any doubt, they didn't vote, and that was almost as good because a lot of people didn't show up, because they felt good about me.[16]

Trump's point was that if black voters did not vote for him, low turnout in their ranks helped doom Hillary Clinton's campaign. Reminiscent of his 2016 campaign engagements, several protestors at the event were escorted out of the venue to Trump's growl "Get 'em outta here," bringing the crowd to its feet.

The carnival atmosphere of the post-election rallies continued in West Allis, Wisconsin outside Milwaukee on December 13. Again firing salvos at political elites, Trump derided Green Party candidate Jill Stein's demand for a recount, calling the effort a waste of money and time and delighting in the fact that his vote count was augmented by 131 ballots. Trump said,

> You know I called it a scam but I won't say that because we want to be nice. OK? So I refuse to say it was a scam tonight. All right? And after all of this money was spent, by the Democrats, believe me, they were behind it. And the Green Party. Wonderful party. She got less than one percent but she thought she was going to catch us.

Touting the support of popular law-and-order, cowboy hat-garbed Milwaukee County Sheriff David Clarke, Trump attempted a half-hearted reconciliation with House Speaker Paul Ryan, a native of the Badger State, who had withdrawn public support for the president-elect when the video of Trump's "locker room" talk regarding women surfaced in October 2016. Trump said he had "come

[16] Quoted in *Chicago Tribune*, "Trump says blacks who stayed home were 'almost as good' as those who voted for him." December 9, 2016. https://www.chicagotribune.com/news/nationworld/politics/ct-trump-rallies-louisiana-michigan-20161209-story.html

to appreciate" Ryan, whom he equated with "fine wine"—it gets better with time. When the crowd spontaneously began chanting "Lock Her Up" in reference to Hillary Clinton as Trump finished a soliloquy on trade policy, he appeared amused and perhaps a little bewildered by the dynamics he had unleashed during the 2016 campaign. "You people don't stop. So I used to say when I used to hear this chant let's just win on November 8th. But now we've won. All right? We've won, big league. So, anyway." Finally, before launching into a redux of his artful interpretation of land-slide victories in Wisconsin and other states in which he narrowly prevailed, Trump took the opportunity to chastise the media, to which he had refused to give interviews in December. Feeling singled out for media rebuke, Trump pointed to the back of the venue and said,

> Look at all those cameras. Look at all that television. Look at that. Who has to do this every night with all those live cameras? Can you imagine if we made a mistake? Would it be a disaster? See other people running for office if they make a mistake, but if I made a mistake, disaster, right? Look at that. You ever see so many cameras? Mr. Vice President? So, but I have to tell you they were devastated on November 8th. They were devastated.[17]

During the last three rallies he held before Christmas, Trump attempted to tone down the rowdiness of his crowds somewhat while continuing to engage in a nationalist narrative and routine attacks on the media and his rival, Hillary Clinton, that only ratcheted up the attendees' fever-pitch outbursts. At some level, the president-elect appeared to underestimate the power of his own rhetoric. In mid-November during an interview with the *New York Times*, to the dismay of many of his most ardent supporters, he walked back the notion of prosecuting Hillary Clinton for her use of a private email server as secretary of state. Trump told Maggie Haberman,

---

[17] *C-SPAN*, "President-elect Donald Trump victory rally in West Allis, Wisconsin." December 13, 2016. https://c-span.org/vicdeo/?420078-1/president-elect-trump-vice-president-elect-pence-deliver-remarks-west-allis-wisconsin

Well, there was a report that somebody said that I'm not enthused about it. Look, I want to move forward, I don't want to move back. And I don't want to hurt the Clintons. I really don't. She went through a lot. And suffered greatly in many different ways. And I am not looking to hurt them at all. The campaign was vicious. They say it was the most vicious primary and the most vicious campaign. I guess, added together, it was definitely the most vicious; probably, I assume you sold a lot of newspapers. I would imagine. I would imagine. I'm just telling you, Maggie, I'm not looking to hurt them. I think they've been through a lot. They've gone through a lot. I'm really looking . . . I think we have to get the focus of the country into looking forward.[18]

But judging from the spontaneous outbreaks of chants to "lock her up," Trump's supporters were scarcely sympathetic to his reversal on Mrs. Clinton's potential fate at the hands of his Justice Department.

In Hershey, Pennsylvania, Trump again suggested lukewarmly that it was time to moderate the rambunctious atmosphere of the campaign. The president-elect said:

But there's something different about a crowd before the election, like when I was here a few weeks ago, and after the election. Before the election, they are brutal, they are so crazed. You're like crazed people, and that's good. I like that. And now, no, and now you're laid back. Hey, babe. Hey, onward, Mr. Trump, onward, right? No, it's great, it's beautiful. In other words, you've won and you feel great about it and you don't have to go totally wild, right?

At the same time, Trump riled up the audience on patriotic grounds. He motivated his spectators by contending that

Patriotism will be celebrated in our cities and taught very, very strongly to our children. And that patriotism will be the foundation of our economic plan, bringing jobs back to America. We're bringing our jobs back, folks. They've been ripped away.

---

[18] *New York Times*, "Donald Trump's New York Times interview: Full transcript." November 23, 2016. http://www.nytimes.com/2016/11/23/us/politics/trump-new-york-times-interviewtranscript

Finally, after celebrating the support he received from women and Hispanics, Trump hit upon the reverie that defines the core of populism. "When Americans are unified," he argued,

> there is nothing we cannot do, no task is too great, no dream too large, no goal beyond our reach. My message tonight is for all Americans, from all parties, all beliefs, all walks of life. Whether you are African American, Hispanic American or Asian American or whatever the hell you are . . . And it's about you, it's not about me. It's about you. I am asking you to dream big and bold and daring things for your family and for your country.[19]

The Orlando rally followed the same essential tack. Alluding once more to the "dishonest media" and exit polling in the Maine contest in 2016, the president-elect returned to conspiracy theory. He asserted that

> We went out and we watched the media, and we believed the media, and the media is [sic] very dishonest. They were even dishonest in their exit polls, right? Now, what's the purpose of being dishonest in an exit poll when you're going to find out the truth in three hours? What are they doing?

Once again trying to calm the effervescent and unruly scene of supporters, he made reference to Hillary Clinton's characterizations of his supporters as "a basket of deplorables." Trump said,

> They're not so deplorable anymore. In fact, the other side is trying to figure out, well, in four years how do we get some of these deplorables to our side, right? . . . But—but now you're mellow and you're cool. And you're not nearly as vicious or violent, right? Because we won, right? And now you sort of laying back, although it doesn't exactly sound like a totally laid-back crowd, but that's OK.[20]

[19] C-SPAN, "President-elect Donald Trump victory rally in Hershey, Pennsylvania," December 15, 2016. https://www.c-span.org/video/?420211-1/president-elect-donald-trump-vice-president-elect-mike-pence-deliver-remarks-hershey-pennsylvania

[20] C-SPAN, "President-elect Donald Trump victory rally in Orlando, Florida," December 16, 2016. https://www.c-span.org/video/?420255-1/president-elect-donald-trump-holds-rally-orlando-florida

In Mobile, Alabama, Trump derided the media and raised the specter of conspiracy theory again. Always sensitive to reporting of the numbers of attendees at his rallies, the president-elect averred: "But the incredible patriots of this stadium today defied the pundits, defied the pollsters and the special interests and delivered a historic win for the American worker and for the American people, totally." His old rival, Hillary Clinton, was resurrected anew by the crowd with chants of "Lock her up! Lock her up! Lock her up!" Amused, Trump said,

> Nah, we won. Let's see, right? We won. But you had the Hillary people on and they were saying, we are going to win the state of Florida, we have information, we're going to win. I mean, maybe their information was how many people voted illegally. Maybe that was the information.[21]

In his later rallies, Trump demonstrated a tacit recognition, perhaps even a prescience that many of his controversial policies would meet significant opposition from Congress or the courts, and certainly from the media. He paid particular attention to laying the groundwork of popular support for a travel ban on select Muslim countries, called for a wall along the southern border with Mexico, and railed against illegal immigrants. Sustained, collective support for these policies would be necessary to combat the elites who would stand in the way. Indeed, subsequent rallies held over the course of 2017 served as a platform to criticize legislators in Congress and the federal judiciary for blocking his most contentious policies.

III. In the style of the Tennessee Tailor? Pontification, political street combat, and presidential norms

Any student of the history of presidential politics struggles to find an analogy to Trump's ten post-inauguration rallies that

---

[21] *C-SPAN*, "President-elect Donald Trump victory rally in Mobile, Alabama," December 17, 2016. https://www.c-span.org/video/?420254-1/president-elect-donald-trump-holds-thank-you-rally-mobile-alabama

took place from February to December 2017. Newly elected presidents in the modern era often make speeches, and increasingly do so strategically outside the Beltway in a search to connect with special audiences and circumvent the national media in exchange for potentially more favorable coverage in the local press.[22] And of course, presidents often stump for candidates of their party in advance of mid-term elections in the fall of their second year in office. But the timing, tenor, and sheer number of Trump's campaign-style rallies are truly *sui generis* in the annals of presidential politics. As Brendan J. Doherty maintains, "[e]arly in their tenure, recent presidents have tried to avoid appearing to be doing anything explicitly electoral" and "holding what the White House press secretary explicitly called a 'campaign event' that was promoted on the president's campaign website is a clear departure from recent presidential practice."[23]

Such overt political rallies also diverge from the norms of presidential comportment in the longer view of history. Andrew Jackson was the nation's first populist president, but Old Hickory is a poor comparison to Trump on the delivery of populist rhetoric from a stylistic perspective. Presidents of the nineteenth century did not campaign actively for themselves or members of Congress. Nor did they engage in public spectacles in which they criticized their political opponents openly. They relied on surrogates, and partisans in the print press, to do their bidding. To have done otherwise would have violated the mores of the era and risked charges of demagoguery.

Alas, one president chose to break with the traditions of a bygone era—the Tennessee Tailor, Andrew Johnson—and with disastrous consequences. Acceding to the presidency upon

---

[22] See, inter alia, Andrew W. Barrett and Jeffrey S. Peake, "When the President Comes to Town: Examining Local Newspaper Coverage of Domestic Presidential Travel." *American Politics Research* 35, no. 1 (2007): 3–31; Jeffrey E. Cohen, *Going Local: Presidential Leadership in the Post-Broadcast Age* (New York: Cambridge University Press, 2010).

[23] Brendan J. Doherty, "Trump isn't really campaigning earlier than other recent presidents. He's just more upfront about it. Here's what the data on presidential travel show us." *Washington Post Blogs*, February 21, 2017.

Abraham Lincoln's assassination in 1865, Johnson imagined himself a populist in the tradition of Jackson. But his style had more in common with Trump, at least tangentially, than his martyred predecessor or the hero of the Battle of New Orleans. "Combining egotism, victimhood and paranoia in a manner similar to Trump, Johnson portrayed himself as the nation's much maligned savior. 'I am your instrument,' he told one audience. 'I stand for the country, I stand for the Constitution'."[24]

Johnson's rhetorical assault on Congress merits scrutiny for the ways in which his "Swing around the Circle" speaking tour compares to Trump's post-inaugural rallies. In Johnson's view Radical Republicans in Congress who sought to punish the South in the aftermath of the Civil War by refusing to seat state delegations were violating their constitutional responsibilities. A proponent of states' rights and an ardent racist, he also opposed civil rights legislation for African Americans. His veto message sending back to Congress a civil rights bill in 1866 was the opening salvo in a war with Congress that would convince him to undertake a calamitous eighteen-day speaking tour several months in advance of the mid-term elections to lambast his enemies in Congress. At the time, the presidential move was an unparalleled break with political conventions.

Johnson set out on public-speaking engagements to build support for his restrained Reconstruction policy stance toward the southern states, which were bent on entrenching discriminatory practices (e.g., "Jim Crow") against blacks and resurrecting the very social structure the Union victory sought to eradicate. Although he sought to manipulate divisions between northern Republicans and Radicals in Congress to his advantage, Johnson wound up entrenching opposition in both camps.[25] In his speeches he typically emphasized

> his rise from the tailor's bench to the presidency [and] he compared himself to Jesus Christ and explained that like the Savior, he, too,

---

[24] Donald Nieman, "Andrew Johnson's failed presidency echoes in Trump's White House." *The Conversation*, February 13, 2018. https://theconversation.com/andrew-johnsons-failed-presidency-echoes-in-trumps-white-house-91139

[25] Eric Foner, *Reconstruction: America's Unfinished Revolution* (New York: Perennial Classics, 1988), pp. 264–5.

liked to pardon repentant sinners. But Congress, and especially Thaddeus Stevens and the radicals, still wanted to break up the Union, an effort he was trying to prevent.[26]

Although his initial stops in Baltimore, Philadelphia, and New York received favorable press coverage, Johnson's speechmaking forays into the Midwest where support for Congress was strong proved his undoing as he savaged his opponents with personal attacks and sank to street-level rants against hecklers. Unable to control his composure in Cleveland, Johnson responded to jeering protestors who called for the hanging of former Confederate President Jefferson Davis with the vituperation, "Why don't you hang Thad Stevens and Wendell Phillips?"[27] In Chicago, in an ode to conspiracy theory, he accused Republicans of starting a deadly riot in New Orleans that cost forty-four African Americans their lives and caused another hundred casualties. And he was ultimately forced to abandon a speaking engagement in Indianapolis amidst growing public discord. Violence broke out and the event degenerated into a fracas with gunfire that left one man dead.

When advisors to Johnson suggested that his tactics were unbecoming, he pugnaciously said "I don't care about my dignity." The remark, as J. Michael Martinez posits, "was widely reported and contributed to a loss of presidential prestige when Johnson needed all the help he could get to gain political support."[28] The *New York Tribune* called the president an "irritated demagogue"[29] and cartoonist Thomas Nast's lampoons of Johnson's tour became legendary in undermining his political clout.[30] For his part, Radical Republican and House Ways and Means Committee Chairman

[26] Hans L. Trefousse, *Andrew Johnson: A Biography* (New York: W. W. Norton, 1989), p. 263.
[27] Foner, *Reconstruction*, p. 255.
[28] J. Michael Martinez, *Coming for to Carry Me Home: Race in America from Abolitionism to Jim Crow* (Lanham, MD: Rowman & Littlefield, 2012), p. 135.
[29] Quoted in Martin E. Mantell, *Johnson, Grant, and the Politics of Reconstruction* (New York: Columbia University Press, 1973), p. 94.
[30] See John Chalmers Vinson, *Thomas Nast: Political Cartoonist* (Athens: University of Georgia Press, 1967).

Thaddeus Stevens described the president's ill-fated speaking odyssey as "the remarkable circus that traveled through the country . . . Sometimes cut outside the circle and entered into street brawls with common blackguards."[31]

The proximate cause of Johnson's ultimate impeachment in 1868 was his violation of the Tenure of Office Act, passed by Congress in 1867 (and repealed in 1887). Congress set a trap for the president, daring him to fire Lincoln's Secretary of War, Edwin Stanton with a statute adopted over a veto that mandated Senate approval for the dismissal of cabinet appointees. But at the heart of Johnson's impeachment was his unseemly behavior in the Swing around the Circle tour and the civil chaos it fomented. The tenth of eleven articles of impeachment against Johnson noted that the president

> did . . . make and declare, with a loud voice certain intemperate, inflammatory, and scandalous harangues, and therein utter loud threats and bitter menaces, as well against Congress as the laws of the United States duly enacted thereby, amid the cries, jeers and laughter of the multitudes then assembled in hearing.[32]

As Jeffrey Tulis details, Johnson violated a fundamental norm of constitutional understanding of the time by appealing over the heads of Congress and communicating directly with the public.[33] Johnson's vitriol and personalization of political conflict on the public stage nearly led to his removal from office had not a handful of Senators sacrificed their political careers to save his embattled presidency.[34]

---

[31] Quoted in Gary Boulard, The Swing around the Circle: Andrew Johnson and the Train Ride That Destroyed a Presidency (New York: iUniverse, Inc., 2008), p. 147.

[32] United States Senate, "The Impeachment of Andrew Johnson (1868) President of the United States," Chapter 7 (Articles of Impeachment). https://www.senate. gov/artandhistory/history/common/briefing/Impeachment_Johnson.htm#7

[33] Jeffrey K. Tulis, *The Rhetorical Presidency* (Princeton, NJ: Princeton University Press, 1987).

[34] See John F. Kennedy, *Profiles in Courage* (New York: Harper & Row, 1964).

Johnson's Swing around the Circle speaking tour is admittedly an imperfect comparison to Trump's "thank-you" rallies in 2017 on several levels. Johnson had no electoral victory to celebrate and the nation had barely survived an unprecedented civil conflict followed by a political assassination of the country's highest elected official. And the timing of his cavalcade of congressional criticism coincided with the mid-term elections. Yet the stylistic similarities in breaking with precedent, recriminations of demagoguery, incidents of street-level combat and bedlam, and calls for impeachment stemming from public rhetoric that defied the accepted bounds of presidential behavior are difficult to overlook. Trump's post-inaugural rallies contained comparable oratory that challenged other co-equal branches of government (specifically the judiciary), personalized political agreements, and gave rise to widespread protests that buttressed an abortive effort in 2017 to remove him from office based on the pretext of obstruction of justice, and again in 2019 for abuse of power and obstruction of Congress, when it was his *conduct* as much as his policies that opponents found most offensive.

Looking back on the Johnson debacle a century-and-a-half ago, many Democrats who were victorious in the mid-term elections of 2018 hoped that history might repeat itself, using extensive investigations and finally impeachment of Trump to discredit his populist appeal at the ballot box in 2020. One must recall that the first attempt at impeaching Johnson in 1867 failed, just as Al Green's bid to oust Trump from the Oval Office flunked exactly 150 years later. For the Tennessee Tailor, the second effort following his violation of a contrived, unconstitutional statute was successful in moving the process forward to the Senate for a trial. The cases of Johnson and Trump suggest that opposition forces in Congress have incentives to engage in the spectacle of impeachment for political gain against populists who call into question the legitimacy of their co-equal status in the constitutional system. Memory of the sizeable gains Republicans made on Capitol Hill in 1868 following the impeachment ordeal, alongside the election of Ulysses S. Grant, surely are were not lost on some House Democrats in the 116th Congress who eagerly sought ways to posture in 2020 and jettison the 45th president from the Oval Office. What contemporary Democrats seem not to realize, however, is the degree to which Trump supporters have become even more energized in the wake of his failed ouster. In sum, Trump's impeachment appears not to have moved the needle much on diametrically opposing views of the president in the electorate.

A. Trump's politics of pre-emption and reactionary rhetoric

Andrew Johnson set out in 1866 to divide and conquer Republicans and Radicals. Stepping foot into hostile political territory, and his inability to maintain his composure when faced by critics, proved his undoing. Trump, on the other hand, seemingly understood the lessons of history in his choice of locales for post-inaugural rallies but underestimated the likelihood of potential violence arising from protests. As Table 5.2 details, the ten rallies in 2017 were held *only* in states where he had prevailed in the presidential election a year earlier, however narrowly. California, Illinois, and New York, for example, where he lost the statewide votes by large margins, did not figure on the schedule. Trump continued the post-campaign strategy of attempting to solidify his base in key states with little regard to the significant number of voters who opposed him on Election Day. In many cases he attempted to shore up support from House Republicans who had expressed reservations about his presidential campaign in 2016. Regardless, moving from the immediate post-election rallies to those post-inauguration, the tone of the rallies shifted to criticism of those in government now poised to impede his agenda. His censure of appointed federal judges was undergirded by a disdain for anti-majoritarian features of the constitutional system. The standard populist narrative of anti-elitism, conspiracy, and nationalism Trump had honed on the campaign trail in 2016 continued unabated, while one protest in Phoenix surely overshadowed his messaging outside the stadium filled with supporters.

Trump typically held rally-style events in several venues where he sought to bolster support from House Republicans who had been guarded during the presidential campaign. Bill Posey (FL-8),

Table 5.2 Post-Inauguration Rallies, 2017

Date	Location	House district	Representative's margin (2016) (%)	Trump's statewide margin (2016) (%)
2/18/2017	Melbourne, FL Orlando-Melbourne Airport	FL-8 Bill Posey	63.1	48.6
3/15/2017	Nashville, TN Nashville Municipal Auditorium	TN-5 Jim Cooper	62.6	60.7
3/20/2017	Louisville, KY Kentucky Expo Center	KY-3 John Yarmouth*	63.5	62.5
4/29/2017	Harrisburg, PA Pennsylvania Expo Center	PA-4 Scott Perry	66.1	48.2
6/21/2017	Cedar Rapids, IA U.S. Cellular Center	IA-1 Rod Blum	53.8	51.1
7/25/2017	Youngstown, OH Covelli Center	OH-13 Tim Ryan*	67.7	51.3
8/3/2017	Huntington, WV Big Sandy Superstore Center	WV-3 Evan Jenkins	67.9	67.9
8/22/2017	Phoenix, AZ Phoenix Convention Center	AZ-7 Ruben Gallego*	75.3	48.1
9/22/2017	Huntsville, AL Von Braun Center	AL-5 Mo Brooks	66.8	62.1
12/8/2017	Pensacola, FL Pensacola Bay Center	FL-1 Matt Gaetz	69.1	48.6
Average	–	–	65.6	54.9

Note:
* Democratic member of Congress

for example, denounced Trump when a video of the president's lewd comments about women surfaced,[35] but later reversed course and said "I support him because he realizes who his enemies are

[35] *USA Today*, "Who supports Trump?" https://www.usatoday.com/pages/interactives/elections/trump-support/

and can protect the country, help turn this economy around and get America headed back in the right direction."[36] House Freedom Caucus member Rod Blum (IA-1) was lukewarm in his support of Trump in the presidential election, saying that he did not like "some of the things Trump does and says" but called for unity around his candidacy.[37] Blum, facing a House ethics investigation, later turned to the president for assistance in a tough midterm race in 2018 and earned his backing on Twitter.[38] Similarly, Mo Brooks (AL-5) unified around Trump and turned to him for aid in 2018, despite criticizing the president's support for Luther Strange in a special election for Senate in the Yellowhammer State in 2017.[39] Evan Jenkins (WV-3) was relatively tepid in his support of Trump in 2016, but ultimately asserted that he was "the only candidate remaining in the presidential contest willing to support our coal miners and stop the Obama-Clinton radical agenda."[40] In 2018 Trump remained non-committal to Jenkins and fellow Republican Patrick Morrissey in the primary race to unseat Democratic Senator Joe Manchin (Morrissey ultimately received the

---

[36] Quoted in James Rosen, "Jump ship on Trump? Florida GOP lawmakers resist national trend." *McClatchy DC Bureau*, October 16, 2016. https://www.mcclatchydc.com/news/politics-government/election/article107611927.html

[37] Cristinia Crippes, "'Never Trump' movement concerns Blum." *The Gazette* (Cedar Rapids, IA), May 6, 2016. https://www.thegazette.com/subject/news/government/elections/never-trump-movement-concerns-blum-20160506

[38] @realDonaldTrump, "Congressman @RodBlum of Iowa got a desperately needed Flood Wall for Cedar Rapids that was almost impossible to get. He makes a BIG difference for Iowa! Border, Military, Vets etc. We need Rod in D.C. He has my Strong Endorsement!" *Twitter*, October 29, 2018, 10:07 p.m. https://twitter.com/realDonaldTrump/status/1057106631652196354?ref_src=twsrc%5Etfw%7Ctwcamp%5Etweetembed%7Ctwterm%5E1057106631652196354&ref_url=https%3A%2F%2Fwhotv.com%2F2018%2F10%2F30%2Fpresident-trump-gives-personal-endorsement-to-iowa-congressman-rod-blum%2F

[39] David M. Drucker, "Brooks chides Trump for endorsing Luther Strange." *Washington Examiner*, August 19, 2017. https://www.washingtonexaminer.com/mo-brooks-chides-trump-for-endorsing-luther-strange

[40] Quoted in Daniel Desrochers, "With Trump victory looming, WV Republicans consider options." *Charleston Gazette-Mail*, May 4, 2016. https://www.wvgazettemail.com/news/politics/with-trump-victory-looming-wv-republicans-consider-options/article_965d0fae-a178-56e3-95a8-a80da498486e.html

nod from voters but did not prevail in the general election).[41] The situation of Matt Gaetz (FL-1) was the exception. Gaetz, whom the president called a "warrior," had long been a key supporter of Trump in the 2016 mid-term elections and his Florida Panhandle district voted for the president by over 39 percent in 2016.[42]

The rallies in Nashville, Louisville, Youngstown, and Phoenix were in districts represented by Democrats, and not one attended. Representative Jim Cooper (TN-5) became a regular critic of the president, disagreeing with Trump on matters as diverse as family separation of illegal immigrants at the southern border to tariffs. John Yarmuth (KY-3) had refused to attend Trump's inauguration "because I didn't think he deserves to be president" and lambasted him at a raucous protest rally in Louisville a day after Trump took the oath of office.[43] In advance of the July rally in Youngstown, Ohio, Tim Ryan (OH-13) opined that Trump had failed his promise to bring jobs back to the Buckeye State and maintained that the president "is the master of the shiny object. You know, 'Hey, look over here,' and don't look at where he doesn't want you to look. I think these campaign-style events are trying to distract people from what's really going on."[44]

The Phoenix rally took place shortly after Trump made controversial comments about the clash between protestors and

[41] Jake Zuckerman, "Trump co-endorses Jenkins, Morrisey; says 'no way' to Blankenship." *Charleston Gazette-Mail*, May 7, 2018. https://www.wvgazettemail.com/news/politics/trump-co-endorses-jenkins-morrisey-says-no-way-to-blankenship/article_22031285-d5b2-59e4-8d6d-8ad36f4edb7b.html

[42] *Washington Post*, "Rep. Matt Gaetz wins Florida's 1st Congressional District seat." November 27, 2016. https://www.washingtonpost.com/election-results/florida-1st-congressional-district/?utm_term=.343976660a57; Ryan Nicol, "'Warrior' Matt Gaetz gets official thumbs-up from Donald Trump." *Florida Politics*, July 13, 2018. http://floridapolitics.com/archives/268704-trump-endorsing-gaetz

[43] Deborah Yetter, "Thousands alarmed by Trump agenda hold rally." *Courier Journal* (Louisville), January 21, 2017. https://www.courier-journal.com/story/news/politics/2017/01/21/local-activists-call-social-justice/96676446/

[44] Quoted in Mary Kilpatrick, "Tim Ryan sounds off on Donald Trump's upcoming Youngstown rally: Ohio Politics Roundup." *Cleveland.com*, July 21, 2017. https://www.cleveland.com/open/index.ssf/2017/07/tim_ryan_sounds_off_on_donald.html

far-right extremists in Charlottesville, Virginia earlier in August 2017 that left one young woman dead when an assailant drove his vehicle into the crowd. Ruben Gallego (AZ-7) criticized the president's timing:

> the question is whether it's appropriate at this time and juncture in this country. You know, we just had an American citizen that was mowed down by a neo-Nazi. The president then proceeded to basically trip over himself to neither condemn the neo-Nazis and white supremacists until finally being pushed. And then to come on the heels of that to Arizona and what I suspect will be a campaign rally filled with rhetoric and not one to actually heal the country, I think it is very dangerous.[45]

In advance of his attendance alongside protestors outside the Phoenix Convention Center at which police used tear gas to disperse crowds, Gallego had called Trump "an abject liar" and a "racist."[46]

Ever distrustful of the print and broadcast media, Trump's post-inaugural rallies—like his extensive use of social media messaging—were, in effect, an ersatz for press conferences and a method to circumvent the putative dishonesty in media coverage of the new administration. Since Eisenhower, newly elected presidents in the modern era have averaged twelve press conferences a year with a standard deviation of eight. Trump gave the fewest press conferences of any president dating to 1953 with just a single gaggle in 2017.[47]

---

[45] Quoted from *NPR All Things Considered*, "Democratic Rep. Ruben Gallego raises concerns about Trump's visit to Phoenix." August 22, 2017. https://www.npr.org/2017/08/22/545314077/democratic-rep-ruben-gallego-raises-concerns-about-trumps-visit-to-phoenix

[46] *AZCentral*, "Live updates: Police release gas on protesters after Trump speech." *Azcentral.com*, August 22, 2017. https://www.azcentral.com/story/news/politics/arizona/2017/08/22/donald-trump-phoenix-arizona-rally/575083001/

[47] Trump's standardized score of first-term presidential press conferences compared to his predecessors is 1.35 standard deviations below the mean ($p = .11$). The average excludes Gerald Ford, who assumed the presidency following Nixon's resignation in August 1974.

The post-inauguration rallies contained many of the themes of the post-election spectacles, including the president's self-congratulatory narratives of major upsets in key swing states that need not be reiterated. However, it is notable that Trump's rhetoric toward elites, the judiciary and media in particular, and toward illegal immigrants became more severe. The events were fora primarily to explicate the lack of policy progress on several fronts as the president took a defensive, reactionary posture while lauding accomplishments like energy development through executive action.

In Melbourne, Florida, Trump condemned the media and the judiciary, linking them together as principal foes to his administration. Indirectly comparing himself to the towering figures of the nineteenth century in the White House, Trump said

> Thomas Jefferson, Andrew Jackson and Abraham Lincoln, and many of our greatest Presidents, fought with the media and called them out, oftentimes on their lies. When the media lies to people, I will never, ever, let them get away with it. I will do whatever I can that they don't get away with it.

Referencing the failure of his first travel ban on select Muslim countries following judicial review, Trump told the audience: "So you probably read where we want to enforce the laws as existing, and so we signed an order a couple of weeks ago, and it was taken over by a court, originally by a judge, and then a—." He continued:

> And I was told—I'll check, but I found it hard to believe—in an over 30-page decision by the appellate court, three judges—and you could tell by the way they were reacting, because it was broadcast on television, and everything we do gets a lot of people watching. So you could tell by the way that phone call went, it wasn't looking good. And when they wrote their decision, as I understand it—maybe I'm wrong—but they didn't write the statute they were making the decision about, because every word of the statute is a total kill for the other side . . . So basically it says the President has the right to keep people out if he feels it's not in the best interest of our country. Right? [Applause.] Unbelievable. Unbelievable. And I listened to these judges talk and talk and talk. So unfair.

272

To reassure his supporters, the president pledged he would "be doing something" about the situation in days to come.[48]

When he appeared before supporters in Nashville in mid-March, Trump was even more livid with the federal judiciary, which had "stayed" a second attempt at a travel ban via executive order. At the outset the president said "I would much rather spend time with you than any of the pundits, consultants, special interests, and certainly reporters from Washington, DC [applause]." After excoriating those who might burn the American flag, the president gave the bad news he had learned just a few moments earlier and even managed to integrate Hillary Clinton gratuitously into the rant.

> I learned that a district judge in Hawaii [booing]—part of much overturned Ninth Circuit Court—I have to be nice otherwise I will get criticized for speaking poorly about our courts. I will be criticized by the most dishonest people in the world. I will be criticized by them for speaking harshly about our courts. A judge has just blocked our executive order on travel and refugees coming into our country from certain countries. The order he blocked was a watered-down version of the first order that was also blocked by another judge and should have never been blocked to start with ... flawed ruling ... this is the opinion of many, an unprecedented judicial overreach. The law and the Constitution give the president the power to suspend immigration when he deems, or she—fortunately it will not be Hillary [applause].[49]

The matter wended its way to the Supreme Court over the next fifteen months and the president ultimately prevailed by a 5–4 decision in *Trump v. Hawaii* (2018).[50] Of course, the president had no foresight into the eventual outcome as his critics charged that

---

[48] *C-SPAN*, "President Trump rally in Melbourne, Florida." February 18, 2017. https://www.c-span.org/video/?424154-1/president-trump-holds-rally-melbourne-florida

[49] *C-SPAN*, "President Trump rally in Nashville, Tennessee." March 15, 2017. https://www.c-span.org/video/?425428-1/president-trump-calls-revised-travel-ban-freeze-unprecedented-judicial-overreach

[50] *Trump v. Hawaii* (2018). https://www.supremecourt.gov/opinions/17pdf/17-965_h315.pdf

the travel ban was at its core discriminatory toward Muslims.[51] The travel ban controversy fed into the president's call for a halt to illegal immigration at the southern border and his plans to build a wall to preclude aliens from entering the United States. If Trump had alluded to Muslims in countries affected by the travel ban as a potential terrorist threat, he also sought to tie illegal immigrants to venomous plans in which they were supposedly engaged to undermine the country's sovereignty.

In Harrisburg, Pennsylvania, in a narrative uncharacteristic from his choppy sentences, he used a metaphor linked to the Biblical image of a serpent to evoke fears of, and villainize, illegals. The event on April 29 marked his 100th day in office, often a key benchmark in media and scholarly analyses of the president's performance. Trump took pains to accentuate that he had broken with tradition and skipped the annual White House Correspondents Dinner:

> A large group of Hollywood actors and Washington media are consoling each other in a hotel ballroom in our nation's capital right now [applause] . . . And I could not possibly be more thrilled than to be more than 100 miles away from Washington Swamp—[applause]— spending my evening with all of you, and with a much, much larger crowd and much better people. Right? [applause]. Right?

As the audience chanted "CNN sucks! CNN sucks!" the president transitioned his narrative of the media from "dishonest" to a new term: "Media outlets like CNN and MSNBC are *fake news*. Fake news. And they're sitting and they're wishing, in Washington—they're watching right now, they're watching. And they would love to be with us right here tonight." It was later that Trump began his soliloquy on illegal immigration. He prefaced his anti-intellectual lesson as follows:

> So I did this a little bit during the rally. Haven't done it in a long time. Who has heard the poem called "The Snake"? So I have it. Does

[51] Josh Gerstein and Ted Hesson, "Supreme Court upholds Trump's travel ban." *Politico*, June 26, 2018. https://www.politico.com/story/2018/06/26/supreme-court-upholds-trumps-travel-ban-673181

anybody want to hear it again? [applause.] You sure? Are you sure? Okay. So let's dedicate this to General Kelly, the Border Patrol, and the ICE agents for doing such an incredible job. [Applause.] This was written by Al Wilson a long time ago. And I thought of it having to do with our borders and people coming in. And we know that we're going to have; we're going to have problems. We have to very, very carefully vet. We have to be smart. We have to be vigilant. . .

On her way to work one morning, down the path along the lake, a tender-hearted woman saw a poor, half-frozen snake. His pretty colored skin had been all frosted with the dew. "Poor thing!" she cried. "I'll take you in and I'll take care of you." *The border.* [Laughter.] "Take me in, oh, tender woman. Take me in for Heaven's sake. Take me in, oh, tender woman," sighed the vicious snake. She wrapped him up all cozy in a comforter of silk, and laid him by her fireside with some honey and some milk. She hurried home from work that night, and as soon as she arrived, she found that pretty snake she'd taken in had been revived. Take me in, oh, tender woman. Take me in for Heaven's sake. Take me in, oh, tender woman, sighed that vicious snake. She clutched him to her bosom, "You're so beautiful," she cried. "But if I hadn't brought you in by now, oh, heavens you would have died." She stroked his pretty skin again and kissed him and held him tight. But instead of saying, "thank you," that snake gave her a vicious bite! Take me in, oh, tender woman. Take me in for Heaven's sake. Take me in, oh, tender woman, sighed the vicious sake. "I have saved you," cried the woman. "And you've bitten me, heavens why? You know your bite is poisonous, and now I'm going to die." "Oh, shut up, silly woman," said the reptile with a grin. "You knew damn well I was a snake before you took me in." [Applause.] Does that explain it, folks? Does that explain it?[52]

Ascribing sinister, conspiratorial motives to immigrants from Central America and Mexico seeking either asylum or a better economic future in the United States, Trump's simplification of a complex, hemispheric problem resonated with the crowd. It is not difficult to comprehend why, as migrant caravans from Honduras and Guatemala made their way to the border in 2018,

---

[52] *C-SPAN*, "President Trump remarks in Harrisburg, Pennsylvania." April 29, 2017. https://www.c-span.org/video/?427466-1/president-fake-news-media-touts-record-100-days

some of his supporters took their cues from the president in efforts to portray the travelers in dehumanizing terms.

Amidst discussion of shared values and the forgotten man and woman, Trump tailored his messaging at many rallies to local issues, lauding his farm policy and executive orders on energy production with the Dakota Access and Keystone pipelines. But of all the rallies, the event in Phoenix was notable for the chaos that took place on the streets and the president's defensive tone. Once again, the president encountered difficulties back-pedaling previous comments that proved controversial and instead chose to blame the media for allegedly misreporting his statements on the tragedy in Charlottesville, Virginia. Trump asserted that

> for the most part, these are really, really dishonest people. These are bad people. And I think they do not like our country. And I do not think it will change. That's why I say this. If they would change, I would never say this. The only people giving a platform to these hate groups is the media itself [*sic*] and the fake news [cheers and applause].[53]

As police fired tear gas into crowds outside the Convention Center, the scene of civil chaos was reminiscent of the pandemonium that characterized Andrew Johnson's conclusion of the Swing around the Circle tour.

IV. At the crossroads of Vaudeville and Main Street, USA: populism meets the permanent campaign

This analysis of the 45th president's post-election and post-inaugural rallies signifies the degree to which "the boundaries of traditional campaign discourse have been breached by Trump"[54]

[53] Quoted in Ian Schwartz, "Trump: Some reporters 'Don't like our country,' don't want to Make America Great Again." *RealClearPolitics*, August 23, 2017. https://www.realclearpolitics.com/video/2017/08/23/trump_some_reporters_dont_like_our_country_dont_want_to_make_america_great_again.html
[54] Kathleen Hall Jamieson, quoted in David Jackson, "Trump's rhetoric is harsher than previous nominees." *USA Today*, June 23, 2016. https://www.usatoday.com/story/news/politics/elections/2016/06/23/donald-trump-hillary-clinton-rhetoric/86293780/

and extended well beyond typical election-year politics. As Edward Appel notes, "[a] near-explicable 'normalization' of Trump's vitriol, fabrication, and threatened mayhem followed the November 2016 vote."[55] Trump's post-election rallies in December 2016 and the broadening of the events into 2017 convey the contemporary reality in American politics that "[g]overning with public approval," as Democratic strategist Pat Caddell posits, "requires a continuing political campaign."[56]

Trump's rallies mark a continuation of presidents governing by targeting grassroots constituents and appealing over the heads of institutional elites in Washington. In his oeuvre entitled *The Permanent Campaign*, journalist Sidney Blumenthal, later an advisor to Bill Clinton, proffered the idea that campaigning had become a form of governing in the context of media- and consultant-driven politics.[57] Walter Dean Burnham suggests that the perpetual campaign that evolved from the late 1960s represents the inverse of historical political realignments insofar as the dynamic has *displaced* political parties rather than reinvigorated them.[58] Indeed, by taking aim at "establishment" Republicans as much as Democrats, Trump's has endeavored to remold the GOP in his own image by accentuating the electorate's personal linkage to him and him alone. This was the central message in the aftermath of the 2018 mid-term elections, which handed Democrats control of the House of Representatives, albeit with a seat gain well below the average loss for incumbent presidents in the post-war era. Reminiscent of one of Marlon Brando's most memorable scenes in *The Godfather*, Trump chastised Republicans who refused to "embrace" him, declined to

---

[55] Edward C. Appel, "Burlesque, Tragedy, and a (Potentially) 'Yuuge' 'Breaking of a Frame': Donald Trump's Rhetoric as 'Early Warning'?" *Communication Quarterly* 66, no. 2 (2018): 168.

[56] Quoted in Joe Klein, "The perils of the permanent campaign." *Time Magazine*, October 30, 2005. http://content.time.com/time/magazine/article/0,9171,1124332,00.html

[57] Sidney Blumenthal, *The Permanent Campaign* (New York: Simon & Schuster, 1982).

[58] Walter Dean Burnham, "The 1984 Election and the Future of American Politics." In Ellis Sandoz and C. V. Crabb, Jr. (eds.), *Election '84: Landslide without Mandate* (New York: New American Library, 1985), p. 206.

kiss the ring symbolized by his agenda, and eschewed his calls to campaign with him. As the president remarked, "you had some that decided to 'let's stay away.' 'Let's stay away.' They did very poorly. I'm not sure that I should be happy or sad, but I feel just fine about it." Citing the losses of a half-dozen Republicans, Trump said, "Those are some of the people that, you know, decided for their own reason not to embrace, whether it's me or what we stand for."[59] For her part, Mia Love (UT-4), whom Trump accused of giving him no "love," opined that the president has "no relationships, just convenient transactions."[60]

If Trump's post-election rallies—full of hubris and histrionics, bluster and buffoonery—appear novel, it is because of the ways in which the populist style has merged with the permanent campaign in conjunction with the president's attempt to reshape, or rather deconstruct, party politics. The congregations of raucous supporters, unyielding in their devotion to the president, represent a unique spectacle that lies at the intersection of Vaudeville and Main Street. Trump is the lightning rod, unpredictable and tragicomedic, to conduct the electrifying antipathy of the forgotten voter in the heartland to disdainful elites in the cesspool of Gomorrah-upon-the-Potomac. "Trump's tactics," writes Jeremy C. Young,

> aren't new, but his agenda is. His emotional campaigning serves solely as a tool for self-aggrandizement, rather than fulfilling its historic function of channeling voter enthusiasm toward a particular legislative program. His rallies, which are notably about him and not about policies, raise deep concerns about a president who uses emotional politics to build a cult of personality rather than to pass laws.[61]

[59] White House, "Remarks by President Trump in press conference after midterm elections." November 7, 2018. https://www.whitehouse.gov/briefings-statements/remarks-president-trump-press-conference-midterm-elections/

[60] Quoted in John Wagner, "Mia Love gives Trump no love as she concedes a narrow loss in Utah." *Washington Post*, November 26, 2018. https://www.washingtonpost.com/politics/mia-love-gives-trump-no-love-as-she-concedes-a-narrow-loss-in-utah/2018/11/26/2062c158-f1a5-11e8-80d0-f7e1948d55f4_story.html?utm_term=.54a0dd9b239e

[61] Jeremy C. Young, "President Trump's rallies are about boosting his ego, not his agenda. The novel purpose behind Trump's road show." *Washington Post*,

The president champions the extravagances of his unorthodox style because it is precisely those qualities that won him the White House. As Trump told his audience in Youngstown, Ohio in July 2017:

> Sometimes they say he doesn't act presidential. And I say, hey look, great schools, smart guy, it's so easy to act presidential but that's not going to get it done. In fact, I said it's much easier, by the way, to act presidential than what we're doing here tonight, believe me. And I said—and I said with the exception of the late, great Abraham Lincoln, I can be more presidential than any president that's ever held this office. That I can tell you. It's real easy, but sadly, we have to move a little faster than that. We will not be beholden to the lobbyists or the special interests. We will never be silenced by the media. I want to protect America. And I want to protect the citizens of America. Your hopes are my dreams. Your dreams are my dreams. I've had a great successful career. I've built a great, great business. This is the only thing that matters. This is the only thing that matters. There is nothing else. Your future is what I'm fighting for each and every day.

The question that remains is whether the populist narrative that Trump so aptly employs to galvanize his base is sufficient to reconcile, or perhaps substitute, the need for policy success. As Doyle McManus maintains, "[t]he new president will continue to campaign, because that's what he knows how to do, and he's good at it. But at some point he needs to deliver."[62]

* * * * *

The next chapter assesses briefly Trump's policymaking efforts and his modus operandi in attempting to navigate through

July 25, 2017. https://www.washingtonpost.com/news/made-by-history/wp/2017/07/25/president-trumps-rallies-are-about-boosting-his-ego-not-his-agenda/?utm_term=.526fd061190f

[62] Doyle McManus, "Trump's permanent campaign won't help him keep his promises." *Los Angeles Times*, January 22, 2017. https://www.latimes.com/opinion/op-ed/la-oe-mcmanus-trump-inauguration-permanent-campaign-20170122-story.html

eÂ

"a rigged system . . . a sick system from the inside."[63] In the policymaking realm, Trump's populist style confronted two prescriptive models of presidential leadership: bargaining and command. Consistent with his election and post-election campaigns against elites, he has largely eschewed efforts at persuasion and instead employed the unilateral levers of the presidency with the accompanying risks such a strategy entails.

[63] C-SPAN, "President Trump rally in Pensacola, Florida." December 8, 2017. https://www.c-span.org/video/?438191-1/president-trump-holds-rally-pensacola-florida

The populist as policymaker

Repubs must not allow Pres Obama to subvert the Constitution of
the US for his own benefit & because he is unable to negotiate w/
Congress.

—Donald Trump, *Twitter*, November 20, 2014

He [Obama] doesn't want to get people together, the old-fashioned
way, where you get Congress. You get the Congress, you get the
Senate, you get together, you do legislation. He just writes out an
executive order. Not supposed to happen that way.

—Donald Trump, January 14, 2016

I would give myself an A+.

—Donald Trump, November 18, 2018

I. Introduction

In his reflection upon Dwight Eisenhower's prospects in the Oval
Office after the Republican's landslide victory in 1952, outgoing
President Harry Truman suggested of his successor that "[h]e'll sit
here, and he'll say, 'Do this! Do that!' *And nothing will happen.
Poor Ike*—it won't be a bit like the Army. He'll find it very frus-
trating."[1] Truman's quip marks a truism of the modern presidency.
Nearly every chief executive has been enticed to lead by command by drawing upon the broad contours of "executive power"
framed in Article II of the Constitution. The appeal of unilateral
action is particularly alluring in view of the wearisome challenges
of persuading Congress, an unenviable task which is often likened

---

[1] Quoted in Richard Neustadt, *Presidential Leadership and the Modern
Presidents* (New York: Free Press, 1960), p. 9.

to herding cats even under the best circumstances. An exasperated Barack Obama, who marshalled his signature Affordable Care Act through Congress in 2010, made the quintessential point as he waged battle against an intransigent opposition majority several years later. Squaring off against the Republican Congress, Obama noted that "I've got a pen and I've got a phone—and I can use that pen to sign executive orders and take executive actions and administrative actions that move the ball forward."[2]

Obama's frustration after losing his partisan majority on Capitol Hill just two years into his term conveys why, according to most scholars, presidents must think big and act boldly early in their term to take the reins of Congress and accomplish their goals quickly. Their influence naturally diminishes across time, and the condition of divided government can further limit the potential for legislative success, particularly in this age of institutional hyper-partisanship. The standard academic prescription is that new presidents "hit the ground running" vis-à-vis Congress.[3] Presidents must capitalize on their brief "honeymoon" period by signaling legislative priorities, quickly shaping the congressional agenda, and persuading members who are likely more deferential in the early days of an administration. Timing is paramount, as the near certainty of mid-term losses for his party looms large over the president's narrow window of opportunity on Capitol Hill. But the other face of the coin—the unilateral prerogatives of the presidency—has far fewer constraints attached. Presidents are naturally tempted to take a path of lesser resistance when confronted with refractory majorities, whatever their partisan composition, on the other end of Pennsylvania Avenue.

Never one to rely on advice from academics, Trump failed in his early efforts to bargain with Congress as much for a lack of structure in the White House and a dearth of policy plans as for

---

[2] Quoted in Rebecca Kaplan, "Obama: I will use my pen and phone to take on Congress." *CBS News*, January 14, 2014. https://www.cbsnews.com/news/obama-i-will-use-my-pen-and-phone-to-take-on-congress/

[3] James P. Pfiffner, *The Strategic Presidency: Hitting the Ground Running* (Lawrence: University Press of Kansas, 1996).

his rhetorical impulses to recriminate legislators who stood in the way of his agenda. In his "honeymoon from hell," the president's chaotic first months in office were compounded by the lowest approval rating of any elected president in seventy years and Twitter diatribes that distracted both Congress and the American public.[4] To make matters worse, "[b]efore and after the November election," write Sarah Binder and Mark Spindel, "Trump outlined a menu of ambitious offerings—including immigration and tax restructuring, infrastructure spending, trade renegotiation, his oft-emphasized southern border wall, as well as Affordable Care Act repeal and Wall Street deregulation," but failed to delineate detailed proposals.[5]

Despite a Republican majority in Congress, albeit with internal and inter-cameral divisions, Trump's opportunities for success were not necessarily bleak. The problem is that the president refused "to put in the time to understand an issue and do the hard work of hashing out solutions with his policy aides, or sitting down with Paul Ryan and Mitch McConnell to hammer out a strategy."[6] Trump's "100 days," a common benchmark used by media and scholars to assess a president's progress in office, was most notable for the failure of health care reform ("repeal and replace" of the ACA) that resulted in the president's frontal assault on the GOP's House Freedom Caucus in March 2017.[7] The months that followed featured continuing offensives against

[4] Karl Rove, "A Presidential honeymoon from hell; This should be a time to notch early wins. But Trump is stalled and distracted." *Wall Street Journal Online*, April 5, 2017.

[5] Sarah Binder and Mark Spindel, "This is why Trump's legislative agenda is stuck in neutral." *Washington Post*, April 26, 2017. https://www.washingtonpost.com/news/monkey-cage/wp/2017/04/26/this-is-why-trumps-legislative-agenda-is-stuck-in-neutral/?utm_term=.f50f174ca7c9

[6] Jamelle Bouie, "Trump can't score a win." *Slate*, September 5, 2017. https://slate.com/news-and-politics/2017/09/trump-cant-score-any-legislative-accomplishments-even-with-a-gop-led-congress.html

[7] Russell Berman, "The Republican majority in Congress is an illusion." *The Atlantic*, March 31, 2017. https://www.theatlantic.com/politics/archive/2017/03/the-republican-majority-in-congress-is-an-illusion/521403/

recalcitrant senators like John McCain (R-AZ) over health care.[8] In fact, Trump's most significant legislative victory on tax cuts did not materialize until the end of his first year amidst threats to shut down the government due to Republicans' inability to forge consensus on immigration and border security.

It is little wonder that Trump turned to executive actions to accomplish many of his goals with all deliberate speed, bypassing Congress where he could and standing ready to litigate in court where necessary. In retrospect, Trump's exchange of the "art of the deal" for unilateral zeal was predictable despite his criticism of Obama's use of executive power ranging from immigration (DACA) to the implementation of the ACA. If Trump's predecessors gravitated toward the exercise of independent executive action due to the particular institutional contexts they faced, the unitary executive model nonetheless fits rather seamlessly with the populist style. Trump's populist style expresses more disdain than patience for institutions like Congress that mediate popular will. Like Nixon before him, Trump views himself as an executive decisionmaker and similarly refused to reach out to the opposition Democrats in Congress.[9] Moreover, it follows that executive actions suit Trump's majoritarian predilections, and he has on more than one occasion challenged the legitimacy of courts to review his policy mandates.

The objective of this chapter is to assess briefly how Trump's populist style intersected with his quest to implement the "Make America Great Again" (MAGA) agenda. The analysis focuses on presidential executive orders and memoranda as key elements of his policymaking efforts. Close scrutiny of these executive actions underscores the degree to which Trump has been largely

---

[8] Julie Hirschfeld Davis, "Trump laces into McCain over his opposition to health care bill." *New York Times*, September 23, 2017. https://www.nytimes.com/2017/09/23/us/politics/trump-mccain-graham-cassidy-health-care-obamacare.html

[9] George C. Edwards III, *Presidential Influence in Congress* (San Francisco: W. H. Freeman, 1980), p. 16; Charles O. Jones, "Presidential Negotiation with Congress." In Anthony King (ed.), *Both Ends of the Avenue: The Presidency, the Executive Branch, and Congress in the 1980s* (Washington, DC: American Enterprise Institute, 1983), pp. 114–15.

successful through the midpoint of his term in reorienting the executive branch, from deregulation and natural resource development to foreign and defense policy despite ample controversy and legal challenges. However, the very real risk to this strategy is that unilateral actions, unlike statutes codified by Congress, are most easily overturned with a stroke of the pen. This is one of the critical lessons of Obama's legacy that Trump may be unwittingly repeating. He has disassembled much of Obama's policies with the same blunt instruments his predecessor used— and Trump's successor could do the same after the billionaire leaves office, whether in 2021 or 2025.

II. The pen versus persuasion: the populist trump card?

Although the Republican majority in Congress in 2017 became increasingly mired in the divisive debate over health care, the budget, and tax reform, Donald Trump wasted no time putting pen to paper in the Oval Office to jump start his MAGA agenda. Front and center were regulatory reform, economic growth, and foreign and defense policy. Analysis of executive orders and presidential memoranda underscores the degree to which Trump steadfastly made unilateral actions a centerpiece of his presidency, in his first 100 days and beyond, more quietly perhaps at times than his continuing anti-elitist harangues against the members of Congress whom he found unpersuadable on the legislative front.

A. Executive orders

The pace of Trump's use of executive orders appears rather unremarkable compared to his most recent predecessors' record. In 2017 and 2018 he issued 55 and 37 executive orders, respectively, for an annual average of 46 through the midpoint of his term. Barack Obama issued an annual average of 35 executive orders over the course of his two terms, and George W. Bush a yearly average of 36. Reaching back to Ronald Reagan, the "Great Communicator" signed an average of 48 executive orders per year, and 50 in 1981. In fact, the substance of the executive orders Trump signed during his inaugural year bear a close resemblance to those of Reagan with an agenda focused on regulatory reform, trade, and foreign and defense policy.

As Kenneth R. Mayer reminds us, however, it is not simply the quantity of executive orders that must be analyzed, but those that go beyond symbolism and the minutiae of departmental administration and embrace the core of the president's policy objectives. Significant executive orders are a tool of control that enables presidents to "shape the institutional and political context in which they sit."[10] In this way, William G. Howell argues, "[p]residents regularly effect policy change outside of a bargaining framework."[11] Such a strategy clearly reflects Trump's approach.

The data in Table 6.1 show Trump's executive orders by policy area from 2017 to 2018. Orders addressing regulation, foreign and defense policy, and management of the executive branch constituted over three-fifths of all orders in 2017. Foreign and defense policy, and executive branch management constituted the

Table 6.1 Executive Orders by Policy Area, 2017–18

Policy area	2017		2018	
Regulatory	12	21.8%	2	5.4%
Foreign/defense	14	25.4%	12	32.4%
Trade	4	7.2%	0	0.0%
Law enforcement	6	10.9%	1	2.7%
Economy	5	9.1%	6	16.2%
Executive branch	9	16.3%	13	35.1%
Other	5	9.0%	3	8.1%
N	55		37	

Note:
$\chi^2 = 20.01$, $p = .003$

Source: *Federal Register*, classification by author.

[10] Kenneth R. Mayer, *With the Stroke of a Pen: Executive Orders and Presidential Power* (Princeton, NJ: Princeton University Press, 2001), pp. 28–9.
[11] William G. Howell, *Power without Persuasion: The Politics of Direct Presidential Action* (Princeton, NJ: Princeton University Press, 2003), p. 13.

lion's share of orders in 2018 and it is notable that Trump issued eighteen fewer orders overall in his second year. From a strategic perspective, Trump used executive orders in his first year to actuate important contours of the agenda he promised voters in 2016. Consolidation of that agenda followed in 2018.

On the regulatory front, Trump signed E.O. 13765 symbolically on his very first day in office. The order empowered the Secretary of Health and Human Services to seek ways to relieve the financial burden of the ACA or "Obamacare" on states, individuals, and families through waivers and exemptions in the implementation of the law pending its repeal by Congress (which did not materialize). E.O. 13772 provided an overlay of the new administration's core principles on regulation, including the rejection of taxpayer bailouts, competition, and placing America first in international regulatory frameworks. Of the more substantive orders in the regulatory realm, E.O. 13771 implemented a "2-for-1" plan by which every new agency regulation required a repeal of two others.[12] E.O. 13789 called for a Treasury Department review of all tax regulations after January 2016 that increase complexity or potentially exceed the statutory authority of the Internal Revenue Service.

Other regulatory executive orders targeted the acceleration of environmental review processes connected to infrastructure projects and a Department of Education review of regulations to preserve state and local control. One of the most detailed orders was E.O. 13783, which sought to promote energy independence and economic growth by implementing a massive, pan-agency review of regulations. Finally, E.O. 13777 mandated the creation of a "regulatory reform officer" in all agencies to enforce the administration's general policies.

In the realm of foreign and defense policy, in 2017 Trump addressed sanctions on Sudan, Venezuela, and North Korea. Other

---

[12] The order was unsuccessfully challenged by Public Citizen and the Natural Resources Defense Council. See *Safety and Health Magazine*, "Judge dismisses lawsuit against '2-for-1' Executive Order on federal regulations." March 1, 2018. https://www.safetyandhealthmagazine.com/articles/16750-judge-dismisses-lawsuit-against-2-for-1-executive-order-on-federal-regulations

orders focused on blocking the property of individuals involved in human rights abuses, reviving the National Space Council, and targeting transnational criminal organizations. But undoubtedly the most controversial orders focused on the president's proposed temporary "travel ban" on individuals from Iran, Iraq, Libya, Somalia, Sudan, Syria, and Yemen, and implementing a process of "extreme vetting" for those seeking visas and refugee status. Although these orders dealt with immigration—a policy area that traverses foreign and domestic affairs—they are classified as foreign/defense policy because Trump justified them on the basis of protecting the nation from potential terrorists attempting to enter the United States at the southern border.

The first travel ban order, E.O. 13769 in January 2017, was immediately confronted with hundreds of lawsuits by opponents who labeled it a "Muslim ban" despite the fact that the countries named were identified as terrorist threats in the Obama administration. Nonetheless, within days of its issuance Trump's order was blocked nationwide when a Seattle judge in the Ninth Circuit Court signed a temporary restraining order.[13] A livid Trump signed a second order, E.O. 13780, that was unveiled in early March and repealed and modified the previous ban. The new order dropped Iraq from the list of countries to which the travel ban applied, but added North Korea and Venezuela. Hours before the ban was to go into effect, another federal judge from the Ninth Circuit Court—this time from Hawaii—issued a nationwide temporary restraining order halting implementation on the basis that the order was discriminatory and violated the Establishment Clause.[14] In a *per curiam*

---

[13] Devlin Barrett and Dan Frosch, "Federal judge temporarily halts Trump order on immigration, refugees." *Wall Street Journal*, February 4, 2017. https://www.wsj.com/articles/legal-feud-over-trump-immigration-order-turns-to-visa-revocations-1486153216

[14] Oliver Laughland, Ed Pilkington, David Smith, and Liz Barney, "Hawaii judge halts new Trump travel ban, setting stage for epic legal battle." *The Guardian*, March 16, 2017. https://www.theguardian.com/us-news/2017/mar/15/trump-travel-ban-blocked-restraining-order-hawaii

decision, the Supreme Court subsequently reinstated elements of the order in June.[15]

The third and final order on "extreme vetting" was issued by Trump in late October as the previous order was set to expire. A year later, a divided High Court took up the matter of the president's authority and ruled in a 5–4 decision that the presidential travel ban was constitutional. Congress had delegated authority to the president on immigration matters in the 1940s, and Chief Justice Roberts argued that "courts should not substitute their own judgment for that of the executive branch on national-security matters, which he characterized as 'delicate,' 'complex,' and involving 'large elements of prophecy'."[16] Trump lambasted his opponents, contending: "This ruling is also a moment of profound vindication following months of hysterical commentary from the media and Democratic politicians who refuse to do what it takes to secure our border and our country."[17]

Law enforcement, the economy, and trade also figured prominently in Trump's first-year executive orders, less for quantity and more for substance. In the legal domain and regarding law enforcement, E.O. 13774 sought to enhance protection of officers by increasing penalties and insuring the application of federal laws. E.O. 13809 rescinded a 2015 Obama order in which certain police equipment, over which the federal government could influence purchase, was identified as potentially harmful to community trust (e.g., armored vehicles, firearms of .50 caliber or more, weaponized vehicles of any kind).[18] E.O. 13778 took

[15] Michael D. Shear and Adam Liptak, "Supreme Court takes up travel ban case, and allows parts to go ahead." *New York Times*, June 26, 2017. https://www.nytimes.com/2017/06/26/us/politics/supreme-court-trump-travel-ban-case.html

[16] Amy Howe, "Opinion analysis: Divided Court upholds Trump travel ban." *SCOTUSBlog*, June 26, 2018. https://www.scotusblog.com/2018/06/opinion-analysis-divided-court-upholds-trump-travel-ban/

[17] Quoted in Adam Liptak and Michael D. Shear, "Trump's travel ban is upheld by the Supreme Court." June 26, 2018. https://www.nytimes.com/2018/06/26/us/politics/supreme-court-trump-travel-ban.html

[18] *Police One*, "What you need to know about Executive Order 13688." August 22, 2016. https://www.policeone.com/jag/articles/210318006-What-you-need-to-know-about-Executive-Order-13688/

aim at the rule of law and balance of federal and state power in regard to the waters of the United States. E.O. 13800 sought to strengthen cybersecurity of federal computers and for critical infrastructure.

On the economic front, no other executive order captured Trump's MAGA emphasis more than "Buy American, Hire American," which focused on restoring elements of the manufacturing industry, in particular. E.O. 13788 sought to maximize use of goods, products, and materials produced in the United States for federal contracts. In addition, the order mandated that agencies "rigorously enforce and administer the laws governing entry into the United States of workers from abroad" and minimize waivers for foreign workers in order to enhance domestic employment. Other first-year orders included promoting rural prosperity, implementing an "America-First" offshore energy policy, expanding apprenticeships, and establishing a task force on infrastructure development.

Executive orders on trade paralleled the president's emphasis on restoring American economic prominence. E.O. 13796 squarely addressed Trump's promise to insure fairness in trade relationships with other countries. The order stated that "It is the policy of the United States to negotiate new trade agreements, investment agreements, and trade relations that benefit American workers and domestic manufacturers, farmers, and ranchers; protect our intellectual property; and encourage domestic research and development." As such, Trump required that government agencies and the U.S. Trade Representative review all bilateral and multilateral trade agreements and report abuses. Other orders targeted "dumping" of goods in the United States by foreign governments and alleged duty violations, mandated a government report on trade deficits stemming from unfair practices by foreign entities, and established an Office of Trade and Manufacturing Policy with the mission "to defend and serve American workers and domestic manufacturers while advising the President on policies to increase economic growth, decrease the trade deficit, and strengthen the United States manufacturing and defense industrial bases."

In 2018 more than a third of Trump's executive orders focused on the executive branch. The president clearly set out to transform the internal operations of the federal level. Orders focused on re-entry of veterans into the workforce, making the postal system more efficient, curbing federal collective bargaining, improving governmental efficiency, enhancing the effectiveness of agency information officers, streamlining federal merit system procedures to facilitate firing employees, and insuring government transparency in terms of the actual number of hours federal workers undertake. In the foreign and defense policy realm, Trump used the pen to address further the socio-political crisis in Venezuela, to reimpose sanctions on Iran, and to authorize sanctions on other of America's adversaries, including those found to have interfered in the 2016 election.

Finally, some of Trump's orders were more symbolic. As a nod to the evangelical Christians who had supported his candidacy, he established a White House Faith and Opportunity Initiative. To address the "skills shortage" in the economy he established the National Council of the American Worker, whose mission is for "private employers, educational institutions, labor unions, other non-profit organizations, and State, territorial, tribal, and local governments to update and reshape our education and job training landscape so that it better meets the needs of American students, workers, and businesses."

B. Presidential memoranda

Scholars have recently noted a decline in presidents' use of executive orders and a concomitant increase in alternative unilateral instruments to accomplish their agenda.[19] The first two years of Trump's presidency arguably solidifies this trend. Presidential memoranda represent another tool in the president's belt, even if this mechanism of command has received little attention in the scholarly literature. Philip J. Cooper suggests that presidential memoranda are "executive orders by another name and yet unique."[20] Presidential memoranda represent "a class of presidential actions that contains

---

[19] Andrew C. Rudalevige, "Executive Orders & Presidential Unilateralism." *Presidential Studies Quarterly* 42, no. 1 (2012): 138–60.

[20] Philip J. Cooper, *By Order of the President: The Use and Abuse of Executive Direct Action* (Lawrence: University Press of Kansas, 2002), p. 80.

orders to administrators and is not subject to the statutory reporting requirements of executive orders and proclamations."[21]

Because memoranda have been used to delegate authority
within the executive branch, interpret the implementation of
statutes, and review policy decisions, inter alia, they are virtually
indistinguishable from executive orders.[22] Yet they are also difficult to tally, as they may or may not be published in the Federal
Register according to the administration's "general applicability
and legal effect."[23] As Cooper notes:

> Until relatively recently, the tendency has been to use memoranda
> in the foreign policy arena to issue findings under various statutes.
> Some were used within the executive branch, sometimes referred to
> as presidential letters, for relatively technical purposes such as del-
> egations of authority. The past three presidents have expanded the
> use of the memorandum for significant purposes and in ways that
> make them appear far more like executive orders than anything else
> in terms of their substantive effect. Indeed, it is common for these
> memoranda to end with a specific statement that the named officials
> are directed by the president to take the actions set forth in the docu-
> ment. As noted earlier, administrations have gone so far as to lump
> orders and memoranda together into a class of actions described as
> *presidential directives.*[24]

There has clearly been an upward tendency in the use of presidential memoranda in the new millennium. Whereas Bill Clinton
published only 14 from 1993 to 2000, George W. Bush wrote a
total of 131 and the number reached 257 for Barack Obama's
eight years. To the midpoint of his term, Donald Trump had
already published a total of 146 presidential memoranda—more

---

[21] Kenneth S. Lowande, "After the Orders: Presidential Memoranda and Unilateral Action." *Presidential Studies Quarterly* 44, no. 4 (2014): 725.

[22] Ibid., p. 729.

[23] Competitive Enterprise Institute, "Presidential Executive Orders and Executive Memoranda," chapter 5. https://cei.org/10KC/chapter-5

[24] Philip J. Cooper, "Presidential Memoranda and Executive Orders: Of Patchwork Quilts, Trump Cards, and Shell Games." *Presidential Studies Quarterly*
31, no. 1 (2001): 127–8.

The populist as policymaker

Table 6.2 Executive Memoranda by Policy Area, 2017–18

Policy area	2017		2018	
Regulatory	1	1.5%	2	2.5%
Foreign/defense	51	76.1%	59	74.4%
Trade	3	4.5%	2	2.5%
Law enforcement	0	0.0%	5	6.3%
Economy	3	4.5%	2	2.5%
Executive branch	5	7.5%	3	3.8%
Other	4	6.0%	6	7.6%
N	67		79	

Note:
$\chi^2 = 6.27$, $p = .394$
Source: *Federal Register*, classification by author.

than half as many as for the entirety of Obama's two terms. As Table 6.2 shows, approximately three-quarters of Trump's memoranda focus on foreign and defense policy.

As with the preceding analysis of executive orders, quantity is less important than what the memoranda signify in terms of the president's efforts to implement his policy agenda. A focus on presidential memoranda places Trump's agenda pursuit through unilateral directives in stark relief to what Congress did not undertake. Embedded within Table 6.2 is the realization of some of the president's most important campaign promises, and many key decisions came within the first 100 days of his administration.

Although foreign and defense policy memoranda dominated Trump's use of this unilateral instrument overall in his first two years, it is significant that six of seven memoranda issued during his first three days in office targeted the federal work force, trade, economics, regulation, and abortion. Two days into his presidency, Trump issued three key memoranda. First, he made good on a campaign promise to overhaul the federal workforce by implementing a hiring freeze. "Critiquing the Washington establishment was central to Trump's campaign," notes Juliet Eilperin, "and he placed federal employees at the center of his effort to 'clean up the corruption and special interest collusion in

Washington, D.C.' His 'Contract with the American Voter' listed a hiring freeze as a key element."[25] Second, in line with previous Republican commanders-in-chief dating to Reagan, Trump reinstituted the so-called Mexico City policy that restricts non-governmental organizations from providing abortion counseling services overseas. The president "signaled his intent to make the order one of his first acts as president, which pleased anti-abortion activists at home."[26] Third, Trump withdrew the United States from the Trans-Pacific Partnership trade negotiations that commenced under his predecessor. Obama had supported a multilateral trade deal in Asia as a means of leveraging U.S. influence vis-à-vis China. Rejecting multilateral trade negotiations in favor of bilateral arrangements, Trump's move "intended to signal that his tough talk on trade during the campaign will carry over to his new administration."[27]

On January 24, 2017 Trump took aim at infrastructure projects that had been put on hold by President Obama. The first memorandum targeted environmental review regulations that Trump called an "incredibly cumbersome, long, horrible permitting process."[28] The following two memoranda paved the way for approval of the Dakota Access Pipeline (DAPL) and the Keystone XL Pipeline to carry oil across the Great Plains and from Canada, respectively. Massive protests by Native Americans on the Standing Rock Sioux Reservation along the Missouri River in North Dakota, and the pleas of environmental groups concerned about climate change, had eventually persuaded Obama to sideline the projects. "The decisions," write Peter Baker and Coral Davenport, "expanded an effort to unravel much of the policy structure left by former President Barack Obama, who

[25] Juliet Eilperin, "Trump imposes immediate federal hiring freeze." *Washington Post*, January 24, 2017, p. A6.
[26] Somini Sengupta, "Trump revives ban on aid to groups that discuss abortion." *New York Times*, January 24, 2017, p. A13.
[27] Yulan Q. Mui, "Demise of TPP shifts U.S. role in world economy." *Washington Post*, January 24, 2017, p. A1.
[28] Steven Mufson and Juliet Eilperin, "Trump seeks to spark action on oil pipelines." *Washington Post*, January 25, 2017, p. A1.

made fighting climate change a central priority."[29] The White House portrayed the expedited review process and approval of the construction of the pipelines as "critical to a strong economy, energy independence, and national security."[30] For his part, Dave Archambault, president of the Standing Rock Sioux Nation, contended of DAPL that "Americans know this pipeline was unfairly rerouted towards our nation and without our consent. The existing pipeline route risks infringing on our treaty rights, contaminating our water and the water of 17 million Americans downstream" and pledged to continue legal challenges to the pipeline's construction.[31]

Trump's early memoranda on foreign and defense policy constituted an admixture of substantive and symbolic undertakings. Within a week of assuming the presidency, Trump issued a memorandum on rebuilding the national defense. In signing the directive he described as a "great rebuilding of the Armed Forces," Trump mandated that the Secretary of Defense commence a thirty-day readiness review focused on defeating ISIS and identifying gaps in materiel and infrastructure alongside an appraisal of ballistic missiles in the nuclear arsenal. The order complemented the president's campaign pledge, hearkening back to the Reagan era, of pursuing "peace through strength."[32] Into the summer of 2017, Trump issued twelve memoranda extending national emergencies in countries from the Central African Republic and North Korea to Somalia and Syria and signed a host of memoranda addressing terrorist threats. But perhaps the most symbolic move came in early December in the decision to

[29] Peter Baker and Coral Davenport, "President revives two oil pipelines thwarted under Obama." *New York Times*, January 25, 2017, p. A1.

[30] White House Statement, "President Trump takes action to expedite priority energy and infrastructure projects." January 24, 2017. https://www.whitehouse. gov/briefings-statements/president-trump-takes-action-expedite-priority-energy-infrastructure-projects/

[31] Press release, "Trump Executive Memorandum on DAPL violates law and tribal treaties." *StandingWithStandingRock*, January 24, 2017. https://stand-withstandingrock.net/trump-executive-order-dapl-violates-law-tribal-treaties/

[32] Dan Lamothe, "Trump calls for 'great rebuilding of the Armed Forces'." *Washington Post*, January 29, 2017, p. A4.

relocate the U.S. embassy in Israel from Tel Aviv to Jerusalem—which Congress authorized in 1995 but which none of his predecessors had completed.[33] Having postponed the decision in May, Trump declared Jerusalem the capital of the Jewish State and signaled his intent to move the embassy. He proclaimed on December 6 that "[w]hile previous presidents have made this a major campaign promise, they failed to deliver. Today, I am delivering."[34] Critics charged the announcement was a major setback for an eventual two-state solution between Israel and the Palestinians, while support from pro-Israel groups, Evangelical Christians, and many members of Congress was solid.[35]

In 2018 a plurality of presidential memoranda on foreign and defense policy included routine delegations of authority to Cabinet heads. Arguably the most significant memoranda targeted the Joint Comprehensive Plan of Action (JCPOA) regarding Iran's nuclear program, upon which the United States and five other countries agreed in 2015. On May 8, 2018 Trump declared that the United States was rescinding participation in the framework and reimposing sanctions on the Iranian regime for its pursuit of ballistic weapon technology. Trump had long criticized the multilateral agreement, lambasting the deal as a "terrible one for the United States and the world. It does nothing but make Iran rich and will lead to catastrophe."[36] With his directive to cabinet heads to cease U.S. involvement in the

---

[33] Sagaar Enjeti, "Flashback: All the times past presidents promised to move US Embassy to Jerusalem." *Daily Caller*, December 6, 2017. https://dailycaller.com/2017/12/06/flashback-all-the-times-past-presidents-promised-to-move-us-embassy-to-jerusalem/

[34] *Political Transcript Wire*, "President Donald Trump delivers remarks on Jerusalem." December 6, 2017.

[35] Ian Lovett, "Evangelical Christians lobbied hard for Trump's move on Jerusalem." *Wall Street Journal (Online)*, December 7, 2017.

[36] @realDonaldTrump, "The Iran nuclear deal is a terrible one for the United States and the world. It does nothing but make Iran rich and will lead to catastrophe." *Twitter*, April 3, 2015, 4:06 p.m. https://twitter.com/realdonaldtrump/status/584129948916514818

agreement, Trump effectively unraveled a major component of Barack Obama's policy legacy by putting pen to paper.[37]

Trump's exit from the JCPOA, or "Iran nuclear deal," and subsequent strategy of imposing a maximum pressure campaign on the mullahs to halt development of weapons-grade nuclear material, has proven one of the most controversial and divisive debates in foreign policy.[38] The economic sanctions, and Iran's inability to sell oil on the world market, has crippled its economy and plummeted the value of the country's currency. Critics contend that Trump's decision to leave the multilateral arrangement "has done nothing to force changes in Iran's regional behavior or push Iran into accepting new U.S. demands. Rather, the policy has sharply increased tensions in the Persian Gulf and decreased Iran's incentives to continue compliance with the JCPOA."[39] In support of that argument, detractors of the president's policy suggest Iran is prone to lashing out in a more bellicose way, including attempts to disrupt oil transports in the Strait of Hormuz and a drone strike on Saudi Arabia's largest oil field and refinery in August 2019. Supporters of Trump's decision posit that the JCPOA framework was fundamentally flawed "because it only paused Iran's nuclear project, instead of ending it, and did nothing to stop Iran's aggression against its neighbors, or its support of terrorism, or its brutal repression of the Iranian people."[40]

Trump also took definitive action in other categories of memoranda. On law enforcement, he issued a memorandum regarding

---

[37] Mark Landler, "Trump abandons nuclear deal he long scorned." *New York Times*, May 8, 2018. https://www.nytimes.com/2018/05/08/world/middleeast/trump-iran-nuclear-deal.html

[38] See Kian Tajbakhsh, "Who Wants What from Iran Now? The Post-Nuclear Deal U.S. Policy Debate." *The Washington Quarterly*, 41, no. 3 (2018): 41–61.

[39] Daryl G. Kimball, "Trump's Failing Iran Policy." *Arms Control Today*, June 2019. https://www.armscontrol.org/act/2019-06/focus/trumps-failing-iran-policy

[40] Joseph I. Lieberman, "2020 Democrats should support Trump's Iran policy, not pledge to rejoin 2015 nuclear deal." *USA Today*, September 9, 2019. https://www.usatoday.com/story/opinion/2019/09/09/2020-democrats-should-support-trump-on-iran-nuclear-deal-olumn/2213275001/

the definition of "bumpstocks" on firearms that effectively transform rifles into semi-automatic weapons. The directive prohibiting the sale of the devices was a direct result of the October 2017 shooting in Las Vegas that claimed the lives of fifty-eight concert-goers and injured more than 400 others.[41] The rule to be enforced by the Bureau of Alcohol, Tobacco, and Firearms (ATF) circumvented the paralysis in Congress over new gun legislation and survived judicial review.[42] In March 2018, Trump issued a memorandum disqualifying transgender individuals from military service under most circumstances, which was challenged successfully in federal courts before the Supreme Court ruled narrowly in a 5–4 decision to uphold the ban in January 2019.[43] In April 2018 the president mandated an end to "catch and release" of illegal aliens, a policy of detaining and then releasing non-criminals he blamed on President Obama and Democrats. The directive fit the president's continuing narrative to take a strict stance on illegal immigration, especially as migrant caravans from Central America headed north to the southern border. As Julie Hirschfield Davis avers,

> The directive does not, on its own, toughen immigration policy or take concrete steps to do so; it merely directs officials to report to the president about steps they are taking to expeditiously end "catch and release" practices. But it is a symbolic move by Mr. Trump to use his executive action to solve a problem that he has bitterly complained Congress will not.[44]

---

[41] Charlie Savage, "Trump administration imposes ban on bump stocks." *New York Times*, December 18, 2018. https://www.nytimes.com/2018/12/18/us/politics/trump-bump-stocks-ban.html

[42] Lawrence Hurley, "U.S. Supreme Court rebuffs bid to block Trump's gun 'bump stock' ban." *Reuters*, March 28, 2019. https://www.reuters.com/article/us-usa-court-guns/u-s-supreme-court-refuses-to-block-trumps-gun-bump-stock-ban-idUSKCN1R9230

[43] David Welna and Bill Chappell, "Supreme Court revives Trump's ban on transgender military personnel, for now." *NPR*, January 22, 2019. https://www.npr.org/2019/01/22/687368145/supreme-court-revives-trumps-ban-on-transgender-military-personnel-for-now

[44] Julie Hirschfield Davis, "Trump signs memo ordering end to 'catch and release' immigration policy." *New York Times (Online)*, April 6, 2018.

C. Orthodox policymaking by an unorthodox president?

This cursory analysis of Trump's use of the unilateral instruments of the presidency does *not* address elements of his rather unconventional style of diplomacy, which is better left to scholars of foreign policymaking. It may well be that in the flotsam and jetsam left behind in his tumultuous steering of the ship of state abroad and acrimonious personal relations with leaders on the world stage, the 45th president has utilized game theory and a set of untraditional stratagems in high-stakes negotiations that provide little of the face-saving opportunities that his predecessors dating to Eisenhower valued in the Cold War era.[45] Regardless, Trump's use of executive orders and presidential memoranda illustrates a general observation on the exercise of presidential power in recent decades and the way in which his populist style intersects with contemporary trends.

For better or for worse, Trump's embrace of unitary executive authority is in keeping with the development of a recent uptick in substantive presidential claims to independent authority. To be sure, "[a] new president of any party," John MacKenzie posits, "might well inventory the accumulated powers—and claims of power—and decide to try hanging on to them."[46] Yet there has been a more pronounced assertion of such claims by presidents of both parties since Ronald Reagan's interpretative construct of broad authority.[47] Like his predecessors, Trump "has shifted policy-making and executive authority to individuals and agencies more directly under presidential control and/or more in line"[48] with his preferences.

---

[45] See Charles Hankla, "Trump could be using advanced game theory negotiating techniques—or he's hopelessly adrift." *The Conversation*, June 8, 2018. http://theconversation.com/trump-could-be-using-advanced-game-theory-negotiating-techniques-or-hes-hopelessly-adrift-97836

[46] John P. MacKenzie, *Absolute Power: How the Unitary Executive Theory Is Undermining the Constitution* (New York: The Century Foundation Press, 2008), p. 57.

[47] Jeffrey Crouch, Mark J. Rozell, and Mitchell A. Sollenberger, "The Unitary Executive Theory and President Donald J. Trump." *Presidential Studies Quarterly* 47, no. 3 (2017): 570.

[48] Jordan T. Cash and Dave Bridge, "Donald Trump and Institutional Change Strategies." *Laws* 7, no. 27 (2018): 6.

The institutionalization and normalization of unitary executive theory, even if the Trump White House never officially adopted such a policy, has enabled the president to "push executive power in even bolder directions than his two predecessors."[49] Accompanying those opportunities has been a concomitant rise in litigation over presidential actions. The hazards are multiple, from potentially stinging blows by federal judges willing to enjoin administration policy to the president's quest to delegitimize justices like those of the Ninth Circuit Court, whom the president routinely condemns for their decisions. Hanging in the balance as well are narrow, 5–4 decisions by the Supreme Court that mirror the divide in public opinion on Trump's agenda for which consensus remains elusive.

As Trump prepares for the 2020 presidential election, his catch-phrases include "Keep America Great" and "Promises Made, Promises Kept." To the extent that he has kept his pledges to restore economic growth, revitalize the manufacturing sector, rebuild the military, exit multilateral trade and foreign policy agreements, and address illegal immigration—and reverse the policy accomplishments of Barack Obama—unilateral actions, rather than congressional legislation, are chiefly responsible for his successes to date. Whether such undertakings survive his term in office remains an open question, and one of the principal perils to his policy legacy if a Democratic candidate prevails in 2020 or 2024.

* * * * *

Of course, Trump faces a host of other possible liabilities as he looks to the 2020 election and beyond. Chapter 7 takes up the potential criminal, constitutional, and political dynamics that threaten the

[49] Crouch *et al.*, "The Unitary Executive Theory and President Donald J. Trump," p. 571; on George W. Bush and the unitary executive, see Michael A. Genovese, "The Foundations of the Unitary Executive of George W. Bush." In Ryan J. Barilleaux and Christopher J. Kelley (eds.), *The Unitary Executive and the Modern Presidency* (College Station: Texas A&M University Press, 2010), pp. 124–44; on Barack Obama and the unitary executive, see Ryan J. Barilleaux and Jewerl Maxwell, "Has Barack Obama Embraced the Unitary Executive?" *PS: Political Science & Politics* 50, no. 1 (2017): 31–4.

viability of his populist presidency in the short and long term. The wider question that looms large over the nation's political landscape is the sustainability of the populist style in the White House, and whether Trump's presidency marks a bold new direction in executive politics, institutional balance, and civic dialogue or an ephemeral phenomenon that will be little more than a footnote in the annals of American political history.

7

The populist in peril

Do you notice the Fake News Mainstream Media never likes covering the great and record setting economic news, but rather talks about anything negative or that can be turned into the negative. The Russian Collusion Hoax is dead, except as it pertains to the Dems. Public gets it!

— Donald Trump, *Twitter*, January 16, 2018

The Economy is one of the best in our history, with unemployment at a 50 year low, and the Stock Market ready to again break a record (set by us many times)—& all you heard yesterday, based on a phony story, was Impeachment. You want to see a Stock Market Crash, Impeach Trump!

— Donald Trump, *Twitter*, January 19, 2019

[I]t was not necessary for me to respond to statements made in the 'Report' about me, some of which are total bullshit & only given to make the other person look good (or me to look bad). This was an Illegally Started Hoax that never should have happened. . .

— Donald Trump, *Twitter*, April 19, 2019

I. Introduction

Less than four months into Trump's term, in May 2017, Congress appointed Special Counsel Robert Mueller to conduct a broadly defined counterintelligence investigation into Russian interference in the 2016 presidential election. Like characters from Beckett's play *Waiting for Godot*, incredulous supporters and anxious detractors of the president breathlessly devoted months to speculating, after two years, whether Mueller would ever show up with a report. At the center of the controversy were charges that Trump and his campaign team had colluded with Russia in the election.

Some of the president's political and media critics even went as far as to suggest the president had committed treason.[1]

When Attorney General William Barr released a four-page precis of the findings of the Mueller investigation to the public in late March 2019, he interpreted the conclusions as having cleared the president of any wrongdoing. There were no indictable crimes. The president took a victory lap, rejoicing that no evidence emerged of any conspiracy or collusion between him or his campaign staff and Vladimir Putin and the Russian government. The report enabled the president to return to his narrative that the entire matter had been a conspiracy and a hoax concocted by his political opponents that unnecessarily cast a dark cloud over his administration for two long years. As Byron York suggests,

> there are indications that special counsel prosecutors mostly knew by the end of 2017, and certainly by a few months later, that the evidence would not establish that conspiracy or coordination—or collusion, to use the popular term—had taken place. Mueller clearly spent a lot of time on the other half of his report—trying to establish that Trump obstructed justice—but on the most explosive and consequential allegation of the Trump–Russia affair, the conspiracy allegation, the Mueller investigation was essentially over long before it officially ended.[2]

With Russia collusion in the rearview mirror, calls by congressional Democrats to analyze the entire report amidst questions about obstruction of justice grew to a deafening level. In April 2019 Barr released it to Congress and the public—a gesture that was not required under existing statute. In the second half of Mueller's report, the special counsel and his team detailed that they were unable to conclude definitively whether Trump had

[1] Harlan Hill, "Don't forget all the Democrats and media who accused Trump of 'treason'." *Daily Caller*, March 29, 2019. https://dailycaller.com/2019/03/29/hill-democrats-media/

[2] Byron York, "When did Mueller know there was no collusion?" *Washington Examiner*, April 29, 2019. https://www.washingtonexaminer.com/opinion/columnists/byron-york-when-did-mueller-know-there-was-no-collusion

obstructed justice during the investigation. Mueller's account of ten potential incidents of obstruction, including the president's consideration of firing him, set off a firestorm of debate among Democratic members of Congress and 2020 presidential contenders about possible impeachment of the president for interference in the inquiry that otherwise found no underlying crime—and the basis of which was suspect for FBI and FISA abuses and perhaps even spying as Barr suggested. Regardless, House Intelligence Committee Chairman Adam Schiff (D-CA) opined that

> [t]he obstruction of justice in particular in this case is far worse than anything that Richard Nixon did, the break in by the Russians of Democratic institutions, a foreign adversary far more significant than the plumbers breaking into the Democratic headquarters so yes, I would say in every way this is more significant than Watergate.[3]

For his part, Trump told Fox News that "[t]his was a coup. This wasn't stealing information from an office in the Watergate apartments. This was an attempted coup. Like a Third World country. Inconceivable."[4]

In sum, Mueller found that there was insufficient evidence to make a legal case beyond a reasonable doubt that the president had engaged in criminal conduct but refused to "exonerate" Trump on obstruction—and thereby left the matter to Congress. White House Special Counsel to the president, Emmet Flood, wrote a stern letter to Attorney General William Barr on April 19, 2019 suggesting that Mueller violated basic norms of the American justice and breached the Department of Justice's own regulations. Anyone under investigation, including the president, is presumed innocent until proven otherwise. Investigators either have enough facts and sufficient evidence to charge a crime or

---

[3] Quoted in Chris Mills Rodrigo, "Schiff: Mueller report 'far worse' than Watergate." *The Hill*, April 21, 2019. https://thehill.com/homenews/sunday-talk-shows/439899-schiff-mueller-report-far-worse-than-watergate

[4] Quoted in Aaron Rupar, "'This was a coup': Trump escalates his authoritarian rhetoric." *Vox*, April 26, 2019. https://www.vox.com/2019/4/26/18517763/trump-hannity-coup-mueller

they do not. In reference to the second half of the Mueller report, Flood argued,

> "conclusively determining that no criminal conduct occurred" was not the SCO's (Special Counsel's Office) assigned task because making conclusive determinations of innocence is never the task of the federal prosecutor. What prosecutors are supposed to do is complete an investigation and then either ask the grand jury to return an indictment or decline to charge the case . . . Prosecutors simply are not in the business of establishing innocence any more than they are in the business of "exonerating" investigated persons.

Flood then indicted Mueller and his team for playing politics. He charged that "inverted-proof standard and exoneration statements can be understood only as political statements, issuing from persons (federal prosecutors) who in our system of government are rightly expected never to be political in the performance of their duties."[5]

Concern about the politicization of the Department of Justice investigations did not begin with Mueller's report. Almost three years earlier, FBI Director James Comey broke with precedent in a similar way. In July 2016 Comey publicly stated that there was insufficient basis to charge Hillary Clinton for crimes relating to her use of a private email server, and then detailed a litany of potential violations that otherwise appeared indictable. Prosecutors never engage in this kind of speculation, at least not publicly. His comments moved the debate to Capitol Hill where House Republicans began their own investigations of the former Secretary of State. In a similar way, the question of obstruction of justice in the Mueller report was moved from the legal arena to committees in the House, now under Democratic control, to make a potential case for impeachment even if the special prosecutor had inadequate evidence of any crime.

---

[5] Full text of the Flood letter to Barr is available at *Fox News*, "Read: White House Counsel Emmett Flood's letter to Attorney General Barr on Mueller report." May 3, 2019. https://www.foxnews.com/politics/read-white-house-counsel-emmett-floods-letter-to-attorney-general-barr-on-mueller-report

Questions about the guiding constitutional principle of the presumption of innocence have clearly been supplanted by politics in this brave new world of extreme polarization. The Mueller report simply reinforced convictions among Trump's most ardent Democratic opponents about the president's alleged corruption and criminal behavior, despite the lack of evidence. Many had made up their minds well before the special counsel's investigation concluded. As Senator Richard Blumenthal (D-CT) predicted a month before Mueller finalized his inquiry, "[t]here are indictments in this president's future. They're coming. Whether they're after his presidency or during it."[6] Whether by impeachment or by potential criminal charges leveled by the assistant attorney general for the Southern District of New York and state-level entities investigating Trump's businesses, some Democrats in Congress remain fixated with either removing the president or insuring his legacy is doomed to criminal and/or civil legal litigation after he leaves office.

It is fitting to this book to consider how impeachment constitutes perhaps the least of Trump's problems compared to other potential perils to his populist presidency—or its redemption—in advance of the 2020 election. There are three distinct challenges he confronts, ranging from constitutional removal to legal jeopardy from possible indictments for past business dealings and key political considerations that may hinder or help his quest for re-election. His impeachment in December 2019 and acquittal in February 2020 may well have backfired on House Democrats, as the president's approval rating increased somewhat and appears to have galvanized his supporters even more. Nonetheless, one cannot help but weigh the legacy of Trump's populist style and the implications both for healthy civic dialogue central to the Republic's democratic endurance and the Founders' vision of the presidency in the political system.

---

[6] Quoted in Tim Hains, "Blumenthal: 'There are indictments in this president's future,' when he leaves office or before." *RealClearPolitics*, March 21, 2019. https://www.realclearpolitics.com/video/2019/03/21/sen_richard_blumenthal_there_are_indictments_in_this_presidents_future.html

II. Pathways to peril

Figure 7.1 is a heuristic that highlights the three axes of potential peril for Trump as he seeks re-election in 2020. As the graphic depicts, one axis is *constitutional*. The House of Representatives has the prerogative to impeach the president, even if the two-thirds vote necessary in the Senate for removal was an unreachable tally in 2020. A less probable peril is use of the 25th Amendment by the Cabinet to remove the president from office for unfitness. The provision has never been employed in the history of the Republic and its invocation, which seems fantastical, would mark an entry into untrodden constitutional terrain. The backlash about a scheme hatched allegedly by Andrew McCabe and/or Rod Rosenstein to surreptitiously record the president's allegedly outrageous conduct behind closed doors and launch what Senator Lindsey Graham called an "administrative coup" solidifies that Trump's potential removal is unlikely to come from untested constitutional provisions.[7] The second axis is *criminal*. The ongoing investigation of Trump and his family

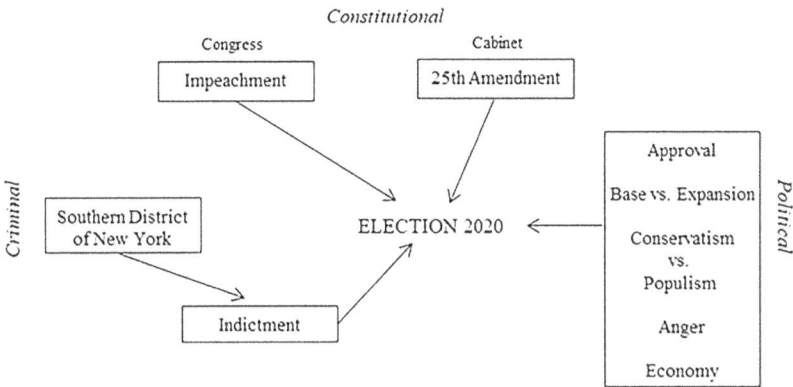

Figure 7.1 The Perils of Trump's Presidency

[7] Tara Law, "McCabe claims Dep. Attorney General Rosenstein first brought up invoking the 25th Amendment against President Trump." *Time*, February 17, 2019. http://time.com/5531496/mccabe-rosenstein-25th-amendment/

by federal prosecutors in the Southern District of New York and other state prosecutors could produce indictments relating to the president's past business practices. While the Justice Department has made the interpretation that a sitting president cannot face a trial, the Constitution is silent on the matter and the rule could be overturned by the courts. Finally, the third axis is *political*. The admixture of Trump's low public approval generally and his focus on shoring up his electoral base from 2016 rather than expanding it raises questions about his ability to replicate a narrow Electoral College victory in 2020. Other questions also hang in the balance. Has Trump effectively "drained the swamp" or do his policies simply reflect a traditional Republican approach that has betrayed elements of his electoral coalition? And is the economic setting commensurate with his campaign pledges to bring back jobs in key states?

A. The constitutional context

Removing the president from office is among the most serious matters, as it is the equivalent of overturning a democratic election. Many Founders, like James Wilson, clearly viewed impeachment, the basis of which is treason, bribery, or other high crimes and misdemeanors, as a political process relating to political crimes relative to a breach of the public trust more than a legal proceeding on issues of standard criminality, per se.[8] As such, the cases of Andrew Johnson and Bill Clinton, and now Trump, suggest the jeopardies to Congress when the legislature overreaches. Johnson was impeached in February 1868 largely as a political ploy by his adversaries to curry favor in the electorate and indict the president for his public criticism of Congress, though the formal charges were based on a statute that was clearly unconstitutional

---

[8] James Wilson, Lectures on Law part 2, No.1, Of the Constitutions of the United States and of Pennsylvania-of the Legislative Department, in *The Works of James Wilson*, edited by Robert G. McCloskey (Cambridge, MA: Belknap Press of Harvard University, 1967). See pp. 399, 426. See also Michael J. Gerhardt, "The Lessons of Impeachment History." *George Washington Law Review* 67 (1999): 611.

and designed solely to entrap him (Tenure of Office Act). He was ultimately saved from removal in the Senate by only a handful of votes of mid-South legislators who sacrificed their own seats to rescue the president.

Bill Clinton was impeached in December 1998 and the Senate failed to convict in February 1999. The pretext for Clinton's impeachment was his sexual liaison with a White House intern, and the two articles adopted by the House were for perjury and for obstruction of justice for allegedly lying about the affair. But prosecutors failed to make the case, which was widely viewed as a political gambit by House Republicans under the leadership of Speaker Newt Gingrich, whose contempt for Clinton's personal behavior as much as his policy stances was undisputable. The Senate vote occurred along partisan lines and fell well short of the two-thirds threshold necessary to remove him.

The dynamics of Trump's impeachment were similarly partisan. When the Mueller report fell flat in summer 2019, the House of Representatives quickly initiated a highly prejudiced investigatory process surrounding the president's July 25 phone conversation with Ukrainian President Zelenskiy. The impeachment investigation was led *not* by the Judiciary Committee, but by House Intelligence Committee Chair Adam Schiff (D-CA), who held closed-door hearings in the bunker of the Capitol from which Republicans had been variably excluded. Schiff also refused initially to release witness transcripts to the public. Ultimately the full House vote on articles of impeachment against the president for abuse of power and obstruction of Congress fell strictly along party lines. House impeachment managers failed to persuade the Republican-controlled Senate of Trump's alleged wrongdoing during the phone call in which the president supposedly abused his power by seeking an investigation of former Vice President Joe Biden's son. The article for obstruction of Congress was particularly weak, based as it was on Trump's refusal to allow certain White House staff to testify before Schiff's committee. Rather than let the question of executive privilege play out in the courts that demand due process, Democrats rushed to impeach and convict the president in the court of public opinion. As expected, Trump was acquitted along a party line vote in the Senate for obstruction of Congress. Only one Republican Senator, Mitt Romney of Utah, voted to convict the president on abuse of power. Trump's phone call with Zelenskiy, which he called "perfect" following release of the transcript, did not rise to any criminal offense, or "other high crime and misdemeanor" in the minds of all but a single senator.

By contrast, Richard Nixon's impeachment was based on clear-cut criminality, and not entrapment, a sex scandal, or a phone call with a foreign leader. He faced certain impeachment in the House in the summer of 1973 in light of irrefutable evidence of misconduct relating to the Watergate scandal. The three articles approved by the Judiciary Committee included obstruction of justice, abuse of power, and contempt of Congress. A pending full House vote to impeach was anticipated to draw widespread bipartisan support and reflected the degree to which congressional support for Nixon had eroded once the Watergate Tapes were made public following the landmark *U.S. v. Nixon* Supreme Court decision. If Trump could reasonably argue that executive privilege attaches to conversations with foreign policy advisors in the White House regarding Ukraine, Nixon's contention that his audio recordings with domestic advisors fell on deaf ears. The overwhelming evidence underscored the president's complicity in the cover-up of the break-in at the Democratic National Committee headquarters in June 1972. Nixon made the ultimate decision to resign from office in August 1973 after a congressional delegation headed by Senator Barry Goldwater went to the Oval Office to accentuate that the president's conviction in the upper chamber was all but a fait accompli.

Even before the release of the Mueller report, many attempted to draw parallels between Nixon and Trump to make the case for the latter's removal from office. "In both cases," argue Marshall Cohen, Annie Grayer, and Tal Yellin,

the President and his White House were enveloped by a sprawling Justice Department investigation. Both times, this led to the departure of senior officials, a slew of criminal charges against people close to the President, and allegations of a cover-up. Nixon and

310

Trump both relished opportunities to proclaim their innocence and go after their opponents.[9]

Some emphasize the sense of anger and grievance that both Nixon and Trump displayed against the individuals and institutions of government investigating them.[10] Still others see a parallel "road map" to impeachment by emphasizing the degree to which Trump, like Nixon, attempted to control the investigation that targeted him and his advisors and the president's quest to gather intelligence on the investigators' tactics. Trump's firing of James Comey, after asking the FBI director to state publicly that he was *not* a focus of the Russia probe, allegedly parallels Nixon's efforts to extract information on the Watergate inquiry from senior Justice Department officials.[11] Finally, others draw comparisons between Nixon and Trump apropos their personal taxes (Nixon cheated; Trump refuses to release his returns), break-ins (the Watergate Hotel for Nixon; the hacking of Democratic National Committee emails by the Russians in 2016 though Trump was not involved), the criminal convictions of advisors surrounding the two presidents (Haldeman, Erlichman, Dean for Nixon; Michael Flynn, Michael Cohen, Paul Manafort for Trump), and apparent disdain for the rule of law—including Nixon's quip to David Frost that "[i]f the president does it, it means that it is not illegal" and Trump's suggestion that he could pardon himself.[12]

[9] Marshall Cohen, Annie Grayer, and Tal Yellin, "In their own words: Nixon on Watergate, Trump on the Russia investigation." *CNN*, March 11, 2019. https://www.cnn.com/interactive/2019/politics/trump-nixon-comparison/index.html

[10] David O. Stewart, "Nixon, Johnson and Trump: America's angry presidents." *Baltimore Sun*, February 19, 2019. https://www.baltimoresun.com/news/opinion/oped/bs-ed-op-0218-angry-presidents-20190215-story.html

[11] Natasha Bertrand, "The eerie parallels between Trump and the Watergate 'road map'." *The Atlantic*, November 20, 2018. https://www.theatlantic.com/politics/archive/2018/11/watergate-road-map-has-parallels-trump-and-flynn/576277/

[12] Jonathan P. Baird, "The Trump–Nixon debate." *Concord (NH) Monitor*, November 22, 2018. https://www.concordmonitor.com/Watergate-parallels-21235599

There are substantive differences between Nixon and Trump. Trump did *not* engage in a "third-rate burglary," as Nixon described Watergate. The Mueller report cleared the White House and the president's campaign staff from any collusion with the Russian government. Moreover, whatever his qualms about the Mueller investigation and his titling of the probe as a "witch hunt," Trump's alleged obstruction contravenes his cooperation in providing hundreds of thousands of documents to the special counsel, some of which related to the Trump Organization.[13] Critically, unlike Nixon who fought the release of tapes documenting the Watergate cover-up tooth and nail, Trump never invoked executive privilege to shield advisors, including White House Counsel Don McGahn, from accommodating Mueller's requests for interviews. Even Attorney General Jeff Sessions' ouster after the mid-term elections of 2018 is scarcely comparable to Nixon's "Saturday Night Massacre" and firing of Special Prosecutor Archibald Cox in October 1973. Frustrated by the Mueller investigation, Trump indubitably wanted to sack the special prosecutor whose team was composed largely of Democratic partisans and Clinton donors—but it may well have been that key advisors' refusals to comply with the president's emotional responses are the difference between a solid case for obstruction and the palpable aggravation expressed by the chief executive for an unremitting inquiry that turned up no criminal conspiracy or collusion, as Trump predicted from the start.[14]

Although only a snapshot in time, in April 2019 public opinion on Trump and impeachment was as inconsistent as Mueller's inconclusive determination of the president's obstruction of justice on ten occasions. Trump's public approval dropped five points following

[13] Lauren Gambino and Stephanie Kirschgaessner, "Mueller subpoenas Trump Organization for documents related to Russia—report." *The Guardian*, March 15, 2018. https://www.theguardian.com/us-news/2018/mar/15/robert-mueller-trump-organization-russia-documents

[14] Zeke Miller and Jill Colvin, "How White House lawyer Don McGahn seems to have saved Trump from himself." *Chicago Tribune*, April 20, 2019. https://www.chicagotribune.com/news/nationworld/politics/ct-don-mcgahn-white-house-lawyer-20190419-story.html

release of the report, sinking to an all-time low of 39 percent for the 45th president.[15] Yet while one poll showed that 56 percent of Americans surveyed believed that Trump had lied about matters pertaining to the investigation, the same percentage did *not* favor impeachment. In effect, the Mueller report only solidified partisan views: 62 percent of Democrats supported impeachment, while 87 percent of Republicans opposed such a tack.

Americans were similarly split on impeachment over the Ukraine phone call. Half the country favored Trump's removal, and opinion divided, as expected, along party lines about a trial for which the acquittal outcome was a foregone conclusion. As of February 2020 following the trial, the president's approval rating has actually ticked up a few points to approximately 46 percent from the mid-summer lows following the release of the Mueller report. The question is whether Democrats will face an electoral backlash for the impeachment ordeal. The stakes for Democratic presidential contenders in 2020 are paramount as they eye the Oval Office: Whoever remains of the nearly two dozen Democratic candidates originally vying for the party's nomination will have to wrestle with the House Democrats' failed and partisan strategy, including Speaker Pelosi's inexplicable, month-long refusal to send the articles of impeachment to the Senate after the House adopted them. For Trump, he has now been acquitted and seeks to vindicate his conspiracy theory argument that the impeachment was based on the same type of hoax as the Russia collusion allegations.

Impeachment has not halted the investigations of the president and his White House by multiple House committees. And on the other side of Capitol Hill, Senate Republicans like Lindsey Graham (R-SC) promise to simultaneously follow the president's calls for probes into potential FISA abuses by the Justice Department on former Trump campaign staff that commenced the entire Russia collusion matter in the first place. House Democrats' efforts to ramp up committee investigations into everything from obstruction of justice to the president's personal finances, and now his comments regarding Justice Department prosecutors' recommendation of a sentence of nine years for the president's former associate Roger Stone for lying to Congress, are aimed at extending the pall over the White House in advance of the 2020 election. Unless something substantive emerges, such investigations are likely only to reinforce partisan views of the president. And little by the way of legislation is likely to develop, prompting Trump to employ unilateral executive authority to solidify his policy accomplishments wherever he can.

Although highly improbable, the president's detractors might hope that Trump's frustration with ongoing congressional probes could lead to his psychological unraveling and inspire the Cabinet to trigger a provision under the 25th Amendment of the Constitution to remove the president from office. Section 4 details that

> Whenever the Vice President and a majority of either the principal officers of the executive departments or of such other body as Congress may by law provide, transmit to the President pro tempore of the Senate and the Speaker of the House of Representatives their written declaration that the President is unable to discharge the powers and duties of his office, the Vice President shall immediately assume the powers and duties of the office as Acting President.

The idea is that if the majority of the fifteen department heads, with the support of the vice president, determined that Trump was so mentally unbalanced and psychologically incapacitated to fulfill his duties, Mike Pence would assume the responsibilities of the Oval Office. Such a prospect would surely delight Never Trumpers in the GOP and perhaps some Evangelicals in light of Pence's credentials as an unabashed social conservative. But it is difficult to conceive how such a turn of events would be welcomed by progressive Democrats, especially considering Pence's views on abortion and gay marriage.

The 25th Amendment, ratified in 1967, grew out of concerns of nightmare scenarios the country endured in the twentieth century, including Woodrow Wilson's incapacitation from a stroke, Franklin D. Roosevelt's failing health during World War II, and the assassination of John F. Kennedy in 1963. But the framers of the amendment never conceived of Section 4 "as a partisan tool to depose a hated president."[16] Rather, the other three sections lay out scenarios "to temporarily transfer power from presidents to vice presidents during medical operations that would leave them incapable of responding to an urgent crisis,"[17] such as when Ronald Reagan and George W. Bush underwent medical procedures. Section 4 has never been employed in the half-century since the 25th Amendment was approved.

The legal and constitutional debate about Section 4 is too lengthy to consider in detail here, but there is ample disagreement on the criteria appropriate to effectively remove a president on the basis of mental or other types of incapacitation. It is highly doubtful that the vice president and Trump's cabinet picks would accede to the provisions of Section 4 in light of the personal loyalty they show to the president, all of whom except the vice president serve at the president's pleasure.[18] Even if they did, "[s]ince the 25th Amendment was written to address temporary disability, it allows the president to announce that he has recovered—presumably Mr. Trump would do so immediately—and force a congressional vote on the finding of unfitness."[19] Moreover,

[i]f Cabinet officers tried to use Section 4, Trump would surely challenge them in court and in the court of public opinion—setting up a constitutional crisis that would make the Clinton impeachment and *Bush v. Gore* look like schoolyard spats.[20]

[16] Jarrett Stepman, "The 25th Amendment: Everything you need to know." *The National Interest*, January 10, 2018. https://nationalinterest.org/blog/the-buzz/the-25th-amendment-everything-you-need-know-24003

[17] Ibid.

[18] Jonathan Turley, "Sorry folks, Trump is not insane." *The Hill*, October 24, 2017. http://thehill.com/opinion/white-house/356842-trump-pales-in-comparison-to-our-history-ofmentally-ill-presidents.

[19] Peter D. Kramer and Sally D. Satel, "Who decides whether Trump is unfit?" *New York Times*, August 29, 2017, p. A27.

[20] David Greenberg and Rebecca Lubot, "Stop talking about the 25th Amendment. It won't work on Trump." *Politico*, September 8, 2018. https://www.politico.com/magazine/story/2018/09/08/trump-25th-amendment-constitutional-crisis-219739

Who else could make the determination about the president's mental capacity beyond the Cabinet? Joel K. Goldstein contends that the framers of the 25th Amendment considered questions of the president's psychological fitness, noting that "[n]umerous comments during hearings and floor debates echoed the assumption that decision-makers at all stages would consult with appropriate medical authorities."[21] But the advocates of Section 4 never identified any entity with which the Cabinet, vice president, or Congress were to consult. Ostensibly, Congress could recognize a medical or non-medical body of experts to diagnose the president's fitness to serve. One pathway might comprise the American Psychological Association (APA) as the "other such body." Indeed, as noted in Chapter 1, members of that elite group testified on Capitol Hill in 2017 and released a lengthy book detailing the president's allegedly forthcoming freefall into mental debility that has yet to occur, all while violating the Goldwater Rule the association adopted in 1973 that prohibits making psychological evaluations from afar.

Another route would be an independent commission of experts of some variety. "For a president who is unfit but not impeachable and who still has the support of his cabinet," Peter D. Kramer and Sally S. Satel suggest,

> the Constitution offers Congress only this one way out, a declaration of impairment presented by a deliberative body of its choice. But that body need not be dominated by doctors. Senator Birch Bayh, the Indiana Democrat who drafted the 25th Amendment . . . specifically opposed relying on physicians to make what he considered a political determination.[22]

In 2017, House Democrat Jamie Raskin (MD) introduced legislation to establish an "Oversight Commission on Presidential Capacity" (H.R. 1987). The Commission would include

---

[21] Joel K. Goldstein, "Talking Trump and the Twenty-Fifth Amendment: Correcting the Record on Section 4." *University of Pennsylvania Journal of Constitutional Law* 21, no. 1 (2018): 113.

[22] Kramer and Satel, "Who decides whether Trump is unfit?"

[t]wo more members [who] would be prominent retired officials—
selected from a list that Raskin suggests might include former presidents, vice presidents, secretaries of state, secretaries of the treasury,
attorneys general, and surgeons general. Once constituted, the 10
members of the commission [drawn from medical and psychiatric
physicians] would select an 11th member to serve as their chair.[23]

Raskin, a constitutional lawyer, asserted that "[t]he 25th Amendment was adopted 50 years ago, but Congress has never set up
the body it calls for to determine presidential fitness in the event
of physical or psychological incapacity. Now is the time to do
it."[24] Needless to say, with the House of Representatives under
the control of Republican Paul Ryan in 2017, Raskin's proposal
was doomed to oblivion. But Katy Tur of MSNBC, herself a
frequent target of the president's attacks on putatively "fake
news," alluded to the ways in which Trump could turn discussion of the bill on its head in an interview with the congressman.
She astutely asked Raskin:

Is this basically giving the sense that this is an anti-Trump, anti-this
president bill and not something where the Democrats are saying
"Here is what we believe in, here is what we are gonna do for the
American people." Are you risking just giving more fodder those
who say that, you know, the deep state or Congress is doing anything they can to make sure that President Trump doesn't succeed?[25]

Discussion of impeachment and the 25th Amendment, in
addition to congressional investigations, accentuates the degree

---

[23] John Nichols, "Congress could establish a commission to see if Trump is
mentally fit to be president." *The Nation*, May 17, 2017. https://www.the-
nation.com/article/many-americans-believe-donald-trump-is-unfit-to-serve-a-
congressman-has-a-plan-to-determine-that/

[24] Quoted in Christina Marcos, "House Dem seeks to create commission on
'presidential capacity'." *The Hill*, May 12, 2017. https://thehill.com/homenews/
house/333193-house-dem-seeks-to-create-commission-on-presidential-capacity

[25] Quoted in Aaron Bandler, "Democrats pushing Commission on Trump's fitness for presidency. Here are 5 things you need to know." *The Daily Wire*,
July 6, 2017. https://www.dailywire.com/news/18327/democrats-pushing-
commission-trumps-fitness-aaron-bandler

to which Democrats' response to the Trump presidency is consistent with the ongoing phenomenon that Ginsberg and Shefter typecast as "politics by other means"[26] that has little to do with populism, per se, though the president's political style may compound the dynamic. It is perhaps here that the Nixon–Trump linkage, or perhaps continuum, is strongest in a different sense. Since Watergate, accusations of wrongdoing, congressional hearings and investigations, special prosecutors, and real or imagined scandals and conspiracies are components of a "post-electoral order" in which elections no longer resolve political conflicts. The result is institutional combat, trench warfare, and scorched-earth tactics—which Trump seems to relish as much as his Democratic opponents. The conflicts appeal to the most zealous partisans while turning off sizeable elements of the electorate. Divided government arguably enhances inter-institutional combat. Scholars like David Mayhew, who contend that split-party government does not lead to *more* investigations of the executive,[27] miss the qualitative change in the way the weapons at the disposal of the majority party in either chamber of Congress are increasingly employed to discredit political opponents, including the president, his staff, and Cabinet members.

If invoking the 25th Amendment against Trump is largely off the table, it is entirely unclear whether House Democrats will pursue impeachment anew and what, if anything, House investigations of the president may reveal that could dissuade the hard core of the president's base of supporters from fleeing his re-election bid. Perhaps a smoking gun of some variety lies in wait to be uncovered, some egregious act of personal or political malfeasance that dooms Trump to impeachment or removal. Buoyed and feeling vindicated by the Mueller report on the question of collusion with Russia, the president has now dug in his heels by arguing that he will *not* cooperate with House investigatory committees in the way he did with the special prosecutor. As a result, as one analyst suggests,

---

[26] Benjamin Ginsberg and Martin Shefter, *Politics by Other Means: The Declining Importance of Elections in America* (New York: Basic Books, 1990).

[27] David R. Mayhew, *Divided We Govern: Party Control, Lawmaking, and Investigations, 1948–2002* (New Haven, CT: Yale University Press, 2005).

[r]ather than indulge the hopes of their most fervently anti-Trump constituents, Democrats might be wiser to press on with investigations while leveling with voters that the best shot at ending Trump's presidency anytime soon will come at the ballot box in 2020.[28]

As the melodrama of congressional investigations unfolds, Trump's populist style is nevertheless well-suited to reinvigorate the palpable anger at the elites whom he placed in his crosshairs to win in 2016 by now targeting those who refuse to accept the legitimacy of his presidency, contend that he is temperamentally unfit for the office, and clamor about his alleged criminal mind. His rhetoric on the Mueller investigation is a case in point. In mid-March 2019, just a month before the report was made public he messaged followers on Twitter to argue that "[t]his was an illegal & conflicted investigation in search of a crime. Russian Collusion was nothing more than an excuse by the Democrats for losing an Election that they thought they were going to win. . ."[29] A few weeks later, Hillary Clinton seemingly played right into Trump's narrative, questioning once again the validity of his electoral victory. On tour with her husband in Los Angeles, she suggested that "[y]ou can run the best campaign, you can even become the nominee, and you can have the election stolen from you."[30] Around the same time Speaker Nancy Pelosi told associates that in regard to 2020 "she does not automatically trust the president to respect the results of any election short of an overwhelming defeat."[31]

---

[28] David Greenberg, "When impeachment works, and when it doesn't." *Politico*, January 20, 2019. https://www.politico.com/magazine/story/2019/01/20/impeachment-history-president-trump-223976

[29] @realDonaldTrump, ". . .should never have been appointed and there should be no Mueller Report. This was an illegal & conflicted investigation in search of a crime. Russian Collusion was nothing more than an excuse by the Democrats for losing an Election that they thought they were going to win. . ." *Twitter*, March 15, 2019, 6:55 a.m. https://twitter.com/realdonaldtrump/status/1106554458383806467

[30] Quoted in Jim Geraghty, "Hillary Clinton's bad habit of questioning election results has spread to all Democrats." *National Review*, May 6, 2019.

[31] Quoted in Daniel W. Drezner, "How good is Nancy Pelosi's threat assessment?" *Washington Post*, May 6, 2019. https://www.washingtonpost.com/pb/

The inexorable quest by Trump and his detractors to dele-gitimize one another has only solidified partisan cleavages that appear dead even in the electorate. Several days after his tweet one survey found that 50 percent of respondents believed that the Mueller inquiry was a "witch hunt" as the president described it. Not surprisingly, the partisan divide was glaring: 86 percent of Republicans and 54 percent of Independents agreed, while only 14 percent of Democrats concurred.[32] Perhaps the most that can be said in the year-and-a-half before the 2020 election is that the marketplace of ideas has been largely supplanted not just by "politics by other means," but "the politics of personal destruc-tion" on which Trump's populist style thrives in equal proportion to Democrats' enmity for him.

B. The criminal context

Just four miles from Trump Tower in New York City, in spring 2017, federal prosecutors in Manhattan representing the South-ern District of New York (SDNY) began an investigation of the Trump Organization. The catalyst for the inquiry into the presi-dent's business dealings stemmed from a referral from the Mueller investigation regarding Michael Cohen, Trump's personal attor-ney and so-called "fixer." Cohen ultimately pled guilty to eight charges, including lying to Congress, lying to a bank to obtain a loan, and failing to pay federal taxes. But the most prominent politically related indictment was his payment of "hush money" to several women who alleged they had affairs with Donald Trump, including adult actress Stormy Daniels and *Playboy* model Karen McDougal, in possible violation of campaign finance rules. The

outlook/2019/05/06/how-good-is-nancy-pelosis-threat-assessment/?nid=menu_
nav_accessibilityforscreenreader&outputType=accessibility&utm_term=.
aa322bcc28b4

[32] Susan Page and Deborah Barfield Barry, "Poll: Half of Americans say Trump is victim of a 'witch hunt' as trust in Mueller erodes." *USA Today*, March 18, 2019. https://www.usatoday.com/story/news/politics/2019/03/18/trust-mueller-investigation-falls-half-americans-say-trump-victim-witch-hunt/3194049002/#

Justice Department concluded that the payments were coordinated by Trump's campaign. Cohen contended he had paid the women off "at the direction" of Trump.[33] While awaiting a three-year sentence in prison, Cohen appeared before a House committee in February 2019 and implicated Donald Trump, Jr., the president's son, and Allen Weisselberg, the chief financial officer for the Trump Organization in the arrangement.[34] The president asserted that Cohen was lying in order to reduce his prison sentence and posited that the money paid to the women was not a campaign contribution, but rather a "personal expense" that did not violate campaign finance regulations.[35] Federal prosecutors maintain that the payments were aimed at influencing the 2016 election.

Many in media and legal circles are of the opinion that ongoing investigations by federal prosecutors in the SDNY and in New York State constitute the most palpable threat to Trump, whether during or after his presidency.[36] It is impossible to know what these investigations will find, if anything, and only limited information is available about their scope at present. Beyond these investigations are lawsuits leveled at Trump. A brief review suggests the extent of potential jeopardy to Trump's presidency and his business empire in the near and long term.

Mueller's report may be concluded, but its tentacles quickly spread north from Washington. "The precise number of federal

---

[33] Brad Heath, William Cummings, and Kevin McCoy, "Michael Cohen said he paid hush money at 'direction' of Trump." *USA Today*, August 21, 2018. https://www.usatoday.com/story/news/politics/2018/08/21/michael-cohen-former-trump-lawyer-feds-reach-plea-deal/1053562002/

[34] Rebecca R. Ruiz, "Even as president, Trump focused on hush money, Cohen says." *New York Times*, February 27, 2019. https://www.nytimes.com/2019/02/27/us/politics/michael-cohen-trump-hush-money.html

[35] David Jackson, "President Trump says hush money does not amount to campaign finance violation." *USA Today*, March 7, 2019. https://www.usatoday.com/story/news/politics/2019/03/07/donald-trump-says-hush-money-doesnt-violate-campaign-finance-law/3089914002/

[36] The subsequent discussion is framed heavily from the analysis of Andrew Prokop, "Mueller is done. Trump's legal woes aren't." *Vox*, March 23, 2019. https://www.vox.com/2019/3/20/18241825/trump-investigations-sdny-inauguration-state-congress

investigations around the country that have grown out of the special counsel's work," write Ben Protess and his colleagues,

> remains unknown because such inquiries are conducted in secret. But the special counsel's office farmed out strands of its inquiry to at least three other United States attorneys' offices, including in Brooklyn, the District of Columbia and the Eastern District of Virginia.[37]

As of early 2019, the SDNY was reported to have an ongoing investigation surrounding the hush-money payments with a particular focus on Trump Organization executives and the president's family. The Justice Department has also undertaken an investigation into the president's inaugural committee and potentially illegal contributions. In August 2018 a GOP lobbyist agreed to a plea arrangement after funneling $50,000 to the inaugural committee from a Ukrainian oligarch.[38] In early 2019, SDNY prosecutors delivered a subpoena to the committee in which they demanded details of donations and expenditures.[39] The subpoena cited possible offenses of conspiracy, money laundering, mail and wire fraud, false statements, and illegal foreign contributions through "straw donors." The SDNY subpoena was followed by a similar request for documents by the Washington, DC attorney general.[40] The SDNY's investigation is complemented by state and

---

[37] Ben Protess, William K. Rashbaum, Benjamin Weiser, and Maggie Haberman, "As Mueller report lands, prosecutorial focus moves to New York." *New York Times*, March 23, 2019. https://www.nytimes.com/2019/03/23/us/trump-investigations-new-york.html

[38] Spencer S. Hsu, "W. Samuel Patten sentenced to probation after steering Ukrainian money to Trump inaugural." *Washington Post*, April 2, 2019. https://www.washingtonpost.com/local/legal-issues/w-samuel-patten-sentenced-to-probation-after-steering-ukrainian-money-to-trump-inaugural/2019/04/12/3dbf2692-5cc1-11e9-9625-01d48d50ef75_story.html?utm_term=.238c86f8af14

[39] Erin Burnett, Erica Orden, Gloria Borger, and Caroline Kelly, "Federal prosecutors subpoena Trump inaugural committee." *CNN*, February 5, 2019. https://www.cnn.com/2019/02/04/politics/sdny-subpoena-trump-inauguration-committee/index.html

[40] Associated Press, "D.C. attorney general subpoenas Trump's inaugural committee." *Politico*, February 27, 2019. https://www.politico.com/story/2019/02/27/trump-inaugural-committee-subpoena-1194641

local prosecutors' inquiries in the District of Columbia and New Jersey to determine whether the committee violated civil statutes.

Other state lawsuits and investigations focus on the Trump Foundation and tax matters pertaining to the Trump Organization. The New York State attorney general filed a civil lawsuit against the Trump Foundation in June 2018, forcing its dissolution, but the lawsuit continues regarding the foundation's tax-exempt status that prosecutors allege was used to fund the 2016 presidential campaign.[41] Additionally, the New York State Department of Taxation and Finance has been conducting a separate criminal investigation into tax matters of the Trump Organization.[42] Some of the basis for the investigations stems from Cohen's testimony in February 2019 on the organization's alleged inflation of asset valuation to obtain loans. Investigators have sent subpoenas to two banks for financial records, which the president is fighting in court. The financial documents investigators seek relate to several hotel properties in Washington, DC, Florida, Chicago, and New York City, and the unsuccessful bid to purchase the Buffalo Bills football team.

Trump also faces several private lawsuits. Summer Zervos, a contestant on Trump's television show *The Apprentice*, accused him of sexual misconduct and filed a defamation lawsuit for an assault that allegedly took place in 2007. Since the statute of limitations expired on sexual misconduct, Zervos' suit claims the president defamed her by calling her a liar in 2016. A New York State appellate court ruled in March 2019 that the lawsuit could move forward.[43] The risk to the president is that a deposition he

---

[41] Shane Goldmacher, "Trump Foundation will dissolve, accused of 'shocking pattern of illegality'." *New York Times*, December 18, 2018. https://www.nytimes.com/2018/12/18/nyregion/ny-ag-underwood-trump-foundation.html

[42] Henry Goldman, "New York Tax Department probes Trump taxes from decades ago." *Bloomberg*, October 2, 2018. https://www.bloomberg.com/news/articles/2018-10-02/new-york-s-tax-department-probes-trump-taxes-from-decades-ago

[43] Kevin McCoy, "NY appeals court rules President Donald Trump must face Summer Zervos' defamation lawsuit." *USA Today*, March 14, 2019. https://www.usatoday.com/story/news/2019/03/14/president-donald-trump-must-face-summer-zervos-defamation-case-ny-court-rules/3162078002/

may be compelled to give under oath might include questions not only related to the Zervos case but also to other women who have made allegations of sexual misconduct. On a different front, Michael Cohen filed suit against the Trump Organization in March 2019 in New York State Court and alleged that the company was in breach of contract by failing to pay his fees to the tune of nearly $2 million.[44] The broader question the suit raises is how, as president, Trump has paid for the legal fees associated with the many investigations he has faced at multiple levels.

Finally, Trump faces lawsuits by states and Congress over the Emoluments Clause in Article II of the Constitution as it relates to his businesses. The District of Columbia and Maryland have sued over the president's renovation of a hotel in Washington and claim that he profited illegally from his political office. A General Services Administration Inspector General Report outlined that lawyers from the agency had not reviewed potential violations in the Emoluments Clause after Trump won the 2016 election.[45] Although a federal appeals court was skeptical of the lawsuit in a hearing in March 2019 and put discovery on hold,[46] a district court judge in Virginia ruled a month later that congressional Democrats' action, based on similar claims, could move forward.[47] The Department of Justice, on behalf of the president, has vowed to fight the lawsuits.

How might indictments in any or all of these investigations and lawsuits affect Trump's re-election prospects in 2020? It is doubtful

[44] John Bowden, "Cohen files lawsuit against Trump Organization." *The Hill*, March 7, 2019. https://thehill.com/policy/national-security/433060-cohen-files-lawsuit-against-trump-organization

[45] Jessica Taylor and Peter Overby, "Federal watchdog finds government ignored Emoluments Clause with Trump hotel." *NPR*, January 16, 2019. https://www.npr.org/2019/01/16/685977471/federal-watchdog-finds-government-ignored-emoluments-clause-with-trump-hotel

[46] Jeff Barker, "Under sharp questioning, Maryland tries to sustain suit over Trump business dealings." *Baltimore Sun*, March 19, 2019. https://www.baltimoresun.com/news/maryland/politics/bs-md-maryland-emoluments-argument-20190318-story.html

[47] Josh Gerstein, "Congressional Democrats notch win in emoluments suit against Trump." *Politico*, April 30, 2019. https://www.politico.com/story/2019/04/30/trump-emoluments-congressional-democrats-1295270

that a challenge to the Justice Department's 2000 opinion that "[t]he indictment or criminal prosecution of a sitting President would unconstitutionally undermine the capacity of the executive branch to perform its constitutionally assigned functions"[48] could be successful in a short period of time. Trump would doubtlessly appeal to the Supreme Court any judicial decisions that contravened the precedential interpretation. The most that can be said is that indictments of, and sworn testimony by, the president could constitute an albatross around his neck in advance of 2020 and beyond. And he could always be prosecuted once he leaves office.

A fitting analogy to consider in a comparative context is Jacques Chirac, president of France from 1995 to 2007. Under indictment for the diversion of public funds as mayor of Paris two decades before he became president of the Fifth Republic, a French court ruled in 1999 that he was immune from prosecution until after he left the presidential office. Chirac fought indictments again in 2009 after leaving office but was ordered to stand trial. He was found guilty of corruption in 2011 and given a suspended sentence in light of his failing health.[49] Nicknamed "Le Bulldozer" for his shrewd and calculating politics that included taking on establishment politicians from Charles de Gaulle to his mentor Valéry Giscard-d'Estaing, Chirac's mixed legacy as president was ultimately overshadowed by the permanent stain of conviction for criminality in the breach of the public trust.

It is doubtful that Trump has seriously considered his homologue's fate across the Atlantic. As he said on Twitter in 2014, "I love taking lawsuits all the way when I'm right."[50] *Caveat emptor.* If he does land in court on the aforementioned matters, "[r]ecords of President Trump's past depositions show a familiar pattern of

[48] White House Office of Legal Counsel, Memorandum to the Attorney General, "A sitting president's amenability to indictment and criminal prosecution." October 6, 2000. https://www.justice.gov/sites/default/files/olc/opinions/2000/10/31/op-olc-v024-p0222_0.pdf

[49] *BBC News*, "French ex-President Jacques Chirac guilty of corruption." December 15, 2011. https://www.bbc.com/news/world-europe-16194089

[50] @realDonaldTrump, "I love taking lawsuits all the way when I'm right. @AGSchneiderman is finding that out the hard way!" *Twitter*, March 12, 2014, 9:11 a.m. https://twitter.com/realdonaldtrump/status/443781419618545664

boasting, sometimes battling opponents and giving little deference to factual details—pitfalls that could all come into play in various legal cases before too long."[51]

C. The political context

Looking toward 2020 the political context of Trump's re-election quest is as indeterminate as the investigations, lawsuits, and some Democrats' quest to impeach the president again. And if polls and voting models of the past failed to predict Trump's victory in 2016 there is justifiable ground to doubt their predictive capacity four years later in light of an electorate as volatile as the rhetoric emanating from the president's tweets.[52] Some considerations include the president's approval, the state of the economy, the relative strength of his voting base, and the president's policy record that raises questions about his populist credentials. The intersection of these factors suggests the possibility of both peril and validation of Trump's populist experiment in the White House.

Approval of Trump's job performance as president is the lowest for any modern chief executive. Although presidents in recent decades have not begun their terms with approval ratings much higher than their share of the national popular vote, Trump's average of 44 percent through early May 2019 represents a nadir compared to any of his predecessors, at least through just a bit beyond the midpoint of his term. From one perspective, Trump's approval rating appears to resemble that of other unpopular presidents like Nixon (average = 49 percent) and one-term presidents like Ford (average = 47%) and Carter (average = 46%). Then again, polarization continues apace: Obama left office with

[51] Tamara Keith, "Trump under oath: Sometimes combative, often boastful, usually lacking details." *NPR*, March 27, 2018. https://www.npr.org/2018/03/27/597015218/trump-under-oath-sometimes-combative-often-boastful-usually-lacking-details

[52] Courtney Kennedy *et al.*, "An Evaluation of the 2016 Election Polls in the United States." *Public Opinion Quarterly* 82, no. 1 (2018): 1–33; James E. Campbell *et al.*, "A Recap of the 2016 Election Forecasts." *PS: Political Science & Politics* 50, no. 2 (2017): 331–8.

an average approval rating of 48 percent after two terms. More ominous perhaps are the contradictions in approval of Trump's handling of the economy and whether voters feel the country is headed in the right or wrong direction. On the economy, the president has consistently had a positive track record, with an average of 54 percent approval through late April 2019. By contrast, at the same time only 37 percent feel the country is on the "right track": 55 percent feel the United States is headed in the wrong direction.[53]

The central puzzle that emerges is how record economic growth and low unemployment, now wholly erased by the 2020 coronavirus pandemic, and Trump's unorthodox behavior will affect his re-election bid as voters weigh an uncertain future. A March 2019 Pew Research Survey found that 70 percent of respondents believed that the president stands up for what he believes. But for a president whose slogan at recent rallies is "Promises Made, Promises Kept" only 45 percent responded that he had kept his pledges. Just 40 percent said he cared about people like them, only 36 percent saw him as trustworthy, and only 28 percent believed he was even-tempered.[54] Still, Trump appears to have held on firmly to his unshakable support from a core base of voters. "For more than two years," Steve Denning argues,

> Trump has defied political gravity, as his base paid little attention to mushrooming criminal investigations, rancid sex scandals, Russian interference in U.S. politics, a rash of cabinet burnouts, a chaotic administration, a neglect of climate change, an undermining of institutions such as the justice system, the FBI and the press and the dismantling of basic international arrangements with allies (like NATO),

---

[53] *RealClearPolitics*, "Direction of the country." https://www.realclearpolitics.com/epolls/other/direction_of_country-902.html; "Job approval on economy." https://www.realclearpolitics.com/epolls/other/president_trump_job_approval_economy-6182.html

[54] Pew Research Center, "Majority says Trump has done 'too little' to distance himself from white nationalists." March 28, 2019. https://www.people-press.org/2019/03/28/majority-says-trump-has-done-too-little-to-distance-himself-from-white-nationalists/

while cozying up to dictators. Trump's base saw these either as irrelevant or even as justified "sticking it" to the status quo.[55]

Yet from raucous rallies to nocturnal tweets, Trump has done precious little to cull support *beyond* his 2016 base—and one hazard is that he has lost critical components of it. As one example, many Republicans were disappointed by the president's signature legislative achievement, tax reform. One poll in March 2019 showed that 65 percent of taxpayers who received larger refunds approved of Trump. Approval of the president by those who obtained about the same in their annual refund or got smaller refunds than expected, however, fell to 46 and 38 percent, respectively.[56] Democratic contenders in 2020 like Kamala Harris have used such findings alongside the cut to the corporate tax rate to make a standard refrain dating to Adlai Stevenson's campaigns against Eisenhower in the 1950s: "Let's call the President's tax cut what it is: a middle-class tax hike to line the pockets of already wealthy corporations and the 1%."[57]

One reason for lower refunds stemmed from the administration's pressure on the Internal Revenue Service to decrease withholding in 2018 as a means of augmenting take-home pay. As a result, the size of annual refunds—the central focus for most taxpayers—dropped for many while few saw noticeably large increases in weekly paychecks. As one analyst suggests, "[i]t *looks* as though the Republican Party implemented their [*sic*] signature tax bill in a manner that will lead many people who received tax

---

[55] Steve Denning, "How Trump's economic chickens are coming home to roost." *Forbes*, February 13, 2019. https://www.forbes.com/sites/stevedenning/2019/02/13/how-trumps-economic-chickens-are-finally-coming-home-to-roost/#234157be2713

[56] Ben Casselman and Jim Tankersley, "Faster tax cuts could be backfiring on Republicans." *New York Times*, March 21, 2019. https://www.nytimes.com/2019/03/21/business/economy/tax-refund-republicans.html

[57] Quoted in Naomi Jagoda, "Smaller tax cuts put GOP on defensive." *The Hill*, February 18, 2019. https://thehill.com/policy/finance/430305-smaller-tax-refunds-put-gop-on-defensive

cuts to believe that Donald Trump *raised* their taxes."[58] Indeed, the tax firm H&R Block found that 47 percent of Americans it surveyed expected that tax cuts would translate into a larger refund, unaware that the IRS had withheld less from their pay-checks over the long haul.[59] Democrats like Ron Wyden (OR) assert that "Republicans deliberately made a decision to goose the tax bill so they could get credit in the fall of 2018 and in effect saying it's a long time until the spring of 2019 and maybe every-body would forget."[60] But the tax cuts did not save the House GOP from disaster in the mid-term elections. And the danger for Trump is that palpable anger across the political spectrum, and critics' charges that the bill only cut taxes for the wealthy and did little to spur job creation,[61] may lead some voters to express their frustration by either abandoning Trump or simply staying home on Election Day 2020.

If Republicans have qualms about the tax cut, however, aggre-gate opinion data from January to April 2019 do not bear out great dissatisfaction with the president. The Gallup Poll reports that for this period Republican support of Trump remained steadfast at 89 percent, a higher mark than for 2017 and 2018. Independents' approval of Trump averaged 35 percent, a figure relatively stable for his first two years. Democratic approval

---

[58] Eric Levitz, "Trump tax cuts are (probably) about to become a political disaster." *New York Magazine*, February 8, 2019. http://nymag.com/intelligencer/2019/02/heres-why-your-tax-refund-is-lower-this-year.html

[59] Laurent Belsie, "For many Americans the Trump tax cut doesn't feel like a boost." *Christian Science Monitor*, February 14, 2019. https://www.csmonitor.com/Business/2019/0214/For-many-Americans-the-Trump-tax-cut-doesn-t-feel-like-a-boost

[60] Quoted in Aaron Lorenzo, "As tax refunds shrink, Republicans scramble to defend Trump tax cut." *Politico*, February 23, 2019. https://www.politico.com/story/2019/02/23/tax-refunds-republicans-1182286

[61] *Public Integrity*, "The secret saga of Trump's tax cuts." April 30, 2019. https://publicintegrity.org/business/taxes/trumps-tax-cuts/the-secret-saga-of-trumps-tax-cuts/; *PBS*, "Did Trump's tax cuts boost hiring? Most companies say no." January 28, 2019. https://www.pbs.org/newshour/economy/making-sense/did-trumps-tax-cuts-boost-hiring-most-companies-say-no

remains at all-time lows, averaging 6.5 percent.[62] The penultimate question is turnout—and whether Trump's GOP base and Independent supporters have similar enthusiasm for him in 2020 as in 2016.

Hanging in the balance is the way in which voters in key states view economic progress and their own situation. There is little doubt that the national economy has been buoyed by deregulation, tax cuts for businesses, wage growth, and a stock market that has made remarkable gains. Unemployment overall (3.6 percent in April 2019) and for key minority groups, including African Americans and Hispanics, is at historic lows and suggests near full employment at the national level. But thinking in terms of the geography of the Electoral College, have job gains occurred in the swing states Trump won in 2016 and that are paramount to a 2020 victory?

One of Trump's central promises in 2016 was to spur the manufacturing sector and bring back jobs that had disappeared. Since he became president the United States added 454,000 manufacturing jobs through early 2019.[63] But the geographic distribution of those jobs is hardly even. Data are scarce given the lag time in gathering them, but one analysis suggests only a modest increase in the Rust Belt.[64] The percentage of manufacturing jobs created from February 2018 to February 2019 grew by more than 13,000 in Michigan, 10,000 in Ohio, and 2,800 in Wisconsin. However, in Pennsylvania, a key state for Trump's electoral victory in 2016, the number of manufacturing jobs created was fewer than 1,000. The large gains in the Democratic strongholds of California and Washington State of more than 10,000 are unlikely to matter for Trump in 2020, while the steady growth in Texas may shore up his support in the Lone Star State. Overall employment increased

---

[62] *Gallup Poll*, "Presidential approval ratings—Donald Trump." https://news.gallup.com/poll/203198/presidential-approval-ratings-donald-trump.aspx

[63] Jane C. Timm, "Fact check: Trump's administration has created 600,000 manufacturing jobs." *NBC News*, February 5, 2019. https://www.nbcnews.com/card/fact-check-we-ve-added-half-million-manufacturing-jobs-n967436

[64] Gay Cororoton, "Manufacturing and housing in the Rust Belt states." *Economists' Outlook Blog*, April 3, 2019. https://economistsoutlook.blogs.realtor.org/2019/04/03/manufacturing-and-housing-in-the-rust-belt-states/

in Wisconsin, Michigan, Ohio, and Pennsylvania by 1 percent or less over the one-year period. Employment increased by just less than 3 percent in Florida, another key state in Trump's 2016 victory.

Beyond assessments of Trumponomics, voters will also have to decide whether Trump's populist style masks old-guard conservatism essentially at odds with his rhetoric. As Rich Lowry posits, "Trump is different from other Republicans on trade and immigration, the issues at the core of his populism, but other than that, he has governed as a fairly typical Republican."[65] His quest to deregulate the economy and his appointment of controversial conservative Supreme Court justices Neil Gorsuch and Brett Kavanagh bring to mind analogies to the Reagan era. Put another way:

> Trump has continued to present himself in populist garb, but it has rarely carried over to policy. Whatever label one might attach to his substantive actions as president, one would be hard pressed to call most of them populist. Trump has filled his administration with a mix of the staggeringly wealthy and the staggeringly reactionary. On the big economic issues of taxes, spending and regulation—ones that have animated conservative elites for a generation—he has pursued, or supported, an agenda that is extremely friendly to large corporations, wealthy families, and well-positioned rent-seekers.[66]

Such a perspective raises the question about the degree to which Trump has "drained the swamp," a pledge largely void of empirical criteria to judge success or failure. Supporters suggest that his attacks on the press, and the "deep state" relating to controversies over alleged FBI spying on his 2016 campaign for which the president has continually delegitimized the nation's top

---

[65] Rich Lowry, "Trump's not populist enough." *Politico*, November 14, 2018. https://www.politico.com/magazine/story/2018/11/14/trump-2020-midterms-populism-222573

[66] Paul Pierson, "American Hybrid: Donald Trump and the Strange Merger of Populism and Plutocracy." *British Journal of Sociology* 68 (November 2017): S106–S107.

law-enforcement agency, are evidence of his commitment.[67] Yet on ethics reform and lobbying to which Trump ultimately tied the refrain at a Wisconsin rally in October 2016, critics underscore that only one proposal had been implemented his first year in office.[68] Others point to the sheer number of former lobbyists in the administration, numbering nearly 200, and Trump's continued appointment of prominent industry officials like Andrew Wheeler at the Environmental Protection Agency.[69] Trump may have altered the rhetoric in Washington, but there is little evidence that the moneyed interest and folkways of the capital have changed substantially. *Plus ça change. . .*

The other three broad pledges Trump made during the 2016 campaign were to "lock her up" in reference to Hillary Clinton (which was more facetious than realistic), to repeal and replace Obamacare, and to build a wall that Mexico would pay for. Clinton is not in jail much to the chagrin of hard-core Trump supporters, House investigations of her email scandal terminated when party control of the House flipped after the 2018 mid-term elections, and she continues to claim that she was robbed of the Oval Office despite her campaign's apparent connection to the origins of the Russia collusion matter. Repeal and replace never materialized in Congress, and Trump's only recourse was an executive action that rescinded the tax penalty for failing to procure health care coverage. And if the proposed wall along the southern border was as much a cultural as a national security issue, supporters also have reason for derision. Mexico has vehemently refused to pay for the barrier and Trump has had his hands tied by prior

[67] Cheryl K. Chumley, "Donald Trump: 'Drain the swamp!' And he is." *Washington Times*, May 21, 2018. https://www.washingtontimes.com/news/2018/may/21/donald-trump-drain-swamp-and-he/?utm_source=GOOGLE&utm_medium=cpc&utm_id=chacka&utm_campaign=TWT+-+DSA&gclid=EAIaIQobChMI5rWovseJ4gIV2UsNCh21qQ-vEAMYASAAEgK7B_D_BwE

[68] Theodoric Meyer, "Has Trump drained the swamp in Washington?" *Politico*, October 19, 2017. https://www.politico.com/story/2017/10/19/trump-drain-swamp-promises-243924

[69] *USA Today*, "EPA nominee showcases how Trump keeps failing to drain the swamp." January 15, 2019. https://www.usatoday.com/story/opinion/2019/01/15/epa-nominee-showcases-how-trump-fails-drain-swamp-editorials-debates/2578903002/

court rulings that prohibit prolonged detention for asylum seekers, effectively cementing a "catch and release" policy at odds with his promise to crack down on illegals.[70]

The disjuncture between Trump's campaign rhetoric and the realities of governing pose a relative liability in his re-election effort. As Denise Bostdorff asserts, "Donald Trump, like past successful candidates who promised political transformation, will also face another hurdle: he is now part of the system he attacked and will find himself held accountable for his performance."[71] He cannot campaign credibly as an "outsider" after four years in the White House, though he will try to do so. Of particular consequence are the retrospective evaluations of Obama voters who switched loyalties in 2016 and supported Trump. If one Ohio focus group's perspectives are widespread in November 2020, the president may have a difficult time forging a successful election coalition in the critical heartland:

> They think President Trump has failed at "draining the swamp." They think the Trump administration is corrupt. They don't think the GOP tax law has helped them and their families. And they're not feeling the "booming" economy . . . He's backed out of so many of his promises.[72]

Trump was clearly more adept at leveraging populist anger for political advantage in 2016 than other candidates.[73] The overarching question is whether his base will forgive his inability

[70] Maria Sacchetti, "Despite vow to end 'catch and release,' Trump has freed 100,000 who illegally crossed the border." *Washington Post*, April 13, 2018. https://www.washingtonpost.com/local/immigration/despite-vow-to-end-catch-and-release-trump-has-freed-100000-who-illegally-crossed-the-border/2018/04/13/839c778e-3754-11e8-acd5-35eac230e514_story.html?utm_term=.76ed6f641516

[71] Denise M. Bostdorff, "Obama, Trump, and Reflections on the Rhetoric of Political Change." *Rhetoric and Public Affairs* 20 (2017): 698.

[72] Quoted in Helaine Olen, "Trump didn't drain the swamp. Supporters are starting to notice." *Washington Post*, September 11, 2018. https://www.washingtonpost.com/blogs/post-partisan/wp/2018/09/11/trump-didnt-drain-the-swamp-supporters-are-starting-to-notice/?utm_term=.a7914d162275

[73] Thomas Rudolph, "Populist Anger, Donald Trump, and the 2016 Election." *Journal of Elections, Public Opinion and Parties* (February 2019). https://doi.org/10.1080/17457289.2019.1582532

to engage successfully in the "art of the deal" and the compromises necessary for governing successfully beyond unilateralism and continue to blame the "establishment" in Washington for his woes. On the other hand, "[t]he temptation for Democrats in the age of Trump," writes David Ignatius,

> is to create a mirror image of his dysfunctional party of rage. Democrats can be as entranced as the GOP by the latest bright, shiny object darting across the political sky. They, too, can mistake social-media energy for real political power.[74]

III. Trump's populist legacy and the decline of civic dialogue

Indeed, the crowded Democratic field of 2020 features populist progressives like Bernie Sanders and Elizabeth Warren—wealthy elites themselves ensconced comfortably in the backwaters of the Potomac—railing against socio-economic inequality and taking up simplified discourse against the "establishment" vis-à-vis complex problems in a fashion similar to Trump. If the president's populist style becomes entrenched in the longer term, it foreshadows the continued disintegration of public trust in the delicate institutional balance the Framers of the Constitution so carefully constructed. The Madisonian model mandates compromise and farsightedness that is anathema to the populist ethos—on the right or left of the political spectrum—which so inelegantly and often crudely captures voter frustration with the immobilism in Washington that precludes the resolution of the nation's challenges, domestic and foreign. At its foundation, the populist style is more often destructive than rehabilitative by delegitimizing the very institutions of republican structures it purports to salvage.

The discursive tendencies of the populist style expressed by Trump impede the type of respectful civic dialogue essential to

---

[74] David Ignatius, "Trump has squandered the opportunity his populist campaign offered." *RealClearPolitics*, January 16, 2019. https://www.realclearpolitics.com/articles/2019/01/16/trump_has_squandered_the_opportunity_his_populist_campaign_offered_139186.html

problem-solving. At one level, Trump's presidency marks the return to an era of paranoid politics. The president and his political opponents see shadowy cabals conspiring to plot their ruin in every corner of the capital, in court rooms, in newspaper offices and on cable television, and at news conferences. Conspiracy theories have run amok to become the norm, embraced as they are by the president, his followers, his detractors, and the media—from nomination politics to foreign affairs and the allegedly "rigged" economy. Such narratives are naturally incongruous with the construction of interpersonal trust necessary for any president to maneuver successfully through the labyrinth of institutional checks and balances. The implication for governance is recourse to unilateralism that satisfies the majoritarian tendency that is a defining feature of the populist style but threatens equilibrium between co-equal branches.

Social media have compounded the gloomy situation. As the first president to employ social media as the primary means of campaigning and governing in such a vigorous way, Trump has moved the nation inexorably away from a style of quiet negotiation and partisan restraint that often characterized the leadership style of his predecessors like Dwight Eisenhower and Lyndon Johnson. In the 1950s and 1960s presidents frequently chose *not* to politicize contentious issues publicly in order to avoid alienating those on the other side of the aisle whose support in Congress was essential. "Hidden-hand" leadership,[75] as Fred Greenstein titles it, is incompatible with the purposeful pursuit of conflict and vilification of opponents on which the populist style thrives. It appears doubtful that a return to the halcyon days of bipartisanship of the 1950s or 1960s characterized by presidents with a different conception of the "art of the deal" is on the horizon. Americans are more polarized than ever, as are the envoys they send to Washington to represent them. The populist style feeds off such polarization.

The ways in which Trump has employed social media have profoundly impacted the already declining state of civic dialogue,

---

[75] Fred I. Greenstein, *The Hidden-hand Presidency: Eisenhower as Leader* (Baltimore, MD: Johns Hopkins University Press, 1994).

and his opponents have followed suit. At the helm of the bully pulpit, and with the largest megaphone in the political system, presidents can utilize this novel medium and its direct channel of communication to the electorate for constructive or destructive purposes. Trump has chosen the latter tack, as have his detractors, in defiance of President Theodore Roosevelt's counsel that for "a republic to be successful we must learn to combine intensity of conviction with a broad tolerance of difference of conviction."[76] But Trump's inflammatory rhetoric, like that of Hillary Clinton in her reference to his supporters as a "basket of deplorables," is a symptom of a much larger problem that should prompt all Americans to undertake self-introspection. "The sins of social media are manifold," posits Scott Garber, "and most of us have contributed to the problem. Social media is a political echo chamber. We outdo each other with incendiary remarks to get the most "Likes," shares and reposts. Outrage is the name of the game, and trolling is everywhere."[77]

If civility among our elected officials is lacking on social media and in public fora, the presidents and members of Congress we elect are a reflection of *us* and it is no mystery why Trump's caustic, populist style resonates with many. Eric Uslaner made an essential point on this front several decades ago in his book entitled *The Decline of Comity in Congress*.[78] He explains that the erosion of civic discourse on Capitol Hill and the resort to name-calling by legislators mirror the incivility of American society at large. The lack of interpersonal trust and dearth of social capital that permeates the nation at the grassroots are replicated within the institutional structures of government. The phenomenon is

[76] Theodore Roosevelt, "Citizenship in a Republic." April 23, 1910, Paris, France. https://www.americanrhetoric.com/speeches/teddyrooseveltcitizen-shipinrepublicarena.htm
[77] Scott Garber, "It's not just a Trump problem—we all have to take responsibility for Twitter." *Vox*, November 8, 2017. https://www.vox.com/2017/11/8/16619178/trump-twitter-tweet-civil-public-discourse-democracy-social-media-responsibility-russia
[78] Eric M. Uslaner, *The Decline of Comity in Congress* (Ann Arbor: University of Michigan Press, 1996).

a product of the disintegration of once-shared values including American exceptionalism, individualism, egalitarianism, and religion. Trump's Twitter feed must be viewed in this light. Why should we expect the president to take the high road when with the push of a button we excoriate people with different views whom we have never met, hurl vile invectives with 280 clicks on the keyboard when most of us would never deign to express such vulgarisms in a face-to-face conversation, and "defriend" on a whim family or longtime friends on Facebook for disagreeing with us? Politicians are following *our* lead. As Hillary Clinton suggested incredulously, "[y]ou cannot be civil with a political party that wants to destroy what you stand for, what you care about."[79]

Trump's manipulation of social media is one of many factors that will determine his legacy. In fact, some have already sought to locate his place in the annals of history, perhaps somewhat prematurely. Political scientists Brandon Rottinghaus and Justin Vaughn conducted a survey on presidential greatness of members of the Presidential and Executive Politics section of the American Political Science Association just less than a year into Trump's term.[80] The results for Trump were scarcely good news. Now, the authors cannot be faulted for confronting an empirical reality to which conservatives are particularly attuned: the supposed liberal bias in the academy. Of the 166 scholars surveyed, only 12.7 percent (n = 21) were affiliated with the Republican Party, and only 17.4 percent (n = 29) considered themselves conservative or somewhat conservative. By contrast, 57.2 percent (n = 95) of the scholars were Democrats and 58.4 percent (n = 97) considered themselves liberal or somewhat liberal. Regardless, the results are unsurprising. Overall, Trump was ranked at the absolute bottom

---

[79] Quoted in Rachel Ventresca, "Clinton: 'You cannot be civil with a political party that wants to destroy what you stand for'." *CNN*, October 9, 2018. https://www.cnn.com/2018/10/09/politics/hillary-clinton-civility-congress-cnntv/index.html

[80] Brandon Rottinghaus and Justin S. Vaughn, "Official Results of the 2018 Presidents & Executive Politics Presidential Greatness Survey." http://www.marioguerrero.info/326/Rottinghaus.pdf

of the barrel—forty-fourth—in terms of presidential greatness, one notch below James Buchanan. He fared only little better among conservative scholars, who ranked him fortieth. And he was considered the most polarizing president in history, just one place above his nineteenth-century populist counterpart, Andrew Jackson, who claimed the second highest number of votes. The results highlight that, as Nick Bryant suggests,

> [a]t the midpoint of Donald Trump's first term, historians have struggled to detect the kind of virtues that offset his predecessors' vices: the infectious optimism of Reagan; the inspirational rhetoric of JFK; the legislative smarts of LBJ; or the governing pragmatism of Nixon . . . Because Donald Trump is unwilling to accept he is anything other than an A+ president, the grade he has bestowed upon himself, he is not prepared to adopt the kind of correctives that have saved troubled presidencies.[81]

Trump has said "I don't like to analyze myself because I might not like what I see."[82] It will be up to American voters on November 3, 2020 to analyze his persona and approach to leadership and decide if *they* like what they see. The electorate will weigh his populist governing style rife with chaos, counterfactuals, and calumnious tweets against his impressive policy record so far on the economic front and juxtapose what his eventual Democratic challenger offers in both style and substance. The ultimate question, however, is not whether Trump the populist is in peril, but whether the populist style, per se, imperils the vision of the presidency the Framers of the Constitution elaborated in Philadelphia in 1787. Looking through this lens, a paramount consideration is Alexander Hamilton's reflection in Federalist #68 on the expected character qualities of our chief executive:

[81] Nick Bryant, "How will history judge President Trump?" *BBC News*, January 17, 2019. https://www.bbc.com/news/world-us-canada-46895634
[82] Quoted in Michael Barbaro, "What drives Donald Trump? Fear of losing status, tapes show." *New York Times*, October 26, 2016. https://www.nytimes.com/2016/10/26/us/politics/donald-trump-interviews.html

The process of election affords a moral certainty, that the office of President will never fall to the lot of any man who is not in an eminent degree endowed with the requisite qualifications. Talents for low intrigue, and the little arts of popularity, may alone suffice to elevate a man to the first honors in a single State; but it will require other talents, and a different kind of merit, to establish him in the esteem and confidence of the whole Union, or of so considerable a portion of it as would be necessary to make him a successful candidate for the distinguished office of President of the United States. It will not be too strong to say, that there will be a constant probability of seeing the station filled by characters pre-eminent for ability and virtue.[83]

It is irresistible to speculate what the Founders might think of Trump's legacy. But sadly "all efforts to transport them into our time zone are misguided, like trying to plant cut flowers."[84] If the candidates who seek the highest office in the land, including Trump and the crowded 2020 Democratic field, do not possess the integrity and moral fiber that Hamilton believed would define the presidency, the complex republican structures he and his colleagues constructed 230 years ago are an insufficient bulwark against the rise of the populist political style. As H. W. Brands suggests, "The virtue of democracy is the legitimacy it confers on those it elects; its vice is the temptation it affords candidates like Trump to inflame the baser passions of the electorate."[85] Jettisoning the Electoral College or impeaching the president is a temporary palliative unlikely to cure the enduring malady that grips us. In this sharply divided era, the contemporary expression of the populist style at campaign rallies and on Twitter redounds too often to the dogma of grudges, scapegoating, and institutional delegitimization that only exacerbates

---

[83] Alexander Hamilton, Federalist #68, "The Mode of Electing the President." http://avalon.law.yale.edu/18th_century/fed68.asp

[84] Joseph J. Ellis, "Historian: What would Founding Fathers think of Donald Trump?" CNN, May 5, 2016. https://www.cnn.com/2016/05/04/opinions/what-would-founding-fathers-think-of-trump-ellis/index.html

[85] H. W. Brands, "How Trump has proved the Founding Fathers right." *Politico*, March 31, 2016. https://www.politico.com/magazine/story/2016/03/trump-founding-fathers-electoral-college-213777

societal cleavages. Politics in the age of Trump clearly run afoul of Abraham Lincoln's enlightened call for the humility and magnanimity required to re-establish and maintain national unity:

> We are not enemies, but friends. We must not be enemies. Though passion may have strained, it must not break our bonds of affection. The mystic chords of memory will swell when again touched, as surely they will be, by the better angels of our nature.[86]

---

[86] Abraham Lincoln, Inaugural Address, March 4, 1861. https://www.gilder-lehrman.org/content/president-lincoln%E2%80%99s-first-inaugural-address-1861

8

Epilogue: Quo vadis?

They (Dems) are scrambling for a theme and narrative. They've gone everywhere from Russian Hoax to Russian Collusion . . . and now they've come to this . . . they think they should have won the 2016 election, they think in their bizarre brains that they did . . .
— Donald Trump, Twitter, September 24, 2019

Many observers might reflect with alarm on the summer of discontent, 2019—the endpoint of the Mueller investigation and the beginning of Trump's impeachment—and compare the contemporary scenes of American politics to the 1951 epic film directed by Mervyn LeRoy. In *Quo Vadis* a corrupt Emperor Nero fiddles while Rome moves toward the precipice of socio-political collapse. His persecution and scapegoating of one group (Christians), after burning the capital himself, ultimately results in his demise at the hands of the angry mob that chases him off to death. But if that film ends with Peter's crosier giving rise to Jesus's flowering words that "I am the way, the light, and the truth," the truth about the direction of the Trump presidency, and the trajectory of the nation, remains very much in the eye of the beholder.

As an embattled President Trump moves inexorably toward his fourth year in office, "fears that once existed only in fiction or in the fevered dreams of conspiracy theorists have become a regular part of the political debate. These days, there is talk of violence, mayhem and, increasingly, civil war."[1] Amidst the

---

[1] Greg Jaffe and Jenna Johnson, "In America, talk turns to something not spoken of for 150 years: Civil war." *Washington Post*, March 2, 2019. https://www.washingtonpost.com/politics/in-america-talk-turns-to-something-unspoken-for-150-years-civil-war/2019/02/28/b3733af8-3ae4-11e9-a2cd-307b06d0257b_story.html

sweltering heat of summer 2019 were senseless mass shootings in Dayton, Ohio, El Paso and Midland/Odessa, Texas, and Gilroy, California. Trump's critics charged that his divisive immigration rhetoric was a key motivator for the El Paso shooting.[2] Democratic presidential candidate Robert Francis ("Beto") O'Rourke called the president a white supremacist and thundered that Trump "poses a mortal threat to people of color" following the gunman's rampage.[3] The president and his supporters, on the other hand, accentuate the connection between the Dayton gunman and his support of Bernie Sanders, Elizabeth Warren, and antifa,[4] and further contend that it is progressives' discrediting of law enforcement that led to multiple attacks on Immigration and Customs Enforcement (ICE) facilities around the country.[5] Such rhetorical salvos by both sides were fired against the backdrop of sporadic violence in cities like Portland, Oregon, where antifa groups squared off against right-wing movements like the Proud Boys.[6] Trump added fuel to the fire of the occasional fisticuffs and brick-throwing by tweeting that he was considering labeling antifa a terror organization, but made no mention of the

[2] Scott Detrow, "Democratic candidates say Trump's rhetoric is partially to blame for mass shootings." *NPR*, "All Things Considered," August 7, 2019. https://www.npr.org/2019/08/07/749164059/democratic-candidates-say-trumps-rhetoric-is-partially-to-blame-for-mass-shootin

[3] Bob Brigham, "Beto O'Rourke calls Trump a white supremacist: 'He poses a mortal threat to people of color'." *Salon*, September 13, 2019. https://www.salon.com/2019/09/13/beto-orourke-calls-trump-as-a-white-supremacist-he-poses-a-mortal-threat-to-people-of-color_partner/

[4] Keith BieryGolick and Cameron Knight, "Dayton shooting: What we know about Connor Betts' politics." *Cincinnati Enquirer*, August 7, 2019. https://www.cincinnati.com/story/news/2019/08/07/dayton-shooting-what-do-we-know-connor-betts-politics/1942122001/

[5] John Hang, "A fourth ICE facility has been attacked: The dangerous consequences of political pandering." *American Spectator*, August 15, 2019. https://spectator.org/a-fourth-ice-facility-has-been-attacked/

[6] Jason Wilson, "Portland rally: Proud Boys vow to march each month after biggest protest of Trump era." *The Guardian*, August 17, 2019. https://www.theguardian.com/us-news/2019/aug/17/portland-oregon-far-right-rally-proud-boys-antifa

right-wing extremist groups they were confronting.[7] Meanwhile both Congress and the president dithered over gun control and legislation on background checks, and neither the White House nor congressional Democrats and Republicans moved the needle on other bills on Capitol Hill.

Democrats' rush to impeachment, which had eroded over the summer months as Robert Mueller gave a lackluster performance in front of Congress and the Russia collusion narrative collapsed, was reignited the day after the autumnal equinox, September 24. Revelations that a whistleblower had alleged that the president attempted to use his office to sully Democratic presidential contender Joe Biden by requesting the Ukrainian president investigate the former vice president's son, who received a lucrative board position on the foreign, state-owned energy company Burisma, prompted House Speaker Nancy Pelosi to announce finally a full impeachment inquiry after earlier trepidation.[8]

The nation was hurriedly subjected to yet another collective Rorschach test when Trump declassified his telephone conversation with Volodymyr Zelenskiy, the Ukrainian comedian-turned-president, who said publicly he did not feel under any pressure from Trump during the call and there was no quid pro quo on military assistance.[9] Nonetheless, to Trump's implacable detractors like Adam Schiff (D-CA), chair of the House Intelligence Committee, the picture is crystal clear and the evidence overwhelming that the president committed high crimes and misdemeanors. According to Schiff, the image painted "a horrible abuse of the oath of office" and presidential actions "damning enough" to

---

[7] Mary Kay Linge, "Trump: US may designate Antifa as terror organization." *New York Post*, August 17, 2019. https://nypost.com/2019/08/17/trump-us-may-designate-antifa-as-terror-organization/

[8] John Haltiwanger and Sonam Sheth, "Trump is facing impeachment over a whistleblower complaint and a phone call with Ukraine's president. Here's what we know." *Business Insider*, September 26, 2019. https://www.businessinsider.com/mysterious-trump-spy-whistleblower-controversy-explained-2019-9

[9] Tara Law, "'Nobody pushed me.' Ukrainian president denies Trump pressured him to investigate Biden's son." *Time*, September 25, 2019. https://time.com/5686305/zelensky-ukraine-denies-trump-pressure/

justify impeachment proceedings.[10] Seizing on conspiracy theory, Speaker Pelosi posited a cover-up by Trump to hide the phone call,[11] even though the president released the transcript publicly. The president and his supporters, however, fail to perceive any image emerging from the inkblot other than another deep state conspiracy. Echoing Gertrude Stein's characterization of Oakland, California, they contend "there's no there there." Trump called the entire affair "another witch hunt"[12] while Devin Nunes (R-CA), ranking member of the House Intelligence Committee, opined that the whistleblower complaint had "all the hallmarks of the Russia hoax" and would end former Vice President Joe Biden's presidential bid.[13] Citing supporter Pastor Robert Jeffress, an angry Trump tweeted that "[i]f the Democrats are successful in removing the President from office (which they will never be), it will cause a Civil War like fracture in this Nation from which our Country will never heal."[14] The more pertinent question, as David Brooks suggests, is the wisdom of impeachment during an election year. Placing the decision to potentially remove the president in the hands of legislators rather than the

[10] Emily Tillett, "Adam Schiff: What Trump said publicly is 'damning enough' for impeachment." *CBS News*, September 25, 2019. https://www.cbsnews.com/news/adam-schiff-whistleblower-what-trump-said-publicly-is-damning-enough-for-impeachment-today-2019-09-25/

[11] Sarah Ferris and Heather Caygle, "Pelosi says Trump engaged in 'cover-up' to hide Ukraine call records." *Politico*, September 26, 2019. https://www.politico.com/story/2019/09/26/pelosi-trump-cover-up-ukraine-call-1514541

[12] Bob Fredericks, "Trump on Ukraine scandal: 'It's another witch hunt'." *New York Post*, September 26, 2019. https://nypost.com/2019/09/26/trump-on-ukraine-scandal-its-another-witch-hunt/

[13] Tim Hains, "Nunes: Whistleblower complaint has 'hallmarks of the Russia hoax'; Ukraine scandal likely end of Biden's campaign." *RealClearPolitics*, September 22, 2019. https://www.realclearpolitics.com/video/2019/09/22/nunes_whistleblower_complaint_looks_like_russia_hoax_ukraine_scandal_likely_end_of_bidens_campaign.html

[14] @realDonaldTrump, "'. . .If the Democrats are successful in removing the President from office (which they will never be), it will cause a Civil War like fracture in this Nation from which our Country will never heal.' Pastor Robert Jeffress, @FoxNews." *Twitter*, September 29, 2019, 6:11 p.m. https://twitter.com/realdonaldtrump/status/1178477539653771264

electorate was a significant gambit by Democrats. Now acquitted, Trump can freely rail against the process and engage his typical anti-elitist arguments against the corrupt Swamp while claiming he was ultimately vindicated.[15]

Whether Donald Trump is impeached a second time by the House, is re-elected, or ousted in 2020, his populist style has had an indubitably profound impact on American politics. His performative politics and divisive discourse are more of an expression of our collective angst, declining trust in institutions at all levels, and deterioration in civil dialogue than the cause of these perturbations, per se. He has seized upon a longstanding socio-political cold war, and his political foes have followed suit, to further tug at the threads that bind citizens together and to their political institutions. Speaker Nancy Pelosi's shredding of Trump's 2020 State of the Union Address symbolizes a larger, troubling dynamic. As Victor Davis Hanson suggests,

> Almost every cultural and social institution—universities, the public schools, the NFL, the Oscars, the Tonys, the Grammys, late-night television, public restaurants, coffee shops, movies, TV, stand-up comedy—has been not just politicized but also weaponized. Donald Trump's election was not so much a catalyst for the divide as a manifestation and amplification of the existing schism.[16]

There is certainly much that divides Americans. Racially, geographically, culturally, and economically the nation's citizenry has increasingly cleaved itself into two camps, purposefully or otherwise. It is relatively easy for populists, whether of Trump's, Elizabeth Warren's, or Bernie Sanders' stripe, to annex longstanding grievances against one or another group of elites or "others"

---

[15] Ian Schwartz, "David Brooks: Trump 'did something impeachable,' but 'impeachment would be a mistake'." *RealClearPolitics*, September 28, 2019. https://www.realclearpolitics.com/video/2019/09/28/david_brooks_trump_did_something_impeachable_but_impeachment_would_be_a_mistake.html

[16] Victor Davis Hanson, "The origins of our Second Civil War." *National Review*, July 31, 2018. https://www.nationalreview.com/2018/07/origins-of-second-civil-war-globalism-tech-boom-immigration-campus-radicalism/

for political gain. Yet the language of populism—the vilification of political foes, the politics of personal destruction, the invention of scapegoats, the simplified solutions—and the consistent delegitimization of electoral processes and the very institutions populists and their detractors seek to lead—is scarcely compatible with the restoration of confidence in elected leaders necessary to a functioning democracy as the Founders envisioned. Trump, and critics who have followed his lead, have pushed the nation further into a conspiratorial mindset that threatens reasoned discussion and has contributed to the severe decline of civil dialogue critical to solve problems. "After all, conspiracism," write the editors of *The Economist*,

> creates a divide deeper than partisan polarisation—an epistemic divide over what it means to know something. Conspiracism comes with a claim to own reality. That's the scenario we worry about most, one that obliterates a common world of facts and public reasoning.[17]

Logic has been sacrificed for political expediency, whether it is a question of "rigged elections," the comparison of immigration detention facilities to Nazi death camps by neophyte members of Congress like Alexandria Ocasio-Cortez (D-NY), or former Vice President Joe Biden's contention that there are three genders. Such examples underscore a stunning inability in our political dialogue to concur on basic, scientific, and/or empirical facts—let alone investigate political controversies objectively.

Of course, Trump is frequently accused of "bigly" exaggerations and outright lies, with a running tally of more than 12,000 by the *Washington Post*.[18] The problem is that intellectual dishonesty, political confutation, and social media have joined forces to

---

[17] *The Economist*, Open Future, "Conspiracy theories are dangerous—here's how to crush them." August 12, 2019. https://www.economist.com/open-future/2019/08/12/conspiracy-theories-are-dangerous-heres-how-to-crush-them

[18] Glenn Kessler, Salvador Rizzo, and Meg Kelly, "President Trump has made 12,019 false or misleading claims over 928 days." *Washington Post*, August 12, 2019. https://www.washingtonpost.com/politics/2019/08/12/president-trump-has-made-false-or-misleading-claims-over-days/

make it much easier for Trump and other politicians to peddle dubious claims absent a media capable of objectively distilling truth and fact from feverish impulses and questionable assertions made at campaign stop photo-ops or in 280 characters or fewer on Twitter. Perhaps solving the dilemma is the citizenry's responsibility, which requires putting down the cellphone and engaging in civic education and meaningful dialogue that is not obfuscated under cover of relative anonymity and electronic hardware.

If the nation is to avoid a descent into the inferno of civil chaos, and come back to a place where citizens and elites can begin talking *to* one another again instead of talking *past* each other, recognizing and eschewing the most noxious aspects of the populist style that appeal to our base instincts, alongside a return to the principles of the Framers of the Constitution, is paramount. Americans must recall that political institutions must survive beyond those who populate them at any particular moment in time, and the loss of decorum and civil discourse betrays the republican ideal. Populism locates what divides us, not what unites us. In the current setting its grammar is exclusionary, not inclusionary. It may be a Sisyphean task ahead of the Republic, but the populist language of institutional delegitimization and personal demonization must be replaced by syntax of unity, a search for common ground, and an avoidance of a rush to judgment that is respectful to our constitutional traditions and consonant with expected behavioral norms of our elected officials. The shrill and impulsive rhetoric of Trump's populism, and those who emulate it, is not easily reconcilable with the core Madisonian assumptions of American institutions: enlightened statesmen, protection of minority opinions, reasoned dialogue, and co-equal branches that must share power in a competitive yet reverent way. Nor is the dehumanizing rhetoric he often employs consistent with the universalism of Jefferson's Declaration. As president, he sets the tone from the top of the political order.

What will Trump's successor in the Republican Party do once the business tycoon leaves the political stage? It is too early to tell whether Trump has managed to rebrand the GOP so successfully in his image that the party of Lincoln and Eisenhower—leaders known for temperance and humility rather than bravado—cannot extricate itself from his populist legacy. Polls suggest that Trump's lack of focus on conventional Republican issues has come at a price, but few GOP lawmakers are prepared to challenge him for fear of electoral reprisal—and for cause. An August 2019 poll found that 70 percent of Republicans wanted Trump to increase or maintain his current level of control over the party, while the traditional, business-oriented wing of the party—some 12 percent—would be upset to see him re-elected.[19] This is bad news for anti-Trump forces in the GOP who suggest that he must be exorcised from the party in a fashion similar to the way Republicans separated themselves from Richard Nixon. The party wandered in the wilderness for an election cycle to reinvent its identity after Watergate, which led to Ronald Reagan's victory six years later and conservatism's ascendency for nearly three decades.[20] Then again, the large number of Republican members of Congress shirking re-election bids out of overt or quiet disagreement with the president's style ahead of 2020 suggests Trump's hold on the GOP may be more precarious than currently recognized.[21]

Donald Trump has clearly shattered norms of presidential behavior. But whatever his short-term fate, his style and allure are not likely replicable by those future GOP leaders who emerge to replace him. As one example, former South Carolina Governor Mark Sanford, who faced insurmountable structural barriers in his brief campaign against Trump for the Republican nomination in 2020, emphasized traditional themes, such as the debt and deficits that the president has failed to address. "Sanford," writes

---

[19] David Lauter, "Trump has remade the Republican Party, but at a price." *Los Angeles Times*, August 22, 2019. https://www.latimes.com/politics/story/2019-08-21/usc-la-times-republican-poll-trump-populism

[20] Sarah Longwell, "Republicans who back impeachment can save the country —and the GOP." *NBC News*, September 30, 2019. https://www.nbcnews.com/think/opinion/republicans-who-back-impeachment-can-save-country-gop-ncna1059896

[21] Rachael Blade, "Trump's takeover of GOP forces many House Republicans to head for the exits." *Washington Post*, September 22, 2019. https://www.washingtonpost.com/politics/trumps-takeover-of-gop-forces-many-house-republicans-to-head-for-the-exits/2019/09/22/d89f99fc-d4bd-11e9-ab26-e6dbebac45d3_story.html

Olivia Nuzzi, "is a conservative from the more innocent time of, like, a few years ago, before Trump and the cultlike creed of his loyal fans supplanted Establishment Republican orthodoxy."[22] What is more, Sanford rejected categorically the anti-intellectual overtures of Trump's presidency. As he stated in one interview,

> if you see a pattern of over and over and over again, wherein facts don't matter and you can just make up anything . . . Our republic was based on reason. The Founding Fathers were wed to this notion of reason. It was a reason-based system. And if you go to a point wherein it doesn't matter, I mean, that has huge implications in terms of where we go next as a society.[23]

Will future GOP leaders follow Sanford's lead? Perhaps. Is Trump's populist presidency a flash in the pan, an experiment with which the electorate will grow tired? Maybe. To be sure, Trump does not share a clear ideological lineage, say, to Ronald Reagan's conservative governing philosophy that spanned generations, though the 45th president's increasingly vocal pro-life stance on abortion, regulatory maneuvers, and court appointments may alter that view. Regardless, Trump's appeal may continue into his post-presidency in ways that are fundamentally dissimilar to his predecessors, much to the dismay of some in the Republican Party, and surely to the abject horror of progressives. Indeed, Trump may sustain influence beyond the White House, regardless of how or when he exits. The strong probability is that he will not retreat from the social media platform that catapulted him to the White House. As Philip Klein contends,

> Trump was an active Twitter user before running for president, throughout his campaign, and during his presidency. He has used

---

[22] Olivia Nuzzi, "Is Mark Sanford's quest for the mythical reluctant Trump voter noble or pathetic?" *New York Magazine*, September 15, 2019. http://nymag.com/intelligencer/2019/09/mark-sanford-2020-presidential-campaign.html

[23] Quoted in Tim Alberta, "'I'm a dead man walking.' Mark Sanford has nothing left to lose. And he's here to haunt Donald Trump." *Politico*, February 17, 2017. https://www.politico.com/magazine/story/2017/02/mark-sanford-profile-214791

the forum to generate controversy and lambaste his critics. There is no reason to believe that will stop when he leaves office and every reason to believe that with more time on his hands and fewer constraints, he'll feel even more freedom to let it rip to his tens of millions of followers. Trump is 73 years old—his mother lived until 88 and his father until 93. It's quite possible that he could be tweeting for a very long time.[24]

Alas, Trump's penultimate legacy has been to master a technology, and show others how to use it in conjunction with his populist style, that is most often antithetical to critical thinking and problem-solving—and to the so-called art of the deal, at least in democratic institutions. As a result, one of Trump's legacies thus far has been to compound the slide toward executive unilateralism. Another has been to push the Democratic Party if not to madness, then clearly further to the left of the ideological spectrum in ways that would have been unthinkable just a decade ago. Regardless, whatever one's political leanings, it is critical to juxtapose Trump's style of anti-intellectualism, majoritarianism, and nativism with the elegant eighteenth-century prose and reasoned arguments of the authors of the Federalist Papers. We would do well, as would future leaders of both parties, to consider Trump's presidency in light of Alexander Hamilton's reminder that "Hard words are very rarely useful. Real firmness is good for every thing. Strut is good for nothing." Unfortunately, Hamilton cannot take to social media from the grave, and it is doubtful he would have found limits of 280 characters sufficient to protest. Still, one can only contemplate the type of demeaning sobriquet Trump might invent for the "little lion," with his wiry stature and fiery red hair, on a medium known as Twitter that defies the sophistication and refinement of the Father of the Federalist Papers. The institution of the presidency that Hamilton endeavored to construct remains in the crosshairs of Trump's deconstructive populism. After all, the Founders were the Republic's first elites.

---

[24] Philip Klein, "How Trump's post-presidential Twitter feed could shape the future of the Republican Party." *Washington Examiner*, September 4, 2019. https://www.washingtonexaminer.com/opinion/columnists/how-trumps-post-presidential-twitter-feed-could-shape-the-future-of-the-republican-party

Bibliography

Books

Allen, Jonathan, and Amie Parnes. *Shattered: Inside Hillary Clinton's Doomed Campaign* (New York: Crown, 2017).

Aristotle. *Aristotle's Politics: A Treatise on Government* (New York: G. Routledge, 1895).

Aristotle. *Aristotle in 23 Volumes*, vol. 21. Translated by H. Rackham (Cambridge, MA: Harvard University Press; London: William Heinemann Ltd., 1944), Book 5, Section 1305(a) [1]. http://www.perseus.tufts.edu/hopper/text?doc=Perseus:abo:tlg,0086,035:5

Aristotle. *The Athenian Constitution* (Cambridge, MA: Charles River Editors, 2018).

Barber, James David. *The Presidential Character: Predicting Performance in the White House* (Englewood Cliffs, NJ: Prentice-Hall, 1977).

Baumgartner, Frank R., and Bryan D. Jones. *Agendas and Instability in American Politics*, 2nd edition (Chicago: University of Chicago Press, 2010).

Berlet, Chip, and Matthew N. Lyons. *Right-Wing Populism in America: Too Close for Comfort* (New York: Guilford Press, 2000).

Blumenthal, Sidney. *The Permanent Campaign* (New York: Simon & Schuster, 1982).

Boulard, Gary. *The Swing around the Circle: Andrew Johnson and the Train Ride That Destroyed a Presidency* (New York: iUniverse, Inc., 2008).

Boyte, Harry. *We the People Politics: The Populist Promise of Deliberative Public Work* (Dayton, OH: Kettering Foundation, 2011).

Carter, Dan T. *The Politics of Rage: George Wallace, the Origins of the New Conservatism, and the Transformation of American Politics* (Baton Rouge: Louisiana State University Press, 2000).

Christman, Henry M. (ed.). *Kingfish to America, Share Our Wealth: Selected Senatorial Papers of Huey P. Long* (New York: Schocken Books, 1985).

Clinton, Hillary. *What Happened* (New York: Simon & Schuster, 2017).

Cohen, Jeffrey E. *Going Local: Presidential Leadership in the Post-Broadcast Age* (New York: Cambridge University Press, 2010).

Conley, Richard S. *The Presidency, Congress, and Divided Government: A Postwar Assessment* (College Station: Texas A&M University Press, 2002).

Cooper, Philip J. *By Order of the President: The Use and Abuse of Executive Direct Action* (Lawrence: University Press of Kansas, 2002).

Corner, John, and Dick Pels (eds.). *Media and the Restyling of Politics* (London: Sage, 2003).

Dallek, Matthew. *The Right Moment: Ronald Reagan's First Victory and the Decisive Turning Point in American Politics* (New York: Free Press, 2000).

Eads, George C., and Michael Fix (eds.). *The Reagan Regulatory Strategy: An Assessment* (Washington, DC: The Urban Institute, 1984).

Edwards, George C., III. *Presidential Influence in Congress* (San Francisco: W. H. Freeman, 1980).

Federici, Michael P. *The Challenge of Populism: The Rise of Right-Wing Democratism in Postwar America* (New York: Praeger, 1991).

Fitzpatrick, John Clement (ed.). *The Autobiography of Martin Van Buren*. Annual Report of the American Historical Association for the Year 1918, vol. 2 (Washington, DC: Government Printing Office, 1920).

Foner, Eric. *Reconstruction: America's Unfinished Revolution* (New York: Perennial Classics, 1988).

Gilmour, John B. *Strategic Disagreement: Stalemate in American Politics* (Pittsburgh: University of Pittsburgh Press, 1995).

Ginsberg, Benjamin, and Martin Shefter. *Politics by Other Means: The Declining Importance of Elections in America* (New York: Basic Books, 1990).

Goffman, Erving. *The Presentation of Self in Everyday Life* (New York: Doubleday Anchor, 1959).

Greenstein, Fred I. *The Hidden-hand Presidency: Eisenhower as Leader* (Baltimore, MA: Johns Hopkins University Press, 1994).

Hatch, Alden. *Franklin D. Roosevelt* (New York: Henry Holt, 1947).

Hofstadter, Richard. *The Paranoid Style in American Politics* (New York: Vintage, 2012).

Hofstadter, Richard. *The Paranoid Style in American Politics and Other Essays* (Cambridge, MA: Harvard University Press, 1996).

Howell, William G. *Power without Persuasion: The Politics of Direct Presidential Action* (Princeton, NJ: Princeton University Press, 2003).

Ionescu, Ghita, and Ernest Gellner (eds.). *Populism: Its Meaning and National Characteristics* (New York: Macmillan, 1969).

Jones, Charles O. *The Trusteeship Presidency: Jimmy Carter and the United States Congress* (Baton Rouge: Louisiana State University Press, 1988).

Judis, John B. *The Populist Explosion: How the Great Recession Transformed American and European Politics* (New York: Columbia World Reports, 2016).

Kazin, Michael. *The Populist Persuasion: An American History* (Ithaca, NY: Cornell University Press, 1998).

Kennedy, John F. *Profiles in Courage* (New York: Harper & Row, 1964).

Kernell, Samuel. *Going Public: New Strategies of Presidential Leadership* (Washington, DC: CQ Press, 2006).

Knight, Peter. *Conspiracy Theories in American History: An Encyclopedia* (Santa Barbara, CA: ABC-CLIO, 2003).

Knollenberg, Bernhard. *Washington and the Revolution, a Reappraisal: Gates, Conway, and the Continental Congress* (New York: Macmillan Company, 1940).

Kristeva, Julia. *Powers of Horror: An Essay on Abjection*. Translated by Leon S. Roudiez (New York: Columbia University Press, 1982).

Laclau, Ernesto. *Politics and Ideology in Marxist Theory: Capitalism—Fascism—Populism* (London: New Left Books, 1977).

Laderman, Charlie, and Brendan Simms. *Donald Trump: The Making of a World View* (New York: I. B. Tauris, 2017).

Lee, Bandy X. *The Dangerous Case of Donald Trump: 27 Psychiatrists and Mental Health Experts Assess a President* (New York: Thomas Dunne Books, 2017).

Leuchtenburg, William E. *In the Shadow of FDR: From Harry Truman to George W. Bush* (Ithaca, NY: Cornell University Press, 2001).

Loeb, Harold. *Life in a Technocracy: What It Might Be Like* (Syracuse, NY: Syracuse University Press, 1996).

MacKenzie, John P. *Absolute Power: How the Unitary Executive Theory Is Undermining the Constitution* (New York: The Century Foundation Press, 2008).

Martinez, J. Michael. *Coming for to Carry Me Home: Race in America from Abolitionism to Jim Crow* (Lanham, MD: Rowman & Littlefield, 2012).

Mantell, Martin E. *Johnson, Grant, and the Politics of Reconstruction* (New York: Columbia University Press, 1973).

Mayer, Kenneth R. *With the Stroke of a Pen: Executive Orders and Presidential Power* (Princeton, NJ: Princeton University Press, 2001).

Mayhew, David R. *Divided We Govern: Party Control, Lawmaking, and Investigations, 1948–2002* (New Haven, CT: Yale University Press, 2005).

Mieczkowsi, Yanek. *Gerald Ford and the Challenges of the 1970s* (Lexington: University Press of Kentucky, 2005).

Mudde, Cas. *Populist Radical Right Parties in Europe* (Cambridge: Cambridge University Press).

Mudde, Cas, and Cristóbal Rovira Kaltwasser. *Populism: A Very Short Introduction* (New York: Oxford University Press, 2017).

Müller, Jan-Werner. *What Is Populism?* (Philadelphia: University of Pennsylvania Press, 2016).

Neubuck, Kenneth J., and Noel Cazenave. *Welfare Racism: Playing the Race Card against America's Poor* (New York: Routledge, 2001).

Neustadt, Richard E. *Presidential Power and the Modern Presidents* (New York: Free Press, 1964).

Neustadt, Richard E. *Presidential Power and the Modern Presidents: The Politics of Leadership from Roosevelt to Reagan* (New York: Free Press, 1990).

Perlstein, Rick. *Before the Storm: Barry Goldwater and the Unmaking of the American Consensus* (New York: Nation Books, 2009).

Pfiffner, James P. *The Strategic Presidency: Hitting the Ground Running* (Lawrence: University Press of Kansas, 1996).

Pious, Richard. *The American Presidency* (New York: Basic Books, 1979).

Plato. *The Republic.* Translated by Alan Bloom (New York: Harper Collins, 1968).

Reedy, George. *The Twilight of the Presidency: From Johnson to Reagan* (New York: Dutton, 1987).

Remini, Robert V. *Andrew Jackson and the Bank War: A Study in the Growth of Presidential Power* (New York: W. W. Norton, 1967).

Rosen, David, and Aaron Santesso. *The Watchman in Pieces: Surveillance, Literature, and Liberal Personhood* (New Haven, CT: Yale University Press, 2013).

Rudalevige, Andrew. *The New Imperial Presidency: Renewing Presidential Power after Watergate* (Ann Arbor: University of Michigan Press, 2005).

Schlesinger, Arthur M. *The Age of Jackson* (Boston: Little, Brown, 1945).

Schlesinger, Arthur M. *The Imperial Presidency* (Boston: Houghton Mifflin, 1973).

Singer, P. W., and Emerson T. Brooking. *Like War: The Weaponization of Social Media* (New York: Houghton-Mifflin, 2018).

Skowronek, Stephen. *The Politics Presidents Make* (Cambridge, MA: Harvard University Press, 1997).

Skowronek, Stephen. *Presidential Leadership in Political Time: Reprise and Reappraisal* (Lawrence: University Press of Kansas, 2008).

Sprague, Richard E. *The Taking of America, 1-2-3* (Self-published, 1976). http://www.denkmalnach.org/download/ToA.pdf

Sundquist, James L. *The Decline and Resurgence of Congress* (Washington, DC: Brookings Institution, 2002).

Trefousse, Hans L. *Andrew Johnson: A Biography* (New York: W. W. Norton, 1989).

Trump, Donald J., and Dave Shiflett. *The America We Deserve* (New York: Renaissance Books, 2000).

Tsebelis, George. *Veto Players: How Political Institutions Work* (Princeton, NJ: Princeton University Press, 2002).

Tulis, Jeffrey K. *The Rhetorical Presidency* (Princeton, NJ: Princeton University Press, 1987).

Tulis, Jeffrey K. *The Rhetorical Presidency* (Princeton, NJ: Princeton University Press, 2017).

Uslaner, Eric M. *The Decline of Comity in Congress* (Ann Arbor: University of Michigan Press, 1996).

Vinson, John Chalmers. *Thomas Nast: Political Cartoonist* (Athens: University of Georgia Press, 1967).

Waterman, Richard, Carol L. Silva, and Hank Jenkins-Smith. *The Presidential Expectations Gap: Public Attitudes Concerning the Presidency* (Ann Arbor: University of Michigan Press, 2014).

White, F. Clifton. *Suite 3505: The Story of the Draft Goldwater Movement* (New Rochelle, NY: Arlington House, 1967).

Wilentz, Sean. *Andrew Jackson*. American Presidents Series (New York: Henry Holt & Co., 2005).

Wilson, James. Lectures on Law part 2, No.1, Of the Constitutions of the United States and of Pennsylvania-of the Legislative Department, in The Works of James Wilson, edited by Robert G. McCloskey (Cambridge, MA: Belknap Press of Harvard University, 1967).

Chapters in edited volumes

Burnham, Walter Dean. "The 1984 Election and the Future of American Politics." In Ellis Sandoz and C. V. Crabb, Jr. (eds.), *Election '84: Landslide without Mandate* (New York: New American Library, 1985), pp. 204–60.

Davidson, Roger H. "The Presidency and the Three Eras of the Modern Congress." In James A. Thurber (ed.), *Divided Democracy: Cooperation and Conflict Between the President and Congress* (Washington, DC: Congressional Quarterly Press, 1991), pp. 61–78.

De Cleen, Benjamin. "Populism and Nationalism." In Cristóbal Rovira Kaltwasser, Paul Taggart, Paulina Ochoa Espejo, and Pierre Ostiguy (eds.), *The Oxford Handbook of Populism* (New York: Oxford University Press, 2017), pp. 342–62.

Destler, I. M. "U.S. Trade Policy-making in the 1980s." In Alberto Alesina and Geoffrey Carliner (eds.), *Politics and Economics in the Eighties* (Chicago: University of Chicago Press, 1990), pp. 251–84.

Edwards, George C., III. "Neustadt's Power Approach to the Presidency." In Robert Y. Shapiro, Martha Joynt Kumar, and Lawrence R. Jacobs (eds.), *Presidential Power: Forging the Presidency for the Twenty-First Century* (New York: Columbia University Press, 2000), pp. 9–15.

Genovese, Michael A. "The Foundations of the Unitary Executive of George W. Bush." In Ryan J. Barilleaux and Christopher J. Kelley (eds.), *The Unitary Executive and the Modern Presidency* (College Station: Texas A&M University Press, 2010), pp. 124–44.

Glad, Paul W. "Bryan and the Progressives." In Paul W. Glad (ed.), *William Jennings Bryan: A Profile* (New York: Hill and Wang, 1968).

Jones, Charles O. "Presidential Negotiation with Congress." In Anthony King (ed.), *Both Ends of the Avenue: The Presidency, the Executive Branch, and Congress in the 1980s* (Washington, DC: American Enterprise Institute, 1983).

Laclau, Ernesto. "Why Populism?" In *New Populisms and the European Right and Far Right Parties* (Milan: Edizioni Punto Rosso, 2012).

Lowndes, Joseph. "Populism in the United States." In Cristóbal Rovira Kaltwasser, Paul Taggart, Paulina Ochoa Espejo, and Pierre Ostiguy (eds.), *The Oxford Handbook of Populism* (New York: Oxford University Press, 2017), p. 232.

Miroff, Bruce. "The Presidency and the Public: Leadership as Spectacle." In Michael Nelson (ed.), *The Presidency and the Political System*, 4th edition (Washington, DC: Congressional Quarterly Inc., 1995), pp. 274, 278.

Nelson, Michael. "Evaluating the Presidency." In Michael Nelson (ed.), *The Presidency and the Political System*, 4th edition (Washington, DC: Congressional Quarterly, Inc., 1995), pp. 3–28.

Owens, Diana. "Twitter Rants, Press Bashing, and Fake News: The Shameful Legacy of Media in the 2016 Election." In Larry J. Sabato,

Kyle Kondik, and Geoffrey Skelley (eds.), *Trumped: The 2016 Election That Broke All the Rules* (Lanham, MD: Rowman & Littlefield, 2017), pp. 167–80.

Panizza, Francisco. "Introduction: Populism and the Mirror of Democracy." In Francisco Panizza (eds.), *Populism and the Mirror of Democracy* (London: Verso, 2005).

Peake, Jeffrey. "Obama, Unilateral Diplomacy, and Iran: Treaties, Executive Agreements, and Political Commitments." In Richard S. Conley (ed.), *Presidential Leadership and National Security Policy: The Obama Legacy and Trump Trajectory* (New York: Routledge, 2018), pp. 142–71.

Journal articles

Akkerman, Tjitske. "Populism and Democracy: Challenge or Pathology?" *Acta Politica* 38, no. 2 (2003): 147–59.

Amenta, Edwin, Kathleen Dunleavy, and Mary Bernstein. "Stolen Thunder? Huey Long's 'Share Our Wealth,' Political Mediation, and the Second New Deal." *American Sociological Review* 59, no. 5 (1994): 678–702.

Appel, Edward C. "Burlesque, Tragedy, and a (Potentially) 'Yuuge' 'Breaking of a Frame': Donald Trump's Rhetoric as 'Early Warning'?" *Communication Quarterly* 66, no. 2 (2018): 157–75.

Baggini, Julian. "How Rising Trump and Sanders Parallel Rising Populism in Europe." *New Perspectives Quarterly* 33, no. 2 (2016): 22–5.

Barilleaux, Ryan J., and Jewerl Maxwell. "Has Barack Obama Embraced the Unitary Executive?" *PS: Political Science & Politics* 50 (2017): 31–4.

Barrett, Andrew W., and Jeffrey S. Peake. "When the President Comes to Town: Examining Local Newspaper Coverage of Domestic Presidential Travel." *American Politics Research* 35, no. 1 (2007): 3–31.

Bimes, Terry, and Quinn Mulroy. "The Rise and Decline of Presidential Populism." *Studies in American Political Development* 18, no. 2 (2004): 136–59.

Bostdorff, Denise M. "Obama, Trump, and Reflections on the Rhetoric of Political Change." *Rhetoric and Public Affairs* 20, no. 4 (2017): 695–706.

Brinkley, Alan. "Huey Long, the Share Our Wealth Movement, and the Limits of Depression Dissidence." *Louisiana History: The Journal of the Louisiana Historical Association* 22, no. 2 (1981): 117–34.

Brinkley, Alan. "Comparative Biography as Political History: Huey Long and Father Coughlin." *The History Teacher* 18, no. 1 (1984): 9–16.

Campbell, James E. "Introduction." Politics Symposium, Forecasting the 2016 American National Elections. *PS: Political Science and Politics* 49, no. 4 (2016): 649–54.

Campbell, James E., *et al.* "A Recap of the 2016 Election Forecasts." *PS: Political Science & Politics* 50, no. 2 (2017): 331–8.

Canovan, Margaret. "Two Strategies for the Study of Populism." *Political Studies* 30, no. 4 (1982): 544–52.

Carter, Dan T. "Legacy of Rage: George Wallace and the Transformation of American Politics." *Journal of Southern History* 62, no. 1 (1996): 3–26.

Cash, Jordan T., and Dave Bridge. "Donald Trump and Institutional Change Strategies." *Laws* 7, no. 27 (2018): 1–21.

Cooper, Philip J. "Presidential Memoranda and Executive Orders: Of Patchwork Quilts, Trump Cards, and Shell Games." *Presidential Studies Quarterly* 31, no. 1 (2001): 126–41.

Cooper, Philip J. "George W. Bush, Edgar Allan Poe, and the Use and Abuse of Presidential Signing Statements." *Presidential Studies Quarterly* 35, no. 3 (2005): 515–32.

Crouch, Jeffrey, Mark J. Rozell, and Mitchell A. Sollenberger. "The Unitary Executive Theory and President Donald J. Trump." *Presidential Studies Quarterly* 47, no. 3 (2017): 561–73.

De Cleen, Benjamin, and Yannis Stavrakakis. "Distinctions and Articulations: A Discourse Theoretical Framework for the Study of Populism and Nationalism." *Javnost—The Public: Journal of the European Institute for Communication and Culture* 24, no. 4 (2017): 301–19.

Dickinson, Matthew J. "Explaining Trump's Support: What We Saw and Heard at His Campaign Rallies." *The Forum* 16, no. 2 (2018): 171–91.

Eiermann, Martin. "How Donald Trump Fits into the History of American Populism." *New Perspectives Quarterly* 33, no. 2 (2016): 29–34.

Endres, Fred F. "Public Relations in the Jackson White House." *Public Relations Review* 2, no. 3 (1976): 5–12.

Enli, Gunn. "Twitter as an Arena for the Authentic Outsider: Exploring the Social Media Campaigns of Trump and Clinton in the 2016 US Presidential Election." *European Journal of Communication* 32, no. 1 (2017): 50–61.

Essig, Todd. "How the Trump Campaign Built a Political Porn Site to Sell the Pleasures of Hate: What Do We Do Now?" *Contemporary Psychoanalysis* 53, no. 4 (2017): 516–32.

Fort, Ilene Susan. "American Social Surrealism." *American Art Journal* 22, no. 3 (1982): 8–20.

Fraser, Steve, and Joshua B. Freeman. "In the Rearview Mirror: History's Mad Hatters: The Strange Career of Tea Party Populism." *New Labor Forum* 19 (2010): 76.

Friedman, Barry D. "A Case-Study Analysis of the Reagan Regulatory Review Program." *Politics and Policy* 21, no. 4 (1993): 705–20.

Gerhardt, Michael J. "The Lessons of Impeachment History." *George Washington Law Review* 67 (1999): 603–25.

Goebel, Thomas. "The Political Economy of American Populism from Jackson to the New Deal." *Studies in American Political Development* 11, no. 1 (1997): 109–48.

Goldstein, Joel K. "Talking Trump and the Twenty-Fifth Amendment: Correcting the Record on Section 4." *University of Pennsylvania Journal of Constitutional Law* 21, no. 1 (2018): 73–152.

Habermas, Jürgen. "Some Distinctions in Universal Pragmatics." *Theory and Society* 3, no. 2 (1976): 155–67.

Hall, Kira, Donna M. Goldstein, and Matthew Bruce Ingram. "The Hands of Donald Trump: Entertainment, Gesture, Spectacle." *Journal of Ethnographic History* 6, no. 2 (2016): 71–100.

Hammond, Bray. "Jackson, Biddle, and the Bank of the United States." *Journal of Economic History* 7, no. 1 (1947): 1–23.

Harrison, Albert A., and James Moulton Thomas. "The Kennedy Assassination, Unidentified Flying Objects, and Other Conspiracies: Psychological and Organizational Factors in the Perception of 'Cover-up'." *Systems Research and Behavioral Science: The Official Journal of the International Federation for Systems Research* 14, no. 2 (1997): 113–28.

Hoekstra, Douglas J. "The Politics of Politics: Skowronek and Presidential Research." *Presidential Studies Quarterly* 29, no. 3 (1999): 657–71.

Holt, Michael F. "The Politics of Impatience: The Origins of Know-Nothingism." *Journal of American History* 6, no. 2 (1973): 309–31.

Hood, Derek. "Racism as Abjection: A Psychoanalytic Conceptualisation for a Post-Apartheid South Africa." *South African Journal of Psychology* 34, no. 4 (2004): 672–703.

Huq, Aziz Z. "The People against the Constitution." *Michigan Law Review* 116 (2018): 1123–44.

Jackson, Clayton. "The Internal Improvement Vetoes of Andrew Jackson." *Tennessee Historical Quarterly* 25, no. 3 (1966): 261–79.

Johnson, Lauren R., Deon McCray, and Jordan M. Ragusa. "#Never-Trump: Why Republican Members of Congress Refused to Support

Their Party's Nominee in the 2016 Presidential Election." *Research & Politics* (January–March 2018): 1–10. http://journals.sagepub.com/doi/pdf/10.1177/2053168017749383

Kaltwasser, Cristóbal Rovira. "The Ambivalence of Populism: Threat and Corrective for Democracy." *Democratization* 19, no. 2 (2014): 184–208.

Kayam, Orly. "The Readability and Simplicity of Donald Trump's Language." *Political Studies Review* 16, no. 1 (2018): 73–88.

Kennedy, Courtney, *et al.* "An Evaluation of the 2016 Election Polls in the United States." *Public Opinion Quarterly* 82, no. 1 (2018): 1–33.

Kersh, Rogan. "The Growth of American Political Development: The View from the Classroom." *Perspectives on Politics* 3, no. 2 (2005): 335–45.

Kreis, Ramona. "The 'Tweet Politics' of President Trump." *Journal of Language and Politics* 16, no. 4 (2017): 607–18.

Lamberty, Pia K., Jens H. Hellmann, and Aileen Oeberst. "The Winner Knew It All? Conspiracy Beliefs and Hindsight Perspective after the 2016 US General Election." *Personality and Individual Differences* 123 (2018): 236–40.

Ledbetter, James. "Has the Famous Populist 'Cross of Gold' Speech Been Unfairly Tarred by Anti-Semitism?" *JSTOR Daily* (Business and Economics), July 6, 2016. https://daily.jstor.org/william-jennings-bryan-cross-of-gold/

Lee, Michael J. "The Populist Chameleon: The People's Party, Huey Long, George Wallace, and the Populist Argumentative Frame." *Quarterly Journal of Speech* 92, no. 4 (2006): 355–78.

Levine, Bruce. "Conservatism, Nativism, and Slavery: Thomas R. Whitney and the Origins of the Know-Nothing Party." *Journal of American History* (September 2001): 455–88.

Long, R. Seymour. "Andrew Jackson and the National Bank." *English Historical Review* 12, no. 45 (1897): 86–7.

Lowande, Kenneth S. "After the Orders: Presidential Memoranda and Unilateral Action." *Presidential Studies Quarterly* 44, no. 4 (2014): 724–41.

Mair, Peter. "Ruling the Void: The Hollowing of Western Democracy." *New Left Review* 42 (November–December 2006).

Marietta, Morgan, Tyler Farley, Tyler Cote, and Paul Murphy. "The Rhetorical Psychology of Trumpism: Threat, Absolutism, and the Absolutist Threat." *The Forum* 15, no. 2 (2017): 313–32.

Marshall, Lynn L. "The Authorship of Jackson's Bank Veto Message." *Mississippi Valley Historical Review* 50, no. 3 (1963): 466–77.

Martinez, Michael D., and Jeff Gill. "The Effects of Turnout on Partisan Outcomes in U.S. Presidential Elections 1960–2000." *Journal of Politics* 67, no. 4 (2005): 1248–74.

Mas, Lluís, Maria-Rosa Collell, and Jordi Xifra. "The Sound of Music or the History of Trump and Clinton Family Singers: Music Branding as Communication Strategy in the 2016 Campaign." *American Behavioral Scientist* 61, no. 6 (2017): 584–99.

McKerns, Joseph P. "The Limits of Progressive Journalism History." *Journalism History* 4, no. 3 (1977): 88–92.

McMahon, Kevin J. "Presidents, Political Regimes, and Contentious Supreme Court Nominations: A Historical Institutional Model." *Law & Social Inquiry* 32, no. 4 (2007): 919–54.

Moffitt, Benjamin, and Simon Tormey. "Rethinking Populism: Politics, Mediatisation and Political Style." *Political Studies* 62, no. 2 (2014): 381–97.

Molyneux, Maxine, and Thomas Osborne. "Populism: A Deflationary View." *Economy and Society* 46, no. 1 (2017): 1–19.

Morrison, James A. "This Means War! Corruption and Credible Commitments in the Collapse of the Second Bank of the United States." *Journal of the History of Economic Thought* 37, no. 2 (2017): 221–45.

Motta, Matthew. "The Dynamics and Political Implications of Anti-Intellectualism in the United States." *American Politics Research* 46, no. 3 (2018): 465–98.

Mudde, Cas. "The Populist Zeitgeist." *Government and Opposition* 39, no. 4 (2004): 542–63.

Mudde, Cas, and Cristóbal Rovira Kaltwasser. "Exclusionary vs. Inclusionary Populism: Comparing Contemporary Europe and Latin America." *Government and Opposition* 48, no. 2 (2013): 147–74.

Murphy, Troy M. "William Jennings Bryan: Boy Orator, Broken Man, and the 'Evolution' of America's Public Philosophy." *Great Plains Quarterly* 40, no. 2 (2002): 83–98.

Nai, Alessandro, and Jürgen Maier. "Perceived Personality and Campaign Style of Hillary Clinton and Donald Trump." *Personality and Individual Differences* 121 (2018): 80–3.

Neustadt, Richard E. "The Contemporary Presidency: The Presidential 'Hundred Days'—An Overview." *Presidential Studies Quarterly* 31, no. 1 (2001): 121–5.

Nichols, Curt. "Reagan Reorders the Political Regime: A Historical–Institutional Approach to Analysis of Change." *Presidential Studies Quarterly* 45, no. 4 (2015): 703–26.

Nichols, Curt. "Modern Reconstructive Presidential Leadership: Reordering Institutions in a Constrained Environment." *The Forum* 12, no. 2 (2014): 281–304.

Nichols, Curt, and Adam S. Myers. "Exploiting the Opportunity for Reconstructive Leadership: Presidential Responses to Enervated Political Regimes." *American Politics Quarterly* 38, no. 5 (2010): 806–41.

Nye, Joseph S., Jr. "Populism is likely to continue in the United States." "Symposium: Why Is Populism on the Rise and What Do the Populists Want?" *The International Economy* (Winter 2019): 12–14.

Perkins, Edwin J. "Lost Opportunities for Compromise in the Bank War: A Reassessment of Jackson's Veto Message." *Business History Review* 61, no. 4 (1987): 531–50.

Pettigrew, Thomas. "Social Psychological Perspectives on Trump Supporters." *Journal of Social and Political Psychology* 5, no. 1 (2017): 107–16.

Pfiffner, James P. "The Constitutional Legacy of George W. Bush." *Presidential Studies Quarterly* 45, no. 4 (2015): 727–41.

Pierson, James. "Why Populism Fails." *The New Criterion* 37, no. 9 (January 2018). https://www.newcriterion.com/issues/2018/1/why-populism-fails

Pierson, Paul. "American Hybrid: Donald Trump and the Strange Merger of Populism and Plutocracy." *British Journal of Sociology* 68 (November 2017): S106–S107.

Price, Bryan D. "Material Memory: The Politics of Nostalgia on the Eve of MAGA." *American Studies* 57, no. 1 (2018): 103–15.

Raum, Richard D., and James S. Measell. "Wallace and His Ways: A Study of the Rhetorical Genre of Polarization." *Communications Studies* 25, no. 1 (1974): 28–35.

Rockoff, Hugh. "The 'Wizard of Oz' as Monetary Allegory." *Journal of Economic Policy* 98, no. 4 (1990): 739–60.

Rohler, Lloyd. "Conservative Appeals to the People: George Wallace's Populist Rhetoric." *Southern Communication Journal* 64, no. 4 (1999): 316–22.

Rozell, Mark J. "Executive Privilege Revived: Secrecy and Conflict during the Bush Presidency." *Duke Law Journal* 52 (2002): 403–21.

Rudalevige, Andrew C. "Executive Orders & Presidential Unilateralism." *Presidential Studies Quarterly* 42, no. 1 (2012): 138–60.

Rudolph, Thomas. "Populist Anger, Donald Trump, and the 2016 Election." *Journal of Elections, Public Opinion and Parties* (February 2019). https://doi.org/10.1080/17457289.2019.1582532

Schoor, Carola. "In the Theater of Political Style: Touches of Populism, Pluralism, and Elitism in the Speeches of Politicians." *Discourse & Society* 28, no. 6 (2017): 657–76.

Schulte-Sasse, Linda. "Meet Ross Perot: The Lasting Legacy of Capraesque Populism." *Cultural Critique* 25 (October 1993): 91–119.

Shogan, Colleen. "Anti-Intellectualism in the Modern Presidency: A Republican Populism." *Perspectives on Politics* 5, no. 2 (2007): 295–303.

Singh, Robert I. "'I, the People': A Deflationary Interpretation of Populism, Trump, and the United States Constitution." *Economy and Society* 46, no. 1 (2017): 20–42.

Sloan, John W. "Meeting the Leadership Challenges of the Modern Presidency: The Political Skills and Leadership of Ronald Reagan." *Presidential Studies Quarterly* 26, no. 3 (1996): 795–804.

Tajbakhsh, Kian. "Who Wants What from Iran Now? The Post-Nuclear Deal U.S. Policy Debate." *The Washington Quarterly*, 41, no. 3 (2018): 41–61.

Tatalovich, Raymond, and Byron Daynes. "Towards a Paradigm to Explain Presidential Power." *Presidential Studies Quarterly* 9, no. 4 (1979): 428–41.

Taylor, Andrew. "Barry Goldwater: Insurgent Conservatism as Constitutive Rhetoric." *Journal of Political Ideologies* 21, no. 3 (2016): 242–60.

Thornton, Russell. "Cherokee Population Losses during the Trail of Tears: A New Perspective and a New Estimate." *Ethnohistory* 31, no. 4 (1984): 289–300.

Thurber, Timothy N. "Goldwaterism Triumphant? Race and the Republican Party, 1965–1968." *The Journal of the Historical Society* 7, no. 3 (2007): 349–84.

Urbinati, Nadia. "The Populist Phenomenon." *Raisons Politiques* 137, no. 3 (2013): 137–54.

Waisbord, Silvio. "Why Populism Is Troubling for Democratic Communication." *Communication, Culture & Critique* 11, no. 1 (2018): 21–34.

Winberg, Oscar. "Insult Politics: Donald Trump, Right-Wing Populism, and Incendiary Language." *European Journal of American Studies* 12, no. 2 (2017). https://journals.openedition.org/ejas/12132

Wirls, Stephen H. "Machiavelli and Neustadt on Virtue and the Civil Prince." *Presidential Studies Quarterly* 24, no. 3 (1994): 461–77.

Woodward, Gary C. "Reagan as Roosevelt: The Elasticity of Pseudo-Populist Appeals." *Central States Speech Journal* 54, no. 1 (Spring 1983): 44–58.

Zompetti, Joseph. "Rhetorical Incivility in the Twittersphere: A Comparative Thematic Analysis of Clinton and Trump's Tweets during and after the 2016 Presidential Election." *Journal of Contemporary Rhetoric* 9, no. 1/2 (2019): 29–54.

Zubovich, Gene. "The Christian Nationalism of Donald Trump." *Religion & Society* (July 17, 2018). https://religionandpolitics. org/2018/07/17/the-christian-nationalism-of-donald-trump/

Polling data

Democracy Fund Voter Study Group. "Views of the Electorate Research Study." August 28, 2017. https://www.voterstudygroup.org/

Duggan, Andrew. "As in 1999, Most Do Not See Trump as Serious Candidate." July 14, 2015. https://news.gallup.com/poll/184115/1999-not-trump-serious-candidate.aspx

Gallup Poll. "Presidential Approval Ratings—Donald Trump." https:// news.gallup.com/poll/203198/presidential-approval-ratings-donald-trump.aspx

Gallup Poll. "Election Polls, Vote by Groups, 1960–1964." https:// news.gallup.com/poll/9454/election-polls-vote-groups-19601964. aspx

Gallup Poll. "Election Polls—Vote by Groups, 1968–1972." https:// news.gallup.com/poll/9457/election-polls-vote-groups-19681972 .aspx

Gallup Poll, July 14, 2015. https://news.gallup.com/poll/184115/1999-not-trump-serious-candidate.aspx

IPSOS News & Polls. "Americans Views on the Media." August 7, 2018. https://www.ipsos.com/en-us/news-polls/americans-views-media-2018-08-07

Pew Research Center. "Majority Says Trump Has Done 'Too Little' to Distance Himself from White Nationalists." March 28, 2019. https://www.people-press.org/2019/03/28/majority-says-trump-has-done-too-little-to-distance-himself-from-white-nationalists/

Pew Research Center, U.S. Politics & Policy, "Views of Trump's Executive Order on Travel Restrictions." February 16, 2017. http://www .people-press.org/2017/02/16/2-views-of-trumps-executive-order-on-travel-restrictions/

Quinnipiac University Poll. April 5, 2016. https://poll.qu.edu/national/ release-detail?ReleaseID=2340

Quinnipiac University Poll. September 10, 2018. https://poll.qu.edu/ national/release-detail?ReleaseID=2567

RealClearPolitics. "Direction of the Country." https://www.realclear-politics.com/epolls/other/direction_of_country-902.html

RealClearPolitics. "Job Approval on Economy." https://www.realclearpol-itics.com/epolls/other/president_trump_job_approval_economy-6182.html

Newspapers, magazines, news websites, and blogs

Abramson, Jill. "Bob Woodward's meticulous, frightening look inside the Trump White House." *Washington Post*, September 6, 2018. https://www.washingtonpost.com/outlook/bob-woodwards-meticu-lous-frightening-look-inside-the-trump-white-house/2018/09/06

Agerholm, Harriet. "Donald Trump asks why other people are called the elite when 'I have a much better apartment and I'm richer than they are'." *The Independent* (UK), June 21, 2018. https://www.independent.co.uk/news/world/americas/donald-trump-elite-better-apartment-richer-minnesota-rally-a8409621.html

Alba, Monica. "Tale of two rallies: How Trump and Clinton events look and sound." *NBC News*, January 25, 2016. https://www.nbcnews.com/politics/2016-election/tale-two-rallies-how-trump-clinton-campaign-n503911

Alberta, Tim. "'I'm a Dead Man Walking.' Mark Sanford has nothing left to lose. And he's here to haunt Donald Trump." *Politico*, February 17, 2017. https://www.politico.com/magazine/story/2017/02/mark-sanford-profile-214791

Algan, Yann, *et al.* "Qui sont les Gilets jaunes et leurs soutiens?" *Observatoire du Bien-être* 3, February 14, 2019. http://www.sciencespo.fr/cevipof/sites/sciencespo.fr.cevipof/files/-Qui-sont-les-Gilets-jaunes-et-leurs-soutiens-1.pdf

Anapol, Avery. "Fox Business drops guest who blamed migrant caravan on 'Soros-occupied State Department'." *The Hill*, October 28, 2018. https://thehill.com/homenews/media/413542-fox-business-exec-condemns-rhetoric-of-guest-who-blamed-migrant-caravan-on

Anderson, Jack, and Dale van Atta. "Trump's art of political giving." *Washington Post*, October 20, 1989, p. E5.

Anderson, Kurt. "How the GOP went crazy." *Slate*, February 2, 2018. https://slate.com/news-and-politics/2018/02/right-wing-conspiracy-theories-from-the-1960s-to-today.html

Anderson, Scott R., and Benjamin Wittes. "Climate change is real at the FBI—and here is the data to prove it." *Lawfare*, July 15, 2018. https://www.lawfareblog.com/climate-change-real-fbi-and-here-data-prove-it

Appelbome, Peter. "The 1992 campaign: Racial politics; Perot speech gets cool reception at N.A.A.C.P." *New York Times*, July 12, 1992. https://www.nytimes.com/1992/07/12/us/the-1992-campaign-racial-politics-perot-speech-gets-cool-reception-at-naacp.html

Arciga, Julia. "James Comey, welcome to the long list of people Donald Trump wants to jail." *Daily Beast*, April 18, 2018. https://www.thedailybeast.com/james-comey-welcome-to-the-long-list-of-people-trump-wants-to-jail

Associated Press. "D.C. attorney general subpoenas Trump's inaugural committee." *Politico*, February 27, 2019. https://www.politico.com/story/2019/02/27/trump-inaugural-committee-subpoena-1194641

Associated Press. "National Enquirer hid Trump secrets in a safe, removed them before inauguration." *CNN*, August 23, 2018. https://www.nbcnews.com/politics/donald-trump/national-enquirer-hid-trump-secrets-safe-removed-them-inauguration-n903356

Axelrod, Tal. "Majority of Americans don't support impeachment: poll." *The Hill*, April 26, 2019. https://thehill.com/homenews/house/440883-majority-of-americans-dont-support-impeachment-poll

Azarian, Bobby. "The psychology behind Donald Trump's unwavering support." *Psychology Today*, September 13, 2016. https://www.psychologytoday.com/us/blog/mind-in-the-machine/201609/the-psychology-behind-donald-trumps-unwavering-support

AZCentral. "Live updates: Police release gas on protesters after Trump speech." *Azcentral.com*, August 22, 2017. https://www.azcentral.com/story/news/politics/arizona/2017/08/22/donald-trump-phoenix-arizona-rally/575083001/

Bailey, Philip M. "Sen. Mitch McConnell: President Donald Trump 'is not a racist'." *Louisville Courier-Journal*, July 16, 2019. https://www.courier-journal.com/story/news/politics/2019/07/16/mitch-mcconnell-president-donald-trump-is-not-racist/1746316001/

Baird, Jonathan P. "The Trump–Nixon debate." *Concord (NH) Monitor*, November 22, 2018. https://www.concordmonitor.com/Watergate-parallels-21235599

Baker, Peter, and Coral Davenport. "President revives two oil pipelines thwarted under Obama." *New York Times*, January 25, 2017, p. A1.

Baker, Ross K. "Dump Trump." *New York Times*, November 24, 1987, p. A23.

Ball, Molly. "Why Hillary Clinton lost." *The Atlantic*, November 15, 2016. https://www.theatlantic.com/politics/archive/2016/11/why-hillary-clinton-lost/507704/

Ballotpedia, September 4, 2018. https://ballotpedia.org/Endorsements_by_Donald_Trump

Bandler, Aaron. "Democrats pushing Commission on Trump's fitness for presidency. Here are 5 things you need to know." *The Daily Wire*, July 6, 2017. https://www.dailywire.com/news/18327/democrats-pushing-commission-trumps-fitness-aaron-bandler

Baquero, Gabby. "Bernie Sanders pushes for free college, health care at rally." *University Wire*, March 10, 2016.

Barabak, Mark C., and Evan Halper. "The real question in the Clinton–Sanders debate? How much change do Democrats want?" *Los Angeles Times*, February 5, 2016. https://www.latimes.com/nation/politics/la-na-0205-new-hampshire-primary-debate-20160205-story.html

Barbanel, Josh. "Trump and city dispute part of $1 billion project." *New York Times*, May 19, 1985, p. 36.

Barbaro, Michael. "After roasting Trump reacts in character." *New York Times*, May 2, 2011, p. A17.

Barbaro, Michael, "Donald Trump clung to 'birther' lie for years, and still isn't apologetic." *New York Times*, September 16, 2016. https://www.nytimes.com/2016/09/17/us/politics/donald-trump-obama-birther.html

Barbaro, Michael. "What drives Donald Trump? Fear of losing status, tapes show." *New York Times*, October 26, 2016. https://www.nytimes.com/2016/10/26/us/politics/donald-trump-interviews.html

Barber, Nigel. "The psychology of insults." *Psychology Today*, November 21, 2016. https://www.psychologytoday.com/us/blog/the-human-beast/201611/the-psychology-insults

Barker, Jeff. "Under sharp questioning, Maryland tries to sustain suit over Trump business dealings." *Baltimore Sun*, March 19, 2019. https://www.baltimoresun.com/news/maryland/politics/bs-md-maryland-emoluments-argument-20190318-story.html\

Barrett, Devlin, and Dan Frosch. "Federal judge temporarily halts Trump order on immigration, refugees." *Wall Street Journal*, February 4, 2017. https://www.wsj.com/articles/legal-feud-over-trump-immigration-order-turns-to-visa-revocations-1486153216

Barrett, Devlin, and Matt Zapotosky, "Inside the FBI: Anger, worry, work—and fears of lasting damage." *Washington Post Blogs*, February 3, 2018. https://www.denverpost.com/2018/02/03/fbi-donald-trump-russia-investigation-nunes-memo/

Barron, James. "Almost everyone's playing stomp-the-Trump." *New York Times*, June 30, 1990, p. 27.

Barrouquere, Brett. "How a fundraiser brought George H. W. Bush, Donald Trump and Don King together." *Chron*, September 16, 2016. https://www.chron.com/news/politics/us/article/A-Bush-a-Trump-and-a-King-How-a-fundraiser-9227763.php

Baylor, Christopher. "Is Trump the last gasp in Reagan's Republican Party?" *Washington Post*, May 11, 2016. https://www.washingtonpost.com/news/monkey-cage/wp/2016/05/11/is-trump-the-last-gasp-of-reagans-republican-party/?utm_term=.8fefbcdfb155

BBC News. "French ex-President Jacques Chirac guilty of corruption." December 15, 2011. https://www.bbc.com/news/world-europe-16194089

Bell, Chris. "Fake news follows migrant caravan's journey north." *BBC News*, October 24, 2018. https://www.bbc.com/news/blogs-trending-45951102

Bellstrom, Kristen. "Carly Fiorna abandons her defense of women for possible Trump cabinet post." *Fortune*, December 13, 2016. http://fortune.com/2016/12/13/fiorina-trump-national-intelligence-women/

Belsie, Laurent. "For many Americans the Trump tax cut doesn't feel like a boost." *Christian Science Monitor*, February 14, 2019. https://www.csmonitor.com/Business/2019/0214/For-many-Americans-the-Trump-tax-cut-doesn-t-feel-like-a-boost

Beres, Louis René. "Trump and the triumph of anti-reason." *U.S. News & World Report*, July 13, 2017. https://www.usnews.com/opinion/op-ed/articles/2017-07-13/donald-trump-and-the-triumph-of-anti-reason-in-america

Berman, Russell. "The Republican majority in Congress is an illusion." *The Atlantic*, March 31, 2017. https://www.theatlantic.com/politics/archive/2017/03/the-republican-majority-in-congress-is-an-illusion/521403/

Bertrand, Natasha. "The eerie parallels between Trump and the Watergate 'road map'." *The Atlantic*, November 20, 2018. https://www.theatlantic.com/politics/archive/2018/11/watergate-road-map-has-parallels-trump-and-flynn/576277/

Betz, Bradford. "Bernie Sanders' income tops $1M for second year in row, reports say." *Fox News*, June 24, 2018. https://www.foxnews.com/politics/bernie-sanders-income-tops-1m-for-second-year-in-row-reports-say

Bierman, Noah. "Anatomy of a Trump rally: The hero (that's him), a jester (also him), villains, damsels, dystopia, and lots of grievances." *Los Angeles Times*, October 10, 2018. https://www.latimes.com/politics/la-na-pol-trump-rally-anatomy-20181010-story.html

Bierman, Noah. "Trump criticizes Sessions and vents frustration at Russia investigation and leaders of the Justice Department and FBI." *Los Angeles Times*, July 19, 2017. https://www.latimes.com/politics/washington/la-na-essential-washington-updates-trump-attacks-attorney-general-sessions-1500514853-htmlstory.html

Binder, Sarah, and Mark Spindel. "This is why Trump's legislative agenda is stuck in neutral." *Washington Post*, April 26, 2017. https://www.washingtonpost.com/news/monkey-cage/wp/2017/04/26/this-is-why-trumps-legislative-agenda-is-stuck-in-neutral/?utm_term=.f50f174ca7c9

Blade, Rachael. "Trump's takeover of GOP forces many House Republicans to head for the exits." *Washington Post*, September 22, 2019. https://www.washingtonpost.com/politics/trumps-takeover-of-gop-forces-many-house-republicans-to-head-for-the-exits/2019/09/22/d89f99fc-d4bd-11e9-ab26-e6dbebac45d3_story.html

Blay, Zeba. "This MLK quote sums up the rise of white supremacy post-Trump." *Huffington Post*, January 15, 2017. https://www.huffingtonpost.com/entry/this-mlk-quote-sums-up-the-rise-of-white-supremacy-post-trump_us_5875426de4b099cdb1000431

Blumenthal, Sidney. "Election '88 and the Wall Street bypass." *Washington Post*, April 21, 1988, p. C1.

Borchers, Callum. "Bernie Sanders tells supporters to knock off the violence." *Washington Post*, June 5, 2016. https://www.washingtonpost.com/news/post-politics/wp/2016/06/05/bernie-sanders-tells-supporters-to-knock-off-the-violence/

Bouie, Jamelle. "Trump can't score a win." *Slate*, September 5, 2017. https://slate.com/news-and-politics/2017/09/trump-cant-score-any-legislative-accomplishments-even-with-a-gop-led-congress.html

Bowden, John. "Cohen files lawsuit against Trump Organization." *The Hill*, March 7, 2019. https://thehill.com/policy/national-security/433060-cohen-files-lawsuit-against-trump-organization

Bowles, Nellie. "Silicon Valley now has its own populist pundit." *New York Times*, August 12, 2017. https://www.nytimes.com/2017/08/12/style/steve-hilton-fox-news-silicon-valley-populist-pundit.html

Boyer, Dave. "Donald Trump to visit home of hero Andrew Jackson." *Washington Times*, March 15, 2017.

Bradner, Eric. "Trump stumbles on David Duke, KKK." *CNN Politics*, February 29, 2016. https://www.cnn.com/2016/02/28/politics/donald-trump-white-supremacists/index.html

Brands, H. W. "How Trump has proved the Founding Fathers right." *Politico*, March 31, 2016. https://www.politico.com/magazine/story/2016/03/trump-founding-fathers-electoral-college-213777

Brant, Danielle. "Bolsonaro uses same fascist tactics as Trump, says Yale professor." *Folha de S. Paulo* (English version), October 4, 2018. https://www1.folha.uol.com.br/internacional/en/world/2018/10/bolsonaro-uses-same-fascist-tactics-as-trump-says-yale-professor.shtml

Brigham, Bob. "Beto O'Rourke calls Trump a white supremacist: 'He poses a mortal threat to people of color'." *Salon*, September 13, 2019. https://www.salon.com/2019/09/13/beto-orourke-calls-trump-as-a-white-supremacist-he-poses-a-mortal-threat-to-people-of-color_partner/

Brookhiser, Richard. "Whigged out." *American History*, September 2016. https://www.historynet.com/deja-vu-whigged-out.htm

Brown, DeNeen L., and Cleve R. Wootson, Jr., "Trump ignores backlash, visits Mississippi Civil Rights Museum and praises civil rights leaders." *Washington Post*, December 9, 2017. https://www.washingtonpost.com/news/post-politics/wp/2017/12/09/amid-backlash-trump-set-to-attend-private-gathering-as-civil-rights-museum-opens-in-mississippi/

Brownstein, Ronald. "Trump may be finished—but Trumpism is just getting started." *The Atlantic*, October 13, 2016. https://www.the-atlantic.com/politics/archive/2016/10/trump-legacy-gop/503813/

Bryant, Nick. "How will history judge President Trump?" *BBC News*, January 17, 2019. https://www.bbc.com/news/world-us-canada-46895634

Bseiso, Faris. "Yang says 'no choice' but to call Trump a white supremacist." *CNN*, August 9, 2019. https://www.cnn.com/2019/08/09/politics/yang-trump-white-supremacist/index.html

Bump, Philip. "A complete timeline of the events behind the memo that threatens to rip D.C. in two." *Washington Post*, February 2, 2018. https://www.washingtonpost.com/news/politics/wp/2018/01/30/a-complete-timeline-of-the-events-behind-the-memo-that-threatens-to-rip-d-c-in-two/?noredirect=on&utm_term=.2878d49a9a25

Bump, Philip. "Why did Trump lose the popular vote? Because he didn't care about it. And because they cheated." *Washington Post*, January 26, 2017. https://www.washingtonpost.com/news/politics/wp/2017/01/26/why-did-trump-lose-the-popular-vote-because-he-didnt-care-about-it-and-because-they-cheated/?noredirect=on&utm_term=.6353f3f54e11

Burke, Melissa Nann, and Chad Livengood. "Huizenga's west Michigan efforts boosted Trump." *Detroit News*, November 13, 2016. https://www.detroitnews.com/story/news/politics/2016/11/12/rep-huizengas-west-michigan-efforts-boosted-trump/93753514/

Burke, Melissa Nann. "'Something is not right here': Michigan pols react to Trump remarks on Russia, 2016 election." *Detroit News*, July 17, 2018. https://www.detroitnews.com/story/news/local/michigan/2018/07/16/trump-putin-election-michigan-reaction/789315002/

Burke, Richard L. "The 1992 campaign: The overview; Perot says he quit in July to thwart G.O.P. 'dirty tricks'." *New York Times*, October 26, 1992. https://www.nytimes.com/1992/10/26/us/1992-campaign-overview-perot-says-he-quit-july-thwart-gop-dirty-tricks.html

Burnett, Erin, Erica Orden, Gloria Borger and Caroline Kelly. "Federal prosecutors subpoena Trump inaugural committee." *CNN*, February 5, 2019. https://www.cnn.com/2019/02/04/politics/sdny-subpoena-trump-inauguration-committee/index.html

Buskirk, Christopher. "While Trump's critics keep talking, our president is fulfilling his promises." *USA Today*, January 18, 2018. https://www.usatoday.com/story/opinion/2018/01/18/while-trumps-critics-keep-talking-our-president-fulfilling-his-promises-christopher-buskirk-column/1041117001/

Butterfield, Fox. "New Hampshire speech earns praise for Trump." *New York Times*, October 23, 1987, p. B3.

Butterfield, Fox. "Trump hints at dreams beyond building." *New York Times*, October 5, 1987, p. B1.

Butterfield, Fox. "Trump turns down Democrats' dinner." *New York Times*, November 24, 1987, p. A18.

Byers, Dylan, and Jeremy Diamond, "Donald Trump's 'sleaze' attack on reporter hits new level of media animosity." *CNN*, May 31, 2016. https://money.cnn.com/2016/05/31/media/donald-trump-reporter-sleaze/index.html

Cannon, Carl M. "Machine politics." *Forbes*, July 2, 1997. https://www.forbes.com/1997/07/02/voting.html#3746835dab69

Carney, Jordain. "Bernie Sanders to fight for campaign finance reform." *The Hill*, August 4, 2015. https://thehill.com/blogs/ballot-box/presidential-races/250187-sanders-campaign-finance-system-amounts-to-legalized

Carter, Dan T. "What Donald Trump owes George Wallace." *New York Times*, January 10, 2016, p. SR6.

Carter, Dan T. "What Donald Trump owes George Wallace." *New York Times*, January 8, 2016. https://www.nytimes.com/2016/01/10/opinion/campaign-stops/what-donald-trump-owes-george-wallace.html

Casselman, Ben, and Jim Tankersley. "Faster tax cuts could be backfiring on Republicans." *New York Times*, March 21, 2019. https://

www.nytimes.com/2019/03/21/business/economy/tax-refund-republicans.html

Cassidy, John. "The problem with the 'Never Trump' movement." *The New Yorker*, March 3, 2016. https://www.newyorker.com/news/john-cassidy/the-problem-with-the-never-trump-movement

Chapman, Steve. "Ross Perot paved the way for Donald Trump." *Chicago Tribune*, July 9, 2019. https://www.chicagotribune.com/columns/steve-chapman/ct-column-ross-perot-trump-chapman-20190709-4ihr3754xrghfohle5jmg7zvsi-story.html

Charen, Mona. "Ross Perot's lessons for today." *RealClearPolitics*, September 2, 2016. https://www.realclearpolitics.com/articles/2016/09/02/ross_perots_lessons_for_today_131686.html

Chavez, Paola, Veronica Stracqualursi, and Meghan Keneally. "A history of the Donald Trump-Megyn Kelly feud." *ABC News*, October 26, 2016. https://abcnews.go.com/Politics/history-donald-trump-megyn-kelly-feud/story?id=36526503

Cheney, Kyle. "No, Clinton didn't start the birther thing. This guy did." *Politico*, September 16, 2016. https://www.politico.com/story/2016/09/birther-movement-founder-trump-clinton-228304

Cheney, Kyle. "Trump blames Sanders for chaos at his rallies." *Politico*, March 12, 2016. https://www.politico.com/story/2016/03/donald-trump-blames-bernie-sanders-rally-protests-220671

Chicago Tribune. "Hillary Clinton promises steady hand in dangerous world." July 28, 2016. https://www.chicagotribune.com/news/nationworld/ct-democratic-national-convention-hillary-clinton-20160728-story.html

Chicago Tribune. "Perot has charged plotting before; proof lacking." October 26, 1992. http://www.chicagotribune.com/news/ct-xpm-1992-10-26-9204070126-story.html

Chicago Tribune. "Trump says blacks who stayed home were 'almost as good' as those who voted for him." December 9, 2016. https://www.chicagotribune.com/news/nationworld/politics/ct-trump-rallies-louisiana-michigan-20161209-story.html

Chumley, Cheryl K. "Donald Trump: 'Drain the swamp!' And he is." *Washington Times*, May 21, 2018. https://www.washingtontimes.com/news/2018/may/21/donald-trump-drain-swamp-and-he/?utm_source=GOOGLE&utm_medium=cpc&utm_id=chacka&utm_campaign=TWT+-+DSA&gclid=EAIaIQobChMI5rWovseJ4gIV2UsNCh21qQ-vEAMYASAAEgK7B_D_BwE

Cillizza, Chris. "The 13 most amazing findings in the 2016 exit poll." *Washington Post*, November 10, 2016. https://www.washingtonpost

.com/news/the-fix/wp/2016/11/10/the-13-most-amazing-things-in-the-2016-exit-poll/?utm_term=.82f37b291451

Cillizza, Chris. "20,000 people came to see Bernie Sanders in Boston. Why aren't we talking more about it?: #FeeltheBern." *Washington Post Blogs*, October 5, 2015.

Cillizza, Chris. "Donald Trump isn't the next Barry Goldwater. It'd be easier for Republicans if he was." *Washington Post,* May 19, 2016. https://www.washingtonpost.com/news/the-fix/wp/2016/05/09/donald-trump-isnt-the-next-barry-goldwater-itd-be-easier-for-republicans-if-he-was/?utm_term=.5ad1317189ec.

Cillizza, Chris. "Trump regrets nothing." *CNN*, October 22, 2018. https://www.cnn.com/2018/10/22/politics/trump-regrets-nothing/index.html

Clark, Tez. "What Donald Trump really means when he hates on Japan." *Vox*, June 23, 2015. https://www.vox.com/2015/6/23/8826245/donald-trump-japan-peril

Clines, Francis X. "Bernie Sanders comes clean." *New York Times Online*, May 26, 2015.

CNN. "Trump makes Pocahontas crack at Navajo code talkers event." November 17, 2017. https://www.youtube.com/watch?v=YAP9vWl0mAk

Cohen, Marshall, Annie Grayer, and Tal Yellin. "In their own words: Nixon on Watergate, Trump on the Russia investigation." *CNN*, March 11, 2019. https://www.cnn.com/interactive/2019/politics/trump-nixon-comparison/index.html

Cohen, Richard. "Duck, Donald!" *Washington Post*, July 22, 1990, p. J7.

Cohen, Richard. "Our next president, the Godfather." *RealClearPolitics*, November 22, 2016. https://www.realclearpolitics.com/articles/2016/11/22/our_next_president_the_godfather_132408.html

Cohn, Nate. "What I got wrong about Donald Trump." *New York Times*, May 5, 2016, A3.

Collins, Eliza. "Trump to Kelly: 'You've been called a lot worse' than bimbo." *USA Today*, May 17, 2016. https://www.usatoday.com/story/news/politics/onpolitics/2016/05/17/trump-kelly-youve-been-called-lot-worse-than-bimbo/84519608/

Collins, Gail. "Reform Party 101." *New York Times*, September 17, 1999, p. A23.

Connor, W. Robert. "A vacuum at the center." *The American Scholar*, Spring 2018.

Conway, Madeline. "Trump: 'Nobody knew that health care could be so complicated.' The president appears to nod to the grim political reality around repealing and replacing Obamacare." *Politico*, February 27, 2017. http://www.politico.com/story/2017/02/trump-nobody-knew-that-health-care-could-be-so-complicated-235436

Coppins, Mckay. "A Faustian bargain pays off for Conservative christians." *The Atlantic*, February 1, 2017. https://www.theatlantic.com/politics/archive/2017/02/conservatives-react-to-trump-scotus-pick/515265/

Corasaniti, Nick. "Partisan crowds at Trump rallies menace and frighten news media." *New York Times*, October 15, 2016.

Cornwell, Rupert. "Perot's dirty tricks paranoia rekindles doubts." *Ottawa Citizen*, October 27, 1992, p. A3.

Cororoton, Gay. "Manufacturing and housing in the Rust Belt states." *Economists' Outlook Blog*, April 3, 2019. https://economistsoutlook.blogs.realtor.org/2019/04/03/manufacturing-and-housing-in-the-rust-belt-states/

Crippes, Cristinia, "'Never Trump' movement concerns Blum." *The Gazette* (Cedar Rapids, IA), May 6, 2016. https://www.thegazette.com/subject/news/government/elections/never-trump-movement-concerns-blum-20160506

Cummings, William. "Andrew Gillum says Ron DeSantis 'monkey' comment is straight out of Trump handbook." *USA Today*, August 29, 2018. https://www.usatoday.com/story/news/politics/onpolitics/2018/08/29/andrew-gillum-ron-desantis-monkey-comment-out-trump-playbook/1139968002/

Cummings, William. "Conspiracy theories: Here's what drives people to them, no matter how wacky." *USA Today*, December 23, 2017. https://www.usatoday.com/story/news/nation/2017/12/23/conspiracy-theory-psychology/815121001/

Daily Beast. "Hannity encourages Trump's JFK–Cruz theory." https://www.thedailybeast.com/hannity-encourages-trumps-jfk-cruz-theory

Dallek, Matthew. "The Conservative 1960s." *The Atlantic*, December 1995. https://www.theatlantic.com/magazine/archive/1995/12/the-conservative-1960s/376506/

Davies, Phil. "The 'Monster' of Chesnut Street." *The Region*, September 2008, p. 45. http://www.minneapolisfed.org/publications_papers/pub_display.cfm?id=4046

Davis, Janet, H. R. Schiffman, and Suzanne Greist-Bousquet. "Semantic context and figure-ground organization." *Psychological Research* 52, no. 4 (1990): 306–9.

Davis, Julie Hirschfeld. "Trump laces into McCain over his opposition to health care bill." *New York Times*, September 23, 2017. https://

www.nytimes.com/2017/09/23/us/politics/trump-mccain-graham-cassidy-health-care-obamacare.html

Davis, Julie Hirschfeld. "Trump signs memo ordering end to 'catch and release' immigration policy." *New York Times (Online)*, April 6, 2018.

Davis, William P. "'Enemy of the People': Trump breaks out this phrase during moments of peak criticism." *New York Times*, July 19, 2018. https://www.nytimes.com/2018/07/19/business/media/trump-media-enemy-of-the-people.html

Dean, John W. "Active-negative Trump is doomed to follow Nixon." *Newsweek*, May 29, 2017. http://www.newsweek.com/activenegative-trump-doomed-follow-nixon-616641

Dean, John W. "Don't compare Trump's presidential campaign to Barry Goldwater's." *Verdict*, May 27, 2016. https://verdict.justia.com/2016/05/27/dont-compare-trumps-presidential-campaign-barry-goldwaters

Decker, Cathleen. "Trump's war against elites and expertise." *Los Angeles Times*, July 27, 2017. https://www.latimes.com/politics/la-na-pol-trump-elites-20170725-story.html

Denning, Steve. "How Trump's economic chickens are coming home to roost." *Forbes*, February 13, 2019. https://www.forbes.com/sites/stevedenning/2019/02/13/how-trumps-economic-chickens-are-finally-coming-home-to-roost/#234157be2713

Derby, Kevin. "Val Demings: President Trump has encouraged, excused, and alluded to violence repeatedly." *Florida Daily*, October 28, 2018. https://www.floridadaily.com/val-demings-president-trump-has-encouraged-excused-and-alluded-to-violence-repeatedly/

Detrow, Scott. "Democratic candidates say Trump's rhetoric is partially to blame for mass shootings." *NPR*, "All Things Considered," August 7, 2019. https://www.npr.org/2019/08/07/749164059/democratic-candidates-say-trumps-rhetoric-is-partially-to-blame-for-mass-shootin

Deseret News (Salt Lake City). "Goldwater calls opposition to gays in military 'dumb'," August 22, 1993. https://www.deseretnews.com/article/306128/GOLDWATER-CALLS-OPPOSITION-TO-GAYS-IN-MILITARY-DUMB.html

Desrochers, Daniel. "With Trump victory looming, WV Republicans consider options." *Charleston Gazette-Mail*, May 4, 2016. https://www.wvgazettemail.com/news/politics/with-trump-victory-looming-wv-republicans-consider-options/article_965d0fae-a178-56e3-95a8-a80da498486e.html

Devroy, Ann. "Perot investigations not very 'American,' Bush says." *Washington Post*, June 23, 1991, p. A12.

Dionne, E. J. "Bernie Sanders: The new St. Nick: His sack of proposals could reframe the popular debate." *Washington Post*, May 15, 2015.

Doherty, Brendan J. "Trump isn't really campaigning earlier than other recent presidents. He's just more upfront about it. Here's what the data on presidential travel show us." *Washington Post Blogs*, February 21, 2017.

Dorrell, Oren. "Nearly 1,000 State Department staffers condemn Trump's travel ban." *USA* Today, January 31, 2017. https://www.usatoday.com/story/news/world/2017/01/31/nearly-1000-state-department-staffers-condem-trumps-travel-ban/97306024/

Dowd, Maureen. "Trump l'oeil tease." *New York Times*, September 19, 1999, p. WK17.

Drezner, Daniel W. "How good is Nancy Pelosi's threat assessment?" *Washington Post*, May 6, 2019. https://www.washingtonpost.com/pb/outlook/2019/05/06/how-good-is-nancy-pelosis-threat-assessment/?nid=menu_nav_accessibilityforscreenreader&outputType=accessibility&utm_term=.aa322bcc28b4

Drucker, David M. "Brooks chides Trump for endorsing Luther Strange." *Washington Examiner*, August 19, 2017. https://www.washingtonexaminer.com/mo-brooks-chides-trump-for-endorsing-luther-strange

Duffy, B. "Perot points the finger at the CIA." *Sunday Herald Sun* (Melbourne, Australia), May 31, 1992.

Economist. "America first and last; Donald Trump's foreign policy." February 4, 2017, p. 17.

Economist. "The big switchover: William Jennings Trump and the monetary elite." February 27, 2017.

Eichel, Larry. "'Draft Trump' committee in N.H. gets visit from the non-candidate." *Philadelphia Inquirer*, October 23, 1987, p. A3.

Eilperin, Juliet. "Trump imposes immediate federal hiring freeze." *Washington Post*, January 24, 2017, p. A6.

Elliott, Philip. "Martha McSally, who learned to love Donald Trump, wins Arizona primary." *Time*, August 29, 2018. http://time.com/5381225/martha-mcsally-arizona-donald-trump/

Elliott, Stuart. "Trump targets: All comers." *USA Today*, May 24, 1989, p. 2B.

Ellis, Joseph J. "Historian: What would Founding Fathers think of Donald Trump?" *CNN*, May 5, 2016. https://www.cnn.com/2016/05/04/opinions/what-would-founding-fathers-think-of-trump-ellis/index.html

Elshtain, Jean Bethke. "A parody of true democracy." *Christian Science Monitor*, August 13, 1992. https://www.csmonitor.com/1992/0813/13181.html

Enjeti, Sagaar. "Flashback: All the times past presidents promised to move US Embassy to Jerusalem." *Daily Caller*, December 6, 2017. https://dailycaller.com/2017/12/06/flashback-all-the-times-past-presidents-promised-to-move-us-embassy-to-jerusalem/

Enten, Henry. "Why Donald Trump isn't a real candidate, in one chart." *FiveThirtyEight*, June 16, 2015. https://fivethirtyeight.com/features/why-donald-trump-isnt-a-real-candidate-in-one-chart/

Faulconbridge, Guy, and Kylie MacLellan. "'I'll make Britain great again, PM Johnson says, echoing Trump." *Reuters*, July 25, 2019. https://www.reuters.com/article/us-britain-eu/ill-make-britain-great-again-pm-johnson-says-echoing-trump-idUSKCN1UK0OG

Farber, M. A., with Diana B. Henriques. "Backstage at the 'Trump-bashing': Despite problems, Donald Trump is as irrepressible as always." *New York Times*, June 10, 1990, p. F6.

Feldman, Linda. "Disrupter in chief: How Donald Trump is changing the presidency." *Christian Science Monitor*, January 4, 2018. https://www.csmonitor.com/USA/Politics/2018/0104/Disrupter-in-chief-How-Donald-Trump-is-changing-the-presidency

Feller, Daniel. "King Andrew and the Bank." *Humanities*, January/February 2008. https://www.neh.gov/humanities/2008/januaryfebruary/feature/king-andrew-and-the-bank

Feigenbaum, Harvey. "Macron the populist." *Social Europe*, February 5, 2019. https://www.socialeurope.eu/macron-the-populist

Ferguson, Joe. "McSally opens up on her relationship with Trump in new interview." *Arizona Daily Star*, June 1, 2018. https://tucson.com/news/local/mcsally-opens-up-on-her-relationship-with-trump-in-new/article_5e071168-65ef-11e8-8d43-1f72f837631a.html

Ferris, Sarah, and Heather Caygle. "Pelosi says Trump engaged in 'cover-up' to hide Ukraine call records." *Politico*, September 26, 2019. https://www.politico.com/story/2019/09/26/pelosi-trump-cover-up-ukraine-call-1514541

Finnegan, Michael. "All the campaign is a stage for Donald Trump." *Los Angeles Times*, January 29, 2016. https://www.latimes.com/nation/politics/la-na-trump-entertainer-20160129-story.html

Forbes. "The definitive net worth of Donald Trump." https://www.forbes.com/donald-trump/#721d32028992

Forster, Katie. "Donald Trump's false claim about illegal votes based on unverified tweet posted on conspiracy website." *The Independent*

(UK), November 28, 2016. https://www.independent.co.uk/news/world/americas/donald-trump-millions-illegal-aliens-voted-greg-phillips-three-million-tweet-infowars-alex-jones-a7443006.html

Fox News, "Read: White House Counsel Emmett Flood's letter to Attorney General Barr on Mueller report." May 3, 2019. https://www.foxnews.com/politics/read-white-house-counsel-emmett-floods-letter-to-attorney-general-barr-on-mueller-report

France, Lisa Respers. "David Letterman wants to put Donald Trump in a home." *CNN*, July 12, 2017. https://www.cnn.com/2017/07/12/entertainment/david-letterman-donald-trump/index.html

Fredericks, Bob. "Trump on Ukraine scandal: 'It's another witch hunt'." *New York Post*, September 26, 2019. https://nypost.com/2019/09/26/trump-on-ukraine-scandal-its-another-witch-hunt/

Friedersdorf, Connie. "When Donald Trump became a celebrity." *The Atlantic*, January 6, 2016. https://www.theatlantic.com/politics/archive/2016/01/the-decade-when-donald-trump-became-a-celebrity/422838/

Gallas, Daniel. "Dilma Rousseff impeachment: How did it go wrong for her?" *BBC News*, May 12, 2016. https://www.bbc.com/news/world-latin-america-36028247

Galston, William A. "Impeachment is not a high priority for voters, recent polls show." *Brookings*, Thursday, January 3, 2019. https://www.brookings.edu/blog/fixgov/2019/01/03/impeachment-is-not-a-high-priority-for-voters-recent-polls-show/

Gambino, Lauren, and Stephanie Kirschgaessner. "Mueller subpoenas Trump Organization for documents related to Russia report." *The Guardian*, March 15, 2018. https://www.theguardian.com/us-news/2018/mar/15/robert-mueller-trump-organization-russia-documents

Garber, Megan. "Mika Brzezinski and Donald Trump's penchant for blood feuds." *The Atlantic*, June 29, 2017. https://www.theatlantic.com/entertainment/archive/2017/06/mika-brzezinski-and-donald-trumps-penchant-for-blood-feuds/532185/

Garber, Megan. "What we talk about when we talk about 'demagogues'." *The Atlantic*, December 10, 2015. https://www.theatlantic.com/entertainment/archive/2015/12/what-we-talk-about-when-we-talk-about-demagogues/419514/

Garber, Scott. "It's not just a Trump problem—we all have to take responsibility for Twitter." *Vox*, November 8, 2017. https://www.vox.com/2017/11/8/16619178/trump-twitter-tweet-civil-public-discourse-democracy-social-media-responsibility-russia

Gass, Nick. "Trump: Ramos was 'like a madman'." *Politico*, August 26, 2015. https://www.politico.com/story/2015/08/donald-trump-jorge-ramos-like-madman-121755

Geraghty, Jim. "Hillary Clinton's bad habit of questioning election results has spread to all Democrats." *National Review*, May 6, 2019.

Gerson, Michael. "Barry Goldwater's warning to the GOP." *Washington Post*, April 14, 2017. https://www.washingtonpost.com/opinions/michael-gerson-barry-goldwaters-warning-to-the-gop/2014/04/17/9e8993ec-c651-11e3-bf7a-be01a9b69cf1_story.html?utm_term=.bd537957feca

Gerstein, Josh. "Congressional Democrats notch win in emoluments suit against Trump." *Politico*, April 30, 2019. https://www.politico.com/story/2019/04/30/trump-emoluments-congressional-democrats-1295270

Gerstein, Josh, and Ted Hesson. "Supreme Court upholds Trump's travel ban." *Politico*, June 26, 2018. https://www.politico.com/story/2018/06/26/supreme-court-upholds-trumps-travel-ban-673181

Gillespie, Patrick. "Trump praises Reagan on trade—but saw it differently in 1989." *CNN Business*, October 19, 2016. https://money.cnn.com/2016/10/19/news/economy/trump-reagan-japan-trade-1989/index.html

Gitlin, Todd. "The Bernie Sanders moment." *New York Times*, July 12, 2015, p. SR3.

Givhan, Robert. "On a different plane." *Washington Post*, December 23, 1999, p. C1.

Glionna, John M. "Couple urge boycott of goods made in Japan." *Los Angeles Times*, November 28, 1989, p. 1.

Goldberg, Jonah. "Can President Trump pardon himself? It's complicated." *Los Angeles Times*, June 5, 2018. http://www.latimes.com/opinion/op-ed/la-oe-goldberg-trump-pardon-20180605-story.html

Goldmacher, Shane. "Trump Foundation will dissolve, accused of 'shocking pattern of illegality'." *New York Times*, December 18, 2018. https://www.nytimes.com/2018/12/18/nyregion/ny-ag-underwood-trump-foundation.html

Goldman, Henry. "New York Tax Department probes Trump taxes from decades ago." *Bloomberg*, October 2, 2018. https://www.bloomberg.com/news/articles/2018-10-02/new-york-s-tax-department-probes-trump-taxes-from-decades-ago

Goldsmith, Jack. "The cost of Trump's attacks on the FBI." *The Atlantic*, December 4, 2017. https://www.theatlantic.com/politics/

archive/2017/12/the-high-price-of-sessionss-failure-to-defend-the-justice-department/547382/

Goldstein, Ian. "Five of David Letterman's best late night Donald Trump takedowns." *Vulture*, March 28, 2017. http://www.vulture.com/2017/03/five-of-david-lettermans-best-late-night-donald-trump-takedowns.html

Golick, Keith Biery, and Cameron Knight. "Dayton shooting: What we know about Connor Betts' politics." *Cincinnati Enquirer*, August 7, 2019. https://www.cincinnati.com/story/news/2019/08/07/dayton-shooting-what-do-we-know-connor-betts-politics/1942122001/

Goodykoontz, Bill. "Donald Trump vs. CNN . . . again. Now on a world stage and with a hint of totalitarianism." *USA Today*, July 15, 2018. https://www.usatoday.com/story/opinion/nation-now/2018/07/15/white-house-cancels-john-bolton-interview-cnn-president-trump-column/786369002/

Gover, Kevin. "American Indians serve in the U.S. military in greater numbers than any ethnic group and have since the Revolution." *Huffington Post*, May 22, 2015. https://www.huffingtonpost.com/national-museum-of-the-american-indian/american-indians-serve-in-the-us-military_b_7417854.html

Graham, David A. "The paradox of Trump's populism." *The Atlantic*, June 29, 2018. https://www.theatlantic.com/politics/archive/2018/06/the-paradox-of-trumps-populism/564116/

Gray, Rosie. "Trump defends white-nationalist protesters: 'Some very fine people on both sides'." *The Atlantic*, August 14, 2017. https://www.theatlantic.com/politics/archive/2017/08/trump-defends-white-nationalist-protesters-some-very-fine-people-on-both-sides/537012/

Greenberg, David, and Rebecca Lubot. "Stop talking about the 25th Amendment. It won't work on Trump." *Politico*, September 8, 2018. https://www.politico.com/magazine/story/2018/09/08/trump-25th-amendment-constitutional-crisis-219739

Greenberg, David. "When impeachment works, and when it doesn't." *Politico*, January 20, 2019. https://www.politico.com/magazine/story/2019/01/20/impeachment-history-president-trump-223976

Greenway, Norma. "Perot's conspiracy allegations just raving of paranoid, Bush camp says." *Montreal Gazette*, October 27, 1992, p. A15.

Greenwood, Max. "Gillum to face tougher road in Florida after primary stunner." *The Hill*, August 29, 2018. http://thehill.com/homenews/campaign/404269-gillum-to-face-tougher-road-in-florida-after-primary-stunner

Greenwood, Max. "Trump inaccurately claims size of rally day before election was 32,000 instead of 4,200." *The Hill*, April 28, 2018. https://thehill.com/homenews/administration/385365-trump-inaccurately-claims-size-of-rally-before-election-was-32000.

Grier, Peter. "The (semi) secret history of Trump's Andrew Jackson portrait." *Christian Science Monitor*, February 9, 2017.

Grove, Lloyd. "Goldwater's left turn." *Washington Post*, July 24, 1994. https://www.washingtonpost.com/wp-srv/politics/daily/may98/goldwater072894.htm

Grynbaum, Michael M., and Emily Baumgaertner. "CNN's Jim Acosta returns to the White House after judge's ruling." *New York Times*, November 16, 2018. https://www.nytimes.com/2018/11/16/business/media/cnn-acosta-trump.html

Gurman, Sadie, and Aruna Viswanatha. "Trump's Attorney General pick criticized an aspect of Mueller Probe in memo to Justice Department." *Wall Street Journal*, December 19, 2018. https://www.wsj.com/articles/trumps-attorney-general-pick-criticized-an-aspect-of-mueller-probe-in-memo-to-justice-department-11545275973

Haberman, Maggie, and Alan Rappeport, "Trump drops false 'birther' claim but offers new one: Clinton started it." *New York Times*, September 17, 2016, p. A10.

Haberman, Maggie, and Alexander Burns. "Trump 2016 bid began in effort to gain stature." *New York Times*, March 13, 2016, p. A1.

Hafner, Josh. "After insulting tweet, Cruz tells Trump: Leave my wife 'the hell alone'." *USA Today*, March 25, 2016. https://www.usatoday.com/story/news/politics/onpolitics/2016/03/24/donald-trump-posted-photo-ted-heidi-cruz/82210692/

Hagle, Courtney. "How Fox News pushed the white supremacist 'great replacement' theory." *MediaMatters*, August 5, 2019. https://www.mediamatters.org/tucker-carlson/how-fox-news-pushed-white-supremacist-great-replacement-theory

Hains, Tim. "Blumenthal: 'There are indictments in this president's future,' when he leaves office or before." *RealClearPolitics*, March 21, 2019. https://www.realclearpolitics.com/video/2019/03/21/sen_richard_blumenthal_there_are_indictments_in_this_presidents_future.html

Hains, Tim. "Nunes: Whistleblower complaint has 'hallmarks of the Russia hoax'; Ukraine scandal likely end of Biden's campaign." *RealClearPolitics*, September 22, 2019. https://www.realclearpolitics.com/video/2019/09/22/nunes_whistleblower_complaint_looks_like_russia_hoax_ukraine_scandal_likely_end_of_bidens_campaign.html

Halpern, Sue. "How he used Facebook to win." *New York Review of Books*, June 8, 2017. http://www.nybooks.com/articles/2017/06/08/how-trump-used-facebook-to-win/

Haltiwanger, John, and Sonam Sheth. "Trump is facing impeachment over a whistleblower complaint and a phone call with Ukraine's president. Here's what we know." *Business Insider*, September 26, 2019. https://www.businessinsider.com/mysterious-trump-spy-whistleblower-controversy-explained-2019-9

Hampson, Rick. "Fox anchor Megyn Kelly describes scary, bullying 'Year of Trump'." *USA Today*, November 15, 2016. https://www.usatoday.com/story/news/politics/elections/2016/11/15/megyn-kelly-memoir-donald-trump-roger-ailes-president-fox-news/93813154/

Hanchett, Ian. "DeSantis: Gillum 'wants to make Florida Venezuela'." *Breitbart*, August 28, 2018. https://www.breitbart.com/video/2018/08/28/desantis-gillum-wants-to-make-florida-venezuela/

Hang, John. "A fourth ICE facility has been attacked: The dangerous consequences of political pandering." *American Spectator*, August 15, 2019. https://spectator.org/a-fourth-ice-facility-has-been-attacked/

Hankla, Charles. "Trump could be using advanced game theory negotiating techniques—or he's hopelessly adrift." *The Conversation*, June 8, 2018. http://theconversation.com/trump-could-be-using-advanced-game-theory-negotiating-techniques-or-hes-hopelessly-adrift-97836

Hanson, Victor Davis. "The origins of our Second Civil War." *National Review*, July 31, 2018. https://www.nationalreview.com/2018/07/origins-of-second-civil-war-globalism-tech-boom-immigration-campus-radicalism/

Harper, Jennifer. "'Classy': Donald Trump to embark on a thank you tour of the heartland." *Washington Times*, November 29, 2016. https://www.washingtontimes.com/news/2016/nov/29/donald-trump-to-embark-on-thank-you-tour-2016/

Harris, John F. "Ross Perot—the father of Trump." *Politico*, July 9, 2019. https://www.politico.com/story/2019/07/09/ross-perot-the-father-of-trump-1404720

Haslam, Nick. "The psychology of insults." *The Conversation*, January 23, 2017. http://theconversation.com/the-psychology-of-insults-71738

Health, Brad, William Cummings, and Kevin McCoy, "Michael Cohen said he paid hush money at 'direction' of Trump." *USA Today*, August 21, 2018. https://www.usatoday.com/story/news/politics/2018/08/21/michael-cohen-former-trump-lawyer-feds-reach-plea-deal/1053562002/

Healy, Patrick, and Amy Chozick. "In Democratic debate, Clinton and Sanders spar over judgment." *New York Times*, April 14,

2016. https://www.nytimes.com/2016/04/15/us/politics/democratic-debate.html;

Heineman, Ben W., Jr. "Goldwater: The record." *Harvard Crimson*, October 9, 1963. https://www.thecrimson.com/article/1963/10/9/goldwater-the-record-pbarry-goldwater-is/

Helmore, Edward. "Green Party candidate Jill Stein calls for climate state of emergency." *The Guardian*, August 20, 2016. https://www.theguardian.com/us-news/2016/aug/20/jill-stein-green-party-climate-state-of-emergency

Helmore, Edward. "How Trump's political playbook evolved since he first ran for president in 2000." *The Guardian*, February 5, 2017. https://www.theguardian.com/us-news/2017/feb/05/donald-trump-reform-party-2000-president

Hemmer, Nicole. "How the right became addicted to conspiracies." *Washington Post Blogs*, July 18, 2018.

Hewitt, Elizabeth, and Anne Galloway, "For a second year, Sanders earns more than $1M." *VTDigger*, June 22, 2018. https://vtdigger.org/2018/06/22/second-year-sanders-earns-1m/

Hill, Harlan. "Don't forget all the Democrats and media who accused Trump of 'treason'." *Daily Caller*, March 29, 2019. https://dailycaller.com/2019/03/29/hill-democrats-media/

Hindustan Times, "Twitter's having a blast comparing Donald Trump to Fredo Corleone, the most dim-witted member of Godfather family." February 14, 2019. https://www.hindustantimes.com/hollywood/twitter-s-having-a-blast-comparing-donald-trump-to-fredo-corleone-the-most-dim-witted-member-of-godfather-family/story-fvl9iXBasqk-0pL64YxRkPN.html

Hoffer, Richard. "USFL awarded only $3 in antitrust decision: Jury finds NFL guilty on one of nine counts." *Los Angeles Times*, July 30, 1986. http://articles.latimes.com/1986-07-30/sports/sp-18643_1_jury-finds-nfl-guilty/2

Hofstadter, Richard. "A long view: Goldwater in history." *New York Review of Books*, October 8, 1964. https://www.nybooks.com/articles/1964/10/08/a-long-view-goldwater-in-history/

Holley, Peter. "KKK's official newspaper supports Donald Trump for president." *Washington Post*, November 2, 2016. https://www.washingtonpost.com/news/post-politics/wp/2016/11/01/the-kkks-official-newspaper-has-endorsed-donald-trump-for-president/?utm_term=.3a55ea1a6e18

Horowitz, Jason. "Over decades, Sanders has stayed on message." *New York Times*, March 26, 2016, p. A11.

Horowitz, Jason. "With palpable sense of conviction, Sanders presses economic message. *New York Times*, October 11, 2015, p. A26.

Horton, Scott. "The paranoid style in American politics." *Harper's*, February 28, 2019. https://harpers.org/blog/2007/08/the-paranoid-style-in-american-politics/

Howe, Amy. "Opinion analysis: Divided Court upholds Trump travel ban." *SCOTUSBlog*, June 26, 2018. https://www.scotusblog.com/2018/06/opinion-analysis-divided-court-upholds-trump-travel-ban/

Howell, William G. "Unilateral politics revisited (and revised) under Trump." *Princeton University Press Blog*, February 6, 2017. http://blog.press.princeton.edu/2017/02/06/william-g-howell-unilateral-politics-revisited-and-revised-under-trump/

Hsu, Spencer S. "W. Samuel Patten sentenced to probation after steering Ukrainian money to Trump inaugural." *Washington Post*, April 2, 2019. https://www.washingtonpost.com/local/legal-issues/w-samuel-patten-sentenced-to-probation-after-steering-ukrainian-money-to-trump-ina ugural/2019/04/12/3dbf2692-5cc1-11e9-9625-01d48d50ef75_story. html?utm_term=.238c86f8af14

Hubbuch, Chris. "Donald Trump: 'Temperament is one of my greatest assets'." *LaCrosse Tribune* (Wisconsin), August 16, 2016. https://lacrossetribune.com/community/vernonbroadcaster/news/local/donald-trump-temperament-is-one-of-my-greatest-assets/article_0d8deb40-48b9-5777-bcb2-739036d76fb9.html

Hurley, Lawrence. "U.S. Supreme Court rebuffs bid to block Trump's gun 'bump stock' ban." *Reuters*, March 28, 2019. https://www.reuters.com/article/us-usa-court-guns/u-s-supreme-court-refuses-to-block-trumps-gun-bump-stock-ban-idUSKCN1R9230

Hyland, Véronique. "An ode to Bernie Sanders' rumpled style." *The Cut*, April 15, 2016. https://www.thecut.com/2016/01/bernie-sanders-fashion-style.html

Ignatius, David. "Trump has squandered the opportunity his populist campaign offered." *RealClearPolitics*, January 16, 2019. https://www.realclearpolitics.com/articles/2019/01/16/trump_has_squandered_the_opportunity_his_populist_campaign_offered_139186.html

Ingraham, Christopher. "America's most gerrymandered congressional districts." *Washington Post*, May 15, 2014. https://www.washingtonpost.com/news/wonk/wp/2014/05/15/americas-most-gerrymandered-congressional-districts/?utm_term=.5b58516379af

Isenstadt, Alex. "Trump purges enemy and reshapes party in his own image." *Politico*, October 24, 2017. https://www.politico.com/story/2017/10/24/trump-republicans-corker-flake-purge-244139

Isikoff, Michael. "FBI investigates alleged wiretapping, attempted sale of Perot phone tapes." *Washington Post*, August 14, 1992, p. A20.

Isikoff, Michael. "Perot tells large rally of death threat; 'mafia-like' group backing NAFTA cited." *Washington Post*, November 8, 1993, p. A4.

Jackson, David. "President Trump says hush money does not amount to campaign finance violation." *USA Today*, March 7, 2019. https://www.usatoday.com/story/news/politics/2019/03/07/donald-trump-says-hush-money-doesnt-violate-campaign-finance-law/3089914002/

Jackson, David. "Trump's rhetoric is harsher than previous nominees." *USA Today*, June 23, 2016. https://www.usatoday.com/story/news/politics/elections/2016/06/23/donald-trump-hillary-clinton-rhetoric/86293780/

Jackson, Raynard. "The monsters Washington created." *Charlotte Post* (North Carolina), November 17, 2016, p. 5A.

Jacobs, Ben. "Florida has to redraw congressional districts because, Florida." *Daily Beast*, July 10, 2014. https://www.thedailybeast.com/florida-has-to-redraw-its-congressional-districts-because-florida?ref=scroll

Jacobs, Ben, and Sabrina Siddiqui. "Bernie Sanders to Clinton: people 'are sick of hearing about your damn emails'." *The Guardian*, October 5, 2015. https://www.theguardian.com/us-news/2015/oct/13/bernie-sanders-hillary-clinton-damn-email-server

Jacobson, Louis, and Linda Qiu. "Donald Trump's Pants on Fire claim linking Ted Cruz's father and JFK assassination." *PolitiFact*, May 3, 2016. https://www.politifact.com/truth-o-meter/statements/2016/may/03/donald-trump/donald-trumps-ridiculous-claim-linking-ted-cruzs-f/

Jacobson, Louis, and Sara Waychoff. "PolitiFact: What's up with Donald Trump and Andrew Jackson?" *Tampa Bay Times*, May 3, 2017.

Jaffe, Greg, and Jenna Johnson. "In America, talk turns to something not spoken of for 150 years: Civil war." *Washington Post*, March 2, 2019. https://www.washingtonpost.com/politics/in-america-talk-turns-to-something-unspoken-for-150-years-civil-war/2019/02/28/b3733af8-3ae4-11e9-a2cd-307b06d0257b_story.html

Jagoda, Naomi. "Smaller tax cuts put GOP on defensive." *The Hill*, February 18, 2019. https://thehill.com/policy/finance/430305-smaller-tax-refunds-put-gop-on-defensive

Jenkins, Holman W. "Prove the tweets were racist." *Wall Street Journal*, July 23, 2019. https://www.wsj.com/articles/prove-the-tweets-were-racist-11563923093

Johnson-Freese, Joan, and Elizabeth Frampton. "The dangers of Donald Trump as an active-negative president." *China US Focus*, July 11,

2017. https://chinausfocus.com/foreign-policy/the-dangers-of-donald-trump-as-an-active-negative-president-to-us-china-policy

Johnston, Chris. "'This is McCarthyism': Trump accuses Obama of 'wire-tapping' his office before election." *The Guardian*, March 4, 2017. https://www.theguardian.com/us-news/2017/mar/04/donald-trump-accuses-obama-of-wire-tapping-his-office-before-election

Johnston, Eric. "Echoes of 1980s trade war seen in Trump comments on Japan." *Japan Times*, January 20, 2017. https://www.japantimes.co.jp/news/2017/01/20/national/politics-diplomacy/echoes-1980s-trade-war-seen-trump-comments-japan/#.W8eYxWhKiyI

Jolin, Dan. "Borat review.' *Empire Online*, September 29, 2006. https://www.empireonline.com/movies/borat/review/

Kabaservice, Geoffrey. "Wild populism has a long history in US politics, but Trump is surely unique." *The Guardian*, January 14, 2017. https://www.theguardian.com/commentisfree/2017/jan/15/wild-populism-long-history-us-politics-trump-surely-unique

Kadner, Phil. "Trump's greatest strength: He speaks 'American'." *Chicago Sun-Times*, August 28, 2018. https://chicago.suntimes.com/columnists/trump-speaks-american-greatest-strength/

Kahn, Chris. "Most Republicans believe FBI, Justice Dept. trying to 'delegitimize' Trump: Reuters/Ipsos poll." *Reuters*, February 5, 2018. https://www.reuters.com/article/us-usa-trump-russia-poll/most-republicans-believe-fbi-justice-dept-trying-to-delegitimize-trump-reuters-ipsos-poll-idUSKBN1FP2UH

Kamisar, Ben. "Poll: 88 percent of voters don't want families separated at border." *The Hill*, June 27, 2018. http://thehill.com/homenews/administration/394480-poll-88-percent-of-voters-dont-want-families-separated-at-border

Kaplan, Rebecca. "Obama: I will use my pen and phone to take on Congress." *CBS News*, January 14, 2014. https://www.cbsnews.com/news/obama-i-will-use-my-pen-and-phone-to-take-on-congress/

Karni, Anne. "Clinton aides blame loss on everything but themselves." *Politico*, November 10, 2016. https://www.politico.com/story/2016/11/hillary-clinton-aides-loss-blame-231215

Kawanami, Takeshi. "The 1980s auto trade wars are back." *Nikkei Asian Review*, February 2, 2017. https://asia.nikkei.com/Economy/The-1980s-auto-trade-wars-are-back

Kazin, Michael. "Donald Trump is no William Jennings Bryan." *Politico*, February 27, 2017. https://www.politico.com/magazine/story/2017/02/william-jennings-bryan-steve-bannon-donald-trump-populist-214822

Kazin, Michael. "How can Donald Trump and Bernie Sanders both be populists?" *New York Times Online*, March 22, 2016. http://www .nytimes.com/2016/03/27/magazine/how-can-donald-trump-and-bernie-sanders-both-be-populist.html

Keating, Joshua. "Conspiracy theorists' on-again-off-again relationship with gold." *Foreign Policy*, April 15, 2003. https://foreignpolicy. com/2013/04/15/conspiracy-theorists-on-again-off-again-relation-ship-with-gold/

Keith, Tamara. "Campaign mysteries: Why don't Bernie Sanders' big rallies lead to big wins?" NPR, April 26, 2016. https://www.npr .org/2016/04/26/475681237/campaign-mystery-why-dont-bernie-sanders-big-rallies-lead-to-big-wins

Keith, Tamara. "Trump under oath: Sometimes combative, often boastful, usually lacking details." *NPR*, March 27, 2018. https://www. npr.org/2018/03/27/597015218/trump-under-oath-sometimes-combative-often-boastful-usually-lacking-details

Kelly, Erin. "Bernie Sanders: 'I am running in this election to win'." *USA Today*, April 30, 2015. https://www.usatoday.com/story/news/ politics/elections/2015/04/29/bernie-sanders-interview-democratic-presidential-race/26576639/

Kelly, Michael. "The 1992 campaign: Candidate's record; Perot shows penchant for seeing conspiracy." *New York Times*, October 26, 1992. https://www.nytimes.com/1992/10/26/us/the-1992-campaign-candidate-s-record-perot-shows-penchant-for-seeing-conspiracy. html

Keneally, Meaghan. "Timeline leading up to Jeff Sessions' recusal and the fallout." *ABC News*, July 26, 2017. https://abcnews.go.com/Politics/ timeline-leading-jeff-sessions-recusal-fallout/story?id=45855918

Keneally, Meaghan. "A look back at Trump comments perceived by some as encouraging violence." *ABC News*, October 19, 2018. https://abcnews.go.com/Politics/back-trump-comments-perceived-encouraging-violence/story?id=48415766

Kessler, Glenn, Salvador Rizzo, and Meg Kelly. "President Trump has made 12,019 false or misleading claims over 928 days." *Washington Post*, August 12, 2019. https://www.washingtonpost.com/ politics/2019/08/12/president-trump-has-made-false-or-misleading-claims-over-days/

Kibasi, Tom. "Nigel Farage's victory gives him the whip hand over British politics." *The Guardian*, May 27, 2019. https://www .theguardian.com/commentisfree/2019/may/27/nigel-farage-brexit-party-elections

Kilgore, Ed. "The spirit of Goldwaterism." *Washington Monthly*, April 18, 2014. https://washingtonmonthly.com/2014/04/18/the-spirit-of-goldwaterism/

Kilgore, Ed. "Trump and the George Wallace tradition of foreign policy." *New York Magazine*, August 30, 2016. http://nymag.com/daily/intelligencer/2016/08/trump-and-the-george-wallace-tradition-of-foreign-policy.html

Kilian, Michael. "Ace of Trump: an artful dealer, usually with the best hand." *Chicago Tribune*, November 22, 1987, p. D1.

Kilian, Michael. "Power shift: D.C. won't stand for dreadfully chic anymore, with Poppy and Bar at the helm." *Chicago Tribune*, December 28, 1988, p. F5.

Kilpatrick, Mary. "Tim Ryan sounds off on Donald Trump's upcoming Youngstown rally: Ohio Politics Roundup." *Cleveland.com*, July 21, 2017. https://www.cleveland.com/open/index.ssf/2017/07/tim_ryan_sounds_off_on_donald.html

Kimball, Daryl G. "Trump's failing Iran policy." *Arms Control Today*, June 2019. https://www.armscontrol.org/act/2019-06/focus/trumps-failing-iran-policy

Klein, Joe. "The perils of the permanent campaign." *Time Magazine*, October 30, 20015. http://content.time.com/time/magazine/article/0,9171,1124332,00.html

Klein, Philip. "How Trump's post-presidential Twitter feed could shape the future of the Republican Party." *Washington Examiner*, September 4, 2019. https://www.washingtonexaminer.com/opinion/columnists/how-trumps-post-presidential-twitter-feed-could-shape-the-future-of-the-republican-party

Knickerbocker, Brad. "Are Donald Trump and his fellow 'birthers' racist?" *Christian Science Monitor*, April 30, 2011. https://www.csmonitor.com/USA/Politics/2011/0430/Are-Donald-Trump-and-his-fellow-birthers-racist

Koronowski, Ryan. "68 times Trump promised to repeal Obamacare. The White House says it's already moving on." *ThinkProgress*, March 24, 2017. http://www. thinkprogress.org/trump-promised-to-repeal-obamacare-many-times-ab9500dad31e

Korte, Gregory. "Trump shrinks Bears Ears, Grand Staircase-Escalante monuments in historic proclamations." *USA Today*, December 5, 2017. https://www.usatoday.com/story/news/politics/2017/12/04/trump-travels-utah-historic-rollback-national-monuments/919209001/

Kramer, Peter D., and Sally D. Satel. "Who decides whether Trump is unfit?" *New York Times*, August 29, 2017, p. A27.

Kreitner, Richard. "What time is it? Here's what the 2016 election tells us about Obama, Trump, and what comes next." *The Nation*, November 22, 2016. https://www.thenation.com/article/what-time-is-it-heres-what-the-2016-election-tells-us-about-obama-trump-and-what-comes-next/

Krieg, Gregory. "14 of Trump's most outrageous 'birther' claims—half from after 2011." *CNN*, September 16, 2016. https://www.cnn.com/2016/09/09/politics/donald-trump-birther/index.html

Krieg, Gregory. "No, Hillary Clinton did not start the 'birther' movement." *CNN*, September 16, 2017. https://www.cnn.com/2016/09/17/politics/hillary-clinton-birther-conspiracy/index.html

Krauthammer, Charles. "The delusional dean." *Washington Post*, December 5, 2003. https://www.washingtonpost.com/archive/opinions/2003/12/05/the-delusional-dean/cbc80426-08ee-40fd-97e5-19da55fdc821/?utm_term=.314e37cbee2f

Kruse, Michael. "I found Trump's diary—hiding in plain sight." *Politico Magazine*, June 25, 2017. https://www.politico.com/magazine/story/2017/06/25/i-found-trumps-diaryhiding-in-plain-sight-215303

Kurtz, Howard. "A Trump jump in the polls despite the media's gloom-and-doom portrayal." *Fox News*, June 8, 2017. http://www.foxnews.com/politics/2018/06/08/trump-jump-in-polls-despite-medias-gloom-and-doom-portrayal.html

Kurtz, Howard. "Between the lines of a millionaire's ad; New Yorker's foreign-policy foray follows political overtures." *Washington Post*, September 2, 1987, p. A4.

Kurtz, Howard. "Donald Trump." *Washington Post*, November 22, 1987, p. 133.

Kurtz, Howard. "Trump weights $2 million ad blitz to defeat Koch." *Washington Post*, December 6, 1988, p. A8; Howard Kurtz, "Trump: The book on the tycoon with the towering ambition." *Washington Post*, November 22, 1987, p. F1.

Kurtzleben, Danielle. "Trade is an identity issue, and Trump knows it." *NPR*, March 10, 2018. https://www.npr.org/2018/03/10/592450875/trade-is-an-identity-issue-and-trump-knows-it

Kuttner, Robert. "Donald Trump's Constitution." *The American Prospect*, Summer 2016: 5–7.

Lambrecq, Maxence. "Pourquoi Emmanuel Macron s'effondre dans les sondages." *Europe1*, August 27, 2019. https://www.europe1.fr/politique/pourquoi-emmanuel-macron-seffondre-dans-les-sondages-3419846.

Lamothe, Dan. "Trump calls for 'great rebuilding of the Armed Forces'." *Washington Post*, January 29, 2017, p. A4.

Landers, Elizabeth, and James Masters. "Trump retweets anti-Muslim videos." *CNN*, November 30, 2017. https://edition.cnn.com/2017/11/29/politics/donald-trump-retweet-jayda-fransen/index.html

Landler, Mark. "Trump abandons nuclear deal he long scorned." *New York Times*, May 8, 2018. https://www.nytimes.com/2018/05/08/world/middleeast/trump-iran-nuclear-deal.html

Laughland, Oliver, Ed Pilkington, David Smith, and Liz Barney. "Hawaii judge halts new Trump travel ban, setting stage for epic legal battle." *The Guardian*, March 16, 2017. https://www.theguardian.com/us-news/2017/mar/15/trump-travel-ban-blocked-restraining-order-hawaii

Lauter, David. "Trump has remade the Republican Party, but at a price." *Los Angeles Times*, August 22, 2019. https://www.latimes.com/politics/story/2019-08-21/usc-la-times-republican-poll-trump-populism

Lavin, Talia. "Conspiracy theories about Soros aren't just false. They're anti-Semitic." *Washington Post*, October 24, 2018. https://www.washingtonpost.com/outlook/2018/10/24/conspiracy-theories-about-soros-arent-just-false-theyre-anti-semitic/?utm_term=.3398ba81953c

Law, Tara. "McCabe claims Dep. Attorney General Rosenstein first brought up invoking the 25th Amendment against President Trump." *Time*, February 17, 2019. http://time.com/5531496/mccabe-rosenstein-25th-amendment/

Law, Tara. "'Nobody pushed me.' Ukrainian president denies Trump pressured him to investigate Biden's son." *Time*, September 25, 2019. https://time.com/5686305/zelensky-ukraine-denies-trump-pressure/

Le Miere, Jason. "Fox News guest claims migrant caravan carries 'leprosy,' 'will infect our people,' offers no evidence." *Newsweek*, November 8, 2018. https://www.newsweek.com/fox-news-migrant-caravan-leprosy-1192605

Lehane, Chris. "Yeah, I wrote the Vast Right-Wing Conspiracy Memo. I stand by every word of it. And it's even worse today." *Politico*, April 27, 2014. https://www.politico.com/magazine/story/2014/04/chris-lehane-right-wing-conspiracy-memo-106059

Lemire, Jonathan. "Trump embraces legacy of Andrew Jackson." *Associated Press: Worldstream*, February 19, 2017.

Lemire, Jonathan, and Ken Thomas. "Trump, unlikely religious favorite, hails Christian values, return of 'Merry Christmas'." *Chicago Tribune*, October 13, 2017. http://www.chicagotribune.com/news/

nationworld/politics/ct-trump-values-voter-summit-20171013-story.html

Levin, Aaron. "Goldwater rules based on long-ago controversy." *Psychiatric News*, August 25, 2016. https://psychnews.psychiatryonline.org/doi/full/10.1176/appi.pn.2016.9a19

Levitz, Eric. "Trump tax cuts are (probably) about to become a political disaster." *New York Magazine*, February 8, 2019. http://nymag.com/intelligencer/2019/02/heres-why-your-tax-refund-is-lower-this-year.html

Liasson, Mara. "Nativism and economic anxiety fuel Trump's populist appeal." *NPR*, September 4, 2015. https://www.npr.org/sections/itsallpolitics/2015/09/04/437443401/populist-movement-reflected-in-campaigns-of-sanders-and-trump

Lieberman, Joseph I. "2020 Democrats should support Trump's Iran policy, not pledge to rejoin 2015 nuclear deal." *USA Today*, September 9, 2019. https://www.usatoday.com/story/opinion/2019/09/09/2020-democrats-should-support-trump-on-iran-nuclear-deal-olumn/2213275001/

Lifson, Thomas. "Maxine Waters goes completely unhinged." *American Thinker*, March 17, 2017. https://www.americanthinker.com/blog/2017/03/maxine_waters_goes_completely_unhinged.htm

Lind, Michael. "Donald Trump, the perfect populist." *Politico Magazine*, March 9, 2016. https://www.politico.com/magazine/story/2016/03/donald-trump-the-perfect-populist-213697

Lind, Michael. "Power to the People." *New Republic*, September 4, 1995, pp. 37–8.

Linge, Mary Kay. "Trump: US may designate Antifa as terror organization." *New York Post*, August 17, 2019. https://nypost.com/2019/08/17/trump-us-may-designate-antifa-as-terror-organization/

Linker, Damon. "Donald Trump's presidency is upon us. But who will President Trump be?" *The Week*, January 17, 2017. http://theweek.com/articles/673549/donald-trumps-presidency-upon-but-who-president-trump

Liptak, Adam, and Michael D. Shear, "Trump's travel ban is upheld by the Supreme Court." June 26, 2018. https://www.nytimes.com/2018/06/26/us/politics/supreme-court-trump-travel-ban.html

Longwell, Sarah. "Republicans who back impeachment can save the country—and the GOP." *NBC News*, September 30, 2019. https://www.nbcnews.com/think/opinion/republicans-who-back-impeachment-can-save-country-gop-ncna1059896

Lopez, German. "We need to stop acting like Trump isn't pandering to white supremacists." *Vox*, August 14, 2017. https://www.vox.com/policy-and-politics/2017/8/13/16140504/trump-charlottesville-white-supremacists

López, Ian Haney, "Why do Trump's supporters deny the racism that seems so evident to Democrats?" *Los Angeles Times*, August 13, 2019. https://www.latimes.com/opinion/story/2019-08-13/trump-voters-racism-politics-white-supremacy

Lorenzo, Aaron. "As tax refunds shrink, Republicans scramble to defend Trump tax cut." *Politico*, February 23, 2019. https://www.politico.com/story/2019/02/23/tax-refunds-republicans-1182286

Los Angeles Times. "Transcripts: What the mics caught Donald Trump saying in 2005 and what he said in his taped apology." http://www.latimes.com/politics/la-na-pol-trump-bush-transcript-20161007-snap-htmlstory.html#

Lovett, Ian. "Evangelical Christians lobbied hard for Trump's move on Jerusalem." *Wall Street Journal (Online)*, December 7, 2017.

Lowndes, Joe. "Populist persuasions." *The Baffler*, October 31, 2018. https://thebaffler.com/latest/populist-persuasions-lowndes

Lowry, Rich. "Bernie's conspiracy theory." *Politico*, October 29, 2015. https://www.politico.com/magazine/story/2015/10/bernies-conspiracy-theory-213307

Lowry, Rich. "Trump's not populist enough." *Politico*, November 14, 2018. https://www.politico.com/magazine/story/2018/11/14/trump-2020-midterms-populism-222573

Lowry, Rich. "Their George Wallace and ours." *National Review*, April 25, 2016, p. 18.

Lueck, Thomas. "Trump City site may be sold, developer says." *New York Times*, October 13, 1988, p. B1.

Lusher, Adam. "Donald Trump's troubled history with the NFL and why his 'take a knee' fight may stem from a grudge held since the 1980s." *UK Independent*, September 28, 2017. https://www.independent.co.uk/news/world/americas/us-politics/donald-trump-take-a-knee-nfl-protest-con-man-huckster-scumbag-american-football-usfl-john-bassett-a7972281.html

Lynch, Conor. "They aren't in it for 'free stuff': What critics get wrong about millennial Bernie Sanders supporters." *Salon*, June 24, 2016. https://www.salon.com/2016/06/24/they_arent_in_it_for_free_stuff_what_critics_get_wrong_about_millennial_bernie_sanders_supporters/

Lynn, Frank. "A closer look at the gorillas of G.O.P. finance." *New York Times*, January 26, 1989, p. B1.

Lynn, Frank. "Investigations will expand in New York." *New York Times*, March 17, 1988, p. B1.

McAdams, Dan P. "The mind of Donald Trump." *The Atlantic*, June 2016. https://www.theatlantic.com/magazine/archive/2016/06/the-mind-of-donald-trump/480771/

McCarthy, Andrew C. "Trump and the 'racist tweets'." *National Review*, July 16, 2019. https://www.nationalreview.com/2019/07/donald-trump-and-the-racist-tweets/

McCoy, Kevin. "NY appeals court rules President Donald Trump must face Summer Zervos' defamation lawsuit." *USA Today*, March 14, 2019. https://www.usatoday.com/story/news/2019/03/14/president-donald-trump-must-face-summer-zervos-defamation-case-ny-court-rules/3162078002/

McDonnell, Patrick J., and Juanita Darling. "Perot's debate statements strike raw nerve in Mexico. Reaction: Blunt exchange impresses many, but Texan comes under fire for what is seen as stereotypical descriptions of poverty." *Los Angeles Times*, November 11, 1993. https://www.latimes.com/archives/la-xpm-1993-11-11-mn-55573-story.html

McGovern, George. "Goldwater: A good friend." *Washington Post*, June 4, 1998. https://www.washingtonpost.com/wp-srv/politics/daily/june98/mcgovern4.htm

McGrory, Mary. "Ross Perot: folksy and frightening." *St. Petersburg Times*, June 29, 1992, p. A7.

McKinless, Ashley. "Bernie Sanders' speech at conservative Christian college a lesson in civility." *America: The Jesuit Review*, September 16, 2015. https://www.americamagazine.org/content/all-things/what-civility-looks-sanders-liberty-university

McManus, Doyle. "It turns out Donald trump is not an Artist of the Deal." *Los Angeles Times*, March 24, 2017. http://www.latimes.com/opinion/op-ed/la-oe-mcmanus-trump-healthcare-failure-20170324-story.html

McManus, Doyle. "Trump's permanent campaign won't help him keep his promises." *Los Angeles Times*, January 22, 2017. https://www.latimes.com/opinion/op-ed/la-oe-mcmanus-trump-inauguration-permanent-campaign-20170122-story.html

McNally, Joel. "Release of Wallace shooter rekindles conspiracy talk." *The Capital Times* (Madison, WI), September 1, 2007, p. A8.

McWhorter, John. "What Trump's speech says about his mental fitness." *New York Times*, February 6, 2018. https://nytimes.com/interactive/2018/02/06/opinion/trump-speech-mental-capacity

393

Marans, Daniel. "In era of Donald Trump, Bernie Sanders sees 'The beginning of a political revolution'." *Huffington Post*, January 31, 2018. https://www.huffingtonpost.com/entry/bernie-sanders-response-donald-trump-state-of-the-union_us_5a715645e4b0ae29f08c1628

Marcin, Tim. "Trump voters, Republicans overall, actually don't care if the president shoots someone on Fifth Avenue: Poll." *Newsweek*, July 18, 2017. https://www.newsweek.com/trump-voters-republicans-overall-actually-dont-care-president-shoots-someone-638462

Marcos, Christina. "House Dem seeks to create commission on 'presidential capacity'." *The Hill*, May 12, 2017. https://thehill.com/homenews/house/333193-house-dem-seeks-to-create-commission-on-presidential-capacity

Marcos, Christina. "Pelosi: Trump is goading us to impeach him." *The Hill*, May 7, 2019. https://thehill.com/homenews/house/442493-pelosi-trump-is-goading-us-to-impeach-him

Marcos, Christina. "The nearly 60 Democrats who voted for impeachment." *The Hill*, December 6, 2017. www.thehill.com/blogs/floor-action/house/363645-the-nearly-60-dems-who-voted-for-impeachment

Margolick, David. "Top state court rules Trump is entitled to tax break for midtown tower." *New York Times*, July 6, 1984, p. B1.

Marimow, Ann E., and Jonathan O'Connell. "Trump can profit from foreign government business at his hotel, if he doesn't do favors in return, Justice Dept. says." *Washington Post,* June 11, 2018. https://www.washingtonpost.com/local/public-safety/obscure-no-more-the-emoluments-clause-is-back-again-in-a-federal-court/2018/06/09/cf052832-6a72-11e8-9e38-24e693b38637_story.html?utm_term=.8d31666b1862

Marquis, Christopher. "Andrew Jackson: Winner and loser in 1824." *American History*, April 2008, p. 56.

Matthews, Dylan. "Zero-sum Trump." *Vox*, January 19, 2017. https://www.vox.com/a/donald-trump-books

Mauldin, John. "3 reasons Brits voted for Brexit." *Forbes*, July 6, 2016. https://www.forbes.com/sites/johnmauldin/2016/07/05/3-reasons-brits-voted-for-brexit/#1a286d501f9d

Mazzei, Patricia, and Jonathan Martin. "A black progressive and a Trump acolyte win Florida governor primaries." *New York Times*, August 28, 2018. https://www.nytimes.com/2018/08/28/us/politics/florida-arizona-election-results.html

Meckler, Laura, and Siobhan Hughes. "Hillary Clinton pitches her vision for America in acceptance speech." *Wall Street Journal*,

July 29, 2016. https://www.wsj.com/articles/hillary-clinton-to-emphasize-experience-steadiness-in-speech-to-democratic-convention-1469747452

Mehren, Elizabeth. "Rich collecting 2nd homes: Owning 2, 3, even 4 houses becoming commonplace." *Los Angeles Times*, May 23, 2000. https://www.sfgate.com/business/article/Rich-Collecting-2nd-Homes-Owning-2-3-even-4-2777678.php

Mehta, Seema, Anthony Pesce, Maloy Moore, and Christine Zang. "Election 2016: Who's giving Sanders all those $27 donations?" *Los Angeles Times*, June 4, 2016, p. A1.

Menand, Louis. "He knew he was right." *The New Yorker*, March 26, 2001. https://www.newyorker.com/magazine/2001/03/26/he-knew-he-was-right

Merica, Dan. "Trump turns to once-mocked executive orders to tout wins." *CNN*, April 27, 2017. https://www.cnn.com/2017/04/27/politics/trump-executive-orders/index.html

Merica, Dan, and Nick Viviani, "Sen. Bernie Sanders is running for president." *WIBW-Channel 13* (Montpelier, VT). https://www.wibw.com/home/headlines/Vermont-independent-Sen-Bernie-Sanders-says-I-am-running-for-president-in-interview-with-AP-301764001.html

Merry, Robert W. "Andrew Jackson's populism: It started with a hatred of crony capitalism." *The American Conservative*, May/June 2017.

Meyer, Theodoric. "Has Trump drained the swamp in Washington?" *Politico*, October 19, 2017. https://www.politico.com/story/2017/10/19/trump-drain-swamp-promises-243924

Michigan Radio. "Some Michigan Republican members of Congress criticize Trump's family separation policy." June 19, 2018. http://www.michiganradio.org/post/some-michigan-republican-members-congress-criticize-trumps-family-separation-policy

Milanova, Iris. "15 life lessons from The Godfather." *Thought Catalogue*, January 5, 2014. https://thoughtcatalog.com/iris-milanova/2014/01/15-life-lessons-from-the-godfather/

Miller, Zeke, and Jill Colvin. "How White House lawyer Don McGahn seems to have saved Trump from himself." *Chicago Tribune*, April 20, 2019. https://www.chicagotribune.com/news/nationworld/politics/ct-don-mcgahn-white-house-lawyer-20190419-story.html

Monkovic, Tom. "Donald Trump and conspiracy theories: A signal from 2012." *New York Times*, May 18, 2016. https://www.nytimes.com/2016/05/19/upshot/donald-trump-and-conspiracy-theories-what-a-poll-in-2011-signaled.html

Montanaro, Domenico. "Is Trump guilty of obstruction of justice? Comey laid out the case." *NPR*, June 10, 2017. https://www.npr.org/2017/06/10/532321287/is-trump-guilty-of-obstruction-of-justice-comey-laid-out-the-case

Montgomery, Lisa Kennedy. "Bernie Sanders' 'Medicare for All' plan would blow up the economy." *Fox Business*, July 31, 2018. https://www.foxbusiness.com/politics/bernie-sanders-medicare-for-all-plan-would-blow-up-the-economy-kennedy

Morin, Rebecca. "Poll: Almost half of voters question Trump's mental stability." *Politico*, January 22, 2018. https://www.politico.com/story/2018/01/22/poll-trump-mental-health-354902

Moss, Bradley P. "Trump's purge of the FBI is complete." *Politico*, August 13, 2018. https://www.politico.com/magazine/story/2018/08/13/peter-strzok-fired-donald-trump-fbi-219355

Mufson, Steven, and Juliet Eilperin. "Trump seeks to spark action on oil pipelines." *Washington Post*, January 25, 2017, p. A1.

Mui, Yulan Q. "Demise of TPP shifts U.S. role in world economy." *Washington Post*, January 24, 2017, p. A1.

Mullen, Jethro. "He said what? A look back at Trump's Japan bashing." *CNN Business*, February 8, 2017. https://money.cnn.com/2017/02/08/news/economy/trump-japan-comments-abe/index.html

Muschamp, Herbert. "A Midas of the gold (yes I do mean gold) cudgel." *New York Times*, November 5, 1997, p. E2.

Musgrave, Paul. "Democracy requires trust. But Trump is making us all into conspiracy theorists" *Washington Post*, March 7, 2017. https://www.washingtonpost.com/posteverything/wp/2017/03/07/democracy-requires-trust-but-trump-is-making-us-all-into-conspiracy-theorists/?utm_term=.7829b95f127a

Nagourney, Adam. "Trump proposes clearing nation's debt at expense of the rich." *New York Times*, November 10, 1999, p. A19.

NBC News. "Pew poll: GOP sours on FBI." July 24, 2018. https://www.nbcnews.com/card/pew-poll-gop-sours-fbi-n894016

NBC News. "The Republicans opposing Donald Trump—And voting for Hillary Clinton." November 6, 2016. https://www.nbcnews.com/politics/2016-election/meet-republicans-speaking-out-against-trump-n530696

Nevins, Buddy. "Millionaire pushing 'Trump for President'." *Fort Lauderdale Sun-Sentinel*, September 17, 1987, p. 3A.

New York Times. "A presidential bid?" July 14, 1987, p. B3.

New York Times. "G.O.P. to ask Trump about mayoral bid." June 16, 1987, p. B2.

New York Times. "Rod Rosenstein's letter appointing Mueller Special Counsel." May 17, 2017. https://www.nytimes.com/interactive/2017/05/17/us/politics/document-Robert-Mueller-Special-Counsel-Russia.html

New York Times. "Ross Perot's 'People'." July 14, 1992. https://www.nytimes.com/1992/07/14/opinion/ross-perot-s-people.html

New York Times. "Scouting." August 5, 1986, p. A20.

New York Times. "The 1992 campaign; transcript of 3rd TV debate between Bush, Clinton and Perot." October 20, 1992. https://www.nytimes.com/1992/10/20/us/the-1992-campaign-transcript-of-3d-tv-debate-between-bush-clinton-and-perot.html

New York Times. "Donald Trump's New York Times interview: Full transcript." November 23, 2016. http://www.nytimes.com/2016/11/23/us/politics/trump-new-york-times-interviewtranscript.html?partner=bloomberg

New York Times. "Text of Goldwater speech on civil rights." June 16, 1964. https://www.nytimes.com/1964/06/19/archives/text-of-goldwater-speech-on-rights.html

Nichols, John. "Congress could establish a commission to see if Trump is mentally fit to be president." *The Nation*, May 17, 2017. https://www.thenation.com/article/many-americans-believe-donald-trump-is-unfit-to-serve-a-congressman-has-a-plan-to-determine-that/

Nicol, Ryan. "'Warrior' Matt Gaetz gets official thumbs-up from Donald Trump." *Florida Politics*, July 13, 2018. http://floridapolitics.com/archives/268704-trump-endorsing-gaetz

Nieman, Donald. "Andrew Johnson's failed presidency echoes in Trump's White House." *The Conversation*, February 13, 2018. https://theconversation.com/andrew-johnsons-failed-presidency-echoes-in-trumps-white-house-91139

Nilsson, Jeff. "How one executive order devastated the country." *Saturday Evening Post*, May 10, 2017. https://www.saturdayeveningpost.com/2017/05/one-executive-order-devastated-country/

Norris, Floyd. "Whom Trump likes (himself) and hates (many)." *New York Times*, August 22, 1990, p. C15.

NPR. All Things Considered. "Democratic Rep. Ruben Gallego raises concerns about Trump's visit to Phoenix." August 22, 2017. https://www.npr.org/2017/08/22/545314077/democratic-rep-ruben-gallego-raises-concerns-about-trumps-visit-to-phoenix

Nuzzi, Olivia. "Inside Trump's make believe presidential addresses." *Daily Beast*, February 29, 2016. https://www.thedailybeast.com/inside-trumps-make-believe-presidential-addresses

Nuzzi, Olivia. "Is Mark Sanford's quest for the mythical reluctant Trump voter noble or pathetic?" *New York Magazine*, September 15, 2019. http://nymag.com/intelligencer/2019/09/mark-sanford-2020-presidential-campaign.html

O'Brien, Timothy L. "Mitch McConnell is Trump's latter-day Ed Koch." *Bloomberg Opinion*, August 24, 2017. https://www.bloomberg.com/opinion/articles/2017-08-24/mitch-mcconnell-is-trump-s-latter-day-ed-koch

O'Connor, Lydia, and Daniel Marans. "Here are 16 examples of Trump being racist." *Huffington Post*, December 13, 2016. https://www.huffingtonpost.com/entry/president-donald-trump-racist-examples_us_584f2ccae4b0bd9c3dfe5566

Olen, Helaine. "Trump didn't drain the swamp. Supporters are starting to notice." *Washington Post*, September 11, 2018. https://www.washingtonpost.com/blogs/post-partisan/wp/2018/09/11/trump-didnt-drain-the-swamp-supporters-are-starting-to-notice/?utm_term=.a7914d162275

Olsen, Henry. "Populism, American style." *National Affairs*, no. 36 (Summer 2018). https://nationalaffairs.com/publications/detail/populism-american-style

Packer, George. "The populists." *The New Yorker*, September 7, 2015. https://www.newyorker.com/magazine/2015/09/07/the-populists

Page, Clarence. "'You people' gaffe shows Perot the perils of populism." *Chicago Tribune*, July 15, 1992. http://www.chicagotribune.com/news/ct-xpm-1992-07-15-9203030818-story.html

Page, Susan, and Deborah Barfield Barry. "Poll: Half of Americans say Trump is victim of a 'witch hunt' as trust in Mueller erodes." *USA Today*, March 18, 2019. https://www.usatoday.com/story/news/politics/2019/03/18/trust-mueller-investigation-falls-half-americans-say-trump-victim-witch-hunt/3194049002/#

Parisi, Albert J. "Trump withdrawal laid to impatience." *New York Times*, August 17, 1986, p. NJ10.

Parker, Ashley. "At rallies, a combustible atmosphere of anger and malice." *New York Times*, March 13, 2016, p. A22.

Pearlman, Jeff. "The day Donald Trump's narcissism killed the USFL." *Sports Illustrated*, September 11, 2018. https://www.theguardian.com/sport/2018/sep/11/the-day-donald-trumps-narcissism-killed-the-usfl

Pearson, Rick, and Kim Geiger. "Sanders: 'Tough' foreign policy: Presidential campaign storms into Chicago." *Chicago Tribune*, February 26, 2016, p. 1.

Persons, Sally. "Trump threatens to pull 'fake news' credentials." *Washington Times,* May 9, 2018. https://www.washingtontimes.com/news/2018/may/9/donald-trump-threatens-to-pull-fake-news-credentia/

Petrishen, Brad, and Craig S. Semon. "Bernin' love warms rally at North High." *Telegram & Gazette* (Worcester, MA), January 3, 2016, p. A1.

Phillips, Tom, and Anna Jean Kaiser, "Brazil must not become a 'gay tourism paradise', says Bolsonaro." *The Guardian*, April 25, 2019. https://www.theguardian.com/world/2019/apr/26/bolsonaro-accused-of-inciting-hatred-with-gay-paradise-comment

Pilkington, Ed. "How does Trump do it? Understanding the psychology of a demagogue's rally." *The Guardian*, December 8, 2015. https://www.theguardian.com/us-news/2015/dec/08/donald-trump-rally-psychology-humor-fear

Pinsolle, Laurent. "Celui qui oserait dire tout haut ce que les électeurs penseraient tout bas: Jean-Marie Le Pen a-t-il raison de penser que les Français ne croient plus à l'étiquette de fasciste qui lui est collée?" *Atlantico*, July 26, 2013. http://www.atlantico.fr/decryptage/celui-qui-oserait-dire-tout-haut-que-electeurs-penseraient-tout-bas-jean-marie-pen-t-raison-penser-que-francais-ne-croient-plus-797623.html.

Police One, "What you need to know about Executive Order 13688." August 22, 2016. https://www.policeone.com/jag/articles/210318006-What-you-need-to-know-about-Executive-Order-13688/

Political Transcript Wire. "President Donald Trump delivers remarks on Jerusalem." December 6, 2017.

Political Transcript Wire. "Sen. Bernard Sanders, I-VT, Democratic candidate, holds a rally." May 19, 2016.

Pollack, Andrew. "Trump on tour; Japan glimpses art of tough talk." *New York Times*, August 19, 1993, p. D2.

Pollock, Cassi. "Where every Republican in Congress stands on Donald Trump." *Washington Examiner*, May 27, 2016. https://www.washingtonexaminer.com/full-list-where-every-republican-in-congress-stands-on-donald-trump

Polsby, Nelson W. "Against presidential greatness." *Commentary*, January 1, 1977. https://www.commentarymagazine.com/articles/against-presidential-greatness/

Press, Bill. "Is Trump mentally fit for office?" *The Hill*, January 18, 2018. http://thehill.com/opinion/white-house/368008-press-is-trump-mentally-fit-for-office

Price, Greg. "Donald Trump mocked both John McCain, who is dying, and George H. W. Bush, who just lost his wife, and Montana rally." *Newsweek*, July 6, 2018. https://www.newsweek.com/donald-trump-mccain-bush-dying-1010966

Price, Michelle L., and Brady McCombs. "Native American tribes sue over Trump's decision to shrink Utah national monument." *Chicago Tribune*, December 5, 2017. http://www.chicagotribune.com/news/nationworld/politics/ct-trump-national-monuments-20171205-story.html

Prokop, Andrew. "Mueller is done. Trump's legal woes aren't." *Vox*, March 23, 2019. https://www.vox.com/2019/3/20/18241825/trump-investigations-sdny-inauguration-state-congress

Protess, Ben, William K. Rashbaum, Benjamin Weiser, and Maggie Haberman. "As Mueller report lands, prosecutorial focus moves to New York." *New York Times*, March 23, 2019. https://www.nytimes.com/2019/03/23/us/trump-investigations-new-york.html

Public Integrity. "The secret saga of Trump's tax cuts." April 30, 2019. https://publicintegrity.org/business/taxes/trumps-tax-cuts/the-secret-saga-of-trumps-tax-cuts/

PBS, "Did Trump's tax cuts boost hiring? Most companies say no." January 28, 2019. https://www.pbs.org/newshour/economy/making-sense/did-trumps-tax-cuts-boost-hiring-most-companies-say-no

Queenan, Joe. "No more Mr. Nice Guy." *Chief Executive* 222 (December 2006).

Quilantan, Bianca, and David Cohen. "Trump tells Dem congress-women: Go back where you came from." *Politico*, July 14, 2019. https://www.politico.com/story/2019/07/14/trump-congress-go-back-where-they-came-from-1415692

Quinn, Melissa. "Tony Perkins: Trump gets a 'mulligan' over Stormy Daniels from Evangelicals." *Washington Examiner*, January 23, 2018. https://www.washingtonexaminer.com/tony-perkins-trump-gets-a-mulligan-over-stormy-daniels-from-evangelicals

Rabinowitz, Jonathan. "Indians issue threats over new casinos." *New York Times*, January 25, 1995, p. B4.

Rafferty, Andrew. "Trump begins debate by attacking Rand Paul." *NBC News*, September 16, 2015. https://www.nbcnews.com/politics/2016-election/trump-begins-debate-attacking-rand-paul-n428761

Raju, Manu. "Trump declared he's running again. Many Republicans aren't ready to back him." *CNN*, April 19, 2018. https://www.cnn.com/2018/04/19/politics/congress-republicans-trump-second-term/index.html

Ramstad, Evan, *Associated Press*, "Perot not new to cries of conspiracy." *Kitsap Sun* (Washington), October 28, 1992. https://products.kitsapsun.com/archive/1992/10-28/249220_perot_not_new_to_cries_of_consp.html

Reicher, Stephen D., and S. Alexander Haslam. "How Trump won." *Scientific American Mind* 28, 2 (2017): 42–50.

Reilly, Katie. "Carly Fiorina: Donald Trump should step aside as presidential nominee." *Time*, October 8, 2016. http://time.com/4523922/carly-fiorina-donald-trump-mike-pence/

Restuccia, Andrew, and Craig Howie. "Trump defends mental health: I'm a 'stable genius'." *Politico*, January 7, 2018. https://www.politico.eu/article/donald-trump-slams-media-over-mental-health-reports/

Restuccia, Andrew. "Trump's baseless assertions of voter fraud called 'stunning'." *Politico*, November 27, 2016. https://www.politico.com/story/2016/11/trump-illegal-voting-clinton-231860.

Reuters. "Jill Stein's election recount ends as Wisconsin finds 131 more Trump votes." *The Guardian*, December 12, 2016. https://www.theguardian.com/us-news/2016/dec/12/pennsylvania-recount-jill-stein-request-denied

Roberts, Sam. "Dinkins gaining support among business executives." *New York Times*, September 26, 1989, p. B1.

Roberts, Sam. "Ed Koch's epic feud with Trump survives the mayor's death." *New York Times*, February 27, 2017.

Robinson, Emerald. "The collapse of the Never-Trump conservatives." *American Spectator*, June 29, 2018. https://spectator.org/the-collapse-of-the-never-trump-conservatives/

Rodrigo, Chris Mills. "Schiff: Mueller report 'far worse' than Watergate." *The Hill*, April 21, 2019. https://thehill.com/homenews/sunday-talk-shows/439899-schiff-mueller-report-far-worse-than-watergate

Rogers, Katie. "The Trump rally: A play in three acts." *New York Times*, October 14, 2018, p. A20.

Rosen, James. "Jump ship on Trump? Florida GOP lawmakers resist national trend." *McClatchy DC Bureau*, October 16, 2016. https://www.mcclatchydc.com/news/politics-government/election/article107611927.html

Rosenberg, Yair. "Conspiracy theories about the Rothschilds are a symptom. The problem is deeper." *Washington Post*, March 21, 2018. https://www.washingtonpost.com/news/posteverything/wp/2018/03/21/conspiracy-theories-about-the-rothschilds-are-a-symptom-the-problem-is-deeper/?utm_term=.cb77a6388fcd

Rosenthal, Max J. "The Trump files: Witness Donald's epic insult fight with the Mayor of New York." *Mother Jones*, August 11, 2016. https://www.motherjones.com/politics/2016/08/trump-files-donalds-epic-battle-with-ed-koch/

Rothenberg, Stuart. "Comparing the GOP divides, 1964 and 2016." *Inside Elections*, May 24, 2016. https://www.insideelections.com/news/article/comparing-the-gop-divides-1964-and-2016

Rothman, Lily. "This is how the whole birther thing actually started." *Time*, September 16, 2016. http://time.com/4496792/birther-rumor-started/

Rothman, Noah C. "Whose violence is it?" *Commentary*, September 2016. https://www.commentarymagazine.com/articles/whose-violence-is-it/

Rothschild, Matthew. "L.A. and Bernie Sanders challenge 'corporate personhood'." *The Progressive*, December 9, 2011. https://progressive.org/dispatches/l.a.-bernie-sanders-challenge-corporate-personhood/

Rove, Karl. "A Presidential honeymoon from hell; This should be a time to notch early wins. But Trump is stalled and distracted." *Wall Street Journal Online*, April 5, 2017.

Rovere, Richard H. "The campaign: Goldwater." *The New Yorker*, October 3, 1964. https://www.newyorker.com/magazine/1964/10/03/the-campaign-goldwater

Rucker, Philip, and Robert Costa, "Bannon vows a daily fight for 'deconstruction of the administrative state'; Trump's chief strategist outlines a nationalist agenda and says the president will fulfill his hard-line promises." *Washington Post Blogs*, February 24, 2017.

Rucker, Philip, Matt Zapotosky, and Carol D. Leonnig, "Trump escalates attacks on FBI." *Washington Post*, March 18, 2018, p. A21.

Ruiz, Rebecca R. "Even as president, Trump focused on hush money, Cohen says." *New York Times*, February 27, 2019. https://www.nytimes.com/2019/02/27/us/politics/michael-cohen-trump-hush-money.html

Rumens, Carol. "Poem of the week: The Darkling Thrush, by Thomas Hardy." *The Guardian*, December 28, 2009. https://www.theguardian.

com/books/booksblog/2009/dec/28/poem-of-the-week-the-darkling-thrush-thomas-hardy

Runciman, David. "The plots against America." *Chronicle of Higher Education*, January 15, 2017. https://www.chronicle.com/article/The-Plots-Against-America/238869

Rupar, Aaron. "'This was a coup': Trump escalates his authoritarian rhetoric." *Vox*, April 26, 2019. https://www.vox.com/2019/4/26/18517763/trump-hannity-coup-mueller

Russell, David. "The Bernie Sanders phenomenon." *The Hill*, June 24, 2015. https://thehill.com/blogs/pundits-blog/presidential-campaign/245937-the-bernie-sanders-phenomenon

Rutsch, Poncie. "Guess how much of Uncle Sam's money goes to foreign aid. Guess again!" *National Public Radio*, February 10, 2015. https://www.npr.org/sections/goatsandsoda/2015/02/10/383875581/guess-how-much-of-uncle-sams-money-goes-to-foreign-aid-guess-again

Ryman, Richard. "'Gunslinger' author breaks down USFL." September 26, 2018. https://www.greenbaypressgazette.com/story/news/2018/09/26/usfl-jeff-pearlman-book-football-buck-recounts-wild-ride/1223195002/

Sacchetti, Maria. "Despite vow to end 'catch and release,' Trump has freed 100,000 who illegally crossed the border." *Washington Post*, April 13, 2018. https://www.washingtonpost.com/local/immigration/despite-vow-to-end-catch-and-release-trump-has-freed-100000-who-illegally-crossed-the-border/2018/04/13/839c778e-3754-11e8-acd5-35eac230e514_story.html?utm_term=.76ed6f641516

Safety and Health Magazine. "Judge dismisses lawsuit against '2-for-1' Executive Order on federal regulations." March 1, 2018. https://www.safetyandhealthmagazine.com/articles/16750-judge-dismisses-lawsuit-against-2-for-1-executive-order-on-federal-regulations

Samuels, Brett. "Lawmakers briefed by Yale psychiatrist on Trump's mental health: Report." *The Hill*, January 3, 2018. https://thehill.com/homenews/administration/367362-lawmakers-briefed-by-yale-psychiatrist-on-trumps-mental-health-report

Samuels, Brett. "2020 Democrats feel more emboldened to label Trump a racist." *The Hill*, August 17, 2019. https://thehill.com/home-news/campaign/457730-2020-democrats-feel-more-emboldened-to-label-trump-a-racist

Sanders, Bernie. "Americans need an economy that supports more than the 1 percent." *The Hill*, January 19, 2019. https://thehill.com/opin-ion/finance/426153-americans-need-an-economy-that-supports-more-than-the-1-percent

Sanger, David E., and Maggie Haberman. "50 G.O.P. officials warn Donald Trump would put nation's security 'at risk'." *New York Times*, August 8, 2016. https://www.nytimes.com/2016/08/09/us/politics/national-security-gop-donald-trump.html

Santhanam, Laura. "FBI support is eroding, but most Americans still back bureau, poll says." *PBS Newshour*, April 17, 2018. https://www.pbs.org/newshour/politics/fbi-support-is-eroding-but-most-americans-still-back-bureau-poll-says

Saunders, George. "Who are all these Trump supporters?" *The New Yorker*, July 11 and 18, 2016. https://www.newyorker.com/magazine/2016/07/11/george-saunders-goes-to-trump-rallies

Savage, Charlie, "Trump administration imposes ban on bump stocks." *New York Times*, December 18, 2018. https://www.nytimes.com/2018/12/18/us/politics/trump-bump-stocks-ban.html

Scherer, Michael, David Weigel, and Karen Tumulty. "Democrats express outrage over allegations of early party control for Clinton in 2016." *Washington Post Online*, November 3, 2017.

Schleifer, Theodore. "Ted Cruz meets with Donald Trump." *CNN*, November 16, 2016. https://www.cnn.com/2016/11/15/politics/ted-cruz-donald-trump-meeting/index.html

Scott, Eugene. "Trump denounces Duke, KKK." *CNN Politics*, March 3, 2016. https://www.cnn.com/2016/03/03/politics/donald-trump-disavows-david-duke-kkk/index.html

Scott, Eugene. "Trump's dislike of—and desire to be a part of—the 'elite'." *Washington Post*, June 21, 2018. https://www.washingtonpost.com/news/the-fix/wp/2018/06/21/trumps-dislike-of-and-desire-to-be-a-part-of-the-elites/?utm_term=.15d5f1e5f8a1

Schwartz, Ian. "David Brooks: Trump 'did something impeachable,' but 'impeachment would be a mistake'." *RealClearPolitics*, September 28, 2019. https://www.realclearpolitics.com/video/2019/09/28/david_brooks_trump_did_something_impeachable_but_impeachment_would_be_a_mistake.html

Seib, Gerald F. "On the world stage, Trump remains disruptor-in-chief." *Wall Street Journal*, June 7, 2017. https://www.wsj.com/articles/on-the-world-stage-trump-remains-disruptor-in-chief-1496677230

Sellers, Frances Stead, and Aaron Blake. "Stephen Bannon's apparent references to anti-immigrant Know-Nothing Party don't seem so coincidental anymore." *Washington Post*, February 2, 2017. https://www.washingtonpost.com/news/the-fix/wp/2017/02/02/stephen-bannons-apparent-references-to-anti-immigrant-know-nothing-party-dont-seem-so-coincidental-anymore/

Sengupta, Somini. "Trump revives ban on aid to groups that discuss abortion." *New York Times*, January 24, 2017, p. A13.

Shapiro, Stuart. "Three views of Trump." *The Hill*, January 6, 2018. http://thehill.com/opinion/white-house/367600-three-views-of-trump

Shear, Michael D., and Adam Liptak. "Supreme Court takes up travel ban case, and allows parts to go ahead." *New York Times*, June 26, 2017. https://www.nytimes.com/2017/06/26/us/politics/supreme-court-trump-travel-ban-case.html

Shear, Michael D., and Ellen Ann Fentress. "Trump, rejecting calls to stay away, speaks at civil rights museum." *New York Times*, December 9, 2017. https://www.nytimes.com/2017/12/09/us/politics/trump-mississippi-civil-rights-museum.html

Shen, Lucinda. "Here's how much you could have won betting on Trump's presidency." *Fortune*, November 9, 2016. http://fortune.com/2016/11/09/donald-trump-president-gamble/

Shephard, Stephen. "Poll: Trump approval sinks 5 points after Mueller report, tying all-time low." *Politico*, April 22, 2019. https://www.politico.com/story/2019/04/22/trump-approval-mueller-report-1286386

Sherman, Brad. "The case for impeaching Donald Trump." *Huffington Post*, October 5, 2017. https://www.huffingtonpost.com/entry/the-case-for-impeaching-donald-j-trump_us_59a5e4a3e4b08299d89d0a9b

Sherman, Brad. "Why I filed articles of impeachment against Trump." *Washington Post*, January 9, 2019. https://www.washington-post.com/opinions/why-i-filed-articles-of-impeachment-against-trump/2019/01/09/aaa59a3c-12c7-11e9-ab79-30cd4f7926f2_story.html?utm_term=.e53ebe4c8297

Shesgreen, Deirde. "Steve Chabot's wild ride on the Trump train." *Cincinnati Enquirer*, April 28, 2017. https://www.cincinnati.com/story/news/politics/2017/04/27/steve-chabots-wild-ride-trump-train/100974626/

Sheth, Sonam. "Obama is the only president since Nixon who didn't face an independent investigation." *Business Insider*, October 23, 2017. https://www.businessinsider.com/obama-nixon-trump-russia-independent-investigation-2017-10

Shrum, Robert. "Donald Trump is not a populist. To be him, Democrats will have to show what real populism is all about." *Politico*, August 29, 2017. https://www.politico.com/magazine/story/2017/08/29/donald-trump-not-a-populist-215552

Siegel, D. "Trump unleashes birther private eyes." *National Enquirer*, April 8, 2011. https://www.nationalenquirer.com/celebrity/trump-unleashes-birther-private-eyes/

Silva, Daniella. "Synagogue massacre suspect pushed caravan conspiracies far-right has embraced." *NBC News*, October 29, 2018. https://www.nbcnews.com/news/latino/synagogue-massacre-suspect-pushed-caravan-conspiracies-far-right-has-embraced-n925921

Silverleib, Alan. "Obama releases long-form birth certificate." *CNN*, April 27, 2011. http://www.cnn.com/2011/POLITICS/04/27/obama.birth.certificate/index.html

Silverstein, Jason. "Donald Trump's fateful campaign announcement speech has really not aged well." *New York Daily News*, June 16, 2017. https://www.nydailynews.com/news/politics/trump-fateful-campaign-announcement-not-aged-article-1.3250165

Smith, Ben, III. "Perot drops out; he asserts election in House 'would be disruptive' to the country, cites 'revitalized' Democratic Party; says he realized it wasn't possible to win three-way presidential race." *Atlanta Journal and Constitution*, July 16, 1992, p. A1.

Smith, Ben, and Byron Tau. "Birtherism: Where it all began." *Politico*, April 24, 2011. https://www.politico.com/story/2011/04/birtherism-where-it-all-began-053563?paginate=false

Smith, David. "Survey: Two in three Trump supporters want a president who breaks the rules." *The Guardian*, December 5, 2017. https://www.theguardian.com/us-news/2017/dec/05/republican-trump-supporters-survey-american-values-rule-breaker

Smith, David. "'Trump derangement syndrome': The week America went mad." *The Guardian*, July 22, 2019. https://www.theguardian.com/us-news/2018/jul/21/trump-derangement-syndrome-putin-summit-republicans

Soble, Jonathan, and Keith Bradsher. "Donald Trump laces into Japan with a trade tirade from the '80s." *New York Times*, March 7, 2016. http://www.nytimes.com/2016/03/08/business/international/unease-after-trump-depicts-tokyo-as-an-economic-rival.html?partner=bloomberg

Soldak, Katya. "Ukrainian humor: A comedian is elected president." *Forbes*, April 21, 2019. https://www.forbes.com/sites/katyasoldak/2019/04/21/ukrainian-humor-a-comedian-is-elected-president/#4129dffcd140

Speros, Bill. "Rand Paul on golfing with Donald Trump: 'The president never loses'." *Golfweek*, October 15, 2017. https://golfweek.com/2017/10/15/rand-paul-on-golfing-with-donald-trump-the-president-never-loses/

St. Louis Post-Dispatch. "Perot persecution by GOP was a hoax, supporter says." March 29, 1997, p. 17.

St. Petersburg Times, "Perot-noia." October 27, 1992, p. 8A.

Stein, Harry. "The Goldwater takedown." *City Journal*, April 2016. https://www.city-journal.org/html/goldwater-takedown-14787.html

Stein, Jeff. "Sanders is beating Obama's 2008 youth vote record. And the primary's not even over." *Vox*, June 2, 2016. https://www.vox.com/2016/6/2/11818320/bernie-sanders-barack-obama-2008

Stepman, Jarrett. "The 25th Amendment: Everything you need to know." *The National Interest*, January 10, 2018. https://nationalinterest.org/blog/the-buzz/the-25th-amendment-everything-you-need-know-24003

Stewart, David O. "Nixon, Johnson and Trump: America's angry presidents." *Baltimore Sun*, February 19, 2019. https://www.baltimoresun.com/news/opinion/oped/bs-ed-op-0218-angry-presidents-20190215-story.html

Stole, Bryn. "Ahead of Trump's State of the Union, Cedric Richmond and the Congressional Black Caucus blast his 'racist rhetoric'." *Baton Rouge Advocate*, January 30, 2018. https://www.theadvocate.com/baton_rouge/news/politics/article_50276bf8-05e9-11e8-afbd-7344421633a8.html

Strauss, Delphine. "Economists reject Trump claims of unfair trade system." *Financial Times*, June 18, 2018. https://www.ft.com/content/2edf26f8-6b28-11e8-b6eb-4acfcfb08c11

Sullivan, Sean, and Jenna Johnson, "Yes, Donald Trump's crowds are big—but not quite as 'yuge' as he often claims." *Washington Post*, October 29, 2016. https://www.washingtonpost.com/news/post-politics/wp/2016/10/29/yes-donald-trumps-crowds-are-big-but-not-quite-as-yuge-as-he-often-claims/

Tani, Maxwell. "The songs that Donald Trump rallies blast to pump up supporters." *Business Insider*, January 9, 2016. https://www.businessinsider.com/donald-trump-rally-songs-2015-12

Tavernise, Sabrina, and Robert Gebeloff. "They voted for Obama, then went for Trump. Can Democrats win them back?" *New York Times*, May 14, 2018. https://www.nytimes.com/2018/05/04/us/obama-trump-swing-voters.html

Taylor, Jessica, and Peter Overby. "Federal watchdog finds government ignored Emoluments Clause with Trump hotel." *NPR*, January 16, 2019. https://www.npr.org/2019/01/16/685977471/federal-watchdog-finds-government-ignored-emoluments-clause-with-trump-hotel

Taylor, Jessica. "Trump calls for unity, healing in Thanksgiving Address." *NPR*, November 23, 2016. https://www.npr.org/2016/11/23/503192654/trump-calls-for-unity-healing-in-thanksgiving-address

Taylor-Coleman, Jasmine. "The dark depths of hatred for Hillary Clinton." *BBC News*, October 12, 2016. https://www.bbc.com/news/magazine-36992955

Tennenhaus, Sam. "The GOP, or Goldwater's Old Party." *The New Republic*, June 11, 2001, p. 33.

Tharoor, Ishan. "Trump's populism is about creating division, not unity." *Washington Post*, February 6, 2017. https://www.washingtonpost.com/news/worldviews/wp/2017/02/06/trumps-populism-is-about-creating-division-not-unity/?utm_term=.5e2d19318d5e

The Economist, Open Future, "Conspiracy theories are dangerous—here's how to crush them." August 12, 2019. https://www.economist.com/open-future/2019/08/12/conspiracy-theories-are-dangerous-heres-how-to-crush-them

Thomsen, Jacqueline. "Trump: My supporters should be called the 'super elite'." *The Hill*, June 27, 2018. http://thehill.com/homenews/administration/394551-trump-my-supporters-should-be-called-the-super-elite

Tillett, Emily. "Trump signs 'religious liberty' executive order." *CBS News*, May 4, 2017. https://www.cbsnews.com/news/trump-signs-religious-liberty-order-to-defend-freedom-of-religion/

Tillett, Emily. "Adam Schiff: What Trump said publicly is 'damning enough' for impeachment." *CBS News*, September 25, 2019. https://www.cbsnews.com/news/adam-schiff-whistleblower-what-trump-said-publicly-is-damning-enough-for-impeachment-today-2019-09-25/

Timm, Jane C. "Fact check: Trump's administration has created 600,000 manufacturing jobs." *NBC News*, February 5, 2019. https://www.nbcnews.com/card/fact-check-we-ve-added-half-million-manufacturing-jobs-n967436

Trump, Donald J. "'Trumped!'" *New York Times*, September 1, 1991, p. BR4.

Trump, Donald J. "There's nothing wrong with America's foreign defense policy that a little backbone can't cure." *Washington Post*, September 2, 1987, p. A9.

Trump, Donald J. "Counting stars." *New York Times*, July 18, 1993, p. V7.

Trump, Donald J. "Downside to upside, all around town." *Wall Street Journal*, September 27, 1991, p. A11.

Trump, Donald J. "I'm back. I'm soaring once again. But enough about you." *New York Times*, November 19, 1995, p. SM58.

Trump, Donald J. "Trump's waistline, from Trump's perspective." *New York Times*, May 2, 1996, p. A22.

Trump, Donald J. "Trump bashing." *Washington Post*, March 8, 1997, p. A21.

Trump, Donald J. "The anti-Trump." *New York Times*, January 17, 1999, p. SM10.

Trump, Donald J. "What I saw at the revolution." *New York Times*, February 19, 2000, p. A15.

Trump, Donald J. "Letters: Character Studies." *New York Times*, September 11, 2005, p. F6.

Tucker, Joshua. "Will global populism continue to erode democracies?" *Washington Post*, September 13, 2017. https://www.washington-post.com/news/monkey-cage/wp/2017/09/13/will-global-populism-continue-to-erode-democracies/

Tumulty, Karen. "How Hillary Clinton helped create what she later called the 'vast right-wing conspiracy'." *Washington Post*, September 3, 2016. https://www.washingtonpost.com/politics/hillary-clinton-was-right-about-the-vast-right-wing-conspiracy-heres-why-it-exists/2016/09/02/4a5e0fba-6879-11e6-99bf-f0cf3a6449a6_story.html?utm_term=.74d34a5ab15a

Tumulty, Karen. "Will Obama's anti-rumor plan work? The Democratic candidate is turning to the Web to disprove the rumors about his faith, his family and his patriotism." *Time*, June 12, 2008. http://content.time.com/time/subscriber/article/0,33009,1813978,00.html

Turley, Jonathan. "Sorry folks, Trump is not insane. *The Hill*, October 24, 2017. http://thehill.com/opinion/white-house/356842-trump-pales-in-comparison-to-our-history-ofmentally-ill-presidents.

USA Today. "Who supports Trump?" https://www.usatoday.com/pages/interactives/elections/trump-support/

USA Today. "EPA nominee showcases how Trump keeps failing to drain the swamp." January 15, 2019. https://www.usatoday.com/story/opinion/2019/01/15/epa-nominee-showcases-how-trump-fails-drain-swamp-editorials-debates/2578903002/

Ventresca, Rachel. "Clinton: 'You cannot be civil with a political party that wants to destroy what you stand for'." *CNN*, October 9, 2018. https://www.cnn.com/2018/10/09/politics/hillary-clinton-civility-congress-cnntv/index.html

Vidal, Gore. "The art and arts of E. Howard Hunt." *The New York Review*, December 13, 1973. Available from the Harold Weisberg Archive, Hood College at http://jfk.hood.edu/Collection/Weisberg

%20Subject%20Index%20Files/V%20Disk/Vidal%20Gore/
Item%2001.pdf

Von Drehle, David. "Ross Perot walked so Trump could run." *Washington Post*, July 9, 2019. https://www.washingtonpost.com/opinions/before-donald-trump-there-was-ross-perot/2019/07/09/284bf7e0-a27b-11e9-bd56-eac6bb02d01d_story.html

Von Schoik, Michael. "Trump 'is not a racist' at all: Ben Carson." *Fox Business News*, July 21, 2019. https://www.foxbusiness.com/economy/trump-is-not-racist-at-all-ben-carson

Wagner, John. "Mia Love gives Trump no love as she concedes a narrow loss in Utah." *Washington Post*, November 26, 2018. https://www.washingtonpost.com/politics/mia-love-gives-trump-no-love-as-she-concedes-a-narrow-loss-in-utah/2018/11/26/2062c158-f1a5-11e8-80d0-f7e1948d55f4_story.html?utm_term=.54a0dd9b239e

Wagner, John. "Two days later, Sanders draws five times as many people as Clinton to event at same university in N.H." *Washington Post Blogs*, September 21, 2015.

Wagner, John, Nick Miroff, and Mike DeBonis. "Trump reverses course, signs order ending his policy of separating families at the border." *Washington Post*, June 20, 2018. https://www.washingtonpost.com/powerpost/gop-leaders-voice-hope-that-bill-addressing-family-separations-will-pass-thursday/2018/06/20/cc79db9a-7480-11e8-b4b7-308400242c2e_story.html?utm_term=.2342240925d0

Walker, Jesse. "One candidate had a foreign policy that anticipated Trump." *Reason*, August 30, 2016. https://reason.com/blog/2016/08/30/trump-wallace-foreign-policy

Walker, Peter. "Barack Obama's Trump-supporting half-brother Malik tweets Kenya birth certificate." *UK Independent*, March 10, 2017. https://www.independent.co.uk/news/world/americas/barack-obama-half-brother-malik-kenya-birth-certificate-tweet-donald-trump-supporter-a7622346.html

Walsh, Edward. "A serene Carter." *Washington Post*, July 22, 1979.

Wartzman, Rick, and Dana Milbank. "Clinton's strengths with business leaders is rare for a Democrat." *Wall Street Journal*, September 24, 1992, p. A1.

Washington Post. "Rep. Matt Gaetz wins Florida's 1st Congressional District seat." November 27, 2016. https://www.washingtonpost.com/election-results/florida-1st-congressional-district/?utm_term=.343976660a57

Washington Post. "Trump on trade: he'd represent; attacking allies, developer says U.S. needs better negotiator." November 1, 1999, p. A20.

Washington Post. "Goldwater's 1964 Acceptance Speech." https://www.washingtonpost.com/wp-srv/politics/daily/may98/goldwater-speech.htm

Weigel, David. "Sanders condemns violence at Trump's San Jose rally." *Washington Post*, June 3, 2016. https://www.washingtonpost.com/news/post-politics/wp/2016/06/03/sanders-condemns-violence-at-trumps-san-jose-rally/

Weisman, Chad. "In US elections, a history of anti-Semitism." *Times of Israel*, August 30, 2016. https://www.timesofisrael.com/the-specter-of-anti-semitism-is-nothing-new-in-us-elections/

Welna, David, and Bill Chappell. "Supreme Court revives Trump's ban on transgender military personnel, for now." *NPR*, January 22, 2019. https://www.npr.org/2019/01/22/687368145/supreme-court-revives-trumps-ban-on-transgender-military-personnel-for-now

Wheeler, Lydia. "Court tosses challenge to Trump's two-for-one regulatory order." *The Hill*, February 26, 2017. http://thehill.com/regulation/court-battles/375617-court-tosses-challenge-to-trumps-two-for-one-regulatory-order

Wicker, Tom. "Johnson swamps Goldwater." *New York Times*, November 4, 1964. https://archive.nytimes.com/www.nytimes.com/books/98/04/12/specials/johnson-goldwater.html

Wilentz, Sean. "Confounding fathers: The Tea Party's Cold War roots." *The New Yorker*, October 18, 2008. https://www.newyorker.com/magazine/2010/10/18/confounding-fathers

Will, George. "Vote against the GOP this November." *Washington Post*, June 22, 2018.

Williams, Katie Bo. "Comey leaked memos to prompt special counsel." *The Hill*, June 8, 2017. https://thehill.com/policy/national-security/336932-comey-leaked-memo-to-prompt-special-counsel

Wilson, Jason. "Portland rally: Proud Boys vow to march each month after biggest protest of Trump era." *Guardian*, August 17, 2019. https://www.theguardian.com/us-news/2019/aug/17/portland-oregon-far-right-rally-proud-boys-antifa

Willstein, Matt. "Inside Sacha Baron Cohen's 13-year feud with Donald Trump, from Ali G to 'Brothers Grimsby'." *Daily Beast*, March 19, 2016. https://www.thedailybeast.com/inside-sacha-baron-cohens-13-year-feud-with-donald-trump-from-ali-g-to-brothers-grimsby

Wisk, Allison, and Julie Westfall. "Democratic National Convention day one: Bernie Sanders tells supporters, 'Hillary Clinton must become the next president of the United States'." *Los Angeles Times*, July 25, 2016. https://www.latimes.com/nation/politics/trailguide/

la-na-democratic-convention-2016-live-sanders-supporters-shout-chants-1469481165-htmlstory.html

Wolf, Z. Byron. "How Donald Trump could delegitimize his own government." *CNN*, March 11, 2017. https://www.cnn.com/2017/03/11/politics/trump-deep-state/index.html

Wolfgang, Ben. "Sanders denies he's 'Santa Claus' and wants to 'give away a bunch of free stuff'." *Washington Times*, February 5, 2016. https://www.washingtontimes.com/news/2016/feb/5/bernie-sanders-denies-hes-santa-claus/

Woodward, Bob, and John Mintz. "Perot launched investigations of Bush; billionaire considered then-vice president, weak, indecisive and possibly corrupt." *Washington Post*, June 21, 1992, p. A1.

Wright, Bruce C. T. "Ross Perot dies 27 years after his infamous NAACP 'You People' speech." *NewsOne*, July 9, 2019. https://newsone.com/3881919/ross-perot-dies-you-people-naacp-speech/

Yan, Holly. "Donald Trump's 'blood' comment about Megyn Kelly draws outrage." *CNN*, August 8, 2015. https://www.cnn.com/2015/08/08/politics/donald-trump-cnn-megyn-kelly-comment/index.html

Yetter, Deborah. "Thousands alarmed by Trump agenda hold rally." *Courier Journal* (Louisville), January 21, 2017. https://www.courier-journal.com/story/news/politics/2017/01/21/local-activists-call-social-justice/96676446/

York, Byron. "When did Mueller know there was no collusion?" *Washington Examiner*, April 29, 2019. https://www.washingtonexaminer.com/opinion/columnists/byron-york-when-did-mueller-know-there-was-no-collusion

Young, Jeremy C. "President Trump's rallies are about boosting his ego, not his agenda. The novel purpose behind Trump's road show." *Washington Post*, July 25, 2017. https://www.washingtonpost.com/news/made-by-history/wp/2017/07/25/president-trumps-rallies-are-about-boosting-his-ego-not-his-agenda/?utm_term=.526fd061190f

Young, Stephen B. "The power of the presidency: Why Trump can't make it go." *Minneapolis Star-Tribune*, March 31, 2017. http://www.startribune.com/the-power-of-the-presidency-why-trump-cant-make-it-go/417835453/

Zapotosky, Matt. "Trump said Mueller's team has '13 hardened Democrats.' Here are the facts." *Washington Post Blogs*, March 18, 2018.

Zauzmer, Julie. "As Trump picks Brett Kavanaugh for the Supreme Court, evangelicals rejoice: 'I will vote for him again'." *Seattle Times*, July 9, 2018. https://www.seattletimes.com/nation-world/

nation-politics/wapoas-trump-picks-kavanaugh-for-the-supreme-court-evangelicals-rejoice-i-will-vote-for-him-again/

Zernike, Kate. "Conspiracies are us: The endless debate over Obama's birth certificate and the paranoid style in American politics." *New York Times*, May 1, 2011, p. WK1.

Zinoman, Jason. "The misunderstood history of Trump on Letterman." *New York Times*, August 15, 2017. https://www.nytimes.com/2017/08/15/arts/television/trump-letterman-misunderstood-history.html

Zuckerman, Jake. "Trump co-endorses Jenkins, Morrisey; says 'no way' to Blankenship." *Charleston Gazette-Mail*, May 7, 2018. https://www.wvgazettemail.com/news/politics/trump-co-endorses-jenkins-morrisey-says-no-way-to-blankenship/article_22031285-d5b2-59e4-8d6d-8ad36f4edb7b.html

Zurcher, Anthony. "The birth of the Obama 'birther' conspiracy." *BBC News*, September 16, 2016. https://www.bbc.com/news/election-us-2016-37391652

Social media

@realDonaldTrump. "@SachaBaronCohen is a moron who should have been pummeled by the weak and pathetic security person who stood watching as he poured ashes over @RyanSeacrest, a wonderful guy, at the Academy Award's red carpet. The security person totally froze—he should be fired." February 27, 2012, 6:58 a.m.

@realDonaldTrump. "Glad to see that Sacha Baron Cohen's new movie is not only a dud but not too good at the box office. He is talentless. @Sacha_B_Cohen." May 22, 2012, 12:31 p.m.

@realDonaldTrump. "I never fall for scams. I am the only person who immediately walked out of my 'Ali G' interview." October 22, 2012, 10:44 a.m.

@realDonaldTrump. "When someone attacks me, I always attack back . . . except 100x more. This has nothing to do with a tirade but rather, a way of life!" *Twitter*, November 11, 2012, 5:56 a.m. https://twitter.com/realdonaldtrump/status/267626951097868289?lang=en

@realDonaldTrump. "I love taking lawsuits all the way when I'm right. @AGSchneiderman is finding that out the hard way!" *Twitter*, March 12, 2014, 9:11 a.m. https://twitter.com/realdonaldtrump/status/443781419618545664

@realDonaldTrump. "The Iran nuclear deal is a terrible one for the United States and the world. It does nothing but make Iran rich and will lead to catastrophe." *Twitter*, April 3, 2015, 4:06 p.m. https://twitter.com/realdonaldtrump/status/584129948916514818

@realDonaldTrump. "Let's Trump the Establishment! We are no longer silent. We will Make America Great Again!" *Twitter*, July 22, 2015, p.m., 12:03 p.m. https://twitter.com/realdonaldtrump/status/623931297698705408

@realDonaldTrump. "Lindsey Graham is all over T.V., much like failed 47% candidate Mitt Romney. These nasty, angry, jealous failures have ZERO credibility!" *Twitter*, March 6, 2016, 8:03 a.m. https://twitter.com/realdonaldtrump/status/706812638215303168?lang=en

@realDonaldTrump. "We cannot let the failing REPUBLICAN ESTABLISHMENT, who could not stop Obama (twice), ruin the MOVEMENT with millions of $'s in false ads!" *Twitter*, March 7, 2016, 9:03 a.m. https://twitter.com/realdonaldtrump/status/706827555562547456?lang=da

@realDonaldTrump. "I love watching these poor, pathetic people (pundits) on television working so hard and so seriously to try and figure me out. They can't!" *Twitter*, August 12, 2016, 4:43 a.m. https://twitter.com/realdonaldtrump/status/764064821000056832

@realDonaldTrump. "In addition to winning the Electoral College in a landslide, I won the popular vote if you deduct the millions of people who voted illegally." *Twitter*, November 27, 2016, 12:30 p.m. https://twitter.com/realdonaldtrump/status/802972944532209664.

@realDonaldTrump. "There is nothing nice about searching for terrorists before they can enter our country. This was a big part of my campaign. Study the world!" *Twitter*, January 30, 2017, 4:27 a.m.

@realDonald Trump. "It is time to take care of OUR people, to rebuild OUR NATION, and to fight for OUR GREAT AMERICAN WORKERS!" *Twitter*, September 27, 2017, 6:55 p.m. https://twitter.com/realdonaldtrump/status/913220484640182272

@realDonaldTrump. "Bob Corker, who helped President O give us the bad Iran Deal & couldn't get elected dog catcher in Tennessee, is now fighting Tax Cuts. . ." *Twitter*, October 24, 2017, 5:13 a.m. https://twitter.com/realdonaldtrump/status/922798321739161600?lang=en

@realDonaldTrump. "Our Steel and Aluminum industries (and many others) have been decimated by decades of unfair trade and bad policy with countries from around the world. We must not let our country, companies and workers be taken advantage of any longer. We want

414

free, fair and SMART TRADE!" *Twitter*, March 1, 2018, 7:12 a.m. https://twitter.com/realdonaldtrump/status/969183644756660224

@realDonaldTrump. "Comey drafted the Crooked Hillary exoneration long before he talked to her (lied in Congress to Senator G), then based his decisions on her poll numbers. Disgruntled, he, McCabe, and the others, committed many crimes!" *Twitter*, April 16, 2018, 5:25 a.m. https://twitter.com/realdonaldtrump/status/985856662866202624

@realDonaldTrump. "How could Jeff Flake, who is setting record low polling numbers in Arizona and was therefore humiliatingly forced out of his own Senate seat without even a fight (and who doesn't have a clue), think about running for office, even a lower one, again? Let's face it, he's a Flake!" *Twitter*, June 7, 2018. https://twitter.com/realdonaldtrump/status/1004722061808427008

@realDonaldTrump. "This is a terrible situation and Attorney General Jeff Sessions should stop this Rigged Witch Hunt right now, before it continues to stain our country any further. Bob Mueller is totally conflicted, and his 17 Angry Democrats that are doing his dirty work are a disgrace to USA!" *Twitter*, August 1, 2018, 6:24 a.m. https://twitter.com/realdonaldtrump/status/1024646945640525826

@realDonald Trump. "Jeff Sessions said he wouldn't allow politics to influence him only because he doesn't understand what is happening underneath his command position. Highly conflicted Bob Mueller and his gang of 17 Angry Dems are having a field day as real corruption goes untouched. No Collusion!" *Twitter*, August 25, 2018, 5:36 a.m. https://twitter.com/realdonaldtrump/status/1033332301579661312

@realDonaldTrump. "Remember, NAFTA was one of the WORST Trade Deals ever made. The U.S. lost thousands of businesses and millions of jobs. We were far better off before NAFTA—should never have been signed. Even the Vat Tax was not accounted for. We make new deal or go back to pre-NAFTA!" *Twitter*, September 1, 2018, 8:12 a.m. https://twitter.com/realdonaldtrump/status/1035908242277376001

@realDonaldTrump. "Many Gang Members and some very bad people are mixed into the Caravan heading to our Southern Border. Please go back, you will not be admitted into the United States unless you go through the legal process. This is an invasion of our Country and our Military is waiting for you!" *Twitter*, October 29, 2018, 7:41 a.m. https://twitter.com/realDonaldTrump/status/1056919064906469376

@realDonaldTrump. "Congressman @RodBlum of Iowa got a desperately needed Flood Wall for Cedar Rapids that was almost impossible to get. He makes a BIG difference for Iowa! Border,

Military, Vets etc. We need Rod in D.C. He has my Strong Endorsement!" *Twitter*, October 29, 2018, 10:07 p.m. https://twitter.com/realDonaldTrump/status/1057106631652196354?ref_src=twsrc%5Etfw%7Ctwcamp%5Etweetembed%7Ctwterm%5E1057106631652196354&ref_url=https%3A%2F%2Fwhotv.com%2F2018%2F10%2F30%2Fpresident-trump-gives-personal-endorsement-to-iowa-congressman-rod-blum%2F

@realDonaldTrump. "...should never have been appointed and there should be no Mueller Report. This was an illegal & conflicted investigation in search of a crime. Russian Collusion was nothing more than an excuse by the Democrats for losing an Election that they thought they were going to win..." *Twitter*, March 15, 2019, 6:55 a.m. https://twitter.com/realdonaldtrump/status/1106554458383806467

@realDonaldTrump. "'If the Democrats are successful in removing the President from office (which they will never be), it will cause a Civil War like fracture in this Nation from which our Country will never heal.' Pastor Robert Jeffress, @FoxNews." *Twitter*, September 29, 2019, 6:11 p.m. https://twitter.com/realdonaldtrump/status/1178477539653771264

Video material, transcripts, and addresses

CNN Transcripts, Anderson Cooper 360 Degrees. "Trump holds Ohio rally." December 1, 2016. http://transcripts.cnn.com/TRANSCRIPTS/1612/01/acd.01.html

C-SPAN. "Bernie Sanders at Liberty University." September 14, 2015. https://www.c-span.org/video/?c4550942/bernie-sanders-liberty-university.

C-SPAN. "President-elect Donald Trump victory rally in Des Moines, Iowa." December 8, 2016. https://www.c-span.org/video/?419792-1/president-elect-donald-trump-holds-rally-des-moines-iowa

C-SPAN. "President-elect Donald Trump victory rally in Hershey, Pennsylvania," December 15, 2016. https://www.c-span.org/video/?420211-1/president-elect-donald-trump-vice-president-elect-mike-pence-deliver-remarks-hershey-pennsylvania

C-SPAN. "President-elect Donald Trump victory rally in Mobile, Alabama," December 17, 2016. https://www.c-span.org/video/?420254-1/president-elect-donald-trump-holds-thank-you-rally-mobile-alabama

C-SPAN. "President-elect Donald Trump victory rally in North Carolina." December 6, 2016. https://www.c-span.org/video/?419634-1/

president-elect-trump-holds-victory-rally-fayetteville-north-carolina

C-SPAN. "President-elect Donald Trump victory rally in West Allis, Wisconsin." December 13, 2016. https://c-span.org/vicdeo/?420078-1/president-elect-trump-vice-president-elect-pence-deliver-remarks-west-allis-wisconsin

C-SPAN. "President-elect Donald Trump victory rally in Orlando, Florida," December 16, 2016. https://www.c-span.org/video/?420255-1/president-elect-donald-trump-holds-rally-orlando-florida

C-SPAN. "President Trump rally in Melbourne, Florida." February 18, 2017. https://www.c-span.org/video/?424154-1/president-trump-holds-rally-melbourne-florida

C-SPAN. "President Trump rally in Nashville, Tennessee." March 15, 2017. https://www.c-span.org/video/?425428-1/president-trump-calls-revised-travel-ban-freeze-unprecedented-judicial-overreach

C-SPAN. "President Trump rally in Pensacola, Florida." December 8, 2017. https://www.c-span.org/video/?438191-1/president-trump-holds-rally-pensacola-florida

C-SPAN. "President Trump remarks in Harrisburg, Pennsylvania." April 29, 2017. https://www.c-span.org/video/?427466-1/president-fake-news-media-touts-record-100-days

C-SPAN. "Senator Bernie Sanders campaign announcement." May 26, 2015. https://www.c-span.org/video/?326214-1/senator-bernie-sanders-i-vt-presidential-campaign-announcement

C-SPAN. "Sen. Bernie Sanders (I-VT): Opening remarks at Liberty University." September 14, 2015. https://www.c-span.org/video/?c4550988/sen-bernie-sanders-opening-remarks-liberty-university

C-SPAN. Transcript, "Donald Trump campaign rally in Hershey, Pennsylvania." November 4, 2016. https://www.c-span.org/video/?418009-1/donald-trump-campaigns-hershey-pennsylvania

C-SPAN. Transcript, "Donald Trump campaign rally in Hilton Head, South Carolina." December 30, 2015. https://www.c-span.org/video/?402610-1/donald-trump-campaign-rally-hilton-head-south-carolina

Diamond Rio. "It's all in your head." 1996. https://www.youtube.com/watch?v=p8Otmhv6YOI

Factbase. "Donald Trump in Baton Rouge, LA, December 9, 2016." https://factba.se/transcript/donald-trump-speech-baton-rouge-la-december-9-2016

Limbaugh, Rush. "An update on Barry's hut brother." *Rushlimbaugh.com*, September 9, 2009. https://www.rushlimbaugh.com/daily/2009/09/15/an_update_on_barry_s_hut_brother/

Lincoln, Abraham. Inaugural Address, March 4, 1861. https://www
.gilderlehrman.org/content/president-lincoln%E2%80%99s-first-
inaugural-address-1861

Media Matters. Video, "Hannity defends birthers: 'Why are they crucified and beaten up and smeared and besmirched?'" March 24, 2011.
https://www.mediamatters.org/video/2011/03/24/hannity-defends-
birthers-why-are-they-crucified/177928

Nixon, Richard M. "Great Silent Majority" speech on Vietnam policy,
November 3, 1969. http://www.americanrhetoric.com/speeches/
richardnixongreatsilentmajority.html

"Republican Convention," 1964. Lyndon Johnson television campaign advertisement. Museum of the Living Image, http://www.
livingroomcandidate.org/commercials/1964/republican-convention
#3991

Schwartz, Ian. "Trump: Some reporters 'Don't Like Our Country,' don't
want to Make America Great Again." *RealClearPolitics*, August 23,
2017. https://www.realclearpolitics.com/video/2017/08/23/trump_
some_reporters_dont_like_our_country_dont_want_to_make_
america_great_again.html

Trump, Donald J. Announcement of Candidacy, Trump Tower, New York,
NY, June 16, 2015. http://www.p2016.org/trump/trump061615sp.html

Trump, Donald J. "Donald Trump remarks on President Obama's
birth certificate." *C-SPAN*, April 27, 2011. https://www.c-span.org/
video/?299230-1/donald-trump-remarks-president-obamas-birth-
certificate

Trump, Donald J. Interview with Larry King at the Republican
National Convention, August, 1988. https://www.youtube.com/
watch?v=Usb0iE5WiZI

Trump, Donald J. "President Donald J. Trump's State of the Union
Address," January 30, 2018. https://www.whitehouse.gov/briefings-
statements/president-donald-j-trumps-state-union-address/

Trump, Donald J. "Remarks by President Trump to the 73rd Session of the
United Nations General Assembly," New York, September 25, 2018.
https://www.whitehouse.gov/briefings-statements/remarks-president-
trump-73rd-session-united-nations-general-assembly-new-york-ny/

Trump, Donald J. Speech to CPAC. February 10, 2011. http://www
.p2012.org/photos11/cpac11/trump021011spt.html

Trump, Donald J. Speech to CPAC, March 15, 2013. http://www
.p2016.org/photos13/cpac13/trump031513spt.html

Wallace, George. 1968 Wallace Campaign advertisement. https://www
.youtube.com/watch?v=4RZ4G251WR4

Wallace, George. George C. Wallace for President 1976 Campaign Brochure. "George C. Wallace has the courage America needs now." http://www.4president.org/brochures/1976/wallace1976brochure.htm

Wallace, George. "The Civil Rights Movement: Fraud, Sham, and Hoax." Address, July 4, 1964. http://www.blackpast.org/1964-george-c-wallace-civil-rights-movement-fraud-sham-and-hoax

Wallace, George. "Segregation Now, Segregation Forever." Inaugural Address as Alabama Governor, January 14, 1963. http://www.blackpast.org/1963-george-wallace-segregation-now-segregation-forever

YouTube. "George Wallace suggests shooter was part of a conspiracy." February 15, 2015. https://www.youtube.com/watch?v=FAxB9WYJN_Q

YouTube. "Sacha Baron Cohen recalls the Ali G—Donald Trump interview." https://www.youtube.com/watch?v=W_ref_Xly7Y

Primary and historical documents

American Party Platform, 1856, Articles III and IX. *HistoryHub*, http://historyhub.abc-clio.com/Support/Display/2144524?sid=2146163&cid=31&view=&tab=3

Anti-Federalist #67. http://www.thisnation.com/library/antifederalist/67.html

Federalist #1. http://avalon.law.yale.edu/18th_century/fed01.asp

Federalist #10. http://avalon.law.yale.edu/18th_century/fed10.asp

Federalist #48. http://avalon.law.yale.edu/18th_century/fed48.asp

Federalist #49. http://avalon.law.yale.edu/18th_century/fed49.asp

Federalist #51. http://avalon.law.yale.edu/18th_century/fed51.asp.

Federalist #68. http://avalon.law.yale.edu/18th_century/fed68.asp

Flood, Emmet. Letter to Attorney General William Barr.

Jackson, Andrew. "Veto message regarding funding of infrastructure development." May 27, 1830. https://millercenter.org/the-presidency/presidential-speeches/may-27-1830-veto-message-regarding-funding-infrastructure

Jackson, Andrew. "President Jackson's veto message regarding the Bank of the United States; July 10, 1832." http://avalon.law.yale.edu/19th_century/ajveto01.asp

"People's Party Platform, 1896." http://www.digitalhistory.uh.edu/disp_textbook.cfm?smtID=3&psid=4067

Shillue, Tom. *Red Eye*, Fox News, September 30, 2015. https://archive.org/details/FOXNEWSW_20150930_070000_Red_Eye

Trump v. Hawaii (2018). https://www.supremecourt.gov/opinions/17pdf/17-965_h315.pdf

United States Senate. "The Impeachment of Andrew Johnson (1868) President of the United States," Chapter 7 (Articles of Impeachment). https://www.senate.gov/artandhistory/history/common/briefing/Impeachment_Johnson.htm#

White House. "Executive Order on the Establishment of a White House Faith and Opportunity Initiative," May 3, 2018. https://www.white-house.gov/presidential-actions/executive-order-establishment-white-house-faith-opportunity-initiative/

White House. "President Trump takes action to expedite priority energy and infrastructure projects," January 24, 2017. https://www.whitehouse.gov/briefings-statements/president-trump-takes-action-expedite-priority-energy-infrastructure-projects/

White House. "Remarks by President Trump in press conference after mid-term elections," November 7, 2018. https://www.whitehouse.gov/briefings-statements/remarks-president-trump-press-confer-ence-midterm-elections/

White House Office of Legal Counsel. Memorandum to the Attorney General. "A sitting president's amenability to indictment and criminal prosecution," October 6, 2000. https://www.justice.gov/sites/default/files/olc/opinions/2000/10/31/op-olc-v024-p0222_0.pdf

Unpublished manuscripts and miscellaneous

Competitive Enterprise Institute. "Presidential Executive Orders and Executive Memoranda," Chapter 5. https://cei.org/10KC/chapter-5

Digital History. "Alexander Hamilton's financial program." http://www.digitalhistory.uh.edu/disp_textbook.cfm?smtID=2&psid=2973

Driesen, David M. "President Trump's Executive Orders and the Rule of Law." Syracuse University. *Social Science Research Network* (SSRN Papers, 2018). https://papers.ssrn.com/sol3/papers.cfm?abstract_id=3114381

"Duck-Rabbit." https://www.illusionsindex.org/i/duck-rabbit

Hunston, Susan. "Donald Trump and the language of populism." Manuscript. April 2016. https://www.birmingham.ac.uk/research/perspective/donald-trump-language-of-populism.aspx

Internet Movie Data Base (IMDB). "Salvatore Corsitto: Bonasera, The Godfather," 1972. https://www.imdb.com/title/tt0068646/characters/nm0181128

Library of Congress. "King Andrew the First." https://www.archives.gov/exhibits/treasures_of_congress/Images/page_9/30a.html

Bibliography

"Optical Illusion, Rubin's Vase, 1915." https://www.sciencesource. com/archive/Optical-Illusion--Rubin-s-Vase--1915-SS2529214.html

Rottinghaus, Brandon, and Justin S. Vaughn. "Official results of the 2018 Presidents & Executive Politics Presidential Greatness Survey." http://www.marioguerrero.info/326/Rottinghaus.pdf

StandingWithStandingRock. Press release. "Trump Executive Memorandum on DAPL violates law and tribal treaties." January 24, 2017. https://standwithstandingrock.net/trump-executive-order-dapl-violates-law-tribal-treaties/

Statista. "Share of Americans who own a second home in 2018, by age." https://www.statista.com/statistics/228894/people-living-in-households-that-own-a-second-home-usa/

Stein, Jill. "The Green New Deal." *Jill Stein 2016*, https://www.jill2016. com/greennewdeal

Index

9/11/2001, 32

Abe, Shinzo, 190
abortion, 115, 166, 237, 293, 294,
    314, 349,
Academy Awards, 181
Access Hollywood video, 90
Acosta, Jim, 216–17
Adams, John, 149
Adams, John Quincy, 95, 96,
    149, 153
Affordable Care Act (ACA), 41, 44,
    153, 208, 282, 283, 284, 287,
    332
Afghanistan, 32, 169
African Americans, 23, 24, 38, 65,
    85, 135, 137, 138, 198, 256,
    257, 260, 263, 264, 330
Alabama, 21, 28, 81, 108, 246,
    249, 261
America First, 17, 52, 141, 142,
    153, 290
American Exceptionalism, 18, 58,
    83, 337
American Party, 15, 134
American Political Science
    Association, 337
American Psychological Association,
    36, 37, 316
Anderson, Pamela Sue, 180
antifa, 342
Anti-Federalist 67, 31
Apprentice (television show), 36,
    168, 225, 323
Archambault, Dave, 295
Aristotle, 69

Arizona, 87, 92, 92n, 134, 168,
    271
Arkansas, 106
Armstrong, Neil, 120
Atlantic City, New Jersey, 175,
    183, 184
Auschwitz, 26
Australia, 181

Baltimore, Maryland, 264
Balzac, Honoré de, 19
Bank of the United States *see*
    Jackson, Andrew
Bannon, Steve, 17, 112, 144
Barr, William, 110, 303, 304,
    305n
basket of deplorables, 42, 114, 242,
    260, 336; *see also* Clinton,
    Hillary Rodham
Baton Rouge, Louisiana, 250, 256
Beckett, Samuel, 302
Benson, Thomas Hart, 97
Biddle, Nicholas, 72, 94, 95, 97, 98,
    100, 101
Biden, Hunter, 39, 309, 343
Biden, Joe, 39, 309, 343, 344, 346
Bill of Rights, 74
Black Panthers, 128
Blum, Rod, 268
Blumenthal, Richard, 306
Blumenthal, Sidney, 277
Bolsonaro, Jair, 11–12, 60
Booker, Corey, 206
Border Patrol, 275
Boston Globe, 187
Boston, Massachusetts, 233, 264

Bradley, Bill, 166
Brando, Marlon, 214, 277
Branstadt, Terry, 255
Brazil, 11–12, 60
Bremer, Arthur, 126
Brexit, 9–11
British Broadcasting Corporations, 130
Broaddrick, Juanita, 191
Brooks, Moe, 268
Bryan, William Jennings, 13, 18–19, 54, 63, 76, 79–80, 87, 113, 117, 121–2, 133, 144, 202, 234; *see also* Cross of Gold Speech, 80, 121
Brzezinski, Mika, 216
Buchanan, James, 63, 149, 153, 338
Buchanan, Pat, 166, 167
Buckley, William F., 123
bumpstocks, 298
Bureau of Alcohol, Tobacco, and Firearms (ATF), 298
Burisma, 39, 343
Burlington, Vermont, 238, 239
Burr, Aaron, 96
Bush, George Herbert Walker, 21, 24, 91, 106, 127, 128, 129, 150, 159, 164, 165, 189
Bush, George Walker, 32, 90, 107, 150, 155, 168, 285, 292, 315
Bush, John Ellis (Jeb), 89, 221
Bush v. Gore, 315

Cable News Network (CNN), 34, 73, 74, 129, 136, 159, 162, 215, 216, 274
Calhoun, John C., 95, 98
Califano, Joseph, 109
California, 2, 167, 248, 267, 330
Cameron, David, 64
Camp Lejeune, North Carolina, 254
Canada, 5, 118, 128, 162, 186, 188, 294
Carlson, Tucker, 17
Carnegie, Andrew, 17

Carson, Ben, 213
Carson, California, 231
Carter, James Earl, 34, 40, 149, 153, 326
Castro, Fidel, 199
Cato *see* Clinton, George
Cats (play), 218
Central America, 275, 298
Central Europe, 11
Central Intelligence Agency (CIA), 107, 126, 127
Chabot, Steve, 250
Charlottesville, Virginia 24, 38, 91, 138, 271, 276
Cherokees, 145
Chicago, Illinois, 187, 220, 264, 323
China, 76, 162, 167, 168, 180, 185–90, 196, 207, 208, 223, 255, 294
Chirac, Jacques, 325
Cincinnati, Ohio, 246, 249, 253
Civil Rights Act (1964), 22, 85, 134
Civil Rights bill (1866), 263
Civil Rights Movement, 21, 81, 135
Civil Rights Museum, 138
Civil War, 263, 344
Clarke, David, 257
Clay, Henry, 15, 94, 95, 98, 100, 101
Cleon, 69
Cleveland, Ohio, 29, 264
Clinton, George, 31, 95
Clinton, Hillary Rodham, 1, 2, 3, 33, 39, 75, 103, 104, 105, 107, 131, 159, 191, 192, 193, 197, 204, 206, 210, 222, 223, 225, 227, 229, 231, 232, 233, 236, 237, 240, 242–4, 247, 249, 258–9, 261, 269, 273, 305, 312, 319, 332, 336, 337
basket of deplorables, 114, 242, 260, 336
"Crooked Hillary," 3, 107, 108, 191, 221
vast right wing conspiracy, 190

Clinton, William Jefferson, 50, 106, 130, 150, 164, 168, 171, 190, 191, 277, 292, 308, 309
Cohen, Michael, 106, 195, 311, 320–1, 323, 324
Cohen, Sacha Baron, 180–3
Colavita, Anthony, 163
Columbia Broadcasting System (CBS), 130, 180
Comey, James, 75, 103, 104, 105, 106, 107, 108, 111, 242, 311
Condon, Richard, 131
Congress, 4, 15, 21, 25, 28, 30, 32, 37, 39, 40–6, 48, 49, 51, 54, 56, 57, 61, 64, 75, 77, 91, 93, 94, 95, 97, 98, 100, 101, 102, 105, 110, 116, 142, 148, 154, 156, 165, 175, 176, 186, 205, 231, 238, 250, 261, 262, 263, 264, 265, 266, 268, 281, 282, 283, 284, 285, 287, 289, 293, 296, 298, 302, 303, 304, 306, 308, 309, 310, 314, 316, 317, 318, 320, 321, 324, 332, 335, 336, 343, 346, 348
Conservative Political Action Committee (CPAC), 168,
Constitution, 3, 16, 52, 71, 85, 95, 97, 98, 100, 102, 156, 176, 204, 263, 273, 281, 308, 314, 316, 324, 334, 338, 347
Constitutional Convention, 27
Conway Cabal, 120
Cooper, Jim, 270
Coppola, Francis Ford, 213
Corker, Bob, 91
Corsi, Jerome, 196–7
Coughlin, Fr. Charles, 20, 134
Cox, Archibald, 312
Crowe, Russell, 246
Cruz, Heidi, 210
Cruz, Rafael, 21, 199–200
Cruz, Ted, 89, 199, 210, 212
Cuba, 199
Cuomo, Mario, 169

Da Ali G Show, 181
Dakota Access Pipeline (DAPL), 50, 276, 294–5
Dallas, Texas, 120, 128, 129
Daniels, Stormy, 320
Davis, Jefferson, 264
Dayton, Ohio (shooting), 342
De Gaulle, Charles, 9, 325
Dean, John, 34
Deep state, 21, 52, 94, 103, 111, 114, 125, 132, 156, 191, 317, 344, 331
Defense, Secretary of, 295
Deferred Action on Childhood Arrivals (DACA), 51, 284
Demings, Val, 250, 251, 252
Democratic National Committee, 241, 310, 311
Democratic Party, 15, 17, 37, 65, 75, 138, 144, 206, 241, 350
Department of Defense, 254
Department of Education, 287
Department of Health and Human Services, 287
Department of Housing and Urban Development, 213
Department of Justice, 52, 94, 104, 107, 110, 111, 114, 132, 191, 192, 259, 308, 310, 311, 313, 314, 321, 322, 325
Department of State, 52, 123, 132, 191, 201
Department of the Treasury, 94, 97, 287
Des Moines, Iowa, 254
DeSantis, Ron, 64–5
Dewey, Thomas, 172
Diamond Rio, 120
Dinkins, David, 164
Dire Straits, 230
Director of National Intelligence, 212
District of Columbia, 137, 323, 324
Dobbs, Lou, 201
Downey, Morton, 189

drain the swamp, 245
Duke, David, 89, 135–6, 167
Duluth, Minnesota, 115
Dunbar, Mike, 187

Eastern Europe, 11, 123
Economist, 346
Ehrlichmann, John, 311
Eisenhower, Dwight David, 21, 84, 93, 122, 123, 271, 281, 299, 328, 335, 347
El Paso, Texas (shooting), 342
El Salvador, 135
Electoral College, 1–3, 8, 87, 95, 227, 229, 247, 248, 308, 330, 339
Emoluments Clause, 3, 324
England, 9
Environmental Protection Agency, 332
Ernst, Jodi, 255
Establishment Clause, 288
establishment (political), 1, 7, 11, 21, 29, 58, 66, 84, 87, 88, 91, 92, 93, 96, 110, 114, 115, 123, 144, 149, 197, 204, 210, 221, 223, 225, 243, 252, 277, 293, 325, 334, 349
Europe, 5, 59, 134, 169
European Parliament, 10
Evangelical Christians, 18, 54, 80, 296

Facebook, 337
Faith Office (White House), 80
fake news, 4, 33, 35, 74, 110, 114, 132, 183, 191, 217, 274, 276, 317
Farage, Nigel, 10
Farah, Joseph, 194
Fargo, North Dakota, 115
Farrell, Chris, 201
Fayetteville, North Carolina, 254
Federal Bureau of Investigation, 2, 6, 75, 94, 102–7, 106, 107, 110, 111, 112, 129, 130, 132, 191, 192, 304, 305, 311, 327, 331
Federal Register, 292
Federalist #1, 70
Federalist #10, 71
Federalist #51, 30
Federalist #68, 338
Federalist #70, 27, 28
Fifth Avenue (New York City), 185, 225
Fillmore, Millard, 15
Fiorina, Carly, 89, 210, 212
firearms, 298
Fitzwater, Marlin, 128
Flake, Jeff, 91
Flood, Emmett, 304–5
Florida, 1, 64–5, 89, 187, 201, 227, 231, 249, 250, 251–3, 260, 261, 270, 272, 323, 331
Flynn, Michael, 104, 105, 311
Forbes Magazine, 179
Forbes, Malcolm, 179
Ford, Gerald Rudolph, 34, 40, 106, 271n, 326
Ford, Henry, 17
Foreign Intelligence Surveillance Act (FISA), 103, 192, 304, 313
Fort Bragg, North Carolina, 254
Foster, Vince, 21, 191
Fox News, 4, 16, 17, 63, 195, 199, 200, 214, 229, 304
France, 8–9, 167
Fulani, Lenora, 167

G7, 142
Gaetz, Matt, 201, 268, 269, 270
Gallego, Rubin, 268, 271
Gallup Poll, 329
gay marriage, 314
gay rights, 88
General Motors, 185
General Services Administration, 324
George III, King, 31
Georgia, 234

Germany, 134, 188
Gilibrand, Kirsten, 206
Gillum, Andrew, 64, 65
Gilroy, California (shooting), 342
Gingrich, Newt, 309
Girard, Stephen, 95
Giscard-d'Estaing, Valéry, 325
Giuliani, Rudy, 164
Gladiator (film), 246
Godfather (film), 213–14, 277
Goldwater, Barry, 20, 21, 22–3, 54,
    63, 83–8, 92–3, 113, 122–4,
    134–5, 139, 140, 141, 142,
    143, 310
Goldwater Rule, 36, 316; *see
    also* American Psychological
    Association
Gore, Albert, 2n, 23,129,
    166, 244
Gorsuch, Neil, 331
Graham, Bob, 64
Graham, Gwen, 64
Graham, Lindsay, 89, 307, 313
Grammys, 345
Grand Old Party (GOP), 1, 43, 44,
    46, 47, 84, 86, 87, 88, 89, 90,
    91, 92, 93, 113, 124, 127, 130,
    131, 153, 159, 162, 163, 168,
    169, 171, 199, 204, 210, 212,
    213, 214, 225, 226, 228, 255,
    257, 277, 314, 322, 329, 330,
    333, 334, 347, 348, 349; *see
    also* Republican Party
Grand Rapids, Michigan, 256
Grant, Ulysses S., 266
Grassley, Charles, 255
Grateful Dead, 224
Great Britain, 95
Great Depression, 19, 28, 37,
    134, 137
Green, Al, 38, 252, 266
Green New Deal, 25, 205
Green Party, 203, 205, 257
Greenwood, Lee, 226
Guatemala, 201, 275

H&R Block, 329
Haiti, 135
Haldeman, H. R. (Harry Robbins),
    311
Hamilton, Alexander, 27, 70, 94,
    338–9, 350
Hamilton (play), 248
Hannity, Sean, 194, 199
Hardy, Thomas, 248
Harriman, Pamela, 184
Harris, Kamala, 206, 328
Harrisburg, Pennsylvania, 274,
Hawaii, 131, 193, 194, 273, 288
Helmsley, Leona, 179
Hermitage, 145
Hershey, Pennsylvania, 222,
    259
Herzog, Arthur, 205
Hewlett-Packard, 212
Hidden-hand leadership, 335
Hilton Head, South Carolina, 222
Hilton, Steve, 64,
Hispanics, 55, 253, 260, 330
Hitler, Adolph, 166
Honduras, 200, 201, 275
Honolulu, Hawaii, 193
Hoover, Herbert, 63, 149, 153
House Freedom Caucus, 269,
    283
House Intelligence Committee, 103,
    304, 309, 343, 344
Houston, Texas, 159
Huffington Post, 256
Humphrey, Hubert, 244
Hungary, 11, 201
Hunt, E. (Everette) Howard, 126

Illegal immigrants/immigration, 2, 3,
    14, 16, 24, 51, 135, 138,
    204, 223, 261, 270, 272, 274,
    298, 299
Illinois, 192, 267
Immigration and Customs
    Enforcement (ICE), 64, 200,
    275, 342

impeachment, 37–9, 43, 106, 152,
    157, 191, 247, 252, 265–7,
    302, 304, 306, 307–13, 315,
    317, 326, 339, 341, 343–4, 345
India, 168
Indian Removal Act (1830), 146
Indonesia, 193
Infowars, 3
Ingraham, Laura, 16, 195
Internal Revenue Service, 287,
    328, 329
Ionescu, Eugène, 6
Iowa, 159, 193, 233, 249, 250, 255
Iran, 50, 118, 140, 288, 291,
    296, 297
Iran nuclear deal *see* Joint
    Comprehensive Plan of Action
Iran–Contra, 106, 128
Iraq, 32, 140, 288
Ireland, 9
Irish Catholics, 15–16, 119, 134
Islamic State in Syria (ISIS), 204,
    207, 223, 295
Israel, 18, 25, 50, 142, 296

Jackson, Andrew, 12, 13, 14, 15, 54,
    58, 63, 68, 72, 76, 82, 93–102,
    112, 117, 133, 144, 144, 148,
    245, 248, 262, 272, 338
Jackson, Mississippi, 138
Japan, 162, 185, 186–90, 208
Jefferson, Thomas, 95, 102,
    148, 272
Jeffress, Robert (Pastor), 344
Jenkins, Evan, 268
Jerusalem, Israel, 50, 142, 296
Jim Crow, 119, 139, 263
John Birch Society, 21, 123–4
Johnson, Andrew, 109, 149, 150,
    247, 262–7, 276, 308
Johnson, Boris, 10–11
Johnson, Lyndon Baines, 31, 34, 86,
    87, 120, 149, 335, 338
Joint Comprehensive Plan of Action,
    50, 296–7

Jong-Un, Kim, 5, 33, 118
Journey, 218
Judicial Watch, 201
Judiciary Committee (House of
    Representatives), 310

Kaepernick, Colin, 38
Kansas, 234
Kasich, John, 253,
Kavanaugh, Brett, 155, 331
Keep America Great, 300
Kelly, John F., 275
Kelly, Megyn, 214–16
Kemp, Jack, 163
Kendall, Amos, 100
Kennedy, Caroline, 190
Kennedy, John Fitzgerald, 21, 34,
    44, 120, 122, 199, 314, 338
Kenya, 21, 193, 194, 195
Keystone XL Pipeline, 50, 276, 294
King, Larry, 159
King, Rev. Martin Luther, 134
Kislyak, Sergei, 105
Know-Nothing Party, 12, 15–17, 76,
    119, 134
Koch, Ed, 161, 163, 164, 173–5
Kristeva, Julia, 198–9
Kruschev, Nikita, 123
Ku Klux Klan, 22, 24, 85, 89, 135,
    136, 167

Lake Champlain, 238
Las Vegas, 1, 84; *see also* shooting,
    298
Latin America, 11, 17, 59
Laurel, Maryland, 126
Le Pen, Jean-Marie, 60, 171
Lee, General Robert E., 138
Lehane, Chris, 191
LeMay, Curtis, 140
Lemon, Don, 215
LeRoy, Mervyn, 341
Letterman, David, 180
Lewinsky, Monica, 191
Liberty University, 234, 236

Libya, 140, 288
Liddy, G. (George) Gordon, 126
Limbaugh, Rush, 194
Lincoln, Abraham, 31, 86, 109, 148,
    263, 265, 272, 279, 340, 347
Lincoln, Nebraska, 117
Llamas, Tom, 216
Long, Huey, 19–20
Los Angeles, California, 319
Louisiana, 19, 249
Louisville, Kentucky, 270
Love, Mia, 278

McAuliffe, Terry, 104
McCabe, Andrew, 104, 108, 111,
    307
McCaghren, Paul, 129
McCain, John, 41, 91, 168, 284
McCarthy, Joseph, 12, 122
McCarthyism, 85, 103
McConnell, Mitch, 43, 283
McDougal, Karen, 320
McGahn, Don, 312
McGovern, George, 87
Macron, Emmanuel, 8–9
McSally, Martha, 92n
Madison, James, 30, 71, 72, 95
Maine, 260
Make America Great Again
    (MAGA), 5, 10, 20, 114–15,
    135, 208, 249, 284, 290
Manafort, Paul, 106, 311
Manchester, New Hampshire, 231
Manchin, Joe, 268
Manhattan (New York City), 202
Manigault, Omarosa, 36
Marine Corps, 254
Martin, Andy, 192
Maryland, 126, 324
Mattis, James "Mad Dog," 254–5
May, Theresa, 10
Maysville Road Bill (Veto, 1830), 97
Medicare, 118, 169, 204, 230
Melbourne, Florida, 272
Mellon, Andrew, 17

Merkel, Angela, 118
Mexico, 14, 15, 23, 51, 135, 153,
    162, 168, 186, 188, 207, 208,
    223, 261, 275, 332; see also
    illegal immigrants
Mexico City policy (abortion), 294
Miami, Florida, 187
Michigan, 1, 93, 227, 249, 251,
    256, 330, 331
Midland-Odessa, Texas (shooting),
    342
Miers, Harriet, 155
migrant caravans, 275, 298; see also
    illegal immigration
Milwaukee, Wisconsin, 126, 257
Mirage Hotel, 184
Missouri River, 294
Mobile, Alabama, 246, 261
Monroe, James, 95, 149
Montgomery, Alabama, 81
Mook, Robby, 244
Moonves, Les, 225
Morales, Evo, 60
Morgan, J. P. (John Pierpont), 17
Morrissey, Patrick, 268
MSNBC, 216, 274, 317
Mueller, Robert, 105, 106, 107, 108,
    109, 110, 191, 192, 302, 304,
    305, 343
Mueller investigation/report, 39,
    107, 110, 302–5, 309, 310,
    312, 313, 318–19, 320, 341
Muslim(s), 50, 52, 90, 162, 192,
    193, 196, 202, 221, 261, 272,
    274, 288; see also travel ban
Myers, Seth, 197

Nashville, Tennessee, 137, 270, 273
Nast, Thomas, 264
National Association for the
    Advancement of Colored
    Persons (NAACP), 22, 23, 134,
    136–7
National Broadcasting Corporation
    (NBC), 89, 174

National Council of the American
  Worker, 291
National Enquirer, 195, 199
National Football League (NFL), 5,
  38, 81, 138, 176, 345
National Front Party (France), 171
National Space Council, 288
NATO *see* North Atlantic Treaty
  Organization
Navajo (code talkers), 145–6
Nazi, 26, 346
Neo-Nazis, 271
Nero, 341
Never Trump movement, 90–1
New Deal, 19, 25, 28, 84, 85
New Hampshire, 187, 196, 231,
  248
New Jersey, 175, 183, 323
New Jersey Generals (USFL), 176
New Orleans, Louisiana, 264; *see
  also* Battle of, 145, 263
New York, 2, 267
New York City, 119, 186, 264,
  320
New Yorker, 184
New York State Department of
  Taxation and Finance, 323
New York Tribune, 264
Ninth Circuit Court, 273, 288,
  299
Nixon, Richard Milhous, 31, 34,
  35, 36, 58, 61, 87, 88, 93, 103,
  126, 150, 284, 304, 310, 311,
  312, 318, 326, 338, 348
North American Free Trade Accord
  (NAFTA), 14, 23, 129, 186,
  189–90
North Atlantic Treaty Organization
  (NATO),76, 140, 186, 327
North Carolina, 1, 249, 253
North Dakota, 115, 294
North Korea, 33, 76, 118, 181, 287,
  288, 295
Norway, 135
Nunes, Devin, 344

Oakland, California, 344
Obama, Barack Hussein, 21, 50,
  51, 55, 89, 102, 103, 106,
  131, 135, 140, 150, 152, 162,
  168, 169, 190, 193–9, 204,
  223, 233, 240, 244, 268, 269,
  281, 282, 284, 285, 288, 289,
  292–3, 297, 298, 300, 326–7,
  333
Obama, Malik, 194
Obama Coalition, 244
Obamacare *see* Affordable Care Act
Ocasio-Cortez, Alexandria, 206, 346
O'Donnell, Jack, 183
Office of Trade and Manufacturing
  Policy, 290
Ohio, 1, 29, 227, 246, 249, 250,
  253, 270, 279, 330, 331,
  333, 342
O'Jays, 168
Orbán, Victor, 11
Organization of Petroleum
  Exporting Countries (OPEC),
  168
Orlando, Florida, 231, 260
O'Rourke, Robert Francis ("Beto"),
  342
Oscars, 345
Oswald, Lee Harvey, 199

Page, Carter, 103
Page, Lisa, 104, 111
Palestinians, 296
Panic of 1819, 95
Panic of 1837, 100
Papadopoulos, George, 106
Paris, France, 123, 325
Paris Climate Accord, 50, 205
Paul, Rand, 210, 213
Paul, Ron, 168
Pavarotti, Luciano, 218
Pelosi, Nancy, 152, 313, 319, 343,
  344, 345
Pence, Mike, 248, 314
Penn, Mark, 193

Pennsylvania, 1, 222, 227, 249, 253, 259, 268, 274, 330, 331
People's Party, 13, 68, 79–80
Pequot Tribe, 176
Pericles, 69
Péron, Juan, 60
Perot, H. Ross, 13, 14, 20, 21, 22, 23–4, 54, 61, 63, 117, 119, 125, 127–30, 138, 144, 165, 191
Persian Gulf, 188, 297
Phantom of the Opera, 218,
Philadelphia, Pennsylvania, 264, 338
Phillips, Wendell, 264
Phoenix, Arizona, 270–1, 276
Pierce, Franklin, 149
Pittsburgh Maulers, 177
Plame, Valerie, 107
Plato, 70
Playboy, 158, 189, 320
Poland, 11
Polk, James, 149
Portland, Oregon, 342
Posey, Bill, 267
Powers, Francis Gary, 123
Presley, Elvis, 120, 167
Prisoners of War (POWs), 127
Progressive Party, 76
Proud Boys, 342
Proust, Marcel, 133
Public Broadcasting System (PBS), 174
Putin, Vladimir, 91, 140, 191, 242, 303

Quo Vadis (film), 341

Radical Republicans, 263, 264, 267
Ramos, Jorgé, 216
Raskin, Jamie, 316–17
Reagan, Ronald Wilson, 38, 40, 42, 49, 53, 88, 106, 124, 127, 133, 150, 151–4, 164, 187, 208, 285–6, 294, 295, 299, 315, 331, 338, 348, 349
reconstruction, 263

Reform Party, 166, 167, 168
R. E. M., 218
Republican National Committee, 29, 129, 158
Republican National Convention (2016), 29
Republican Party, 6, 57, 65, 86, 88, 93, 129, 165, 168, 170, 171, 204, 207, 228, 328, 337, 347, 349
Revolutionary War, 95, 120
Richmond, Cedric, 250, 251, 252
Roberts, Barbara, 88
Roberts, Bill, 124
Roberts, John (Chief Justice), 289
Rockefeller, Nelson, 86, 93
Rolling Stones, 179
Romney, George, 86, 93
Romney, Willard (Mitt), 54, 89, 169, 257, 310
Roosevelt, Franklin Delano, 19, 27–8, 31, 34, 134, 148, 172, 205, 314
Roosevelt, Theodore, 149, 336
Rosenstein, Rod, 105, 307
Rothschilds, 121
Rouseff, Dilma, 11
Rozelle, Pete, 176
Rubin's vase, 22
Rubio, Marco, 89, 210, 229
Russia, 2, 3, 75, 103, 104, 105, 106, 107, 108, 167, 191, 192, 303, 304, 311, 312, 313, 318, 327
Russia collusion, 302–3, 311, 319, 327, 332, 341, 343, 344
Ryan, Paul, 257–8, 283, 317
Ryan, Tim, 270

San Francisco 49ers, 38
Sanders, Bernie, 19, 56, 57, 64, 65, 79, 118, 203, 204, 211, 219, 229–41, 334, 242, 243, 345
Sanford, Mark, 348, 349
Saudi Arabia, 162, 188, 297
Scavino, Dan, 249

Schiff, Adam, 304, 309, 343
Schlafly, Phyllis, 123
Scotland, 9
Scott, Rick, 65
Scott, Ridley, 246
Scranton, William, 86
Seacrest, Ryan, 181
Seattle, Washington, 288
Second Party Era, 12
Seminoles, 145
Senate Intelligence Committee, 105
Sensenbrenner, James, 251
Sessions, Jeff, 91, 108, 109,
    110, 312
Seventh Day Adventist, 213
Sherman, Brad, 39
Shillue, Tom, 229–30
Social Security, 86, 167, 230
Somalia, 288, 295
Soros, George, 201
South America, 11
South Korea, 168
Southern District of New York
    (attorney general for, SDNY),
    306, 308, 320–4
Soviet Union, 40, 123
Special Counsel's Office (White
    House), 305
Specie Circular (1836), 100
Spencer, Stu, 124
Speyer, Jerry, 185
Spicer, Sean, 52
Sprague, Richard, 126
Squad (House of Representatives),
    25
Stand Up for America, 135
Standing Rock Sioux, 294–5
Stanton, Edwin, 109, 265
Starr, Kenneth, 191
State of the Union Address (2018),
    142, 251, 345
Steele, Christopher, 103
Stein, Gertrude, 344
Stein, Jill, 203, 205, 206, 257
Stevens, Thaddeus, 264–5

Stevenson, Adlai, 328
Stone, Roger, 314
Stormer, Richard, 122
Strange, Luther, 268
Strauss, Johann, 249
Strzok, Peter, 6, 104, 111
Sudan, 287, 288
Supreme Court, 43, 125, 151, 155,
    175, 273, 289, 298, 299, 300,
    310, 325, 331
Syria, 10, 140, 169, 288, 295

Taft, Robert, 172
Tea Party, 124
Tel Aviv, Israel, 50, 142, 296
Tennessee, 145
Tenure of Office Act (1867), 265,
    309
Texas, 38, 74, 129, 159, 168, 169,
    199, 210, 212, 330, 342
Time Magazine, 256
Tony Awards, 345
Trail of Tears, 146
transgendered, 298
Trans-Pacific Partnership (TPP), 50,
    294
travel ban, 50, 52, 74, 90, 114, 135,
    261, 272–4, 288–9; *see also*
    Muslims
Trudeau, Gary, 179
Trudeau, Justin, 118
Truman, Harry, 34, 44, 149,
    281
Trump, Donald John,
    anti-elitism, 12, 16, 27, 47, 52,
        56, 61, 78, 82–3, 88, 93, 119,
        160–1, 172, 189, 197, 202,
        206, 209
    anti-intellectualism, 4, 7, 20, 54,
        76–7, 118–19, 145, 162, 206,
        221, 224, 274, 349, 350
    Apprentice (television show), 36,
        168, 225, 323
    birther controversy (Obama),
        190–8

Trump, Donald John, (*cont.*)
 border wall with Mexico, 15, 43,
  47, 51, 153, 209, 223, 261,
  274, 283, 332
 conspiracy theory, 2, 27, 54, 55,
  66, 77, 114, 118, 161, 152,
  191, 192, 197, 199, 202, 222,
  228, 256, 260, 261, 313
 illegal immigrants, 2, 3, 14, 15,
  17, 24, 51, 135, 138, 171,
  198–202, 204, 221, 223, 261,
  270, 272, 274, 275
 impeachment of, 38–9, 43, 157,
  247, 266–7, 304–5, 309–10,
  311–13, 317, 318, 341, 343–4
 nativism, 15, 16, 21, 27, 54, 63,
  83, 134, 139, 145, 146, 161,
  206, 222, 350
 ordinary Americans, 13, 76–8,
  113, 138, 146, 159, 161, 170,
  172, 178, 203, 206, 217,
  254, 255
 racism, 15, 21–2, 25, 39, 131,
  134, 135, 136–7
 Surviving at the Top, 179
 The America We Deserve, 171
 trade policy, 14, 17, 29, 47, 66,
  75, 142–4, 151, 153, 159, 161,
  162, 165, 167, 169, 186–7,
  189, 190, 202, 208, 223–4,
  255, 256, 258, 283, 286, 289,
  293, 294, 300, 331
Trump, Jr., Donald, 321
Trump, Fred, 171
Trump, Ivana, 160
Trump, Ivanka, 74, 209
Trump, Melania (née Knauss), 74,
 166, 207
Trump Derangement Syndrome, 26,
 37
Trump Foundation, 323
Trump Organization, 320, 323, 324
Trump Plaza Hotel, 178
Trump Tower, 103, 207, 320
Trump v. Hawaii, 273

Twenty-Fifth Amendment, 35, 307,
 314–19
Twisted Sister, 218
Twitter, 2, 4, 34, 38, 89, 92, 103,
 104, 107, 109, 114, 158, 182,
 185, 209, 215, 217, 226, 249,
 269, 281, 283, 302, 319, 325,
 337, 339, 341, 347, 349, 350
Tyler, John, 150

US v. Nixon, 310
Ukraine, 11, 310, 313, 322
unitary executive theory, 28, 284,
 299–300
United Kingdom, 5, 9, 81
United Nations, 142, 185
United States Football League
 (USFL), 162, 176–7
United States Trade Representative,
 290
United We Stand, 127
University of Central Florida, 231
Univision, 216
Urban League, 22

Van Buren, Martin, 98, 100
Venezuela, 65, 287, 288, 291
Vidal, Gore, 126
Vietnam War, 81, 82, 86, 127, 139,
 140, 239
Virginia, 24, 38, 91, 104, 138, 213,
 248, 271, 276, 322, 324
Voting Rights Act, 251

Wales, 9
Wall Street, 205, 231–2, 233,
 236, 283
Wall Street Journal, 184
Wallace, George, 12, 20, 21, 54,
 63, 76, 81–2, 113, 119, 125–6,
 134, 135, 138, 139, 140, 141,
 142, 202, 223, 252
War of 1812, 95
Ward, David, 200
Warren Commission, 122

Index

Warren, Elizabeth, 19, 66, 145–6, 206, 334, 342, 345
Washington, DC, 238, 273, 323
Washington, George, 31, 95, 139
Watergate, 32, 36, 40, 88, 103, 304, 310, 311, 312, 318, 348
Waters, Maxine, 37
Weicker, Lowell, 175, 176
Weisselberg, Allen, 321
Welch, Robert, 123–4
West Allis, Wisconsin, 257
Wheeler, Andrew, 332
Whig Party, 15
White House Correspondents Dinner, 169, 197, 274
White House Faith and Opportunity Initiative, 291
Wilkie, Wendell, 123, 171, 172
Wilson, Al, 275
Wilson, Frederica, 38
Wilson, James, 308
Wilson, Woodrow, 34, 150, 314
Winfrey, Oprah, 166, 189

Wirt, William, 100
Wisconsin, 1, 205, 227, 249, 250, 251, 257, 258, 330, 331, 332
Wolf, Naomi, 166
Worcester, Massachusetts, 230
World War II, 123, 134, 145, 189, 314
Wray, Christopher, 111, 112
Wright, Jim, 163
Wyden, Ron, 329

Yarmuth, John, 270
Yates, Sally, 52
Yemen, 288
Young, David, 250
Young, Neil, 207
Youngstown, Ohio, 270, 279
YouTube, 112, 181, 227

Zakaria, Fareed, 190
Zelenskiy, Volodymyr, 11, 39, 309, 310, 343
Zervos, Summer, 323–4

EU representative:
Easy Access System Europe
Mustamäe tee 50, 10621 Tallinn, Estonia
Gpsr.requests@easproject.com

www.ingramcontent.com/pod-product-compliance
Lightning Source LLC
Chambersburg PA
CBHW070841300326
41935CB00039B/1325